'"Coalitions of the willing" or "governance by posse" were prevalent metaphors among US geopolitical rhetoricians only for the first few years of the twenty-first century, but Alejandro Rodiles makes a convincing case that the interweaving of formal international law with designed informality of operational commitments has become ubiquitous. This excellent study, informed equally by legal theory and early experience as a Mexican diplomat, probes the challenges posed for lawyers by a phenomenon that extends from the Proliferation Security Initiative to contemporary partnerships and network governance and perhaps even China's Belt and Road.'

Benedict Kingsbury, New York University School of Law

'Whoever is interested in process of global lawmaking should read this book. Provocatively building on the notion of the "coalitions of the willing", Professor Alejandro Rodiles shows how the interplay between formal and informal law shapes the development of international law across a range of fields. The book is theoretically innovative and empirically rich and last but not least, it is a very good read.'

Professor Wouter Werner, Vrije Universiteit Amsterdam

COALITIONS OF THE WILLING AND INTERNATIONAL LAW

Global action and regulation is increasingly the result of the interplay between formality and informality. From the management of state conduct in international security to the coordination of national policies in climate change, international organizations work ever closer with coalitions of the willing. This book carefully describes this dynamic game, showing that it consists of transformative orchestration strategies and quasi-formalization processes. On the institutional plane, coalitions of the willing turn into 'durable efforts', while international organizations perform as 'platforms' within broader regime complexes. On the normative level, informal standards are framed in legal language and bestowed with the force of law, while legal norms are attached to multilayered schemes of implementation, characterized by pragmatic correspondences, persuasion tactics, and conceptual framing. Understanding how this interplay alters the notion of 'international legality' is crucial for the necessary recalibrations of the political ideals that will inform the rule of law in global governance.

ALEJANDRO RODILES is an associate professor of international law at the Instituto Tecnológico Autónomo de México (ITAM), Mexico City. He undertook his doctoral studies at the Humboldt University of Berlin and is a member of the International Law Association's study groups on UN sanctions and on cities and international law. In addition to his academic pursuits, he has extensive diplomatic experience, including as legal advisor of Mexico's Mission to the UN, as *sous-sherpa* to the Nuclear Security Summit, at the Office of the Legal Advisor, and at the Policy Planning Staff of the Foreign Minister.

CAMBRIDGE STUDIES IN INTERNATIONAL AND COMPARATIVE LAW: 135

Established in 1946, this series produces high quality, reflective and innovative scholarship in the field of public international law. It publishes works on international law that are of a theoretical, historical, cross-disciplinary or doctrinal nature. The series also welcomes books providing insights from private international law, comparative law and trans-national studies which inform international legal thought and practice more generally.

The series seeks to publish views from diverse legal traditions and perspectives, and of any geographical origin. In this respect it invites studies offering regional perspectives on core *problématiques* of international law, and in the same vein, it appreciates contrasts and debates between diverging approaches. Accordingly, books offering new or less orthodox perspectives are very much welcome. Works of a generalist character are greatly valued and the series is also open to studies on specific areas, institutions or problems. Translations of the most outstanding works published in other languages are also considered.

After seventy years, Cambridge Studies in International and Comparative Law sets the standard for international legal scholarship and will continue to define the discipline as it evolves in the years to come.

Series Editors
Larissa van den Herik
Professor of Public International Law, Grotius Centre for International Legal Studies, Leiden University

Jean d'Aspremont
Professor of Public International Law, University of Manchester and Sciences Po Law School

A list of books in the series can be found at the end of this volume.

COALITIONS OF THE WILLING AND INTERNATIONAL LAW

The Interplay between Formality and Informality

ALEJANDRO RODILES

CAMBRIDGE
UNIVERSITY PRESS

University Printing House, Cambridge CB2 8BS, United Kingdom

One Liberty Plaza, 20th Floor, New York, NY 10006, USA

477 Williamstown Road, Port Melbourne, VIC 3207, Australia

314-321, 3rd Floor, Plot 3, Splendor Forum, Jasola District Centre, New Delhi - 110025, India

79 Anson Road, #06-04/06, Singapore 079906

Cambridge University Press is part of the University of Cambridge.

It furthers the University's mission by disseminating knowledge in the pursuit of
education, learning and research at the highest international levels of excellence.

www.cambridge.org
Information on this title: www.cambridge.org/9781108463263
DOI: 10.1017/9781108680431

© Alejandro Rodiles 2018

This publication is in copyright. Subject to statutory exception
and to the provisions of relevant collective licensing agreements,
no reproduction of any part may take place without the written
permission of Cambridge University Press.

First published 2018
First paperback edition 2020

A catalogue record for this publication is available from the British Library

Library of Congress Cataloging in Publication data
Names: Rodiles, Alejandro, 1975- author.
Title: Coalitions of the willing and international law : the interplay between formality
and informality / Alejandro Rodiles, Instituto Tecnologico Autonomo de Mexico
Description: Cambridge, United Kingdom ; New York, NY, USA : Cambridge University
Press, 2018. | Series: Cambridge studies in international and comparative law ;
135 | Based on author's thesis (doctoral - Humboldt-Universitat zu Berlin, Juristische
Fakultat, 2015) issued under title: Coalitions of the willing and the role of law
in multilayered governance : an analysis of informality in international law. |
Includes bibliographical references and index.
Identifiers: LCCN 2018009846 | ISBN 9781108493659 (hardback) |
ISBN 9781108463263 (paperback)
Subjects: LCSH: Alliances. | Intervention (International law) | Security, International.
Classification: LCC KZ4053 .R63 2018 | DDC 341.3–dc23
LC record available at https://lccn.loc.gov/2018009846

ISBN 978-1-108-49365-9 Hardback
ISBN 978-1-108-46326-3 Paperback

Cambridge University Press has no responsibility for the persistence or
accuracy of URLs for external or third-party internet websites referred to in
this publication, and does not guarantee that any content on such websites is,
or will remain, accurate or appropriate.

Para Natalia y Sofía, con todo mi amor

[W]e are the hub of alliances unrivalled in the history of nations.

Barack H. Obama

In this era of international relations, we may need to start thinking less about formal international treaties and agreements and much more about what you might describe as coordinated national policies.

Richard N. Haass

Managing States turns centrally on information ... for example through cognitive framing[.]

Kenneth W. Abbott

CONTENTS

Foreword   xi
Acknowledgements   xiii
List of Abbreviations   xviii

1 Introduction   1
The Plan of the Book   7

2 The Conceptual Metaphor 'Coalition of the Willing'   10
2.1 Catchphrase Analysis   12
2.2 Frame Theory   16
2.3 Conceptual Metaphor Theory   20
2.4 Why Resort to Framing and Conceptual Metaphors?   28
2.5 Conclusion   33

3 Testing the Frame: The Genealogy of a Catchphrase   38
3.1 The Western Missionary Deep Frame   41
3.2 The Genealogy of the Concept   45
3.3 Concluding Remarks on Coalitions of the Willing in a Non-Polar Post-11/8 Global Environment   83

4 Global Security Governance by Posse: The Proliferation Security Initiative & Co.   92
4.1 The Proliferation Security Initiative   93
4.2 The PSI at the Intersection of US Border Security and Global Maritime Security   124
4.3 Concluding Remarks on the *PSI & Co.*: The Amorphous Nature of Coalitions of the Willing   146

5 Coalitions of the Willing in Context: The Interplay between Formality and Informality   148
5.1 Coalitions' Evolution by Mimesis: More Than Just 'Activities'   153
5.2 Coalitions' Jurisgenerative Capacity Arising from the Interplay with (Formal) Institutions   168

CONTENTS

5.3 Concluding Remarks on the Interplay among Coalitions of the Willing and Institutions: Outside Orchestration   202

6 Coalitions of the Willing and the Role of Law in the Deformalized Global Complex   210

6.1 The Interplay between Formality and Informality: Promoting Informal Hierarchies   211

6.2 Concluding Remarks on Coalitions' Impact on International Legality   248

7 Conclusion   250

Bibliography   259
Index   283

FOREWORD

This book fascinatingly portrays the encounters of an evocative political concept with international law and its manifestations in practice. Alejandro Rodiles describes 'coalitions of the willing' as a widespread paralegal phenomenon that leaves international law formally intact but may decisively determine its interpretation and application, and which may even go so far as to undermine international law. Such coalitions are more than a subset of the many informal arrangements that are part of what is often called global governance. Coalitions of the willing represent a quintessentially modern driving force for the development, implementation, and supplementation of international law, as exercised by influential states. Originally developed as an operative political concept in and for the United States of America, the concept of 'coalitions of the willing' is analyzed and presented as a category with considerable explanatory force.

The author is both a theory-minded academic and an experienced international legal practitioner. Alejandro Rodiles first works on the concept of 'coalitions of the willing', its purpose, and effects – including a discussion of the political subconscious through the application of language theory. It is only after having developed a proper theoretical foundation and perspective that he explores certain regimes at the edges of international security law and policy. In describing the creation and working of regimes like the Proliferation Security Initiative (PSI), the Container Security Initiative (CSI), the Global Initiative to Combat Nuclear Terrorism (GICNT), the Nuclear Security Summit (NSS), the Global Counterterrorism Forum (GCTF), and the Financial Action Task Force (FATF), he extracts their symptomatic character for the way in which international security relations are conducted behind the more visible events.

The book connects several debates in international law and political science. Although most of the examples for coalitions of the willing are taken from United States–dominated security regimes, the analytical force of it is limited to neither elucidating a particular manifestation of US policy nor to the area of security law.

The main challenge for any author who wishes to fruitfully address 'coalitions of the willing' is to remain between the Scylla of a – legally or politically – constructive approach that, consciously or subconsciously, uses the concept to achieve particular goals, and the Charybdis of a critical approach for which the concept merely serves to unmask hegemonic designs. Alejandro Rodiles has, in my view, succeeded in maintaining such a fruitful balance. He sees the hegemonic dimension, but he also identifies the law-creating and implementing functions of coalitions of the willing. He combines the virtues of realist and critical political scientists and of positivist and deconstructionist lawyers. He is thereby able to capture one of the most important aspects of the 'modern condition' of international law.

Georg Nolte
Humboldt University of Berlin, Member of the
International Law Commission

ACKNOWLEDGEMENTS

When I defended my 'little dissertation' in order to get my law degree, at the National Autonomous University of Mexico (UNAM), the Iraq War of 2003 had just started. The impact was profound, informing my whole approach to the discipline I came to embrace, first as a practitioner at Mexico's Foreign Ministry, and then as an academic. The 'coalition of the willing' forged by the George W. Bush administration, and the whole framing of it as *the* means to deal with threats to international peace and security in face of the alleged inefficacy of the United Nations and international law, shook my whole belief in law as a meaningful and contestable articulation of power. As a junior advisor at the Policy Planning Staff of Mexico's Foreign Minister, my agnosticism was only exacerbated. I began to work in international law as a 'translator', so to speak, from the legal into the political dialects, noticing that both share etymology and grammar. In this sense, well before reading David Kennedy and Martti Koskenniemi, I could grasp that law is politics by other means. But dialects are expressions of life, and translation is therefore useful in order to overcome (contingent but real) boundaries. That was the beginning of the imaginary of this book, even if I was not aware of it. I thank Arturo Sarukhán, my former boss at the Policy Planning Staff, with whom I learned to communicate in different dialects and who has profoundly shaped my sensibilities in foreign policy and international relations. He also introduced me to the work of Richard N. Haass, the intellectual father of 'coalitions of the willing' and a US foreign policy strategist whose ideas have exercised an important and not sufficiently acknowledged impact on world politics and law in the post- and post-post Cold War environments – I hope to remedy this attention deficit a bit in the pages to come.

I then moved to the Office of the Legal Advisor, where I had the fortune to work with Juan Manuel Gómez Robledo and Joel Hernández, fine international lawyers who taught me what I know about the craft of the discipline, as well as the value of organized multilateralism. Faith

xiv ACKNOWLEDGEMENTS

reinstalled but plagued with doubts, nonetheless, after writing legal memoranda, I read with fervour *Der Nomos der Erde*. I could not get the thought out of my head that I was working on premises that were vanishing as I began to learn how to articulate and work with them. At that time, I luckily acquired *US Hegemony and the Foundations of International Law*, edited by Michael Byers and Georg Nolte. At the same time, I also read Andreas Paulus' 'The War against Iraq and the Future of International Law', a wonderful article that shaped many thoughts contained in this book. I wrote Andreas about my intentions to write a doctoral dissertation on coalitions of the willing and international law. He read carefully my very long emails, understood my motivations, and brought me into contact with Georg Nolte, making this journey possible in the first place. That journey would have been materially impossible without the scholarship that was generously provided to me by Mexico's Council on Science and Technology (CONACYT), and administrated by the German Academic Exchange Service (DAAD).

As my doctoral supervisor, Georg Nolte motivated me and believed in my project even when I was more than sceptical. His door was literally always open for advice and thoughtful debates. We may have different views on certain issues of law and politics, but our communication flows as if there were no political or cultural barriers. I have come to think of him as an enlightened positivist who knows the law and defends it with passion, but a passion that is grounded in a genuine understanding of the world where this law acquires its meaning. And he has a dialectical mind, always willing and able to overcome the theses and anti-theses of the politics of law. This book benefited enormously from his example and guidance. Most important, he and Elena Nolte-Borovkova always cared for me and my family in Germany, alleviating homesickness as only they can.

In Munich, I had the fortune of becoming part of a wonderful environment – academic but, most of all, human – in which many of the thoughts in this book started to take shape as the project of my doctoral dissertation. I thank Georg Nolte, Bruno Simma, Bardo Fassbender, Thilo Rensmann, and Andreas Paulus for providing institutional support and invaluable advice. I am especially thankful to Christine Schuhbeck-Schmidt, who was always helpful and gentle. During my time in Munich was also when I met colleagues who became good friends, particularly Helmut Aust and Christian Djeffal. Helmut discussed with me almost every aspect of this book, read several chapters, and gave most valuable

ACKNOWLEDGEMENTS

feedback. He accompanied me and my work along the trip from Munich to Berlin, and this book owes a lot to him: *danke mein Freund!*

Eyal Benvenisti spent some time in Munich when I was starting to write the dissertation. We discussed my project in some length. Those conversations are an essential part of this story, and he continued throughout the years to listen to my ideas and give great and gentle advice. His thoughts have had a profound impact on this book, as the reader will immediately notice. Also in Munich, I took part in a research project on informality in international relations, conducted by Christopher Daase, which was extremely useful for many ideas developed in this book as well.

Still in Munich, I was invited to join the Mexican Mission to the UN, in New York, for the third participation of my country in the United Nations Security Council. I thank Juan Manuel Gómez Robledo and Claude Heller for giving me the opportunity to be part of a great team in the Mexican Mission. While there, I could not write a single page for the dissertation, but the experience proved to be crucial for the whole book, and for what it should turn into. The insights I gained as a Sixth Committee delegate, as well as an 'expert' to the Counter-Terrorism and Al-Qaida and Taliban Sanctions Committees, as well as my role as the Mexican *sous-sherpa* to the Nuclear Security Summit, informed many of the present findings and assessments. I experienced the United Nations as a platform, with the Security Council being at many edges of a growing network of governance. In New York, I was very lucky to have had the opportunity of exchanging views on these incipient observations with Benedict Kingsbury, who helped me understand the proper dimensions of these practical experiences for my academic work; he became a powerful source of inspiration far beyond this book.

After finishing my assignment in New York, Georg Nolte invited me to work with him in Berlin. He is not only an excellent doctoral supervisor, but also a wonderful person to work with. There is no other way to put it: I have learned so much from him that I cannot thank him enough.

I finished the dissertation at Humboldt University, a great institution I came to embrace as my second *alma mater*. The Chair for Public Law, Public International Law, and European Law was full of inspiring and friendly people, many of whom contributed in several ways to bringing my dissertation to a good end. For very fruitful discussions, I thank Helmut Aust, Christian Djefall, Chris Gutmann, and Peter Staubach. We also had a great time together. My profound gratitude goes to Kerstin Schuster who made life easier and brought much life into work. My family and I also benefited much from the friendship and generosity of Johanna Aust.

I have discussed certain parts and aspects of this book with many friends and colleagues in several settings or bilaterally, and all have been relevant for the final outcome. Beyond those already mentioned, let me express my gratitude to Markus Jachtenfuchs, the second reader of my dissertation, who made helpful criticisms I hope I could address properly; Carlos Montemayor, who read the second chapter and provided great feedback; Alfonso Ascencio, who commented on several aspects of the Proliferation Security Initiative and the law of the sea treated in Chapter 4; Larissa van den Herik and the International Law Association (ILA) Working Group on UN Sanctions that gave me the opportunity to discuss some aspects of Chapter 5; Mattias Kumm and the Rule of Law group at the WZB, in Berlin, where I presented parts of Chapter 3; the Grakov Center at Humboldt University, where I received valuable comments on first drafts of Chapter 6 and found the time to write 'the whole thing' down (for PhD purposes); as well as Guadalupe Barrena, Arnulf Becker Lorca, Konrad Bühler, Jorge Cerdio, Rodrigo Chacón, Anne Peters, Ulises Schmill, and Gavin Sullivan.

I would also like to thank my splendid research assistant at the Instituto Tecnológico Autónomo de México (ITAM), María José Flores Ramírez, who has also been one of the brightest students I have ever had. She has put tremendous effort into the finishing of this book, and has worked with remarkable professionalism, I am profoundly indebted to her! The anonymous readers made inspiring suggestions to improve the manuscript – I hope to have met some of their expectations. The team at Cambridge University Press has been extremely helpful, professional, and kind: I sincerely thank Larissa van den Herik and Jean d'Aspremont for their impetus, as well as Finola O'Sullivan, Tom Randall, Laura Blake, and Gemma Smith for all their help and patience along the process. I also thank Elizabeth Kelly and Sindhujaa Ayyappan for the careful copy-editing process.

There are people with whom I did not directly exchange views about the pages of this book, but without the inspiration I gained from their friendship, I could never have written it. My gratitude goes to my dear friend Armin Keller, Alexander Bruck, Santiago Chacón, Nicolás Vázquez, Alvar Saenz, David Schoffel, Arturo Berumen, Fernando Serrano, and above all, Peter Lueb, my beloved teacher in literature and life.

Most of all, I am deeply grateful to my innermost circle, my family that gives me motivation in each and every sense. I thank my wife, life companion, and motor of life, Paola Karam, for her patience, support, and love. Her skills and knowledge in intellectual property also taught me a lot about the routines of informality in the law. Matías and David have sacrificed time with their dad, and I can only apologize to them. David was a newborn when I finished the dissertation. Because of family reasons, Matías and I stayed alone in Berlin right before the defence of the dissertation. He was only four, but he showed such a strength in face of 'Papa's big day' I will never forget: thank you! And I thank my mother, Sofía Rodiles, for her unconditional love and support. She is also partly responsible for this: as a former member of Mexico's foreign service, she awakened very early in my life my desire to understand *the global*.

ABBREVIATIONS

CBP	Customs and Border Protection of the US Department of Homeland Security
CMF	Combined Maritime Forces
CoCom	Coordination Committee on Multilateral Export Controls
COP	Conference of the State Parties
CSI	Container Security Initiative of the US Customs and Border Protection
CTC	Counter-Terrorism Committee of the United Nations Security Council
CTED	Counter-Terrorism Executive Directorate of the Counter-Terrorism Committee of the United Nations Security Council
CTF-150	Combined Task Force-150
CTF-151	Combined Task Force-151
CTF-152	Combined Task Force-152
CTITF	Counter-Terrorism Implementation Task Force of the United Nations General Assembly
C-TPAT	Customs Trade Partnership against Terrorism
DHS	US Department of Homeland Security
DIS	Detailed Implementation Assessment of the Counter-Terrorism Executive Directorate
DoD	US Department of Defense
DoS	US Department of State
DPRK	Democratic People's Republic of Korea
ECHR	European Court of Human Rights
ECOWAS	Economic Community of West African States
FAST	Free and Secure Trade program
FATF	Financial Action Task Force
FIUs	Financial Intelligence Units
FSRBs	Financial Action Task Force Style Regional Bodies
FTF	foreign terrorist fighters
GA	United Nations General Assembly
GAL	global administrative law

GCTF	Global Counterterrorism Forum
GICNT	Global Initiative to Combat Nuclear Terrorism
GMP	Global Maritime Partnership
HEP	highly enriched plutonium
HEU	highly enriched uranium
HLPM	High Level Political Meetings of the Proliferation Security Initiative
IAEA	International Atomic Energy Agency
IAG	Implementation Assessment Group of the Global Initiative to Combat Nuclear Terrorism
IATA	International Air-Transport Association
ICAO	International Civil Aviation Organization
ICJ	International Court of Justice
ICRG	International Co-Operation Review Group of the Financial Action Task Force
ILC	International Law Commission
IMCMEX	International Mine Countermeasures Exercise
IMO	International Maritime Organization
IN-LAW	informal international law-making project
IS	Islamic State
ITLOS	International Tribunal for the Law of the Sea
MEF	Major Economies Forum on Energy and Climate Change
MoU	memoranda of understanding
MSO	Maritime Security Operations
NAM	Non-Aligned Movement
NATO	North Atlantic Treaty Organization
NDCs	nationally determined contributions of the Paris Agreement on Climate Change
NNSA	US Department of Energy's National Nuclear Security Administration
NNWS	non-nuclear weapon states
NPT	Treaty on the Non-Proliferation of Nuclear Weapons
NSG	Nuclear Suppliers Group
NSCG	Nuclear Security Contact Group
NSS	Nuclear Security Summit
OECD	Organization for Economic Cooperation and Development
OEF	Operation Enduring Freedom
OEG	Operation Expert Group of the Proliferation Security Initiative
OEWG	Operational Experts Working Group of the Proliferation Security Initiative
OGS	Office of Global Strategies of the US Department of Homeland Security

ABBREVIATIONS

OIA	Overview of Implementation Assessment of the Counter-Terrorism Executive Directorate
OIF	Operation Iraqi Freedom
PACOM	US Pacific Command
PCIJ	Permanent Court of International Justice
PIA	Preliminary Implementation Assessment of the United Nations Counter-Terrorism Committee
PRST	Statement by the President of the United Nations Security Council
PSI	Proliferation Security Initiative
RMSI	Regional Maritime Security Initiative
ROEG	Regional Operational Experts Groups of the Proliferation Security Initiative
SC	United Nations Security Council
SG	United Nations Secretary General
SIP	Statement of Interdiction Principles of the Proliferation Security Initiative
SOP	Statement of Principles of the Global Initiative to Combat Nuclear Terrorism
SOUTHCOM	United States Southern Command
SUA	2005 Protocol to the 1988 Convention for the Suppression of Unlawful Acts against the Safety of Maritime Navigation
TSA	US Transportation and Security Administration
UNCLOS	United Nations Convention on the Law of the Sea
UNFCCC	United Nations Framework Convention on Climate Change
USNSS	US National Security Strategy
VCLT	Vienna Convention on the Law of Treaties
WMD	weapons of mass destruction

1

Introduction

Coalitions of the willing are strongly associated with the Iraq War of 2003. Indeed, it was this event that so fundamentally questioned the efficacy and future of international law and brought the phenomenon into public awareness. Symbolic as it may be, the United States–led military alliance is only one of the various phenomena designated by the term. 'Coalition of the willing' is a political catchphrase that receives different meanings depending on who is using it. The Iraq War of 2003 and the military operation to combat terror, crime, and piracy, Operation Enduring Freedom; diplomatic partnerships among liberal democracies like the proposed League of Democracies; transgovernmental, non-governmental, and hybrid networks in all conceivable fields, such as the fight against transnational organized crime; the stabilization of the global financial architecture; the fight against global warming; and the pursuit of human security all seem to be part of the steadily growing collection of coalitions of the willing acting in the global realm. In the domestic realm, the expression is also occasionally employed, but the present book is concerned with the usages of the term within international discourses and the implications of the phenomenon for international law or, more precisely, for the role of law in global affairs.

Due to the negative connotations that the catchphrase acquired after the illegal intervention in Iraq, the broader 'global war on terror', and the aggressive international rhetoric of the government of George W. Bush, especially during his first term in office, it has been largely replaced by euphemisms like 'partnership', 'platform', or 'initiative'; at times, reference is made just to 'coalitions'. However, the idea behind these labels has not changed significantly, and 'coalition of the willing' is the expression that best captures the motivations, strategies, and goals involved in the concept. This is the reason why I have deliberately chosen to keep this term throughout the present study, although the book is not about the Iraq War of 2003.

2   INTRODUCTION

Without engaging in the analysis of the concept at this point, it can be said that coalitions of the willing are informal groups of like-minded actors – though the like-mindedness of all participants is questionable in several ways, as I will argue. This notion is not restricted to states and has been applied to transnational NGOs, as well as to diplomatic joint ventures in which governments have worked together with civil society in the pursuit of humanitarian aims, such as the Humanitarian Initiative that played a crucial role in the recent adoption of the Treaty on the Prohibition of Nuclear Weapons. Still, we are dealing mainly with groupings of states that often, but not always, integrate the private sector into their functions. In the end, coalitions of the willing are states' creatures, and states – rather, a few in particular – are the principal actors assembling and leading them. Hence, this book is about informal coordination mechanisms among states,[1] which are often but not exclusively led by the United States of America (USA).

International co-operation outside institutions and treaty structures is certainly not a new phenomenon, and informally co-ordinated state conduct can be traced back to at least the Congress of Vienna and the concert system put in place by it. A net of informal mechanisms in the field of exports control of weapons of mass destruction (WMDs) and dual-use materials began to operate in the 1950s with the Coordination Committee on Multilateral Export Controls (CoCom), which was replaced by the Wassenaar Arrangement after the Cold War. These groups, as well as other trans-governmental networks[2] in the financial sector, like the Basel Committee on Banking Supervision, are the direct precedents of the type of coalitions of the willing I will discuss in this book. An important point of clarification is due in regard to the relationship of coalitions of the willing with trans-governmental networks as those studied in Anne-Marie Slaughter's *New World Order*.[3] I will discuss in some detail, for example, the Financial Action Task Force (FATF), a trans-governmental network *par excellence*, and also other schemes of agency-to-agency co-operation at the transnational level. I will analyze closely related phenomena and their current evolutions while tracing,

---

[1] See Eyal Benvenisti, 'Coalitions of the Willing and the Evolution of Informal International Law', in Christian Calliess, Georg Nolte, and Peter-Tobias Stoll (eds.), *Coalitions of the Willing: Avantgarde or Threat?* (Cologne/Munich: Carl Heymanns Verlag, 2007), p. 1.

[2] See Robert O. Keohane and Joseph S. Nye, 'Transgovernmental Relations and International Organizations' (1974) 27 *World Politics* 39, at 42-50.

[3] Anne-Marie Slaughter, *A New World Order* (Princeton: Princeton University Press, 2004).

INTRODUCTION 3

explaining, and always maintaining awareness of the linkages they have with a whole conceptual framework where the coalition of the willing approach has actually been developed and refined over the years as an integral part of a global governance strategy. This strategy has been mainly designed by US foreign policy circles in the government, think tanks, and academia, and Professor Slaughter has played a prominent role in this regard in Princeton as well as in Washington, D.C. This is a strategy concerned with the maintenance of US hegemony in a rapidly changing world. It emerged in the early post-Cold War years, particularly in the writings of the influential international relations (IR) scholar Richard N. Haass, and has been adjusted since then to other tectonic shifts in world order, such as the 9/11 situation, and more recently to the increasing non-polarity in world affairs. As part of this strategy, the coalition of the willing approach offers greater flexibility and expediency in comparison to slowly incremental and politically contested traditional multilateral diplomacy, as well as the rigidity of international law-making processes. It is not clear how this strategy will unfold under President Donald Trump. What can be said is that Trump's foreign policy so far seems to lack a coherent route,[4] which makes the pursuit of this approach as part of an integral strategy questionable. But even under such a scenario, the US-led coalitions with which I will deal here continue to perform until this very day, and quite intensely so. Moreover, the coalition of the willing approach is no longer exclusive to the USA or the West but has become part and parcel of global governance in a non-polar age.[5]

One perception of coalitions of the willing is that they perform outside international organizations, thus being 'better understood as an activity than an organization'.[6] As such, they pose a serious challenge to organized multilateralism; they are certainly part of a broader 'move from institutions'.[7] It is important to clarify that 'organized multilateralism' does not only refer to international organizations (IOs) but also to the idea of an international community organized through law. Here, of course, the United Nations (UN) occupies a pivotal position, but it is more the notion of the post-war order *qua* legal order that I have in

---

[4] On this, see Chapter 3, p. 76, and pp. 89–90.

[5] See Section 3.3.

[6] Richard N. Haass, *The Reluctant Sheriff. The United States after the Cold War* (New York: Council on Foreign Relations/Brookings Institution Press, 1997), p. 95.

[7] See the contributions to the ASIL symposium, 'The Move from Institutions?' (2006) 100 *Proceedings of the Annual Meeting (American Society of International Law)*, pp. 287–302.

4   INTRODUCTION

mind. This is not to ignore the limitations of the 'international community'. However, the ideal of a *Rechtsgemeinschaft* is at the core of rule of
law aspirations at the international level; i.e., it fulfils a purpose for the
legitimacy and credibility of international law as a universal *project*.
I speak consciously of a 'project' as I do not pretend to portray a picture
of international law as an inclusive and transparent legal system that is
now being threatened in its integrity by coalitions of the willing. These
and other manifestations of global governance are, nevertheless, threats
in the sense that they can reverse some of the achievements constructed
over time and take the faith away from important aspirations, including
rule of law aspirations, which are crucial as political ideals in order for
international law not to stagnate. As we will see in the course of this
book, one of the achievements that is seriously jeopardized by 'coalitions
of the willing and the evolution of informal international law'[8] is international law's foundational principle of sovereign equality. This
principle, all its shortfalls notwithstanding and even taken as a fiction,
remains of the utmost importance for less powerful states.[9] Coalitions of
the willing are thus conceived in this book as instruments that contribute
to the further loosening of control of powerful states,[10] which take
advantage of the selectivity awarded by coalitions in order to define the
priorities in the implementation and evolution of international law –
nothing more but nothing less.

Legal certainty and predictability are seriously affected by informality
in global affairs. Now, it is also true that the strength of these values in
international law tends to be overestimated. Formal international lawmaking – i.e., the processes of rule creation that can be traced back to a
valid source of international law – already entails a great deal of instances
that are opaque in the sense that their genesis is not always clear.

---

[8] This is the title of the first comprehensive legal essay addressing coalitions of the willing
from an international law perspective, see Benvenisti, 'Coalitions of the Willing'.

[9] See Benedict Kingsbury, 'Sovereignty and Inequality' (1998) 9 *European Journal of
International Law* 599; see also B. S. Chimni, 'Legitimating the International Rule of
Law', in James Crawford and Martti Koskenniemi (eds.), *The Cambridge Companion to
International Law* (Cambridge: Cambridge University Press, 2012), p. 290, at p. 294; in
relation to coalitions of the willing, see Heike Krieger, 'Coalitions of the Willing –
A Résumé from the General Public International Law Point of View', in Christian
Calliess, Georg Nolte and Peter-Tobias Stoll (eds.), *Coalitions of the Willing: Avantgarde
or Threat?* p. 43, at pp. 46–47.

[10] Benvenisti, 'Coalitions of the Willing', pp. 22–23; and Brad R. Roth, 'Coalitions of the
Willing and the International Rule of Law', in Calliess, Nolte, and Stoll (eds.), p. 33, at
pp. 41–42.

INTRODUCTION

Customary international law is a prime example; another is the normative evolutions of treaties through conferences of the states' parties and their subsidiary organs, including the cross-references they tend to make to the work of expert bodies through 'best practices' and the like. This also reveals a certain degree of informality, or semi-formality, and the opaqueness that it produces also tends to favour those who have the resources to impose their own standards. However, the informality that characterizes coalitions of the willing has evolved over time. It is worth commenting in this context that in 2000, memoranda of understanding (MoUs) were still conceived as 'the standard building block of the informal international order'.[11] Today, states that wish to circumvent legal constraints by opting for informal arrangements are better advised to avoid the signing of MoUs, as the US Department of State explicitly encourages its negotiators to do.[12] More importantly, the informality that is actively promoted by coalitions contributes to a further deformalization of international law and, therefore, increases the dislocation of authority in the global realm. This happens primarily through the replacement of competent authorities and legal powers with regime complexes, where fluid 'spheres of authority' are juxtaposed in multi-layered global governance schemes.[13] And this is made by the intense interplay of coalitions with formal institutions and law, the interplay between formality and informality that this book is about.

Closely related to the implications for sovereign equality, the principle of state consent is also experiencing important changes through coalitions of the willing and their jurisgenerative potential.[14] Furthermore, the norms that are produced within coalitions are paradigmatic examples for the rise of informal international law-making.[15] From thoroughly negotiated 'working plans' specifying concrete normative expectations on the behaviour of participant states (Nuclear Security Summit, – NSS) and

---

[11] Anne-Marie Slaughter, 'Governing the Global Economy through Government Networks', in Michael Byers (ed.), *The Role of Law in International Politics* (New York: Oxford University Press, 2001), p. 177, at p. 189.

[12] See US Department of State (DoS), Office of the Legal Advisor, Treaty Affairs, Guidance on Non-Binding Documents, at www.state.gov/s/l/treaty/guidance/.

[13] See James N. Rosenau, 'Governing the Ungovernable: The Challenge of a Global Disaggregation of Authority' (2007) 1 *Regulation & Governance* 88.

[14] See Nico Krisch, 'The Decay of Consent: International Law in an Age of Global Public Goods' (2014) 108 *The American Journal of International Law* 1.

[15] See Joost Pauwelyn, Ramses A. Wessel, and Jan Wouters (eds.), *Informal International Lawmaking* (Oxford: Oxford University Press, 2012).

6   INTRODUCTION

recommendations for legal reform and harmonization of regulations (FATF), to 'principles of conduct' that systematize existing legal powers under both national and international law in order to carry out in a co-ordinated manner specific activities like the interdiction of vessels on the high seas (Proliferation Security Initiative – PSI), these examples demonstrate the extent to which coalitions are shaping the ways international and transnational law are made today, and they invite us to revisit the notion of soft law.

We will see throughout the case studies that will be conducted in Chapters 4 and 5 that coalitions of the willing are powerful instruments for implementing international legal rules, something that, in a system that lacks central enforcement authorities, can contribute to the strengthening of international law. Indeed, for some authors, the proliferation of informal trans-governmental mechanisms is a positive evolution towards a more 'effective World Order'.[16] Apart from the fact that this implementation will prove to be highly selective,[17] this feature of coalitions may suggest that what is needed is the development of mechanisms for improving transparency and accountability;[18] namely, what global

[16] See Slaughter, *A New World Order*, pp. 166 et seq.; see also Kal Raustiala, 'The Architecture of International Cooperation: Transgovernmental Networks and the Future of International Law' (2002) 43 *Virginia Journal of International Law* 1, at 90 (mentioning in 2002 that '[o]n balance, the most plausible prediction about the future is that networks will strengthen the traditional tools of international law and organization').

[17] Already skeptical on the purported advantages of transnational networks, see José E. Alvarez, 'Do Liberal States Behave Better? A Critique of Slaughter's Liberal Theory' (2001) 12 *European Journal of International Law* 183, at 211 et seq.; and Stephen J. Toope, 'Emergent Patterns of Governance and International Law', in Byers, *The Role of Law in International Politics*, p. 91, at pp. 96–97 (mentioning that '[n]etworks, like regimes, and regardless of their membership, are sites of power, and potentially of exclusion and inequality').

[18] This is probably the oldest and still most common critique of coalitions and informal networks. In her early writings on trans-governmental networks, Anne-Marie Slaughter, although already very enthusiastic, focused on the accountability problems, which however, she also saw as the result of misperceptions by critics, see Anne-Marie Slaughter, 'Agencies on the Loose? Holding Government Networks Accountable', in George A. Bermann, Matthias Herdegen, and Peter L. Lindseth (eds.), *Transatlantic Regulatory Cooperation: Legal Problems and Political Prospects* (Oxford: Oxford University Press, 2001), p. 521; for an early warning on accountability, transparency and participation problems raised by then new forms of governance, see Philip Alston, 'The Myopia of the Handmaidens: International Lawyers and Globalization' (1997) 8 *European Journal of International Law* 435.

administrative law (GAL) has been searching for.[19] Efforts to constrain coalitions and to provide some sort of accountability and transparency are related to the following, more fundamental question: to what extent is the interplay between formality and informality spurred by coalitions capable of developing international law towards a global law, which can better respond to dynamic global risks and needs without renouncing its quality as law?

The Plan of the Book

In order to address these questions, I will proceed as follows. In the next chapter, I will analyze the concept of 'coalition of the willing'. The aim is not to provide a fixed definition, which contains the elements of the concept once and for all, but to understand and explain how the concept has emerged and evolved, by whom it is used and for what purposes, and in what sense it relates to international legal and political discourses. Accordingly, I will base my analysis in frame and conceptual metaphor theory. Given that coalitions of the willing function on the premise of voluntary state behaviour, renouncing legal obligation, frame analysis as developed by cognitive linguist George Lakoff will also prove to be useful for better understanding how coalitions of the willing work – i.e., how do they induce and persuade states to perform certain conduct. This will prove to be useful again in Chapter 6, where the implications of informal international law for international legality will be assessed.

In Chapter 3, the frames involved in the conceptual metaphor 'coalition of the willing' and the ideas transmitted by these frames will be tested. In identifying the different instances where coalitions of the willing have played an important role, I will not try to write a history of the phenomenon, but rather a genealogy of the catchphrase – i.e., to sketch an account of the distinct usages the term has experienced in international political and legal discourses over time. Special attention will thus be paid to the legal doctrines related to 'coalitions of willing and able states' acting in the framework or at the margins of collective security – i.e., the multinational forces authorized and unauthorized by the UN Security Council to use all necessary means to maintain or restore international peace and security. I will then show how the notion of 'coalition of the willing and able states' that emerged in the 1990/1991

---

[19] See Benedict Kingsbury, Nico Krisch, and Richard B. Stewart, 'The Emergence of Global Administrative Law' (2005) 68 *Law and Contemporary Problems* 15, at 17 et seq.

8 INTRODUCTION

Gulf War was further elaborated and refined as part of a US foreign policy and global governance strategy, but which has been appropriated by other states, mainly powerful ones and beyond the West.

Chapters 4 and 5 contain case studies. There, I will analyze some concrete manifestations of coalitions of the willing. The principal aim of Chapter 4 will be to show how the ideas that are entailed in the conceptual metaphor 'coalition of the willing' (Chapter 2) have materialized over time. Therefore, I will take a closer look at the PSI and other 'sister initiatives' like the Global Initiative to Combat Nuclear Terrorism (GICNT), as well as the bilaterally operating Container Security Initiative (CSI). In Chapter 5, the FATF, the NSS, and its continuation under what might be termed the 'NSS 2.0', as well as the Global Counterterrorism Forum (GCTF), will be analyzed in light of their interplays among themselves and with IOs, and of the jurisgenerative work arising from the latter.

In Chapter 6, an assessment of the findings of the case studies will be made. The interplay revealed in Chapters 4 and 5 intensifies the global complex as a system of rule, an assemblage of informal and formal schemes of co-operation and ruling. Therefore, in a first step, some of the salient features of regime complexity will be analyzed and problematized. Indeed, while the literature on governance and regime complexity has shed light on the mysterious ways through which conduct is steered today at the global level, it is to a large degree eulogistic in that it uncritically celebrates the intricacies of the network. Instead, my focus will be on portraying the *complexities of complexity*, with a view to unravelling the power games it enables. The formal–informal interplay spurred by coalitions of the willing has concrete consequences for international law as we know it. Building on some of the main theses developed in the informal international law-making project (IN-LAW),[20] I will argue that we are witnessing the emergence of an *anti-law law* as a consequence of this interplay. Coalitions of the willing are characterized by a *fluctuant informality* that consists of *orchestration* strategies, as well as *quasi-* and *reformalization* processes that take place in a dynamic game with formal law and institutions. The consequence of playing this game is the transformation of the players: coalitions turn into durable efforts and IOs into platforms; informal standards are framed in legal language; legal norms are attached to informal frames;

---

[20] See Pauwelyn, Wessel, and Wouters (eds.), *Informal International Lawmaking.*

and implementation occurs through an efficient multilayered mechanism characterized by pragmatic correspondences, persuasion, conceptual framing, and nudging.

In Chapter 7, I will make some tentative remarks on how this *anti-law law* might be transforming our understanding of international legality. While state consent-based legality is shrinking to a few chessboard domains of classical inter-state disputes,[21] the new inter-normativity that dynamically arises from the ongoing formal–informal interplay predominates in more and more fields, including such crucial areas as global security and climate change governance, and it is spreading beyond. It is a sort of new *resilience normativity* that is extremely difficult to accommodate into a system. Whether or not this can be achieved is not something I can answer, nor do I intend to make normative assertions on how the world should be ruled instead. My aim is rather to contribute to a better understanding of these transformations of law in the global realm so that the political contestation through which the ideas of a global rule of law have to emerge can be more attuned, thus keeping alive the old dream of international law as a universal project, willing and able to constrain power.

---

[21] See Anne-Marie Slaughter, *The Chessboard & the Web – Strategies of Connection in a Networked World* (New Haven: Yale University Press, 2017).

2

The Conceptual Metaphor 'Coalition of the Willing'

[T]he orator must ... put his hearers, who are to decide, into the right frame of mind.

Aristotle[1]

... every definition stretches into an open horizon.

Friedrich Waismann[2]

The essence of metaphor is understanding and experiencing one kind of thing in terms of another.

George Lakoff & Mark Johnson[3]

The expression 'coalition of the willing' is strongly associated with the Iraq War of 2003. Indeed, it was the same event that posed such fundamental questions as to the efficacy and future of international law, which brought the phenomenon into public awareness. Symbolic as it may be, this United States–led military alliance represents only one of the various phenomena designated by the term, which has been used in various contexts and accordingly received different meanings. Other examples include maritime coalitions patrolling the high seas like the *Combined Maritime Forces* (CMF), diplomatic partnerships among liberal democracies such as the proposed *League of Democracies*, as well as intergovernmental, non-governmental and hybrid networks in all conceivable fields, such as the fight against transnational organized crime, the stabilization of the global financial architecture, the fight against global warming, or the pursuit of the most diverse humanitarian aims.

---

[1] Aristotle, *Rhetoric* (New York: Dover Publications, 2004), 1377b.
[2] Friedrich Waismann, 'Verifiability' (1945) sup. vol. XIX *Proceedings of the Aristotelian Society* 119, at 125.
[3] George Lakoff and Mark Johnson, *Metaphors We Live By*, second edition (Chicago: The University of Chicago Press, 2003), p. 5.

THE CONCEPTUAL METAPHOR 'COALITION OF THE WILLING' 11

All these phenomena seem to be part of a steadily growing collection of coalitions of the willing acting in the international realm.[4]

'Coalition of the willing' is an abbreviated form of the expression 'coalition of the willing and able', thus indicating that willing and able actors, primarily states but in no way restricted to them, come together (coalesce) in order to pursue certain common objectives. The goals pursued are usually pressing global threats and challenges, and the endeavours to address them therefore of an urgent and case-specific nature, assigning coalitions of the willing an *ad hoc* character that distinguishes them from standing alliances.[5] Related to this ad hocism, coalitions tend to be informal,[6] which represents another element of differentiation from standing alliances, international organizations (IOs), and other institutionalized forms of international cooperation. This prima facie description gives a clue of what we are talking about but not much more; it does, in fact, equally apply to other related manifestations of global governance, especially transnational networks. The difficulty of defining the concept 'coalition of the willing' lies, *inter alia*, in that it is not a *terminus technicus* of international law or international relations (IR) theory but a disputed political catchphrase.

Therefore, an analysis of political catchphrases is required. A brief overview into rhetoric, and especially into cognitive linguistics shall give us an account of how these linguistic tools are created, how they work, and by which means they pursue their goals. On this basis, I will try to achieve a better understanding of the expression 'coalition of the willing' and of the phenomenon(a) actually named by it. I will show that a particular representation of international co-operation is advanced strategically through this catchphrase, which can be explained best by observing its metaphorical structure, and, in particular, the surface and deep frames involved in it.

---

[4] In the domestic realm, the expression is employed too, but I focus in this book on the usages of the term within international discourses.

[5] See Jolyon Howorth, 'From Alliances to Coalitions of the Willing: The New Regional Dynamics of Transatlantic Relations', paper delivered to the Annual Conference of International Studies Association (ISA) (Hawaii, March 2005) on file with the author; see also Elke Krahmann, 'American Hegemony or Global Governance? Competing Visions of International Security' (2002) 7 *International Studies Review* 531, at 537 and 542.

[6] In the juridical sense, coalitions of the willing are necessarily informal since they are not grounded in legal instruments. However, as we shall see in the course of this book, this issue is not always crystal clear, but rather different shades of informality are involved depending on the coalition at hand.

12 THE CONCEPTUAL METAPHOR 'COALITION OF THE WILLING'

2.1 Catchphrase Analysis

According to the classical theory of concepts[7] (and traditional juridical thought), one is tempted to believe that through a meticulous examination of the term, one would be able to extract its definitional elements – i.e., its fixed properties. In a first conceptual approach, I have proceeded just in that manner by proposing definitional properties (i.e., the concept's intension) and defining coalitions of the willing as 'global, amorphous, and *ad hoc* groupings';[8] other characterizations speak of 'coordination efforts of "like-minded states"'.[9] Both descriptions contain important elements of the phenomenon. However, the difficulties of differentiating 'the proper usage' of the term from those that 'artificially stretch the concept'[10] is hardly overcome by these approaches. The uncertainty underlying its possible extension – i.e., the range of things it may denote – and which may vary over time, makes the verifiability of its intension a major problem, leading thus to a *phenomenological trap*. Reliance on contingent differences, such as the distinct goals that coalitions pursue, in order to analytically differentiate what a coalition of the willing is and what not, fails to comprehend the phenomenon by prejudicing from the outset the research agenda. In other words, the methodological obsession of defining the concept – though driven by the honest intention of bringing clarity into the debate – leads to overlook some of its important features while over-emphasizing others.

A similar approach to socio-legal phenomena is taken by Mariana Valverde. Following the notion of 'chronotopes' developed by Russian literary critic Mikhail Bakhtin (i.e., the relational spatial-temporal configurations that give each literary genre its specificity), Valverde commits to a fluid and dialogical analysis, emphasizing the need

> to produce concrete analyses in an open-ended manner, remembering that our first commitment is not promoting the prestige or the theoretical

---

[7] For an overview, see Eric Margolis and Stephen Laurence, 'Concepts', in Edward N. Zalta, *The Stanford Encyclopedia of Philosophy* (2012), at http://plato.stanford.edu/archives/fall2012/entries/concepts/.

[8] See Alejandro Rodiles, '*Coalitions of the Willing*: Coyuntura, Contexto y Propiedades. Un Primer Esbozo' (2007) 7 *Anuario Mexicano de Derecho Internacional* 675, at 693.

[9] In this sense, one of the first comprehensive studies on coalitions of the willing and international law by Benvenisti, 'Coalitions of the Willing and the Evolution of Informal International Law'.

[10] See Rodiles, '*Coalitions of the Willing*: Coyuntura, Contexto y Propiedades', 693.

2.1 CATCHPHRASE ANALYSIS

> rigour of our chosen disciplines or fields – much less sour chosen neologisms – but rather understanding the world we live in.[11]

I share the same methodological concern, therefore seeking a phenomenological approach to coalitions of the willing that shares many features with Valverde's theses – and, as she mentions, translations from Bakhtin's concepts. In this sense, I am devoted to respect the complexity and indeterminacies of the phenomenon under study, as well as its relational characteristics, and will not artificially simplify it for the sake of 'academic rigour'. I will do this, however, by resorting to frame and metaphor theory, because I believe that understanding the metaphorical structure of the concept 'coalition of the willing' enables a better comprehension of the ways in which international action is framed today and how the frames involved are highly instrumental in shaping behaviour at the global level, thus performing a normative function.

For now, it is important to underline that the concept of our concern does not have *a* meaning that hermetically contains its elements once and for all, but it is of an open texture. This means that its definition is '*always* corrigible or emendable ... [and that] we cannot foresee completely all possible conditions in which [it is] to be used'.[12] Nonetheless, this does not mean that everything can be described randomly by it. In the following, I will show that despite the absence of a clear and pure definition, there is a coherent set of ideas and ideals that are transmitted through the catchphrase 'coalition of willing'. This becomes clearer once we think of it not as a single concept but as a conceptual structure. As we shall see, this structure is built by a metaphor according to which international cooperation is understood in terms of friendship and resoluteness. This reveals much more than what fixed definitions like that of 'like-minded states', or 'global amorphous groupings', actually can do. In doing this, I will follow George Lakoff's and Mark Johnson's conceptual metaphor theory, where '[c]oncepts are not defined solely in terms of inherent properties; instead, they are defined primarily in terms of interactional properties'.[13]

---

[11] Mariana Valverde, *Chronotopes of Law – Jurisdiction, Scale and Governance* (Oxon and New York: Routledge, 2015), p. 27.

[12] On the open texture of concepts (the German original is '*Die Porosität der Begriffe*'), see Waismann, 'Verifiability', 123.

[13] Lakoff and Johnson, *Metaphors We Live By*, p. 125. The interactional properties described here are similar to the relational approach taken by Mikhail Bakhtin under his notion of

14 THE CONCEPTUAL METAPHOR 'COALITION OF THE WILLING'

Before explaining the conceptual metaphor 'coalition of the willing', it is important to underline that we are dealing, at the same time, with a political catchphrase. In other words, the conceptual metaphor 'coalition of the willing' is used strategically. But what does this exactly mean? Besides the fact that catchphrases are fashionable expressions, frequently used in the media, one should bear in mind that a catchphrase is a *parole*, where the system of signs and rules of the *langue* is individualized through particular and ephemeral utterances.[14] This basic characterization reveals an important aspect of catchphrases: they reflect a particular way of using words since they are intended to *catch* attention. We are talking about a metaphor that links acts of speech – in a broader sense – to the physical activity of catching, thus representing particular and often peculiar utterances that are highly capable of getting the audience's attention – i.e., *to catch it*.[15] But when it comes to 'political catchphrases', attention is not the ultimate intention, but rather connected to a specific political goal: someone or something is to be supported or rejected. This implies that they contain a message, and an element of inducement. Hence, they are linguistic means to convince major audiences to agree with the political message they encapsulate. In this sense, they belong to the field of rhetoric.[16]

Two interesting questions arise by looking closer at the proposed description: how do catchphrases encapsulate political messages, and how do they try to convince the audience? As both aspects are strictly related with each other, it is convenient to approach these two questions at the same time. A first explanation consists in that catchphrases summarize political messages and ideas through short and snappy

'intertextuality', suggesting 'that language be regarded as always already social, as always already dialogical' (Valverde, *Chronotopes of Law*, p. 5).

[14] The distinction between *langue* and *parole* was established by Ferdinand de Saussure in his classical *Course de Linguistique Générale* (1916); for a succinct summary of this distinction, see John Phillips and Chrissie Tan, 'Langue and Parole', in *The Literary Encyclopedia*, at www.litencyc.com/php/stopics.php?rec=true&UID=662.

[15] For a detailed analysis of how metaphors work in our everyday life, see Lakoff and Johnson, *Metaphors We Live By*; see also Zoltan Kövecses, *Metaphor: A Practical Introduction*, second edition (Oxford: Oxford University Press, 2010).

[16] This is also the conclusion to which Patrick Honecker arrives after reviewing the evolution of political catchphrase research in Germany, see P. Honecker, 'Vorreformatorische Schlagwörter, Spiegel politischer, religiöser und sozialer Konflikte in der frühen Neuzeit', PhD thesis, University of Trier (2002), pp. 19–28, at http://ubt.opus.hbz-nrw.de/volltexte/2004/149/pdf/20021212.pdf. Regarding the general importance of persuasion in rhetoric, Aristotle said that this art 'may be defined as the faculty of observing in any given case the available means of persuasion'. Aristotle, *Rhetoric*, 1355b.

expressions that are easier to understand and to remember than elaborated discourses. Details are intentionally left aside, as the point is to recognize only the bigger lines of such discourses and, of course, only those that are helpful for the political goal to be achieved. In other words, they perform what can be called a *partial briefing function*. Thus, it is tempting to compare 'catchphrases' to 'keywords'.[17] Both tell only about some parts of a broader idea or message. However, a keyword reflects only the *key* elements of a subject matter. A catchphrase, on the other hand, entails a subtler selection of the parts to be reflected; it is partial. By looking further into the functions that catchphrases perform, it becomes clear that they go beyond the partial briefing function. In order to convince the audience, it is not enough to brief about the parts of a discourse the creator or user of the expression wants the audience to bear in mind. The audience must be also emotionally touched. Catchphrases are emotionally loaded, evoking strong feelings in the addressees, negative or positive, leading them so to take a stand on the particular issue. In Aristotle's words, it is the art to put the audience 'into the right frame of mind'.[18]

So far, it can be said that catchphrases combine a partial briefing function and emotional persuasion. This description matches with early studies in the field of catchphrases, especially with the research developed in Germany during the late nineteenth and early twentieth centuries. These studies already stressed catchphrases' concise form, their attachment to present political discourse and events, as well as their affective character.[19] This still holds true. However, developments in cognitive

---

[17] The expression 'coalition of the willing' has been described elsewhere as a 'dodgy keyword', see Maximilian Malirsch and Florian Prill, 'The Proliferation Security Initiative and the 2005 Protocol to the SUA Convention' (2007) 67 *Zeitschrift für ausländisches öffentliches Recht und Völkerrecht* 229. However, this is insofar misleading as 'coalition of the willing' does not only entail the key elements of an idea or subject but also encapsulates a more complex political message or idea.

[18] Aristotle, *Rhetoric*, 1377b. The philosopher further noted that there are three inherent forms of persuasion: first, the one that stems from the personal character of the speaker, or what we would call today charisma; the second is 'putting the audience in a certain frame of mind'; and the last one consists of the proof or apparent proof of the argument. It is the second mode of persuasion, which is strictly related to emotional speech, I am referring to here; see Aristotle, *Rhetoric*, 1356a.

[19] According to Honecker, in 1863, when the word 'catchphrase' ('*Schlagwort*') was first introduced in a German dictionary, linguists were already aware of the conciseness of these fashionable expressions. By the beginning of the twentieth century, their emotional character and their intention to persuade the audience to adopt certain points of view became clear too. After World War I, the historian Wilhelm Bauer demonstrated the

16 THE CONCEPTUAL METAPHOR 'COALITION OF THE WILLING'

linguistics have introduced important insights into the way catchphrases function, particularly in regard to the means by which they try to convince the audience.

An illustrative way to explain these insights is by looking closer at a metaphor, the meaning of which is strictly related to that of the 'catchphrase' metaphor: 'buzzword'. This term denotes a word or phrase that sticks in the audience's awareness just like a continuous low sound remains in the hearing of a person. Buzzwords become what they are by repetition, that is, by continuously appearing in public debate, especially in the media. And just like the buzzing of a bee immediately evokes whatever comes along with bees, buzzwords and catchphrases resemble broader meanings; they carry with them encapsulated messages, so to speak. But to the point, we only have a vague idea of how this works. Further explanation can be found in frame theory.

2.2   Frame Theory

According to frame theory,[20] every word comes along with a conceptual background called 'frame' – i.e., a mental structure of which we are not necessarily consciously aware, but which shapes the way we understand the world around us. This can be best explained by providing an example. The word 'coalition' immediately activates (literally speaking,

---

importance of catchphrases in opinion forming and, hence, for the media; see Honecker, *Vorreformatorische Schlagwörter*, pp. 19–20.

[20] Framing analysis already existed in social sciences, especially in sociology, since the mid 1970s; for a *locus classicus*, see Erving Goffman, *Frame Analysis: An Essay on the Organisation of Experience* (New York: Harper Colophon, 1974). For an interesting application of this kind of framing theory to the advancement of indigenous rights in international law, see Rhiannon Morgan, *Transforming Law and Institution: Indigenous Peoples, the United Nations and Human Rights* (Farnham: Ashgate, 2011), pp. 35 et seq., and pp. 117 et seq. Although related, the framing theory I use in this book has been developed in the field of linguistics, especially by Charles Fillmore (see Charles Fillmore, 'Frame Semantics and the Nature of Language' (1976) 280 *Annals of the New York Academy of Sciences* 20), and subsequently by George Lakoff. For an informal but precise account, see George Lakoff, *Don't Think of an Elephant! Know Your Values and Frame the Debate* (Vermont: Chelsea Green Publishing, 2004); id., *Thinking Points, Communicating Our American Values and Vision* (New York: Farrar, Straus and Giroux, 2006); for a systematic application of metaphor and frame theory to political debate, see id., *Moral Politics. What Conservatives Know that Liberals Don't*, second edition (Chicago: The University of Chicago Press, 2002); and id., *Whose Freedom: The Battle over America's Most Important Idea* (New York: Picador/Farrar, Straus and Giroux, 2006).

that is through neural automatic or even unconscious processes)[21] other concepts and ideas instantiated in our brains, which are related to the concept 'coalition', such as 'partnerships', 'co-operation', 'shared interests', 'common action', and so on. Semantic roles are also activated by the 'coalition frame' as shown by ideas about political parties or governments acting together in order to achieve common goals.[22] Taken together, all these ideas form a framework, a 'conceptual frame' that says much more than the lexical definition of the word 'coalition'. A frame includes, so to speak, a package of knowledge, but – and this is very important – it is a specific knowledge that depends on the particular cultural and experiential environment of the listener.[23] Most probably, the 'coalition frame' would not be the same for a person familiarized with a parliamentary democracy as, say, for someone raised within a one-party system. In the second case, it would be no surprise if the activated frame entailed labour unions and other forms of corporate organizations associated with the party apparatus[24] instead of coalitions among different and sometimes differing political forces, common to parliamentary systems.

In the international realm, a human rights activist would think most probably first of non-governmental, global networks that are committed to humanitarian aims worldwide, whereas many states' representatives would conceive the word 'coalition' predominantly in terms of intergovernmental cooperation, temporary diplomatic groupings, or, especially after the Iraq invasion of 2003, multinational forces. And yet, other diplomats and scholars would associate the expression with new forms of diplomacy that champion human security issues, involving

---

[21] On the relationship between implicit social cognition, conceptual metaphor theory, and frame analysis, see John A. Bargh, 'What Have We Been Priming All These Years? On the Development, Mechanisms, and Ecology of Nonconscious Social Behavior' (2006) 36 *European Journal of Social Psychology* 147; see also Ronald Chen and Jon Hanson, 'Categorically Biased: The Influence of Knowledge Structures on Law and Legal Theory' (2004) 77 *Southern California Law Review* 1103, at 1211–1215.

[22] For the explanation of how semantic roles, scenarios, and scripts function, and how they matter to social organization, see Goffman, *Frame Analysis*.

[23] See Lakoff, *Metaphors We Live By*, pp. 185–194; *id.*, *Thinking Points*, pp. 9–19.

[24] An example of this is Mexico's political system during the seven decades of one-party rule (1929–2000) governed by the *Institutional Revolutionary Party* (PRI). There, 'corporativism' was one of the most effective forms of social control performed by the PRI/government.

18 THE CONCEPTUAL METAPHOR 'COALITION OF THE WILLING'

partnerships among like-minded non-governmental organizations, IOs, and states.[25] It is in this sense that a concept like 'coalition' receives its meaning(s) through different and evolving frames; thus it makes little sense to try to resort to or elaborate lexicographic definitions (although this definitely would make the linguistic analysis easier, it would not help in understanding the phenomenon that is referred to by the linguistic expression).

Catchphrases and buzzwords are not the only linguistic tools capable of framing. Actually, every word carries a conceptual baggage with it.[26] The distinctive element of catchphrases and buzzwords is that they are there to frame. Framing is not only more obvious when it comes to them, but it is the very reason they are created. In order to activate particular frames, catchphrases and buzzwords often come in form of neologisms[27] or metaphors; as I will show later in this chapter, metaphorical thought is of the utmost importance in regard to the creation and function of catchphrases. This should come as no surprise since new expressions and figurative speech are appropriate means to get and maintain the audience's attention. As a result, whole political discourses, programmes, statements, and messages can be encapsulated in a single word, an appealing metaphorical expression, or in a short and snappy phrase.

Now, it should be reconsidered whether 'catchphrases' and 'buzzwords' are different expressions for the same thing. It is not easy to set forth a clear distinction between them, as they are often used synonymously. Nevertheless, whilst the principal function of most buzzwords consists in getting more complex discourses and ideas to the audience via framing, political catchphrases are created in order to induce the addressee, also via framing, to think of an issue in a particular way. Hence, a subtler form of framing is involved in the latter case. The fact

---

[25] See Lloyd Axworthy, 'Human Security and Global Governance: Putting People First' (2001) 7 *Global Governance* 19, at 20–23; Andrew F. Cooper, 'Stretching the Model of "Coalition of the Willing"', in Andrew F. Cooper, Brian Hocking and William Maley (eds.), *Global Governance and Diplomacy: Worlds Apart?* (London: Palgrave Macmillan, 2008), p. 257.

[26] See Lakoff, *Don't Think of an Elephant*, pp. 3 et seq.

[27] Although many catchphrases are newly coined expressions, one should not confuse neologisms with catchphrases, since not every neologism is a catchphrase and vice versa. What is distinctive about catchphrases is that they receive a special meaning and are used strategically. Early studies in the field of political catchphrases in Germany (*Schlagwortforschung*) already pointed in this direction. Wilhelm Bauer, for example, noted that "a catchphrase is not a catchphrase but is used as a catchphrase"; quoted in Honecker, *Vorreformatorische Schlagwörter*, p. 20.

2.2 FRAME THEORY

that buzzwords are commonly created and used by the media, while political catchphrases are normally the direct product of political discourse (and think tanks!), speaks in favour of this distinction. It is of course true that catchphrases are frequently reproduced by the media, and the ones who promote them want this very much to happen, but still: 'evil empire', 'axis of evil', 'rogue states', and 'war on terror', to name but a few catchphrases in the field of international politics, were all created by administrations of the United States of America (USA),[28] not by *Fox News*. The present analysis is limited to catchphrases.

The subtler form of framing takes place through the interplay of what are called 'surface frames' and 'deep frames'. The former are the ones that I have been referring to so far: words carry a conceptual package associated with its ordinary sense. But when a political catchphrase is formulated with the intention to reflect a particular message and to induce the audience to take a certain stand on an issue, a more complex kind of mental representation has to be activated – one that contains not only related ideas and semantic roles but also whole ideals and value systems. This is what is meant by 'deep frames' – i.e., the mental structures through which the *Weltanschauung* of an individual is organized, as they contain hers or his basic moral representations. As George Lakoff says, 'slogans do not make sense without the appropriate deep frames in place'.[29] Socio-psychological studies on nonconscious cognition point in the same direction, showing that the priming of cues – i.e., the exposure to semantic stimuli – can have a broad effect on individuals' subsequent behaviour and choices through the activation of 'deep cultural ideologies'[30] and 'knowledge structures that likely shape, among other things, our policy preferences'.[31]

---

[28] It is worth recalling that only the last of these examples is a creation of the Bush Jr. administration. Ronald Reagan frequently referred to the former Soviet Union as the 'evil empire', whereas the label 'rogue state' was coined by the Clinton administration in order to classify unfriendly nations suspected of sponsoring terrorism. For an analysis of President Reagan's freedom rhetoric, see Gerhard Besier and Gerhard Lindemann, *Im Namen der Freiheit: Die amerikanische Mission* (Goettingen: Vandenhoeck & Ruprecht, 2006), pp. 219 et seq.; for a concise study of the Clinton administration's foreign policy concepts, see Peter Rudolf and Jürgen Wilzewski, 'Beharrung und Alleingang: Das außenpolitische Vermächtnis William Jefferson Clintons' (2000) 44 *Aus Politik und Zeitgeschichte*.

[29] Lakoff, *Thinking Points*, p. 10.

[30] Bargh, 'What Have We Been Priming All These Years?', 148.

[31] Jon D. Hanson and Mark Yeboah, 'The Policy IAT', in Jon D. Hanson (ed.), *Ideology, Psychology, and Law* (Oxford: Oxford University Press, 2012), p. 265, at p. 268.

20 THE CONCEPTUAL METAPHOR 'COALITION OF THE WILLING'

Political catchphrases link particular issues to certain moral and political ideals, so that the former are viewed and understood in terms of the latter.[32] Lakoff explains this through different contemporary catchphrases, such as 'tax relief'[33] or 'gay marriage',[34] or the 'war on terror'.[35] Actually, his explanation of how 'the war on terror-frame' works is highly interesting for lawyers, in particular for constitutional, penal, and international lawyers. This metaphor activates ideas that support presidential war powers like the notion of a strong commander in chief, capable of defending the nation against its enemies. At the same time, it deactivates 'the law enforcement-frame' – i.e., the idea that terrorism ought to be addressed through police action and criminal law mechanisms domestically and by means of legal and judicial cooperation abroad.[36] Similarly, the interplay between surface and deep frames has important consequences for understanding the phenomenon called 'coalition of the willing': it is a metaphor, rooted in a particular way of conceiving international cooperation, that can be better understood by analyzing the deep frames it activates. Before explaining this, it is important to say a little bit more about the specific role of metaphors in this context.

2.3 Conceptual Metaphor Theory

Subtle framing is closely related to metaphorical thought. And this is quite obvious since metaphors can be very powerful tools in activating deep frames, schemas, and categories.[37] The strength of figurative speech in political rhetoric is of course nothing new, known at least since ancient

---

[32] The significant role of framing in US political debate, as well as the importance of frame theory in elucidating this, has been commented, *inter alia*, by: Matt Bai, 'Notion Building', *The New York Times Magazine* (12 October 2003), at www.nytimes.com/2003/10/12/magazine/notion-building.html?pagewanted=print; id., 'The Framing Wars', *The New York Times Magazine* (17 July 2005), at www.nytimes.com/2005/07/17/magazine/17DEMOCRATS.html?pagewanted=all&_r=0 (the latter essay takes a critical stance on Lakoff's theses).

[33] Lakoff, *Don't Think of an Elephant*, pp. 3 et seq..

[34] Ibid., pp. 46–51.

[35] Ibid., pp. 69–78.

[36] Lakoff, *Don't Think of an Elephant*, pp. 69–78. Among the international legal scholars who have observed this, though without referring to frame theory, see Mireille Delmas-Marty, 'The Paradigm of the War on Crime: Legitimating Inhumane Treatment?' (2007) 5 *Journal of International Criminal Justice* 584, at 586; and David Kennedy, 'Lawfare and Warfare', in James Crawford and Martti Koskenniemi (eds.), *The Cambridge Companion to International Law* (Cambridge: Cambridge University Press, 2012) p. 158, at p. 165.

[37] See Chen and Hanson, 'Categorically Biased', 1211–1212.

2.3 CONCEPTUAL METAPHOR THEORY

Greek philosophy.[38] Early catchphrase analysis (*Schlagwortforschung*) was aware of this, stressing the important role that metaphors occupy in the specific field of political catchphrases. For German historian Wilhelm Bauer, catchphrases are often figurative because they are directed to the masses, and according to his early twentieth century view, masses are 'only capable of thinking through pictures'.[39] Pejorative as it is, Bauer's statement entails, nonetheless, an embryonic understanding of what cognitive linguistics later explained to be a fundamental part of human understanding (and not only of the 'masses', whatever that means): the way metaphors shape our knowledge and comprehension in day-to-day life.[40]

Cognitive metaphor theory postulates that we all think to a very considerable extent via metaphors. This can be best explained through what Lakoff and Johnson call 'persistent fallacies'.[41] These refer to certain myths in traditional Western epistemology and linguistics, according to which metaphorical thought does not play a significant role in

---

[38] See Aristotle, *Rhetoric*, 1410b. On Aristotle's early account of the importance of poetry and metaphors 'to induce insight', see Lakoff and Johnson, *Metaphors We Live By*, p. 190.

[39] Wilhelm Bauer, *Die öffentliche Meinung in der Weltgeschichte* (Potsdam, 1930), pp. 21 et seq., cited in Honecker, *Vorreformatorische Schlagwörter*, p. 20.

[40] Lakoff and Johnson's book, *Metaphors We Live By*, was first published in 1980. It has had a considerable impact on linguistics, philosophy, and psychology. In political science, it has been Lakoff himself who has applied cognitive linguistics to contemporary US political discourse (see note 20). In jurisprudence, Steven L. Winter has written a book that brings the advances of cognitive science in connection to persistent questions of legal theory. Cognitive metaphor theory plays a crucial role in this regard, since 'an understanding of metaphor as *cognitive* and *conceptual* transforms the basic assumptions about reason upon which standard accounts of categorization and law both depend' (Steven L. Winter, *A Clearing in the Forest: Law, Life and Mind* (Chicago: The University of Chicago Press, 2001), p. 43); see also Anthony G. Amsterdam and Jerome Bruner, *Minding the Law: How Courts rely on Storytelling, and How their Stories Change the Ways we Understand the Law – and Ourselves* (Cambridge, USA: Harvard University Press, 2000). For a critical review of these two books and of the application of 'cognitivism' to legal thought in general, see Dennis Patterson, 'Fashionable Nonsense' (2003) 81 *Texas Law Review* 841, at 858–878. Other legal writings that make use of Lakoff and Johnson's theory include Chen and Hanson, 'Categorically Biased'; in the field of international law, see Andrea Bianchi, 'Textual Interpretation and (International) Law Reading: The Myth of (In)Determinacy and the Genealogy of Meaning', in Pieter H.F. Bekker, Rudolf Dolzer and Michael Waibel (eds.), *Making Transnational Law Work in the Global Economy, Essays in Honour of Detlev Vagts* (Cambridge: Cambridge University Press, 2010), p. 34, at pp. 42–47; see also Alejandro Rodiles, 'Law and Violence in the Global South: The Legal Framing of Mexico's "NARCO WAR"', *Journal of Conflict & Security Law* (2018, forthcoming).

[41] Lakoff and Johnson, *Metaphors We Live By*, pp. 243–274.

22 THE CONCEPTUAL METAPHOR 'COALITION OF THE WILLING'

knowledge, nor in the way the latter is communicated through language. According to this view, metaphorical thought is rather limited in its scope and potential to the realms of the unreal and the emotions. The fallacies are the following:

(a) metaphors are solely a matter of words – i.e., metaphors are not concepts;
(b) metaphors are strictly based on similarity;
(c) all concepts are literal – i.e., they have a proper, fixed meaning; and
(d) rational thought is in no way shaped by the nature of our brains and bodies; it is disembodied.

All these assumptions are based on *a priori* conceptions of the way human reasoning and thought function. And it is precisely in this regard that cognitive science has shown that meaning and reasoning, as well as language as a source of evidence for them, are to a great extent matters of empirical study and not only of *a priori* theorization.[42] Let me explain this.

Take fallacy (a), which basically states that 'metaphor is only about the ways we *talk* and not about conceptualization and reasoning'.[43] Empirical psychological studies point quite to the contrary. People often reason through what is called 'metaphorical mappings' – i.e., the inference from one conceptual domain (source domain) to another (target domain), which means that 'most concepts are partially understood in terms of other concepts'.[44] This proves to be a highly intuitive proposition once we consider how we usually explain abstract concepts through those that are closer to our concrete experiences.[45] The authors of *Metaphors We Live By* exemplify this mental process on the hand of a variety of everyday life metaphors, like 'argument is war',[46] 'love is a journey',[47] and so on. These examples show clearly how metaphors perform a very important role in determining the ordinary significance and scope of concepts, being thus called 'conceptual metaphors'. This thesis can be summarized by saying that metaphors do not only matter when it comes to giving a word a meaning beyond its ordinary usage but are often

---

[42] Ibid., pp. 3, 246 et seq..
[43] Ibid., p. 245.
[44] Ibid., p. 56.
[45] I remember when my then two-year-old son called a garage a 'car house' ('*casa de autos*'), which is not a word in Spanish (at least not in Mexican Spanish).
[46] Lakoff and Johnson, *Metaphors We Live By*, pp. 4–6.
[47] Ibid., pp. 44–45.

unavoidable in understanding what a word means in the very first place, thus *occupying* a very important *position* within our conceptual system. Actually, 'occupy a position' is an orientational metaphor without which many concepts related to mental, social, economic, juridical, and many other sorts of structures would not be understood.

The above mentioned also trumps fallacy (b), since the correlations involved in metaphorical mappings are systematic and not mere similarities of the sort *A* is like *B*.[48] In the case of a conceptual metaphor, concept *A* has not only some commonalities with concept *B*, but *A* is also partly defined in terms of *B*, which in turn means that *B* constitutes part of the meaning of *A*. Conceptual metaphors are coherently structured through systematic cross-domain correspondences from one conceptual domain to the other – i.e., constituent properties of one domain come from the other, thus *creating* similarities and not merely relying on pre-existing ones. By regarding a very common metaphor like 'understanding is grasping', it becomes clearer that metaphorical mappings are not only about projection but also about expansion, 'in the sense that it is a nonreductive function: to conceive of understanding as grasping, for example, is to gain a sense of 'grasp' as a cognitive operation without losing or supplanting its physical meaning'.[49] This shows also that metaphors are dependent on particular languages, and cultures as exemplified by the metaphor 'catching the flavour' ('*agarrar el gusto*'), very common in Mexico. Here, the physical meaning is expanded to sensory and emotional perceptions, which in turn are also relevant for cognitive processes of understanding: 'catching the flavour' of something means not only to start liking it, but also to begin understanding it; in other words, by starting to understand something, you begin to like it, and by liking it, you can better understand it. For these reasons, it is highly questionable to affirm that concepts do always have inherent properties.[50] Metaphorical mappings, hence, also contradict fallacy (c).

---

[48] See ibid., pp. 147–155. According to the traditional understanding of metaphors, '*A* is *B*' is interpreted as '*A* is like *B* in regard to *c, d, e*', where *c, d, e* are pre-existing properties of *A* and *B*: '*A* court of law is a battlefield', e.g., is interpreted as 'a court of law is like a battlefield *in that* it is the place where a struggle between opponent parties takes place, etc.'.

[49] Winter, *A Clearing in the Forest*, p. 65.

[50] These questions and the 'multidimensional *gestalts*' Lakoff and Johnson refer to in order to describe interactional properties that are not inherent to objects themselves but relate to the ways we mentally interact with objects – perceptual, motor-activity, purposive and functional properties – (see Lakoff and Johnson, *Metaphors We Live By*, pp. 119–124),

24 THE CONCEPTUAL METAPHOR 'COALITION OF THE WILLING'

Stephen Pinker, who advocates a middle-ground position between those who think of metaphors' role in language and thought as 'semantic fossils' and cognitive linguists like Lakoff and Johnson, regards conceptual metaphors as analogies of the sort *A is like B*, noticing though that the similarities are between the relations among the parts of *A* and *B*.[51] So far, he acknowledges the importance of conceptual metaphors in rhetoric, communication, and even thought. However, he does not seem to accept that conceptual metaphors can *create* similarities. This is due to his notion that, in the end, they 'can be learned and used only if they are analyzed into more abstract elements like 'cause', 'goal', and 'change', which make up the real currency of thought'.[52] Lakoff and Johnson do not deny that 'things in the world do play a role in constraining our conceptual system', but this happens '*only through our experience of them*'.[53] Pinker's 'real currency of thought', in contrast, is thoroughly aprioristic. In this context, I cannot help but to be reminded of Friedrich Waismann's words:

> How reassuring it would be to say that nature must obey causal laws – and so on, you know the tune. The question is only whether Nature will conform to Kant.[54]

---

remind of Hegel's 'Perception: Or Things and Their Deceptiveness' of the *Phänomenologie des Geistes*: 'The simple and true fact, which I perceive, is, however, in virtue of this result, not a universal medium either, but the particular property by itself, which, again, in this form, is neither a property nor a determinate being, for it is now neither attached to a distinct "one" nor in relation to others. But the particular quality is a property only when attached to a "one", and determinate only in relation to others. By being this bare relation of self to self, it remains merely sensuous existence in general, since it no longer contains the character of negativity; and the mode of consciousness, which is now aware of a being of sense, is merely a way of "meaning" (*Meinen*) or "intending" – i.e. it has left the attitude of perception entirely and gone back into itself. But sense existence and "meaning" themselves pass over into perception: I am thrown back on the beginning, and once more dragged into the same circuit, that supersedes itself in every moment and as a whole'. G. F. W. Hegel, *The Phenomenology of the Mind* (1807), translated by J. B. Baillie (London: Harper & Row, 1967), p. 41, at https://ebooks.adelaide.edu.au/h/hegel/phenom enology_of_mind/complete.html. For the German original, see G. F. W. Hegel, *Phänomenologie des Geistes* (Frankfurt a.M.: Suhrkamp, second edition, 1989), p. 98. I am indebted to the late philosophy professor José Ignacio Palencia (UNAM) as well as to Alexander Bruck Santos for drawing my attention to this.

[51] See Steven Pinker, *The Stuff of Thought. Language as a Window into Human Nature* (New York: Penguin Books, 2008), pp. 253–261.

[52] Ibid., p. 259.

[53] Lakoff and Johnsons, *Metaphors We Live By*, p. 154.

[54] Waismann, 'Verifiability', 135.

2.3 CONCEPTUAL METAPHOR THEORY

Finally, fallacy (d) probably entails the most fundamental misunderstanding underpinning scepticism in regard to cognitive metaphor theory. The metaphor 'catchphrase'[55] actually is a good example for explaining this. The word 'catchphrase' relates the more abstract concept 'phrase' (and other linguistic expressions) to the concrete physical experience of 'catching'. This is a prominent characteristic of conceptual metaphors, and the reason for it *lies* in that the manner of our thought is *shaped* by our body and the experiences we make with it.[56] Physical experiences are the first phenomena we realize in our lives. Therefore, they permeate not only the way we perceive sense data, but also the way we understand and construct conceptually the world in which we live. 'Metaphorical systems' can explain this situation. Beyond particular conceptual metaphors, where one concept is partially explained in terms of another, metaphorical systems are sets of concepts organized in respect to one another.[57] Most of these systems are rooted in physical experiences and objects, as is demonstrated by the example of the fundamental metaphorical system of 'orientational metaphors' – i.e., a structured set of conceptual metaphors that are based on spatial orientations like 'up', 'down', 'in' and 'out'. From these spatial references a whole range of metaphors are derived, beginning with basic ones like 'more is up', 'less is down', leading to more elaborate ones such as 'having control over someone/something', 'being on top of a situation' or 'feeling down', etc. Hence, we can talk of more complex mappings that connect a whole range of metaphors by means of relating physical domains (source) to mental (target) domains. The metaphor 'catchphrase' is part of such a system, where ideas are explained in terms of objects, expressions in those of containers, and communication through sending – i.e., the so-called conduit metaphor.[58] In the frame of the conduit metaphor, it makes perfect sense to catch a phrase.

The conduit metaphor is a basic metaphorical system that is highly important in structuring metalanguage. This applies to several languages, and the etymology of the word 'metaphor' itself is emblematic in this

---

[55] 'Catchphrase' as such is a conduit metaphor, like 'sending a message', 'getting a meaning', and so on. Particular catchphrases need not be conduit metaphors, nor metaphors at all, though they usually come in form of metaphors.

[56] Lakoff and Johnson, *Metaphors We Live By*, pp. 56–60.

[57] Ibid., pp. 14 et seq..

[58] Ibid., pp. 10–13.

26 THE CONCEPTUAL METAPHOR 'COALITION OF THE WILLING'

respect: *'meta pherein'* or 'to carry over'.[59] It is important to recall that the conduit metaphor system stresses some aspects of concepts while hiding others: 'The very systematicity that allows us to comprehend one aspect of a concept in terms of another ... will necessarily hide other aspects of the concept'.[60] In the case of the 'catchphrase' metaphor, it can be observed that a simple phrase, metaphor or snappy expression *contains* ideas or ideals, which are *sent* to the audience, whose attention is to be *caught*. At the same time, this metaphor hides other aspects of the concept, such as that the meaning depends very much on the one who uses the expression, and, most importantly, that this meaning is not objectively out there but framed in accordance with the interests of the creator or disseminator of each particular catchphrase. That certain aspects of the target domain concept are not comprehended in the source domain concept also means that conceptual metaphors can and do often perform a strategic function, consisting in undermining those relevant aspects of the target domain that are not comprised in the source domain. I have referred to this as the partial briefing function.

Another fundamental aspect of conceptual metaphors is that, just as physical experiences do matter, so does the cultural environment to which people belong.[61] I mentioned this earlier in the chapter in regard to the different semantic roles involved in the 'coalition frame', depending on the specific politico-cultural environment where the frame operates.[62] Since conceptual metaphors are special cases of framing, the same applies to them. The metaphor 'coalition of the willing' is a case in point. As exemplified by the often unnatural translations, it does not

---

[59] See Winter, *A Clearing in the Forest*, p. 52. (reminding the reader that in modern Greek 'metaphora' ('μεταφορά') means 'metaphor' *and* 'transport').

[60] Lakoff and Johnson, *Metaphors We Live By*, p. 10.

[61] Ibid., pp. 22–24. It is interesting to observe in this context that Dipesh Chakrabarty links his personal experience as a migrant to the explanation of how ideas and concepts that are commonly acknowledged as abstract and universal, 'look utterly different in different historical contexts', and thus, '[n]o country ... is a model to another country, though the discussion of modernity that thinks in terms of "catching-up" precisely posits such models'. He further questions the 'universality' and 'purity' of concepts, especially political ideas, on the basis that the distinction 'between the figurative (how a concept is visualized in practice) and the discursive sides of a concept – its abstract purity, as it were – is itself a partial and overdrawn distinction'. (Dipesh Chakrabarty, *Provincializing Europe: Postcolonial Thought and Historical Difference*, reissue with a new preface by the author (Princeton: Princeton University Press, 2008), *preface*, pp. xii–xiii). This critique, as we shall see in Chapter 3, has important implications for the way the 'coalition of the willing' metaphor operates.

[62] See note 24.

2.3 CONCEPTUAL METAPHOR THEORY

easily work in languages rooted in other cultures. A look into how the expression has been translated into Spanish or French, for example, is quite revealing. Inconsistent terms, like '*coalition des prêts*' ('coalition of the willing') and '*coalition des volontaires*' ('coalition of volunteers') are equally used in French; in Spanish, some references can be found to '*coaliciones de los voluntarios*' ('coalitions of volunteers'), or even '*coaliciones de buena voluntad*' ('coalitions of good will'), but most of these terms hardly fit into the intuitive notion of coalition of the willing. The expression '*coalición de los dispuestos*' ('coalition of the willing') reflects the idea best but sounds quite unappealing and odd.[63] No doubt, such unnatural translations can be slowly familiarized by constant repetition into the importing language and culture, but this process often shows that conceptions, ideas, and values are being transferred rather than translated.[64]

This is important as it makes clear that the concept 'coalition of the willing' is rooted in a particular political culture and reflects a specific way of understanding international cooperation. However, due to the force of attraction of the actors who have created and disseminated the term, it has slowly become part of the vocabulary of international political and legal discourses. This is, of course, not new to international politico-legal vocabularies, and one may ask if conceptual metaphor analysis and, more generally, cognitive linguistics are at all required to demonstrate this. People observe such transfers to happen all the time without referring to theory and linguistic analysis whatsoever, and public international lawyers are very much accustomed to domestic, regional, and private vocabularies nurturing their 'common language'. However,

---

[63] For a description of the problems that the term raises in Spanish, see Rodiles, '*Coalitions of the Willing*: Coyuntura, Contexto y Propiedades', 678. There, I reach the conclusion that it is best to refer to the term in English, not only because no translation is convincing but also because thereby the reader is reminded that the term reflects a particular way of thinking about international cooperation, which is far from universal.

[64] In saying this, I do not pretend to suggest that translatability in international legal and political discourses is or ought to be an easy task of matching equivalents. As Lydia Liu explains, it consists rather in the making of such equivalents *between* languages and cultures, and this is performed through historical encounters that much reveal the incidental nature of international law. Cases like that of the concept of our concern, where the translation is so weak, might be seen as an instance where the encounter is marked by such a strong asymmetry that meaning is straightforwardly transferred, making the weakness of the encounter clear. On translatability in international law, see Lydia H. Liu, *The Clash of Empires: The Invention of China in Modern World Making* (Cambridge, USA: Harvard University Press, 2004), pp. 108–139.

28 THE CONCEPTUAL METAPHOR 'COALITION OF THE WILLING'

framing analysis and conceptual metaphor theory are insofar useful as they help to reveal those ideas and ideals that are involved in a given concept and that are often hidden or distorted through deliberate framing. In doing this, they significantly contribute to acknowledging that terms (and ideas) are not only often coined in a particular place, and then make their way to the international domain, but that they might be also, or even fundamentally, about something else which makes its way in silence through the back door. As I will argue in Chapter 3, a closer look at the frames involved in the expression 'coalition of the willing' reveals that we are not exclusively dealing with a pragmatic notion about the need of employing flexible mechanisms of international cooperation here and there, but also with a broader idea of how the globe should be ruled, as well as with hegemonic anxieties.

2.4 Why Resort to Framing and Conceptual Metaphors?

To state that each particular culture and subculture matters in the way people understand the world and frame their world-views should not be confounded with radical subjectivism, according to which meaning is entirely private and no objectivity can be achieved at all. Conceptual metaphors are grounded on non-metaphorical physical experiences, as well as cultural environments:

> Concepts emerge both from constant direct interaction with our environment and from knowledge we gain as members of our culture. Concepts have certain natural dimensions of structure, each of which is based on some aspect of our personal or cultural experience.[65]

Hence, understanding is about how we interact with these experiences and environments, and it is not unconstrained or arbitrary. But just as this notion distances itself from subjectivism, it also rejects the objectivists' paradigm according to which things and experiences have inherent properties (i.e., fixed to the objects and outside our minds), and their definition is about identifying them in terms of necessary and sufficient elements. Instead, conceptual metaphor theory understands properties as predominantly *interactional* – i.e., they emerge from the interaction with our experiences, primarily physical but also cultural. Understanding concepts partially in terms of other concepts consists precisely in

---

[65] George Lakoff and Mark Johnson, 'The Metaphorical Structure of the Human Conceptual System' (1980) 4 *Cognitive Science* 205.

assigning properties to the concepts involved that emerge from the correlations among the experiences on which each of the concepts is grounded; it is in this sense that similarities are created, not just compared.[66] One of the most ardent critiques to conceptual metaphor theory (and to cognitive linguistics more generally, as well as to its application to legal thought) states that it supposedly denies objective knowledge, reducing rational reasoning to rival framings.[67] Indeed, the said theory denies absolute objectivity in the sense of objective truths, but it postulates a different kind of objectivity that is relative to the conceptual systems grounded on our physical experiences and cultural environments.

This has been deceptively described as 'cognitive relativism',[68] suggesting that it abandons rationality altogether and advocates indeterminacy of knowledge and communication. However, this term also does quite accurately reflect the strength of the idea underlying the theory it criticizes, namely that truth is relative to understanding, and understanding relative to our experiences and conceptual systems; this could be called equally *experientialist objectivity*. Understanding is metaphorical, and hence imaginative and rational at the same time: it is about explaining things in terms of others through 'categorization, entailment and inference';[69] it 'means, quite simply, that we use physical and social experience and general cultural knowledge to categorize and understand'.[70]

It is important to underline that cognitive linguistics does not embrace indeterminacy in communication and understanding. As a legal scholar who applies it, I am emphatic in clarifying that I reject both the myth of textual determinacy and the doctrines of legal indeterminacy. Meaning in law is constrained and enabled by social

---

[66] 'Love' and 'affection' are paramount examples of how the properties we assign to these concepts emerge from the correlations involved in the metaphors that explain them: e.g., 'love is a journey' and 'affection is warmth'. This is by no means restricted to concepts dealing with emotions. See Lakoff and Johnson, *Metaphors We Live By*, pp. 119–125, 151–155, 255–257.

[67] For such a critique in regard to the conceptual metaphor theory of Lakoff and Johnson, see Pinker, *The Stuff of Thought*, pp. 245–278; for a similar critique concerning the application of cognitive linguistics in jurisprudence, see Patterson, 'Fashionable Nonsense', 845–867; 885–892.

[68] Steven Pinker, 'Block That Metaphor!', *The New Republic Online* (8 October 2006), at https://newrepublic.com/article/77730/block-metaphor-steven-pinker-whose-freedom-george-lakoff.

[69] Lakoff and Johnson, *Metaphors We Live By*, p. 193.

[70] Winter, *A Clearing in the Forest*, p. 12.

30 THE CONCEPTUAL METAPHOR 'COALITION OF THE WILLING'

experiences and cultural knowledge, and, therefore, determinacy is relative to social interactions.[71] In the words of Andrea Bianchi, legal meaning is a 'social construct',[72] and in those of Steven Winter, law is 'the product of an interaction between particular, situated historical actors'.[73] This is not far away from an important tendency in critical legal studies that 'rejects both the idea of global indeterminacy and the idea that there is always a correct interpretation, [and] it also rejects the idea that determinacy and indeterminacy are 'qualities' or 'attributes' inherent in the norm, independently of the work of the interpreter'.[74] Taking the idea of interactional properties a step further, it becomes also clear that not only specific legal norms but whole 'different legal orders, both formal and informal, and both past and present, constitute each other's practical meaning'.[75] This is to what Boaventura de Sousa Santos refers to as 'interlegality',[76] a notion I shall come back to in Chapter 7 when ascertaining what the interplay between formality and informality channelled through coalitions of the willing means for the role of law in today's global complex.

What may be called *imaginative rationality* represents a viable alternative for explaining socio-political issues where absolute truths grounded on formal logic and the assumption of inherent, fixed properties usually fail to comprehend the complexities of the phenomena, often leading to a disparity between theory and reality, and to the design of ineffective or even counter-productive responses. In regard to concepts that operate in the realm of international law and politics, conceptual metaphor theory is particularly valuable since it openly acknowledges that concepts, arguments, and theories highlight *and* hide

---

[71] I have observed this elsewhere, together with my coauthors, in relation to treaty interpretation by domestic courts; see Helmut P. Aust, Alejandro Rodiles and Peter Staubach, 'Unity or Uniformity? Domestic Courts and Treaty Interpretation' (2014) 27 *Leiden Journal of International Law* 75, at 78–79.

[72] Andrea Bianchi, 'Textual Interpretation and (International) Law Reading', pp. 51 et seq.

[73] Winter, *A Clearing in the Forest*, p. 317 (further stating, 'the fact that constraint in law is a dynamic social phenomenon rather than an immovable, external fact should be a scandal only to those still operating within the two-dimensional framework of objectivity versus subjectivity', p. 330).

[74] Duncan Kennedy, 'A Left Phenomenological Alternative to the Hart/Kelsen Theory of Legal Interpretation', in *id.*, *Legal Reasoning: Collected Essays* (Aurora: The Davies Group Publishers, 2008), p. 160.

[75] Valverde, *Chronotopes of Law*, p. 5.

[76] See Boaventura de Sousa Santos, 'Law: A Map of Misreading. Toward a Postmodern Conception of Law' (1987) 14 *Journal of Law and Society* 279, at 288.

2.4 WHY RESORT TO FRAMING AND CONCEPTUAL METAPHORS? 31

properties of phenomena instead of proposing that they articulate universal and absolute truths. Moreover, it makes clear that conflicting conceptual systems often render definitive standpoints about the world untenable. Most importantly, it emphasizes that understanding is very often only possible through the negotiation and renegotiation of meaning.[77] Such conceptual contestation is the essence of multilateral diplomacy and can only be in the interest of searching for some clarity and objectivity indeed.

I do not intend to deny that reframing arguments and concepts helps putting forward one's own views, values, and ideologies.[78] It is a choice, no doubt. But it is also about unravelling political, economic, and cultural choices already made by deconstructing the elements that are hidden.[79] Hence, framing analysis and conceptual metaphor theory help to make choices visible, and this is crucial for discovering the particular behind the universal, the 'false universals'[80] Martti Koskenniemi calls upon international lawyers to identify,[81] and which I believe to be one of the

---

[77] See Lakoff and Johnson, *Metaphors We Live By*, pp. 227, 231.

[78] There is an important difference between framing and reframing on the one hand and spin and propaganda on the other. The latter are manipulative uses of framing, where the meaning of something is purposively turned into something else (the opposite or an innocent version of it). Lakoff rejects these manipulative uses of framing, see Lakoff, *Don't Think of an Elephant!*, pp. 100–101. Probably, he would thus accept that using frames in which one believes and that express the moral views of the beholder implies a choice, and, thus, a certain rivalry is undeniable. It is also quite clear that distinguishing framing from spin and propaganda is not always an easy task.

[79] It has been criticized that framing analysis applied to unravelling the political, economic, and cultural choices made by judges and other law-applying authorities 'sounds like classical Legal Realism [and that] there is nothing here that can be identified or characterized as "cognitive"' (see Patterson, 'Fashionable Nonsense', at note 89 and accompanying text, referring to Amsterdam and Bruner, *Minding the Law*). It should come as no surprise that cognitive linguistics can be a powerful tool for legal analyses inspired or rooted in legal realism, nor does this deny its character as what it is. Winter actually is very clear on this: 'It is not difficult to imagine that if Llewellyn and the other legal realists were alive today, they would be the firsts to turn to the study of the mind better to understand life and law' (Winter, *A Clearing in the Forest*, p. 42).

[80] This expression is employed by Jeffrey Dunnoff in order to describe this recurrent theme in Koskenniemi's work; see Jeffrey L. Dunnoff, 'From Interdisciplinarity to Counterdisciplinarity: Is There Madness in Martti's Method?' (2013) 27 *Temple International and Comparative Law Journal* 309, at 328.

[81] See, e.g., Martti Koskenniemi, 'Hegemonic Regimes', in Margaret A. Young (ed.), *Regime Interaction in International Law: Facing Fragmentation* (Cambridge: Cambridge University Press, 2012), p. 305, at p. 324. As mentioned, this is a recurrent theme in Koskenniemi's work. I have chosen this text because it relates to regime complexes, which, as will become clear in Chapters 5 and 6, are the spaces where coalitions of the willing assemble

32 THE CONCEPTUAL METAPHOR 'COALITION OF THE WILLING'

most important tasks of the scholar concerned with the possibilities of construing an international law that is truly international.[82]

In fact, the contestation involved in framing analysis is not far away from other approaches in jurisprudence regarding the meaning(s) of certain juridical concepts and their function within legal systems. For instance, German legal philosopher and former constitutional judge, Ernst-Wolfgang Böckenförde, explains that many fundamental legal concepts, like '*Rechtsstaat*' or 'public security', can be best characterized through the metaphor '*Schleusenbegriffe*', which means 'floodgate concepts', which signifies that they cannot be defined once and for all, but are open to the 'flood' of changing political and constitutional ideas. For Böckenförde, it is the knowledge of their rival usages throughout history that enables a more systemic understanding of them.[83] This dialectical understanding calls to mind the thesis of 'essentially contested concepts', which Jeremy Waldron employs to analyze the concept of the rule of law.[84] The notion was originally conceived by philosopher W. B. Gallie, for whom this contestation 'implies recognition of rival uses ... as not

and interact with other mechanisms and institutions. Koskenniemi highlights there the importance of translating the vocabularies of managerialism of regimes and regime complexes, in order to 'undermine the propensity of such languages to present themselves as the global Esperanto ... [and to] highlight the partial and contestable nature of the knowledge we have about the world'.

[82] This is one of the main tasks of the comparative international law project; for an early articulation, see Martti Koskenniemi, 'The Case for Comparative International Law' (2009) 20 *Finnish Yearbook of International Law* 1; for a comprehensive volume uniting different voices, see Anthea Roberts, Paul B. Stephen, Pierre-Hughes Verdier and Mila Versteeg (eds.), *Comparative International Law* (Oxford: Oxford University Press, 2018); see also Anthea Roberts, *Is International Law International?* (Oxford: Oxford University Press, 2017). By focusing on the differences and similarities in the ways international law is taught in different places, Roberts helps debunk the myth of the universality of the academic discipline of international law, which has been very much centred on Western scholarship.

[83] See Ernst-Wolfgang Böckenförde, 'Entstehung und Wandel des Rechtsstaatsbegriffs', in id., *Recht, Staat, Freiheit. Studien zur Rechtsphilosophie, Staatstheorie und Verfassungsgeschichte*, second edition (Frankfurt a.M.: Suhrkamp 2006), p. 143, pp. 143–144.

[84] Jeremy Waldron, 'Is the Rule of Law an Essentially Contested Concept (in Florida)?' (2002) 21 *Law and Philosophy* 137. Elsewhere, I have compared Böckenförde's and Waldron's theses and applied them to the 'rule of law' at the international level, particularly in relation to the so-called 'thinner' and 'thicker' versions of it; see Alejandro Rodiles, 'Non-Permanent Members of the United Nations Security Council and the Promotion of the International Rule of Law' (2013) 5 *Goettingen Journal of International Law* 333, at note 38.

only logically possible and humanly 'likely', but as of permanent critical value to one's own use or interpretation of the concept in question'.[85]

The conceptual contestation involved in framing analysis, and the fact that conceptual metaphor theory does not focus on defining concepts but instead on how to 'get a handle' on them (i.e. on how they are understood by those using them, how they function, and make the ones using them function themselves)[86] is what makes this approach so appealing and useful for the present book. In other words, when dealing with a contested catchphrase circulating international legal and political discourses like 'coalition of the willing', it does not sound like a promising intellectual enterprise to concentrate efforts in order to state that 'coalitions of the willing are x and y'. It seems far more fruitful to take a close look into how the concept has been used by whom and for what purposes, how it functions in international politics and law, and how it affects international political and legal discourses. Also, in the coming chapters, I will show that coalitions' most appealing working method is persuasion and that some of their outcomes are themselves products of framing: innovative regulatory devices are created for inducing the international audience to voluntarily adopt this or that measure. These devices are very efficient and becoming a general trend in international affairs. Framing, like nudging,[87] may thus be part of an increasing arsenal of ruling devices where the fundamental distinction between legal and illegal is losing ground.

2.5   Conclusion

This *excursus* into framing analysis and conceptual metaphor theory has shown that searching for a clear definition of the phenomenon that is referred to as 'coalition of the willing' is not as important as it may have seemed before. What matters is to know under which circumstances the phenomenon came into being, on which surface and deep frames the concept is grounded, how it works, and what are the main goals pursued by it.

---

[85] W. B. Gallie, 'Essentially Contested Concepts' (1955–1956) 56 *Proceedings of the Aristotelian Society* 193, cited in Waldron, 'Is the Rule of Law an Essentially Contested Concept?', 151.

[86] See Lakoff and Johnson, *Metaphors We Live By*, p. 116.

[87] See Cass R. Sunstein, *Why Nudge? The Politics of Libertarian Paternalism* (New Haven/London: Yale University Press, 2014).

34 THE CONCEPTUAL METAPHOR 'COALITION OF THE WILLING'

On this basis, the point is made here that 'coalition of the willing' is a metaphorical concept by means of which instances of international co-operation (the target domain 'coalition') are to be understood and experienced in terms of the willingness and the ability to do the right thing (the source domain 'willingness and ability'); let us keep in mind that 'coalition of the willing' is the abbreviated form of the expression 'coalition of the willing and able'. The metaphor consists in a personification whereby human characteristics (willingness and ability) are attributed to non-human entities (coalitions). The personification of groups of states and other collective actors goes back to one of the principal metaphors structuring international political, economic, and legal discourses, namely the personification of the state.[88] Willingness and ability entail the ideas (surface frames) of friendship and virtue, as well as those of expediency, flexibility, and efficiency. Hence, the metaphor is about understanding international co-operation as performed by selective groups of states and other actors, which come together in a very flexible (i.e., informal) manner to efficiently pursue their goals. Inclusiveness is subordinated to selectiveness since those who are to coalesce are the ones who share an affinity in means and goals – i.e., the 'friendship frame' that implies exclusion. The *efficiency paradigm*, on its part, overrides procedural fairness and form; coalitions are instrumental and amorphous.[89] No one has described this in more precise terms than former US Secretary of Defense Donald Rumsfeld: '*the mission must determine the coalition, the coalition must not determine the mission*, or else the mission will be dumbed down to the lowest common denominator'.[90]

This shows that the surface frames involved in the conceptual metaphor 'coalition of the willing' are grounded in the predominantly Western ideal (deep frame) that certain values are intrinsically good, and, therefore, achieving them justifies the means. I call this the *Western missionary deep frame*. By appealing to the concepts and values reflected in the surface frames of 'friendship' and 'efficiency', this catchphrase is

---

[88] See Paul Chilton and George Lakoff, 'Foreign Policy by Metaphor', in Christina Schäffner and Anita L. Wenden (eds.), *Language & Peace* (Aldershot: Ashgate, 1995), p. 37. See also Martti Koskenniemi, 'Miserable Comforters: International Relations as New Natural Law', (2009) 15 *European Journal of International Relations* 395, at 402 (referring 'the anthropomorphic metaphor of states acting in the international world as "moral entities"' back to Samuel von Pufendorf's international law vocabulary).

[89] See Rodiles, '*Coalitions of the Willing*: Coyuntura, Contexto y Propiedades', 684–700.

[90] Rumsfeld made this point several times, I refer here to Donald A. Rumsfeld, 'Transforming the Military' (May/June 2002) *Foreign Affairs* 20, at 31. Emphasis added.

2.5 CONCLUSION

intended to distract from some of the central motivations behind its uses, thus performing a *partial briefing function*. Once these concealed motivations come to the surface, it will be easier to distinguish coalitions of the willing from other related phenomena. I will do this in the following chapter by situating the concept within the political and legal discourses where it has been articulated in a more systematic way.

Before doing that, however, it should be stressed that the fact that the concept of our concern does not have *a* meaning that hermetically contains its elements once and for all, does not mean that everything can be named randomly by it. As mentioned previously, framing analysis and conceptual metaphor theory do not embrace absolute indeterminacy. Despite the absence of a clear and pure definition, the conceptual metaphor 'coalition of the willing' transmits a coherent picture of the ideas and ideals involved in this instance of international co-operation.[91] Engaging into a theoretical speculation that would take as a starting point some *a priori* characterizations (and typologies) as working hypotheses is a tempting method, which would seem to offer a clearer way ahead. But this could soon turn out to be a *phenomenological trap*, as mentioned earlier. With this I mean that the analysis of the phenomenon would be prejudiced from the outset precisely because its characteristics (the properties of the phenomenon) would be taken for granted on the basis of little evidence (the 'proper elements' that allow one to speak of x and not z). Instead, in the next chapter, I will observe the discourses and situations where the expression has been used, paying special attention to those where it has played a strategic role, and how it has evolved within them; in short, the genealogy of the catchphrase will be traced.

A final remark must be made in relation to the contemporary usages and actual appeal of the expression. As mentioned at the beginning of this chapter, the Iraq War of 2003 brought the phenomenon into public awareness and made the catchphrase 'coalition of the willing' common currency in the media and beyond. Before that, the term was pretty much reserved to American foreign policy and international politics and law specialists. As could be expected, once the expression was extensively associated with the illegal invasion carried out by the USA and its

---

[91] Coherence is to be understood here as the inferences that permit correlating the target domain ('coalition') to the source domains ('willingness' and 'ability') – i.e. the metaphorical entailments that make the imparting of characteristics from one domain to the other fit together; see further Lakoff and Johnson, *Metaphors We Live By*, pp. 89–96; see also Kövecses, *Metaphor: A Practical Introduction*, pp. 121–132.

coalition partners, and later on with the pictures of Abu-Ghraib and Guantanamo and the overall aggressive foreign policy rhetoric and actions of the George W. Bush administration, the catchphrase acquired very negative connotations among laypersons, diplomats, and international law and relations scholars. Accordingly, the notion of 'effective multilateralism'[92] originally attached to the catchphrase started to lose credibility, and coalitions of the willing were more and more perceived as paramount examples of disguised US unilateralism,[93] as well as a sign of the imperial overstretch experienced during those years. Since then, and during the second term of President George W. Bush,[94] the catchphrase 'coalition of the willing' slowly lost its prominence in US foreign policy discourse and in international politics.[95] Today, it is more common to hear just about 'coalitions', 'initiatives', 'platforms', and increasingly about 'partnerships'. However, and as I will show in the following chapters, the ideas behind these words are pretty much the same as those

[92] Although 'effective multilateralism' is mostly associated with European Union foreign policy, here I am referring to the conception advocated by the United Kingdom and the United States in the aftermath of the Iraq War of 2003, and which is closely related to the 'coalition of the willing approach'; see George W. Bush and Tony Blair, 'Effective Multilateralism to Build a Better World: Joint Statement by President George W. Bush and Prime Minister Tony Blair, November 20, 2003', reprinted in US Government Printing Office, *Weekly Compilation of Presidential Documents*, vol. 39, issue 47 (2003), pp. 1658–1660.

[93] See, for example, Thomas Risse, 'The Crisis of the Transatlantic Security Community', in Dimitris Bourantonis, Kostas Ifantis and Panayotis Tsakonas (eds.), *Multilateralism and Security Institutions in an Era of Globalization* (New York: Routledge, 2008) p. 78, at p. 91.

[94] Of course, this was due also to internal political reasons. As the American public began to be increasingly pessimistic about the war in Iraq, the second Bush Jr. administration began to resort to euphemisms to replace the metaphors still employed during its first term. Another example is the 'struggle against violent extremism' instead of the 'war on terror'; see Eric Schmitt and Thom Shanker, 'Washington recasts terror war as "struggle"', *The New York Times* (27 July 2007), at www.nytimes.com/2005/07/26/world/americas/26iht-terror.html.

[95] This change in rhetoric is further documented in Chapter 3. For now, suffice it to mention that whereas the US National Security Strategy 2002 uses the term 'coalition of willing' or 'coalitions of the willing and able' four times, the 2006 Strategy does this only once, and the National Security Strategy of the Obama administration abandons the term altogether; see *The National Security Strategy of the United States of America* (September 2002), preface and pp. 11, 25, at www.state.gov/documents/organization/63562.pdf; *The National Security Strategy of the United States of America* (March 2006) [hereinafter '*US National Security Strategy 2006*'], p. 48, at www.comw.org/qdr/fulltext/nss2006.pdf; and *National Security Strategy* (May 2010), at http://nssarchive.us/NSSR/2010.pdf.

involved in the 'old' catchphrase, and coalitions of the willing are not only still being employed in the international realm but also are actually proliferating in the various fields of global governance. Thus, the usage of the said euphemisms clearly reveals reframing efforts, in particular by the principal advocates of the idea, the USA – also during the Obama administration. This is a clear case of 'spin', whereby innocent frames are put on something embarrassing that has been said or happened, trying to distract from such arguments, evaluations and events, but without changing the basic idea(s) that led to those arguments, evaluations, and events.[96] Hence, I consciously make the choice of maintaining the term 'coalition of the willing' throughout the present book in order to remind the reader that we are still in presence of the same concept (and phenomenon).[97]

---

[96] See note 78.

[97] Occasionally, when referring to concrete manifestations that carry such names (e.g., the *Proliferation Security Initiative*), I will use terms like 'initiative' or 'partnership' but in the understanding that we are still in the presence of coalitions of the willing, no matter how they have been renamed.

3

Testing the Frame: The Genealogy of a Catchphrase

The mission must determine the coalition, the coalition must not determine the mission.

Donald A. Rumsfeld[1]

In Chapter 1, we saw that it is very difficult, if not futile, to search for an exact definition of the concept 'coalition of the willing'. People understand different things by it, and there is no way to divine the 'right' meaning. But I argued also that finding a clear definition is not as important as it may have seemed before. In the end, what matters is to understand how the phenomenon called 'coalition of the willing' works in the international realm, and to that end, it is much more helpful to know how the concept is used, by whom, and for what purposes – in other words, to 'get a handle' on it.[2] Following the conceptual metaphor theory of George Lakoff and Mark Johnson, I looked at the expression not as a single concept in the traditional sense of having inherent properties but instead as a conceptual (metaphorical) structure, where properties emerge from the interactions with the phenomenon – i.e. how it is experienced, in which contexts, and by whom.

In this vein, I propose to understand 'coalition of the willing' as a conceptual metaphor according to which international co-operation is understood and experienced in terms of the willingness and the ability to do 'the right thing'. The target (coalition) and source domains (willing and able) of this metaphor evoke the notions of co-operation, as well as those of friendship, virtue, and efficiency. One of the main ideas that is put forward by this conceptual metaphor is that like-minded actors share a sense for what values are worth protecting and pursuing, and they are therefore better suited to perform resolutely the mission: they are the

---

[1] Rumsfeld, 'Transforming the Military', 31.
[2] Lakoff and Johnson, *Metaphors We Live By*, p. 116.

TESTING THE FRAME: THE GENEALOGY OF A CATCHPHRASE   39

force to carry out the task.[3] Capability and willingness go hand in hand under this notion: it is about the ability to do the right thing, and the 'right thing' is determined by the values friends hold in common. This is crucial inasmuch as it denotes the underlying representation of a division between friends – i.e. 'those ... to whom the same things are good and evil'–[4] and foes. In other words, borrowing from Antony Anghie, we are talking about a 'dynamic of difference'[5] between those who share certain values and are willing to defend them, and those who are unwilling or unable.[6] Depending on the seriousness of the issues at hand, especially when these are related to international security, unwilling or unable actors are often perceived as 'outlaws', 'rogue', or 'evil'.[7] Selectiveness and exclusion are the corollaries of efficiency and affinity. Hence, according to the coalition of the willing frame, international co-operation is not understood as an inclusive enterprise of a larger community (or aimed at building that community), based on the (formal) requirements that enable equal participation, but rather as selective and expedient co-operation. This model of ad hoc international co-operation is driven by what can be called the *efficiency paradigm*, which calls for a high degree of flexibility: co-operation is not to be stacked in any regular form; for the sake of efficiency, it is to remain amorphous.[8]

---

[3] Not coincidentally, coalitions are sometimes called 'task forces'; on the *Financial Action Task Force* (FATF), see Chapter 5.

[4] Aristotle, *Rhetoric*, 1381a.

[5] See Antony Anghie, *Imperialism, Sovereignty and the Making of International Law* (Cambridge: Cambridge University Press, 2007), pp. 9 and 315–316; for a similar approach, focused on how the distinction between the 'self' and the 'other' in European representations has informed the foundations and the evolution of international law, see Siba N'Zatioula Grovogui, *Sovereigns, Quasi Sovereigns and Africans* (Minneapolis: The University of Minnesota Press, 1996).

[6] The distinction between 'willing/able' and 'unwilling/unable' states is certainly not new to international legal and political discourses, but it has experienced an important revival in the era of the 'global war on terror', leading, *inter alia*, to the controversial 'unwilling or unable test' in the framework of the right to self-defence (see Section 3.2.1.3). However, its implications are not restricted to self-defence issues; they play an important role in relation to other concepts and doctrines that have a bearing on legal, economic, and military interventions, such as the notions of failed states, the responsibility to protect (R2P), and human security.

[7] For instance, states that have been perceived as unwilling or unable to prevent the proliferation of weapons of mass destruction (WMDs) have been described by US administrations as 'outlaw' (George H.W. Bush), 'rogue' (Clinton), or 'evil' – i.e. belonging to the 'axis of evil' (George W. Bush). See Lee Feinstein and Anne-Marie Slaughter, 'A Duty to Prevent', (January/February 2004) *Foreign Affairs* 136, at 139.

[8] See Rodiles, '*Coalitions of the Willing*: Coyuntura, Contexto y Propiedades', 693–695.

The resort to Anghie's 'dynamic of difference' suggests that international law has always been selective, based on exclusion rather than inclusion, and therefore that one of the fundamental characteristics identified in this book in regard to coalitions of the willing is not new, perhaps not even specific to them. It is precisely this sort of continuum in the history of international law to which I want to draw attention by invoking the conceptual frameworks of authors like Anghie and N'Zatioula Grovogui. As will become clear in the course of the book, coalitions of the willing are interactional mechanisms that are shaping the ways in which international law is made today. They do this through innovative means of co-ordinated action and regulation at the global level – i.e. at the international and transnational levels. The two fundamentals mostly affected by coalitions and other related phenomena are the principle of sovereign equality and the notion of organized multilateralism – i.e. the post-war architecture of the international community as represented by the United Nations (UN) and other international organizations (IOs). Sovereign equality has always been a fiction, no doubt, but one that nevertheless has contained the exercise of sheer power to a certain extent and has afforded some degree of participation to all states.[9] International institutions, and the UN in particular, reflect inequalities and have also served to institutionalize hegemonies; the composition of the Security Council being only one example, albeit the most notorious one. But, to some extent, decolonization and concerted moves by the less powerful have transformed the UN into a more democratic institution.[10] It should not be underestimated how much states that are represented in the G77 and the Non-Aligned Movement (NAM), as well as others that do not qualify as powerful players, cherish this institution as their common asset. This goes beyond state representatives; members of civil societies of less powerful states also see a venue to articulate their demands in the UN. What this shows is not that the international legal order is inherently inclusive, transparent, and just, as opposed to coalitions of the willing, but rather that this exclusive and opaque legal order has been corrected over time; it has offered room to insert the interests of the less powerful, or just the 'other'; its language has also favoured the articulation of broader demands beyond power politics. In sum, the

---

[9] See Kingsbury, 'Sovereignty and Inequality'.

[10] See Mark Mazower, *No Enchanted Palace: The End of Empire and the Ideological Origins of the United Nations* (Princeton: Princeton University Press, 2008), pp. 149 et seq.

question of *whose international law are we talking about*, is subject to an ongoing contestation.[11]

I conceive coalitions of the willing as part of these struggles about the historical project of international law. I regard them as a newer attempt at shifting the balance in favour of the interests of power. Thus, the dynamic of difference is neither new nor something specific to them, but coupled with the efficiency paradigm, as it is within the coalition of the willing approach, this dynamic acquires a new strength in times of rapidly evolving global risks.

3.1 The Western Missionary Deep Frame

The coalition of the willing frame reflects a highly instrumentalist understanding of international co-operation and law as it is driven by a strong conviction that the achievement of specific objectives, as well as the defence and promotion of certain values, override form and processes. To say that 'the mission must determine the coalition'[12] is to postulate that the end justifies the means. This can be described as the maximization of the particular rationalities[13] that motivate each coalition (and each case of coalition building), a driving force in the proliferation of instances of global governance. At the same time and perhaps at a more fundamental level, it is the expression of a mission-driven thinking, according to which the mission is about defending, promoting, and achieving higher values. Thus, the mission itself becomes intrinsically good. I call this the *Western missionary deep frame*. With this, I am not suggesting that every coalition of the willing is necessarily driven by (or actively engages in) a 'civilizing mission' that is in 'a mission to elevate

---

[11] Elsewhere, I use the same argument in order to show that the aspiration of *one* universal international law has been a major struggle for Latin American international lawyers for whom this historical project is an existential political question related to the place of Latin American countries in the international community; see Alejandro Rodiles, 'The Great Promise of Comparative Public Law for Latin America – Toward *Ius Commune Americanum?*', in Anthea Roberts, Paul B. Stephen, Pierre-Hughes Verdier, and Mila Versteeg (eds.), *Comparative International Law* (Oxford: Oxford University Press, 2018), p. 501, at 521–522.

[12] Rumsfeld, 'Transforming the Military', 31.

[13] On the 'maximization of inherent rationality', see Andreas Fischer-Lescano and Gunther Teubner, *Regime-Kollisionen. Zur Fragmentierung des globalen Rechts* (Frankfurt a.M.: Suhrkamp, 2006), pp. 25 et seq.

the other' unwilling or unable ones.[14] However, there is indeed a 'dynamic of difference' inherent to this approach to international action.

As mentioned in the previous chapter, the coalition of the willing metaphor is a personification of groups of states and other collective actors, which are attributed human characteristics (willingness and ability, and whatever comes along with that). This goes back to one of the principal metaphors structuring international political, economic, and legal discourses – namely the personification of the state.[15] Under this structure of thought, the willing and able state is considered the responsible adult (the moral person), whereas the unwilling or unable is either thought of as a child who still needs to be educated or as an irresponsible adolescent whose actions cannot be trusted. The willing and able have the self-awareness of holding a special responsibility in the international community, and in the absence of a broader agreement on the concrete configurations of that community, they consider themselves as having the privilege and duty to take the initiative to uphold the common goods that are considered indispensable – be it security, the environment, or the stability of trade and finance, to name but a few. In doing this, they not only claim the self-arrogation in the determination of the global public goods and values to be defended (to determine the mission),[16] but also to act on behalf of the unwilling or unable (to build and assemble coalitions, and engage in the capacity building – i.e., education – of the unable ones), if the case so requires.[17] And here, we can observe how, in the reconfiguration of the international landscape over time, 'colonial structures' are – partially but fundamentally – reproduced in new forms and vocabularies. Antony Anghie and Siba N'Zatioula Grovogui have argued that there is a continuum in the civilizing mission: from colonies to mandates over development to good governance. The distinction between willing/able and unwilling/unable can be regarded as part of

---

[14] Grovogui, *Sovereigns, Quasi Sovereigns, and Africans*, p. x.

[15] See Chapter 1, note 88, and accompanying text.

[16] For an overview on global public goods and international law (and the need to better conceptualize these in our field), see Gregory Shaffer, 'International Law and Global Public Goods in a Legal Pluralist World' (2012) 23 *European Journal of International Law* 669.

[17] On the role of global public goods in the articulation and justification of the effective international action required, which often leads to informal and flexible mechanisms in disregard of state consent, see Krisch, 'The Decay of Consent', 3–7. Noting that 'one reason policy-makers arguably have developed a broader definition of global public goods is to enhance the scope for global governance projects and thus legitimize their pursuit', see Shaffer, 'International Law and Global Public Goods', 674.

3.1 THE WESTERN MISSIONARY DEEP FRAME

this continuum: the idea of the coalition of the willing is informed by a division of the international community between responsible, efficient global actors and the rest. And the prerogative of the initiative to determine the mission and assemble coalitions clearly belongs to the former.

If this dynamic of difference informs the idea behind coalitions of the willing, then there is a clear analogy to the missionary thinking that post-colonial scholars denounce. But the missionary deep frame is also about a strong sense of pragmatism: if a goal is important – as the maintenance of international security, the protection of the global environment, and the stability of global finance are – ideas of inclusion, procedural fairness, certainty, and even accountability are regarded as only supplementary values and norms, which can be circumvented for the sake of the achievement of substantive values and the protection of global public goods. This pragmatism is inevitably anti-formalistic, but it is not the sort of pragmatism that rejects the faith in an unequivocal way to conceptualize things and ideas –[18] quite to the contrary. It is premised on the assumption of the existence of higher, intrinsic, and universal (i.e. universally valid and with universal meaning) values and goods that justify the means that enable their achievement. It is, in this sense, a newer, post–Cold War version of natural law.[19]

The reason to situate this trend in the post–Cold War era will become clearer once the genealogy of the concept 'coalition of the willing' is traced (in the next section). For now, it should be recalled that the end of the major blocs' opposition generated a series of great expectations, epitomized in the reappearance of the grand formula of a 'new world order'.[20] The advent of the unipolar moment and the apparent triumph of liberal democracy gave rise to what Sundhya Pahuja pointedly calls 'much more evangelical possibilities'.[21] Pahuja identifies two forms of

---

[18] Following the tradition of Charles Sandars Pierce, Willian James and John Dewey; see Christopher Hookway, 'Pragmatism', in Edward N. Zalta (ed.), *The Stanford Encyclopedia of Philosophy* (Winter 2013 Edition), at http://plato.stanford.edu/archives/win2013/entries/pragmatism/.

[19] Cf. Koskenniemi, 'Miserable Comforters'.

[20] Strategically advanced by former US President George H. W. Bush, for example, in his 'new world order speech': George H. W. Bush, *Address before a Joint Session of Congress* (11 September 1990), at http://www.presidency.ucsb.edu/ws/?pid=18820.

[21] Sundhya Pahuja, *Decolonising International Law: Development, Economic Growth and the Politics of Universality* (Cambridge: Cambridge University Press, 2011), p. 179.

44 TESTING THE FRAME: THE GENEALOGY OF A CATCHPHRASE

this post–Cold War evangelism: the human rights project and putative realism, both asserting 'the universality of liberal democracy ... in a new world order'.[22] On his part, Martti Koskenniemi recalls that, at the same time, 'the inherited language of the modern states-system, and international law, no longer seem[ed] able to give voice to important groups and interests'.[23] This 'old' language of sovereign equality and formal legal principles was – and is – 'challenged by the new idioms of globalization and transnational governance'.[24]

The missions that determine coalitions of the willing are of many different kinds, ranging from counter-terrorism and non-proliferation of weapons of mass destruction (WMDs) to the stabilization of global finance to the fight against climate change. Thus, the new and several idioms of globalization and transnational governance nurture the rationalities that underlie each coalition. But could it be that, beyond each of these rationalities, there is an underlying theme that upholds the idea of coalition of the willing over time? In the ensuing section, I will show that its different usages reflect an intense preoccupation with losing control in today's global disorder. This anxiety started within US foreign policy discourse with the collapse of the bipolar structure – if only because the USA found itself as the remaining superpower. It has been shaped over time by the same foreign policy elite according to other tectonic shifts in world affairs. Hence, the ideals and specifics of the coalition of the willing approach are genealogically tied to US foreign policy grand strategy as developed from the early 1990s until the administration of Barack Obama. In today's non-polar world, the multilayered and flexible global governance strategy – of which coalitions of the willing are an essential component – has been appropriated by other powers, including the so-called 'Global South'. The (current) retreat of the USA from world ordering projects since the elections of 8 November 2016 (11/8) may enhance this tendency. However, states from the Global South reveal often an ambivalent attitude towards the informality inherent to this strategy and thus to the instrumentalist understanding of multilateralism and international law. The following genealogy will conclude with some brief remarks on the future of coalitions of the willing in this non-polar, post-11/8 global environment.

[22] Ibid.
[23] Koskenniemi, 'Miserable Comforters', 396.
[24] Ibid.

3.2 The Genealogy of the Concept

It is not my intention to write a brief history of coalitions of the willing but to sketch an account of the distinct usages the term has experienced throughout different phases of international relations. Coalitions of the willing are mainly post–Cold War creatures, but besides that, it is very difficult to delineate a chronology of their different appearances. The catchphrase is contested and of an open texture, where evolving views on international order have a deep impact on how the concept is concretized over time. It is in this sense that a genealogy of the catchphrase can contribute to a more comprehensive understanding of the concept.[25]

The notion of 'genealogy' used here is inspired by Michel Foucault's understanding of it – itself inspired by Friedrich Nietzsche – as the provenance and emergence of singular events and not as linear history in search for origins.[26] In other words, in tracing the descent of coalitions of the willing, I will give an account of the events, discourses, and practices in which these post–Cold War creatures have been deployed.[27] So understood, this genealogy has also the intention of deneutralizing the seemingly neutral vocabularies and spins that are employed to label the form of international co-operation that underlies the conceptual meta-phor 'coalition of the willing'. In other words, the following pages shall serve to translate the neutral or technocratic semantics of 'partnerships', 'platforms', and 'initiatives', back into political terms, precisely by asking where these partnerships and initiatives come from and whom they serve. Indeed, as Koskenniemi mentions, '[v]ocabularies have histories that are tied with the genealogies of particular forms of rule'.[28]

---

[25] This passage owes much to Ernst-Wolfgang Böckenförde's 'Entstehung und Wandel des Rechtsstaatsbegriffs' in E.W. Böckenförde, *Recht, Staat, Freiheit* (Frankfurt a.M.: Sur-kamp, 2006), pp. 143–144 (referring to the concept of '*Rechtsstaat*', which he describes as a 'flood-gate-concept' ('*Schleusenbegriff*'), open to evolving representations that cannot be defined once and for all but has to be analyzed through the historical development of its usages in order to arrive at a 'systemic understanding of the concept'; other examples of 'flood-gate-concepts' include 'public security' and 'public order'); see also Chapter 1, note 83. and accompanying text.

[26] See Michel Foucault, 'Nietzsche, Genealogy, History', in Donald F. Bouchard (ed.), *Language, Counter-Memory, Practice* (Ithaca: Cornell University Press, 1977), p. 139, at pp. 140–141.

[27] Cf. David-Olivier Gougelet and Ellen K. Feder, 'Genealogies of Race and Gender', in Christopher Falzon, Timothy O'Leary and Jana Sawicki (eds.), *A Companion to Foucault* (Chichester: Willey-Blackwell, 2013), p. 472, at p. 473.

[28] Koskenniemi, 'Hegemonic Regimes', 324.

46 TESTING THE FRAME: THE GENEALOGY OF A CATCHPHRASE

3.2.1 The First Uses of the Catchphrase: Collective Security and 'New World Order'

There is no reliable evidence regarding the exact origin of the expression 'coalition of the willing'. The first documented usages, which date back to the first Clinton administration, refer to it as *'what has been called* a "coalition of the willing"',[29] without specifying the matter any further. However, it is plausible to link these references to a phenomenon that has its roots in the Korean War of 1950 but only became common in the 1990s, coinciding with the beginning of the post–Cold War era. The new international activism resulting from the weakening and partial disappearance of bipolar structures has often been exemplified by the Gulf War of 1991 and the US-led 'coalition', as President George W. H. Bush called *Operation Desert Storm*,[30] which removed Iraqi troops from Kuwait. In this sense, this military operation and its predecessor, *Operation Desert Shield*, are regarded as the early models of coalitions of the willing and are, most probably, the phenomena to which the early usages of the catchphrase, especially within the US administration, refer to as *'what has been called* a coalition of the willing'.[31]

This can be regarded from two perspectives. First, coalitions of the willing are viewed as manifestations of a new and more decisive US activism in world affairs, made possible by the collapse of the Soviet Union in the early 1990s;[32] an era characterized as the 'unipolar moment'.[33] Second, coalitions are seen as a sign of the new possibilities of international co-operation and of a reinvigorated collective security system.[34] In the latter case, the emphasis is on international law and the UN: an era 'where the rule of law supplants the rule of the jungle'.[35] In the end, both perspectives are expressions of the same: the promises of a

---

[29] William J. Clinton, *Interview of the President by Sam Donaldson, ABC* (5 June 1994), at www.ibiblio.org/pub/archives/whitehouse-papers/1994/Jun/1994-06-05-Presidents-ABC-Interview-on-USS-George-Washington. Emphasis added.

[30] George H.W. Bush, *Address to the Nation on the Invasion of Iraq* (16 January 1991), at http://www.americanrhetoric.com/speeches/ghwbushiraqinvasion.htm.

[31] See note 29.

[32] SC resolutions concerning Iraq's invasion of Kuwait are regarded as manifestations of the ending of the Cold War precisely because of the collaboration of the former Soviet Union in the Council in the course of 1990.

[33] See only Charles Krauthammer, 'The Unipolar Moment' (1990) 70 *Foreign Affairs* 23.

[34] Cf. Oscar Schachter, 'United Nations Law in the Gulf Conflict' (1991) 85 *The American Journal of International Law* 452.

[35] George H. W. Bush, *Address before a Joint Session of Congress* (11 September 1990).

3.2 THE GENEALOGY OF THE CONCEPT

new era for organized multilateralism and international law under the leadership of the 'indispensable nation'.[36] It is important to highlight this because it is a recurrent theme of coalitions of the willing: they are means to promote international law's efficacy *and* instruments of power. This tension will accompany us throughout the book. In the course of the book, I shall make the case that the conception of international law advanced through this approach is a highly instrumental one that is ultimately at the service of power.

3.2.1.1 Charter Adaptation through Coalitions

Chapter VII resolutions of the United Nations Security Council (SC) authorizing the use of force to multinational forces have experienced a well-documented growth since 1990,[37] and SC resolution 678[38] is commonly regarded as the starting point of this evolution.[39] Notwithstanding, an important episode of this story can already be found at the beginning of the Cold War, namely the US-led intervention in the Korean War, in 1950. As commented in 1991 by Thomas Franck and Faiza Patel:

> the practice of the Security Council has evolved other means of taking coercive measures, including the use of police forces raised ad hoc in response to a specific threat to the peace. Both the Korean and the Kuwaiti situations are examples.[40]

---

[36] Catchphrase commonly attributed to former US Secretary of State Madeleine Albright; see Secretary of State Madeleine K. Albright, *Interview on NBC-TV "The Today Show" with Matt Lauer* (19 February 1998), at www.state.gov/1997-2001-NOPDFS/statements/1998/980219a.html.

[37] See David M. Malone (ed.), *The UN Security Council, From the Cold War to the 21st Century* (Colorado: International Peace Academy/Lynne Rienner Publishers, 2004), pp. 653–668; see also Vaughan Lowe et al. (eds.), *The United Nations Security Council and War: The Evolution of Thought and Practice since 1945* (Oxford: Oxford University Press, 2008), pp. 672–677.

[38] SC Res. 678 (29 November 1990).

[39] See, for example, Christine Gray, *International Law and the Use of Force*, third edition (Oxford: Oxford University Press, 2008), pp. 327, 366.

[40] Thomas M. Franck and Faiza Patel, 'UN Police Action in Lieu of War: "The Old Order Changeth"' (1991) 85 *The American Journal of International Law* 63, at 66. At the same time, Oscar Schachter derived important implications from the fact that 'Article 43 has become a dead letter', which point in a similar direction; see Schachter, 'United Nations Law in the Gulf Conflict', 463–465.

48 TESTING THE FRAME: THE GENEALOGY OF A CATCHPHRASE

Although the treatment of the Korean crisis within the SC occurred under specific circumstances, where the Soviet Union was largely absent,[41] SC resolutions 83[42] and 84[43] represent, nevertheless, the first authorization to UN member states on the use of force pursuant to Article 42 of the UN Charter.[44] In particular, resolution 83 of June 1950

> [r]ecommends that Members of the United Nations furnish such assistance to the Republic of Korea *as may be necessary* to repel the armed attack and to restore international peace and security in the area.[45]

The Council's call on UN member states to provide military forces 'to a unified command under the United States of America' in order to conduct operations against North Korea is also the first case of an US-led coalition of able and willing states acting on behalf of the UN collective security system, although it was not called that way.[46] And it should remain a rather lonely precedent until the Soviet Union once again disappeared from the SC,[47] though this time for longer than a couple of months.

From 1990 onwards,[48] chapter VII authorizations to UN member states to use force for the maintenance or restoration of international

---

[41] SC resolutions on the Korean crisis were all, with the exception of SC Res. 88 (8 November 1950) (deciding to invite the People's Republic of China to the discussions on the issue) and SC Res. 90 (31 January 1951) (regarding the removal of the topic from the Council's agenda), released during the Soviet Union's blockade to the UN due to the refusal to accept the People's Republic of China in the world organization instead of the Republic of China (Taiwan).

[42] SC Res. 83 (27 June 1950).

[43] SC Res. 84 (7 July 1950).

[44] Charter of the United Nations (UN Charter) 1 UNTS (1946) xvi. The language of these resolutions suggests that the Council was making a call to exercise the right of collective self-defence, so that the legal basis of that intervention is also to be found in Art. 51 UN Charter.

[45] SC Res. 83 (27 June 1950). Emphasis added. The expression 'as may be necessary' can be regarded as the first precedent of today's common formula 'all necessary means/measures', which represents the agreed language within the Council on use of force authorizations.

[46] SC Res. 84, operative paragraph (op.) 3.

[47] One exception must however be noted. In 1966, the SC authorized the United Kingdom of Great Britain and Northern Ireland (UK) to use its naval force to prevent the delivery of oil to the racist regime of Southern Rhodesia. Although it did neither involve the USA nor a coalition of states, this case constitutes a clear example of SC authorizations to member states on the use of force. See SC Res. 221 (9 April 1966), op. 5.

[48] To be exact, from 25 August 1990 onwards: SC Res. 665 (25 August 1990), op. 1, already authorizes 'Member States co-operating with the Government of Kuwait ... to use such measures ... as may be necessary under the authority of the Security Council to halt all

3.2 THE GENEALOGY OF THE CONCEPT 49

peace and security have become a common procedure of the Council. The reason for this is well known. Article 43 of the UN Charter establishes that:

> I. All Members of the United Nations, in order to contribute to the maintenance of international peace and security, undertake to make available to the Security Council, on its call and in accordance with a special agreement or agreements, armed forces[.][49]

Due to the unwillingness of member states, such agreements have not come into being. Some states, however, have demonstrated their willingness to act together in the pursuit of international peace, but only without a standing agreement, which would have to be negotiated with permanent and non-permanent members of the SC, submitted to domestic ratification procedures, and which would govern such sensitive issues as numbers, types, and the location of their forces. Their willingness is rather attached to ad hoc authorizations – i.e., to more or less broad and vague mandates by the SC to use 'all necessary means' –[50] given on a case-by-case basis.[51]

Hence, multinational forces gathered for specific cases have become *the* model for collective security action. This model was already predicted by Myers McDougal and Florentino Feliciano in 1961 based on the experience of the Korean crisis. However, due to the paralysis within the Council during the Cold War, they predicted that the UN General Assembly (GA) would be the appropriate organ to activate enforcement action:

> The agreements envisaged in Article 43 of the United Nations Charter ... have never been concluded, and in all likelihood will not be concluded in the foreseeable future ... As a result, the participants in a police action probably will consist of individual members or groups of members acting

---

inward and outward maritime shipping ...', giving authorization to coalition forces in *Operation Desert Shield* to enforce the shipping embargo imposed on Iraq in SC Res. 661 (6 August 1990).

[49] UN Charter, 1 UNTS xvi, Art. 43.

[50] As Christine Gray observes, this 'euphemistic formula', which has been frequently used by the Council since the Gulf crisis of 1990–1991, is clearly understood to mean the use of force. This was already clear when China abstained to vote on SC Res. 678 precisely because this formula entailed the use of military force; see Gray, *International Law and the Use of Force*, pp. 264–265, and 333.

[51] For an early description of these multinational forces as '*ad hoc* police forces, gathered instance by instance', see Franck and Patel, 'UN Police Action in Lieu of War', 74.

50   TESTING THE FRAME: THE GENEALOGY OF A CATCHPHRASE

> as agents of the organized community upon the basis of a permissive authorization or delegation from the General Assembly.[52]

It was not the GA but the Council, which, once liberated from the confrontation between the great blocs, activated the model that has been characterized by international lawyers as 'the franchise model',[53] the 'privatization model',[54] the 'decentralized military option',[55] the 'delegation model',[56] the 'authorization model',[57] and, more and more frequently, 'coalitions of the willing'.[58] The SC itself has never used the expression 'coalition of the willing', although references to the 'willingness of Member States' acting in multinational forces are quite common in the authorization resolutions concerning the former Yugoslavia.[59] It is

---

[52] Myres S. McDougal and Florentino P. Feliciano, *Law and Minimum World Public Order: The Legal Regulation of International Coercion* (New Haven: Yale University Press, 1961), p. 254.

[53] See Thomas Franck, 'The United Nations as Guarantor of International Peace and Security: Past, Present and Future', in Christian Tomuschat (ed.), *The United Nations at Age Fifty: A Legal Perspective* (The Hague: Kluwer Law International, 1995), p. 25, at pp. 31–33. Though a few years later, Franck talked about 'coalitions of the willing', see note 58.

[54] See John Quigley, 'The "Privatization" of Security Council Enforcement Action: A Threat to Multilateralism' (1996) 17 *Michigan Journal of International Law* 249.

[55] See N. D. White and Özlem Ülgen, 'The Security Council and the Decentralized Military Option: Constitutionality and Function' (1997) 44 *Netherlands International Law Review* 378.

[56] See Danesh Sarooshi, *The United Nations and the Development of Collective Security: The Delegation by the UN Security Council of Its Chapter VII Powers* (Oxford: Clarendon Press, 1999).

[57] See Frank Berman, 'The Authorization Model: Resolution 678 and Its Effects', in Malone (ed.), *The UN Security Council, From the Cold War to the 21st Century*, p. 653.

[58] See Niels Blokker, 'Is the Authorization Authorized? Powers and Practice of the UN Security Council to Authorize the Use of Force by "Coalitions of the Able and Willing"' (2000) 11 *European Journal of International Law* 541; Thomas M. Franck, 'When, If Ever, May States Deploy Military Force Without Prior Security Council Authorization?' (2001) 5 *Washington University Journal of Law & Policy* 51, at 54; Nico Krisch, 'Article 43', in Bruno Simma, Daniel-Erasmus Khan, Georg Nolte and Andreas Paulus (eds.), *The Charter of the United Nations, A Commentary*, third edition, vol. II (Oxford: Oxford University Press, 2012), p. 1351, at p. 1356; Gary Wilson, 'The Legal, Military and Political Consequences of the "Coalition of the Willing" Approach to UN Military Enforcement Action' (2007) 12 *Journal of Conflict and Security Law* 295; Christine Gray, 'The Charter Limitations on the Use of Force: Theory and Practice', in Lowe *et al.* (eds.), *The United Nations Security Council and War*, p. 89.

[59] SC Res. 1031 (15 December 1995), op. 12; SC Res. 1088 (12 December 1996), op. 16; SC Res. 1174 (15 June 1998), op. 8; SC Res. 1247 (18 June 1999), op. 8. These authorizations, however, do not constitute typical cases of 'coalitions of able and willing States' as they refer to authorizations to regional organizations under chapter VIII.

3.2 THE GENEALOGY OF THE CONCEPT   51

only logical to describe participating states in these multinational enter-prises as 'willing',[60] since they join them voluntarily, following rather unaddressed calls of the Council.[61] Accordingly, international legal scholars have also chosen the same semantics: 'In the absence of Article 43 agreements ... action under Article 42, by those who are *willing* to participate, can properly be authorized by the United Nations and carried out under UN command'.[62] At the same time, multinational forces acting on behalf of the SC were described with the noun 'coalition' from the Gulf War of 1991 onwards; first, as we have seen, by the US adminis-tration,[63] subsequently by international legal scholars,[64] and increasingly by the media.[65] Today, the term is used often in this sense by the UN Secretariat,[66] though considerably less often by member states during formal meetings.[67] As a result, at the beginning of the new millennium,

---

[60] In the *Supplement to an Agenda for Peace*, the UN Secretary-General describes multi-national forces authorized by the SC as 'group[s] of willing Member Sates'. UN Doc A/50/60-S/1995/1 (3 January 1995), *Report of the Secretary-General on the Work of the Organization*, para. 78.

[61] The Council has expressly referred, e.g., to the US (SC Res. 84), the UK (SC Res. 221), and 'French forces' to take the necessary means to support African-led or UN missions in Côte d'Ivoire (SC Res. 2101 [25 April 2013] and SC Res. 2112 [30 July 2013]); Mali (SC Res. 2100 [25 April 2013]); and the Central African Republic (SC Res. 2127 [5 December 2013]). However, this remains rather an exception or occurs when forces of a specific state are already operating in the zone of concern. Regarding regional organizations, the Council is more inclined to name the organization authorized.

[62] Rosalyn Higgins, *Problems & Process, International Law and How We Use It* (Oxford: Clarendon Press, 1995), p. 266. Emphasis added.

[63] See note 30.

[64] See, e.g., Eugene V. Rostow, 'Until What? Enforcement Action or Collective Self-Defense?' (1991) 85 *The American Journal of International Law* 505, at 514; Burns H. Weston, 'Security Council Resolution 678 and Persian Gulf Decision Making: Precar-ious Legitimacy' (1991) 85 *The American Journal of International Law* 516, at 526–27 (speaking actually of a 'US-led coalition'); Franck, 'The United Nations as Guarantor', 32; N. D. White and Ülgen, 'The Security Council and the Decentralized Military Option', 386.

[65] See, v.g.: Thomas L. Friedman, 'Running the Gulf Coalition Is Tricky Business', *The New York Times* (23 September 1990); Alan Cowell, 'Syria, Baking Coalition, Is Still Insistent on Golan', *The New York Times* (15 February 1991).

[66] Former UN Secretary General (SG) Ban Ki-moon made usage of this terms in relation to Somalia, see UN Doc. S/2007/204 (20 April 2007), *Report of the Secretary-General on the Situation in Somalia pursuant to paragraphs 3 and 9 of Security Council resolution 1744 (2007)*, para. 6; UN Doc. S/2007/658 (7 November 2007), *Report of the Secretary-General on the Situation in Somalia*, para. 34.

[67] However, see South Africa on behalf of the Non-Aligned Movement (NAM), as well as Mongolia, supporting a proposal by former SG Kofi Annan on the creation of a multinational force for the Middle East, see UN Doc S/PV.4515 (18 April 2002),

52 TESTING THE FRAME: THE GENEALOGY OF A CATCHPHRASE

the term 'coalition of the willing' was commonly used among international lawyers to describe the UN Charter's *manqué* collective security system in the post–Cold War era; or as mentioned by Thomas Franck:

> The failure to realize the aims of Article 43 caused the Charter system to invent an alternative: the "coalition of the willing" authorized by the Council to use force collectively.[68]

3.2.1.2 From Charter Adaptation to Charter Violation

It might seem too obvious to recall that in order to be categorized as an 'Article 42 coalition of the willing', the respective military operation must count with a previous SC mandate; this is the '*conditio sine qua non* for the lawful operation by a coalition of the able and willing'.[69] However, what seems to be a superfluous remark has not been always as obvious as it should be.

In the aftermath of the Gulf War of 1991, US-led coalition forces conducted air strikes over Iraq in order to enforce no-fly zones to protect Kurdish and Shiite populations from attacks by Saddam Hussein's regime, in what became known as *Operation Provide Comfort* and *Operation Southern Watch*.[70] In December 1998, US and United Kingdom (UK) air forces launched another bombardment on Iraq's territory with the aim of reducing the chances of Hussein's regime to further develop WMDs. Apart from alleged humanitarian reasons, coalition members relied on the so-called 'implied-authorization thesis' – i.e., the assumption that due to the continuous non-compliance of Iraq with SC resolutions, the coalition was implicitly authorized to take enforcement action. Of course, the argument put forward by the USA and the UK was more complex than that.[71] It relied, for instance, on a supposedly revived authorization to use force according to SC resolution 678, since Iraq did not comply with the disarmament obligations that conditioned

---

pp. 12, 21; Singapore referring to the International Assistance Force in Afghanistan, see UN Doc. S/PV.4541 (23 May 2002), p 19.

[68] Franck, 'When, If Ever', 57.

[69] Blokker, 'Is the Authorization Authorized?', at note 3 and accompanying text.

[70] See Brian Frederking, *The United States and the Security Council: Collective Security since the Cold War* (London/New York: Routledge, 2007), p. 87.

[71] For a critical evaluation of these arguments, see Nico Krisch, 'Unilateral Enforcement of the Collective Will: Kosovo, Iraq and the Security Council' (1999) 3 *Max Planck Yearbook of United Nations Law* 59, at 64 et seq.

3.2 THE GENEALOGY OF THE CONCEPT   53

the cease-fire resolution.[72] In the end, however, all these considerations are based on the premise that member states can deduce from SC resolutions the existence of an implied authorization to use force when such an authorization is not given explicitly by the Council. And this line of reasoning was used again by the same military powers in the Iraq War of 2003. As is well known, in *Operation Iraqi Freedom* (OIF), the USA and UK once again relied, *inter alia*, on an alleged material breach by Iraq of the cease-fire conditions established in SC resolution 687.[73]

The implied authorization thesis is wrong and dangerous for the integrity of the post-war collective security system. Implying that there is an authorization by the SC is tantamount to take a decision on the authorization itself – i.e., to presume that the Council has delegated its power to authorize. It is therefore crucial to be clear about what the Council does when it 'authorizes' willing and able states to use 'all necessary measures' in a given situation. The legal basis for these author-izations lies in the expressed and implicit powers given to the Council by the UN Charter to decide on enforcement actions involving the use of force, especially in Article 42, but also in Articles 39 and 48, 1.[74] As Kelsen mentioned in 1950:

> The wording of Articles 39, 42, 47 and 48 does not exclude the possibility of a decision of the Security Council to the effect that Members which have not concluded a special agreement under Article 43 shall take a definite enforcement action[.][75]

Thus, the Council is not delegating powers to member states when it makes these authorizations, and there is no need to derive delegation powers from general principles of law.[76] However, there is some confu-sion about this, as is shown by the European Court of Human Rights'

---

[72] See SC Res. 687 (3 April 1991).

[73] For an excellent appraisal of this argumentation and its implications for international law, see Andreas Paulus, 'The War against Iraq and the Future of International Law: Hegem-ony or Pluralism?' (2004) 25 *Michigan Journal of International Law* 691, at 697 et seq.

[74] Art. 39 establishes that the SC 'shall ... decide what measures shall be taken in accord-ance with Arts. 41 and 42 ...', and Art. 48.1 prescribes that 'the action required to carry out decisions of the Security Council for the maintenance of international peace and security shall be taken by all Members of the United Nations or some of them, as the Security Council may determine'. UN Charter, 1 UNTS xvi.

[75] Hans Kelsen, *The Law of the United Nations. A Critical Analysis of Its Fundamental Problems* (Clark, New Jersey: The Lawbook Exchange, LTD., 1950, eighth reprint, 2009), p. 756.

[76] A position originally held by Sarooshi, *The United Nations and the Development of Collective Security*.

54 TESTING THE FRAME: THE GENEALOGY OF A CATCHPHRASE

(ECHRs') decision on the *Behrami & Behrami* and *Saramati* cases.[77] There, the Court determined the admissibility of two claims related to actions and omissions of the North Atlantic Treaty Organization's (NATO) forces operating in Kosovo (Kosovo Force – KFOR), as well as of the UN Interim Civil Administration Mission for Kosovo (UNMIK), both authorized by SC resolution 1244.[78] The Strasbourg Court noted that despite the fact that resolution 1244 'used the term "authorize", that term and the term "delegation" are used interchangeably'.[79] Hereby, the Court supported the delegation-thesis:

> The UNSC was thereby delegating to willing organisations and members states (see paragraph 43 as regards the meaning of the term "delegation" and paragraph 24 as regards the voluntary nature of this State contribution) the power to establish an international security presence as well as its operational command.[80]

One should ask: *who* uses these terms interchangeably? This may be the case of some authors but not of the SC. [81] It is true that the latter does not usually mention the exact legal basis for the authorizations in the relevant resolutions – referring in more general terms to chapter VII – but it has a long-standing and coherent practice in *authorizing* member states and regional organizations to use all necessary means in the pursuit of enforcement action. The relevant provisions of the Charter represent a solid legal ground for the authorization practice of the Council. In this sense, every authorization must be exactly that, *authorized* by the Council through a mandate in a valid resolution. The expressed and implied competences given to the SC by the Charter do not empower it to delegate these powers, for these are given to the Council and only to the Council. These competences entitle the SC to permit that willing and able states assist it in the performance of its primary duty.

For these reasons, as Bardo Fassbender mentions, it is more appropriate to describe these situations as circumstances where the SC decides that measures according to Article 42 need to be performed, and for that

---

[77] See Kjetil Mujezinović Larsen, 'Attribution of Conduct in Peace Operations: The "Ultimate Authority and Control" Test' (2008) 19 *European Journal of International Law* 509.

[78] S/RES/1244, op. 7 and 10, respectively.

[79] European Court of Human Rights (ECHR), *Agim Behrami and Bekir Behrami v. France, and Ruzhdi Saramati v. France, Germany and Norway*; Application Nos. 71412/01 and 78166/01, Grand Chamber, Decision on Admissibility (2 May 2007), 133 ILR 1, para. 43.

[80] Ibid., para. 129 (whereby the court also relies on Sarooshi's theses, see para. 130).

[81] See, for example, Gray, *International Law and the Use of Force*, pp. 328, 332, and 333.

3.2 THE GENEALOGY OF THE CONCEPT

purpose it gives a specific 'mandate' to those states who are willing and able to carry out the actions determined by the Council.[82] That the correlation between the terms 'authorization' and 'mandate' is the proper one in public law (and not between 'authorization' and 'delegation'), is supported by long-standing legal doctrine,[83] the Council's own practice,[84] and the International Court of Justice (ICJ) when referring in passing to a 'mandate or authorization' stipulated in any given resolution adopted 'purportedly for the maintenance of international peace and security'.[85]

The implied authorization thesis favours a general delegation to individual states to determine the existence of a threat or breach of the peace, since this is a precondition for enforcement action.[86] Almost needless to say, this determination is a discretionary competence given to the Council, and only to the Council, in order to permit it to fulfil its primary responsibility, which happens to be at the same time the main purpose of the UN. Implied authorizations are tantamount to implied delegations alleged by the want-to-be delegate. And this is counter-intuitive. In other words, if the thesis that the competent organ has implicitly given away its most important competence or primary responsibility, to individual states, then we would be more in the presence of a *transfer* of Charter competences to those individual states gathered in coalitions of the

---

[82] See Bardo Fassbender, 'Review Essay: *Quis judicabit*? The Security Council, Its Powers and Its Legal Control' (2000) 11 *European Journal of International Law* 219, at 230.

[83] See Heinrich Triepel, *Delegation und Mandat im Öffentlichen Recht. Eine Kritische Studie* (Berlin/Stuttgart: Kohlhammer Verlag, 1942) (mentioning that 'delegation' entails a deferral of a competence, whereas a 'mandate' is the execution by the mandatary of a competence in the name of the mandator; see pp. 23–27).

[84] Fassbender quotes SC Res.1264 to illustrate that the Council itself uses the term 'mandate' (see above note 82); other examples include the authorization to the US-led *Operation Iraqi Freedom*, see SC Res. 1511 (16 October 2003); SC Res.1546 (8 June 2004); SC Res.1637 (11 November 2005); SC Res. 1723 (28 November 2006); and SC Res. 1790 (18 December 2007).

[85] ICJ Reports (1962) *Certain Expenses of the United Nations*, Advisory Opinion (20 July 1962) [hereinafter 'ICJ, *Certain Expenses*'], p. 151, at p. 168.

[86] Michael Wood recognizes that even in the case in which individual states make a convincing claim that they are acting in the aid of a common purpose previously laid down by the SC (as opposed to purely national interests), 'there is surely a risk that, if this were accepted, the Council's work could be inhibited because of fears that if it laid down a "common purpose" this could be interpreted as indirectly sanctioning the unilateral use of force'; see Michael Wood, 'The Law on the Use of Force: Current Challenges' (2007) 11 *Singapore Year Book of International Law* 1, at 10.

56 TESTING THE FRAME: THE GENEALOGY OF A CATCHPHRASE

willing than in that of a delegation implicitly or explicitly foreseen in the Charter. And this is a serious hypothesis, as it would mean that the collective security system of the UN Charter would be replaced by another system. This distinction between 'delegation' and 'transfer' of competences is based on the criterion established by Alf Ross in reference to a problem of constitutional law, namely the problem of self-reference in constitutional reform procedures. Ross concludes that a norm establishing the amendment procedure of the constitution can be reformed by the same procedure, without transitioning into a new legal order. As he observes, the amended reformatory norm $N_R{}^1$ derives ultimately its legal validity from the same constituting authorities who instituted the reform procedure N_R, since $N_R{}^1$ is reformed though N_R. Applied to our problem, it is clear that the constituting authorities – i.e. the drafters of the Charter – did entrust the Security Council, and only the Security Council, the principal responsibility for maintaining and restoring international peace and security. If the Council decided to delegate this faculty, it is problematic; if individual states arrogated this delegation, then it is clear that this arrogation would not derive its legal validity from the same authorities who entrusted the Council with discretionary competences. For it cannot be that the same authority on which the legal powers of an organ rest is the basis for the circumvention of such competences. Such an arrogation is either a clear violation of the Charter or, if it would succeed and be accepted by all UN member states, a transition from the legal order established by the Charter to a different legal system.[87]

It is noteworthy that on the occasion of the use of chemical weapons by the al-Assad regime in Syria, in 2013, SC resolution 2118 explicitly mentions that in case of non-compliance by Syria (to depose these weapons), the Council will decide to 'impose measures under chapter VII of the United Nations Charter'.[88] Compared to the formula used in resolution 687 (1991) on Saddam Hussein's Iraq, according to which the Council decided 'to take further steps as may be required for the implementation of the present resolution and to secure peace and security in the region',[89] resolution 2118 can be interpreted as rejecting or foreclosing any future reading on the resolution that would suggest an implied authorization. Criticisms of that resolution lamenting that it

---

[87] Cf. Alf Ross, 'On Self-Reference and a Puzzle in Constitutional Law' (1969) 78 *Mind* 1.

[88] SC Res. 2118 (27 September 2013), op. 21.

[89] SC Res. 687, op. 34.

3.2 THE GENEALOGY OF THE CONCEPT 57

contains no automatism – i.e., no immediate enforcement mechanism against eventual non-compliance by the regime in Damascus – seem to confirm this.[90]

The implied authorization thesis has not been the only attempt to legally justify the actions of military coalitions of willing states acting without SC authorizations – or of regional organizations like NATO's[91] *Operation Allied Force* in Kosovo in 1999.[92] Doctrines of necessity and humanitarian intervention have been used in this sense in Kosovo, as well as in the late summer of 2013 in regard to the Syrian civil war, as the attempts made by the British government to forge a coalition against the Assad regime made clear,[93] which, however, never came to being. Here is not the place to engage in a legal analysis of the doctrine of humanitarian intervention.[94] In the end, I am of the opinion that the

---

[90] These criticisms were raised, among others, by Republicans in the US Senate, see Nick Paton Walsh and Elise Labott, 'Security Council Oks Syria Resolution, Warns of Consequences', *CNN* (28 September 2013), at http://edition.cnn.com/2013/09/27/world/meast/un-syria-resolution/.

[91] Although questions have been raised about whether NATO can be regarded as a regional arrangement for the purposes of Art. 53 (1) UN Charter (see Bruno Simma, 'NATO, the UN and the Use of Force: Legal Aspects' (1999) 10 *European Journal of International Law* 1, at 10; and Erika de Wet, *The Chapter VII Powers of the United Nations Security Council* (Oxford/Portland: Hart, 2004), pp. 290–293), the practice of the UN, including that of the Council and of the SG, as well as state practice (including, for example, the jurisprudence of the German Federal Constitutional Court, in the *AWACS/Somalia Case* – BVerfGE 90, 286, 353 et seq., as well as in the *AWACS/Turkey Case* – BVerfG 121, 135, 157), indicate the contrary (see, in this sense, Hans Kelsen, 'Is the North Atlantic Treaty a Regional Arrangement?' (1951) 45 *The American Journal of International Law* 162, and Georg Nolte, 'Die "neuen Aufgaben" von NATO und WEU: Völker- und verfassungsrechtliche Fragen' (1994) 54 *Zeitschrift für ausländisches öffentliches Recht und Völkerrecht* 95, at 99–101, and 111–114).

[92] Some treated this case as a coalition of the willing acting under NATO's umbrella, see Richard A. Falk, 'What Future for the UN Charter System of War Prevention?' (2003) 97 *The American Journal of International Law* 590, at 591 (mentioning that '[t]he burning issue in the Kosovo setting was whether "a coalition of the willing" acting under the umbrella of NATO was legally entitled to act as a residual option').

[93] See *Chemical Weapon Use by Syrian Regime – UK Government Legal Position*, at http://i2.cdn.turner.com/cnn/2013/images/08/29/chemical-weapon-use-by-syrian-regime-uk-government-legal-position.pdf.

[94] See Georg Nolte, 'Kosovo und Konstitutionalisierung: Zur humanitären Intervention der NATO-Staaten' (1999) 59 *Zeitschrift für ausländisches öffentliches Recht und Völkerrecht* 941; Simon Chesterman, *Just War or Just Peace? Humanitarian Intervention and International Law* (Oxford: Oxford University Press, 2001); as well as Philip Alston and Euan Macdonald (eds.), *Human Rights, Intervention, and the Use of Force* (Oxford: Oxford University Press, 2008).

58 TESTING THE FRAME: THE GENEALOGY OF A CATCHPHRASE

discussion can still be summarized as one where reasons of legitimacy are opposed to those of legality.[95] The 'illegal but legitimate' formula still raises the same questions as it did in 1999: who decides what is legitimate?[96] Even in the presence of compelling reasons of humanity, what is the price for relaxing the legal bases of the UN Charter's system of collective security?[97] The contemplated but unexecuted intervention in Syria in 2013 can be regarded as a blow-back to that doctrine, reminding us of the limitations of the related concept of the R2P, the endorsement of it by the SC in Libya 2011 notwithstanding – or perhaps precisely because of how resolution 1973[98] was interpreted and implemented by Western states.

What the doctrines of implied authorization and humanitarian intervention have in common is that they put in jeopardy the collective security system and with it the post-war's international legal order through self-arrogation and the advancement of rules of another game (of morality and politics) defined only by a few in the name of the international community. The cases where coalitions of the willing have acted on such grounds have to be categorically distinguished from those instances where multinational forces have performed with the authorization of the SC: the latter is a perfectly legal and necessary Charter adaptation; the former is the circumvention or even violation of the UN Charter.

---

[95] The legality of this doctrine can hardly be sustained in light of the rejection of 130 States after Kosovo; see Group of 77 South Summit, *Declaration of the South Summit* (Havana, Cuba, 10–14 April 2000), para. 54: 'We reject the so-called "right" of humanitarian intervention, which has no legal basis in the United Nations Charter or in the general principles of international law', at www.g77.org/summit/Declaration_G77Summit.htm.

[96] Independent International Commission on Kosovo, *Kosovo Report: Conflict, International Response, Lessons Learned* (Oxford: Oxford University Press, 2000), p. 4. See also Bruno Simma's 'thin red line' in Simma, 'NATO, the UN and the Use of Force', 6 (mentioning that 'in any instance of humanitarian intervention a careful assessment will have to be made of how heavily such illegality weights against all the circumstances of a particular concrete case'); as well as Thomas M. Frank, *Recourse to Force: State Action against Threats and Armed Attacks* (Cambridge: Cambridge University Press, 2002) pp. 174–191.

[97] For a powerful argument on the perils of the 'illegal but legitimate' approach, see Anthea Roberts, 'Legality vs Legitimacy: Can Uses of Force be Illegal but Justified?', in Alston and Macdonald (eds.), *Human Rights, Intervention, and the Use of Force*, p. 179.

[98] SC Res. 1973 (17 March 2011), op. 4.

3.2.1.3 Concluding Remarks on 'SC Coalitions of Willing and Able States': The Thin Line between Collective Security and Self-Defence

When Kelsen acknowledged that, 'as a matter of fact, the armed forces, which are the essential factor in the system of collective security, are not yet at the disposal of the Security Council',[99] he was not only lamenting the absence of Article 43 agreements but also foreseeing what would turn into a major defiance of the post-war order – i.e., to prevent an eventual paralysis of the UN collective security system. He did not regard what later became known as coalitions of willing and able states as panaceas, as his comments on the US-led coalition in the Korean War make clear.[100] Nevertheless, to permit the Council to be made unable to perform its primary responsibility in the absence of Article 43 agreements would have been tantamount to transform an international order based on a centralized collective security system into one of decentralized collective self-defence and to return to the old system of the League of Nations.[101] In the face of the UN Charter's *manqué* collective security system, states form coalitions because they are willing and able to support the Council for a specific mandate given by the Council, and only by the Council. This happens on an ad hoc basis, and one might regret that the Council has turned ad hocism into a normal way of procedure, not only in regard to Article 42 authorizations. Yet, there are very good reasons to believe that the Council is bound to act on such a basis if it wants to act at all. This is collective security adapted, and as almost every contemporary commentator, Kelsen saw in Articles 39, 42 and 48 of the UN Charter a sufficient ground to render such empowerments legally valid. This interpretation has been supported by the practice of the Council and other organs of

---

[99] Hans Kelsen, 'Collective Security and Collective Self-Defense under the Charter of the United Nations' (1948) 42 *The American Journal of International Law* 783, at 795.

[100] Kelsen, *The Law of the United Nations*, pp. 927–949.

[101] Cf. Kelsen, 'Collective Security and Collective Self-Defense', 793–796 (explaining that the only difference between self-defence under general international law and collective security under the Covenant was that in the latter case states were bound to assist the attacked state, whereas in the former they were only entitled to do so). See *1919 Covenant of the League of Nations* (LNTS No. 34), Art. 16. On the tensions between self-defence and collective security in the charter system, see Nico Krisch, *Selbstverteidigung und kollektive Sicherheit* (Heidelberg: Springer, 2001).

60   TESTING THE FRAME: THE GENEALOGY OF A CATCHPHRASE

the UN, reaffirmed by the ICJ,[102] as well as by national courts.[103] Hence, there is ample support for this interpretation, whether it is a matter of the 'established practice' of the SC which forms part of the 'relevant rules of the organization',[104] a case of subsequent practice of the SC *and* the states parties to the UN Charter that establishes the agreement of the latter on this interpretation,[105] or both.[106]

---

[102] Although concerned with traditional peace-keeping operations, the advisory opinion of the ICJ in the *Certain Expenses* case made it generally clear that in the absence of Art. 43 agreements, the Charter cannot be interpreted as hindering the Council to perform its primary responsibility, see ICJ, *Certain Expenses*, p. 167.

[103] The German Federal Constitutional Court has also referred to this, expressing in its *AWACS/Somalia* case of 1994 that the application of Art. 42 does not necessarily require the existence of troops according to Art. 43; see BVerfGE 90, 286, 380.

[104] Art. 5 of the *1969 Vienna Convention on the Law of Treaties*, 1115 UNTS 331 [hereinafter 'VCLT'] mentions that the Convention applies to any constituent treaty of an international organization, 'without prejudice to the rules of the organization'. According to the *1986 Vienna Convention on the Law of Treaties between States and International Organizations or between International Organizations* [VCLT-IO], UN Doc A/CONF.129/15 (21 March 1986) (not yet in force), Art. 2 (j), as well as to Art. 2 (b) of the International Law Commission's (ILC) *Draft Articles on the Responsibility of International Organizations* [DARIO], the 'established practice' of an organization forms part of its rules (see UN Doc A/66/10, Supplement No. 10 (2011), *ILC, Report on the Work of Its Sixty-Third Session (26 April to 3 June and 4 July to 12 August 2011)*, chapter V).

[105] Art. 31 (3) (b) VCLT mentions: '*Any* subsequent practice in the application of the treaty which establishes the agreement of the parties regarding its interpretation'. Therefore, the practice in the application of the treaty itself does not have to be exclusively that of the parties – as opposed to the agreement (understanding) regarding the interpretation that arises from this practice. See the work of the ILC's Special Rapporteur, Georg Nolte, on subsequent agreements and subsequent practice in relation to the interpretation of treaties, in particular UN Doc. A/68/10, Supplement No. 10 (2013), *ILC, Report on the Work of Its Sixty-Fifth Session (6 May to 7 June and 8 July to 9 August 2013)*, chapter IV.

[106] The interplay among the organ's practice and that of UN member states supports the view that we are in presence of a 'general practice of the Organization'; see ICJ Reports (1971) *Legal Consequences for States of the Continued Presence of South Africa in Namibia (South West Africa) Notwithstanding Security Council Resolution 276 (1970)*, Advisory Opinion (21 June 1971), p. 16, at p. 22 (stating that the procedure followed by the SC regarding the application of Art. 27 (3) UN Charter, requiring only that the permanent members do not vote in the negative ('concurring votes') for a decision of the Council to be adopted, 'has been generally accepted by Members of the United Nations and evidences a general practice of that Organization'). Elsewhere, I argue that the established practice of an organ and the subsequent practice of the member states of an organization are interacted and mutually reinforcing instances of relevant practice for the interpretation of the constituent treaty; see Alejandro Rodiles, 'Non-Permanent Members of the United Nations Security Council and the Promotion of the International Rule of Law' (2013) 5 *Goettingen Journal of International Law* 334, at 336.

3.2 THE GENEALOGY OF THE CONCEPT 61

When a military coalition of the willing acts without a SC mandate, it usually claims its legality either on the basis of individual or collective self-defence under Article 51 of the Charter or on a (mis)conception of the right to self-defence, like the pre-emptive self-defence doctrine most clearly articulated by the USA after 9/11.[107] Claims of self-defence are at times supported by the 'unwilling or unable test', the role of which can be expected to increase due to the growing presence of non-state actors in armed conflicts, and the absence of protests after the USA delivered its legal justification on the air strikes conducted by coalition forces on Syrian territory against the Islamic State (IS).[108] According to the letter submitted to the UN Secretary General (SG) by the US Permanent Representative to the UN, on 23 September 2014, the USA coupled the right of individual and collective self-defence with the unwilling or unable test:

> States must be able to defend themselves, in accordance with the inherent right of individual and collective self-defense, as reflected in Article 51 of the UN Charter, when, as is the case here, the government of the State where the threat is located is unwilling or unable to prevent the use of its territory for such attacks. The Syrian regime has shown that it cannot and will not confront these safe-havens effectively itself. Accordingly, the United States has initiated necessary and proportionate military actions in Syria in order to eliminate the ongoing ISIL threat to Iraq[.][109]

---

[107] *National Security Strategy of the United States of America (September 2002)* [hereinafter '*US National Security Strategy 2002*'], pp. 13–16, at www.state.gov/documents/organization/63562.pdf. Two major precedents being the pre-emptive strike by Israel on Iraq's nuclear reactor Osirak, in 1981 and condemned by the SC in SC Res. 487 (19 June 1981), and the air strikes conducted by the USA on a pharmaceutical plant in Khartoum, Sudan, and on Al-Qaida training camps in Afghanistan, in 1998, see Frederic L. Kirgis, 'Cruise Missile Strikes in Afghanistan and Sudan', *ASIL Insight* (18 August 1998), at www.asil.org/insights/volume/3/issue/11/cruise-missile-strikes-afghanistan-and-sudan.

[108] Probably due to the general condemnation of the IS, the legal justification of the USA has not been questioned so far by other states. The SG acknowledged it by noting 'that the strikes took place in areas no longer under the effective control of that [Syrian] Government' (reproduced in Ryan Goodman and Sarah Knuckey, 'Remarkable Statement by UN Secretary General on US Airstrikes in Syria', blog contribution, *Just Security* (23 September 2014), at http://justsecurity.org/15456/remarkable-statement-secretary-general-airstrikes-syria/).

[109] UN Doc. S/2014/695 (23 September 2014), *Letter Dated 23 September 2014 from the Permanent Representative of the United States of America to the United Nations Addressed to the Secretary General.*

62 TESTING THE FRAME: THE GENEALOGY OF A CATCHPHRASE

It is true that this test has some support in state practice beyond the USA,[110] and it has been recognized as a basis for self-defence by the UN Special Rapporteur on Extrajudicial, Summary or Arbitrary Executions in the context of targeted killings.[111] However, even outspoken proponents of this test admit that those instances of state practice are not supported by *opinio iuris*,[112] and that the test 'remains controversial under international law'.[113] There are very important reasons explaining the scepticism towards this doctrine. First, it is a very lax test in which the already porous notions of 'unwilling' and 'unable' are combined by a disjunction, 'according to which *both* the inability and the unwillingness scenarios separately warrant forcible intervention'.[114] Second, although 'unwilling' would seem to hint towards the direction of a harbouring, tolerating, or even colluding state, one should nonetheless remain aware that unwillingness is a concept vague enough to be interpreted in another light whenever the international political ambiance so allows. Thirdly, the 'unable test' seems to be even more vague since no standards (e.g., due diligence) are in place for conducting it. What consequences would this have for states doing everything in their reach in order to prevent hostile actions towards other states from non-state actors acting within their territory but which eventually fail to prevent an attack by the latter?

---

[110] Russia's use of force against Chechen rebels in Georgia, in 2002, Turkey's incursions into Iraq against members of the Kurdish Worker's Party (PKK), Israel's attacks on Hezbollah and Hamas in Lebanon, as well as the incursion of Colombia's forces into Ecuador to fight members of the *Fuerzas Armadas Revolucionarias de Colombia* (FARC), in 2008, are the most cited examples in which individual states other than the USA have claimed to exercise the right to self-defence due to the unwillingness or inability of other states concerning the actions of non-State actors acting from within their territory. See Ashley S. Deeks, '"Unwilling or Unable": Toward a Normative Framework for Extraterritorial Self-Defense' (2012) 52 *Virginia Journal of International Law* 483, at 486–491. For a pointed critique, see Kevin Jon Heller, 'Ashley Deeks' Problematic Defense of the "Unwilling or Unable" Test', blog contribution, *Opinio Juris* (15 December 2011), at http://opiniojuris.org/2011/12/15/ashley-deeks-failure-to-defend-the-unwilling-or-unable-test/.

[111] See UN Doc. A/HRC/14/24/Add.6 (28 May 2010) *Report of the Special Rapporteur on Extrajudicial, Summary or Arbitrary Executions, Philip Alston*, para. 35.

[112] See Deeks, '"Unwilling or Unable"', at note 70 ('I have found no cases in which states clearly assert that they follow the test out of a sense of legal obligation').

[113] Ryan Goodman, 'International Law on International Airstrikes against ISIS in Syria', blog contribution, *Just Security* (28 August 2014), at http://justsecurity.org/14414/international-law-airstrikes-isis-syria/.

[114] Theresa Reinold, 'State Weakness, Irregular Warfare, and the Right to Self-Defense Post 9/11' (2011) 105 *The American Journal of International Law* 244, at 256. Emphasis added.

3.2 THE GENEALOGY OF THE CONCEPT   63

Under the 'unwilling *or* unable' logic, any successful terrorist attack would justify the use of force. In practice, however, it is very doubtful that this sort of 'strict liability'[115] would apply on an equal ground to all states.[116]

To be sure, it can hardly be sustained today that the traditional criteria for the attribution of responsibility of an armed attack favoured by the ICJ in the *Nicaragua* case and subsequently reaffirmed, most clearly in the *Bosnian Genocide* case,[117] have remain unaltered after 9/11. But the 'preferable view still seems to be'[118] that attribution, although a 'more lenient standard of attribution',[119] is still required.[120] The unwilling or

---

[115] See Arnulf Becker Lorca, 'Rules for the "Global War on Terror": Implying Consent and Presuming Conditions for Intervention' (2012) 45 *New York University Journal of International Law and Politics* 1, at 35–44.

[116] For a similar view, see Dawood I. Ahmed, 'Defending Weak States against the "Unwilling or Unable" Doctrine of Self-Defense' (2013) 9 *Journal of International Law and International Relations* 1, at 16 (relying, on his part, on an article by Anghie and Chimni on how the lack of clarity 'rarely works in favour of Third World interests', see Antony Anghie and B. S. Chimni, 'Third World Approaches to International Law and Individual Responsibility in Internal Conflicts' (2003) 2 *Chinese Journal of International Law* 77, at 101).

[117] See ICJ Reports (1986) *Military and Paramilitary Activities in and against Nicaragua (Nicaragua v. United States of America)*, Merits, Judgment (27 June 1986), p. 14, at pp. 64–65 (para. 115); and ICJ Reports (2007) *Application of the Convention on the Prevention and Punishment of the Crime of Genocide (Bosnia and Herzegovina v. Serbia and Montenegro)*, Judgment (26 February 2007), p. 43, at pp. 206–211 (paras. 396–407) (referring to the 'effective control test' as developed in *Nicaragua* as its 'settled jurisprudence'; at para. 407).

[118] Albrecht Randelzhofer and Georg Nolte, 'Article 51', in Simma, Khan, Nolte and Paulus (eds.), *The Charter of the United Nations*, p. 1397, at p. 1417.

[119] Christian J. Tams, 'The Use of Force against Terrorists' (2009) 20 *European Journal of International Law* 359, at 386 (referring to the criminal law notion of 'aiding and abetting', as developed in this context by Tom Ruys and Sten Verhoeven, 'Attacks by Private Actors and the Right of Self-Defence' (2005) 10 *Journal of Conflict & Security Law* 289, at 315 et seq.; for an analysis of the (not very clear) relationship between this concept and complicity in the law of state responsibility, see Helmut Philipp Aust, *Complicity and the Law of State Responsibility* (Cambridge: Cambridge University Press, 2011), p. 226.

[120] As noted by Randelzhofer and Nolte, such a reassessment of the secondary rules of attribution would have to be 'in the light of the applicable primary rules', see Randelzhofer and Nolte, 'Article 51', pp. 1417–1418. Perhaps, as James Crawford mentions, the rules of attribution need not be broadened or relaxed at all, but reliance on primary rules of international law would be the 'preferable approach', since 'an array of customary and treaty-based norms exist which render state participation in or co-ordination of terrorists acts an international wrong for which state responsibility may arise ...'; see James Crawford, *State Responsibility: The General Part* (Cambridge: Cambridge University Press, 2013), p. 158.

64 TESTING THE FRAME: THE GENEALOGY OF A CATCHPHRASE

unable test does not provide clear criteria for the attribution of an armed attack (current or imminent). It is at least as amenable and open to subjective judgments as the doctrine of humanitarian intervention, thus leaving the doors wide open for military actions without SC authorizations. In the words of Eric Posner:

> [T]he "unable and unwilling" doctrine, and the exception for humanitarian intervention all whittle away at whatever part of the law on United Nations use of force blocks U.S. goals.[121]

Kelsen's reading of Article 51 UN Charter 'as a provisional and temporary measure, permitted only "until" the Security Council takes necessary measures to restore peace, especially until collective security comes into action, and not as a substitute for it',[122] may sound too strict today.[123] However, his insistence on taking the difference between collective security and self-defence seriously should not fall into oblivion, especially in times of a perpetual war on terror, which keeps offering grounds for self-defence. In *Reine Rechtslehre*, Kelsen describes self-defence as the case limit of any legal order;[124] in international law, a fall-back into a highly decentralized international order would mean that every state, or group of states, 'may claim to wage a just war'.[125]

3.2.2 The Coalition of the Willing Approach in US Foreign Policy Discourse: Rivalry or Integration?

The US-led coalition in the Gulf War of 1991 is often regarded as a sign for a new multilateral era, which vanished away only a decade later with the tragic events of 9/11 and the reaction by the superpower, especially the invasion of Iraq in 2003. However, the promise of a 'new world order' of organized multilateralism and respect for the international rule of law was already called into question by the unipolar moment itself and the

---

[121] Eric Posner, 'Obama's Drone Dilemma', Slate (8 October 2012), at www.slate.com/articles/news_and_politics/view_from_chicago/2012/10/obama_s_drone_war_is_prob ably_illegal_will_it_stop_.html (referring to what he calls 'coerced consent' in connection with the 'inferred' or 'implied consent' alleged by the Obama administration in relation to targeted killings, mostly by means of drone strikes, in Pakistan).
[122] Kelsen, 'Collective Security and Collective Self-Defense', 795.
[123] For a more balanced approach, see Derek W. Bowett, *Self-Defence in International Law* (Manchester: Manchester University Press, 1958), pp. 195–197.
[124] See Hans Kelsen, *Reine Rechtslehre*, second edition (1960) (Vienna: Österreichische Staatsdruckerei, 1992), p. 41.
[125] Kelsen, 'Collective Security and Collective Self-Defense', 795.

3.2 THE GENEALOGY OF THE CONCEPT 65

increasing resort to unilateralism by the sole superpower.[126] As stated by Michael Byers and Georg Nolte in the preface to their 2003 edited volume on US hegemony and international law, the project that led to their book started well before 9/11 with the fundamental question of 'whether the current predominance of the United States is leading to foundational change in the international legal system'.[127] Political scientists and IR scholars were asking similar questions in regard to multilateralism and world order.[128]

In parallel to these evolutions, a complex system of global ruling under which international law is conceived in instrumentalist terms and the UN as an important yet another platform in a semi-formal network of global governance gradually gained in strength.[129] Beyond the hopes of a new order based on international law and centred on the UN, post–Cold War anxieties began very soon to pave the way for the conception of a coming global disorder that needed to be addressed urgently by resorting to innovative approaches. In the following sections, I will show that coalitions of the willing have been a crucial component of these innovative approaches, which have been constructed primarily within US foreign policy circles. Thus, the coalition of the willing approach is part of the design of a larger strategy, the main concern of which has been the maintenance of US predominance in a rapidly changing global environment.

3.2.2.1 From a Coalition Authorized to a Coalition Unauthorized: Framing Matters

Although the catchphrase 'coalition of the willing' was advanced most aggressively by the Bush Jr. administration, and it was the Iraq War 2003 that brought the term into the public's awareness, it has been

---

[126] See the contributions in Michael Byers and Georg Nolte (eds.), *United States Hegemony and the Foundations of International Law* (Cambridge: Cambridge University Press, 2003) p. xv; see also Georg Nolte, 'Die USA und das Völkerrecht' (2003) 78 *Die Friedens-Warte* 119.

[127] See M. Byers and G. Nolte, 'Preface', in Byers and Nolte (eds.), *United States Hegemony*, p. xv.

[128] See Stewart Patrick and Shepard Forman (eds.), *Multilateralism & U.S. Foreign Policy: Ambivalent Engagement* (London/Boulder: Lynne Rienner Publishers, 2002).

[129] Cf. Martti Koskenniemi and Päivi Leino, 'Fragmentation of International Law? Postmodern Anxieties' (2002) 15 *Leiden Journal of International Law* 553, at 559 (arguing that 'liberalism and globalisation did not bring about coherence, to the contrary. The structure provided by the East–West confrontation was replaced by a kaleidoscopic reality in which competing actors struggled to create competing normative systems').

66 TESTING THE FRAME: THE GENEALOGY OF A CATCHPHRASE

present in US foreign policy discourse since the early 1990s. One of the first documented uses of the expression can be found in an interview with President William J. Clinton by *ABC News*, in June 1994. Asked on the possibility of acting unilaterally against North Korea, if Pyongyang hindered UN inspections regarding its nuclear program of the late 1980s and if the SC failed to establish tough sanctions in that event, President Clinton answered that the USA would not need 'to go it alone' because the real question was instead if 'we [could] have what has been called a *coalition of the willing*'.[130] He continued: 'we would certainly consider that if we failed at the United Nations'.[131]

These were not isolated remarks. The *National Security Strategy of Engagement and Enlargement 1995* establishes the following:

> We must also use the right tools – being willing to act unilaterally when our direct national interests are most at stake; in alliance and partnership when our interests are shared by others; and multilaterally when our interests are more general and the problems are best addressed by the international community.[132]

Here, we have already the basic idea underlying the US foreign policy notion of coalitions of the willing, namely that they are conceived as alternative means to traditional multilateralism. This notion is in no way limited to issues of war and peace – i.e. to military alliances – but extends to international security matters more broadly and to practically any conceivable field of international co-operation where the stakes are high enough to resort to alternative venues if the traditional ones proved unable. If, for whatever reason, vital US foreign policy objectives cannot be achieved in a standing multilateral forum, then a coalition can and should be assembled to pursue the respective aims. The fact that the 1995 Security Strategy uses the word 'partnership' instead of 'coalition' should not distract from the basic idea – 'alliance' is most probably used here to refer to NATO. The 'coalition' surface frame entails the concept of 'partnership', which corresponds to the 'friendship frame'. In this order, 'partnerships' are gathered according to the issues at hand. In contrast to standing international organizations (IOs), they are conceived as ad hoc – i.e. strictly issue oriented – and their composition does not

---

[130] President William J. Clinton, *Interview of the President by Sam Donaldson*, ABC (5 June 1994). Emphasis added.

[131] Ibid.

[132] *A National Security Strategy of Engagement and Enlargement* (February 1995), p. 7, at www.au.af.mil/au/awc/awcgate/nss/nss-95.pdf.

3.2 THE GENEALOGY OF THE CONCEPT 67

obey requirements of universal, equal membership but is selective and driven by a dynamic of difference according to the willingness and ability of potential participants.

President Clinton's conception is quite similar to the one that his successor would use in the aftermath of 9/11: the idea that there are higher values that should not be hindered, not even by the basic rules of the game. It is, in fact, already a notion of global governance where (world) government is absent (unable or unwilling), informed by the need to respond efficiently to urgent global threats. The resort to the word 'coalition' by Presidents Clinton and Bush, Jr., offered legitimacy as it stood in clear allusion to the Gulf War alliance assembled in 1990/91 by George H. W. Bush,[133] which counted on a sound legal basis (collective self-defence and a SC mandate) and stood as an example of ample international co-operation and consensus. It is thus a matter of framing to call selective groups of states 'coalitions'. Even if these are designed to perform outside legal structures, or precisely because of that, the early-1990s 'coalition frame' proved to be the right choice for presenting an idea of international co-operation that should progressively but significantly depart from the promises of the new world order of the early 1990s. However, it should be recalled that the idea of 'a narrower, less formal grouping that would pressure Iraq' in the event that the SC should have failed to respond in the face of Saddam Hussein's aggression against Kuwait was also an option that was discussed inside the Bush Sr. administration.[134] Thus, there is a lineage relationship between *Operation Desert Storm* and *Operation Iraqi Freedom*.

In the ensuing section, I will trace the genesis of the ideas underlying coalitions of the willing as they have been developed mainly by US IR scholar, diplomat, and influential foreign policy thinker (and, since 2003, president of the New York–based Council on Foreign Relations), Richard N. Haass. His theses are not the only relevant ones in developing this approach, and I will also draw on other writings from the inner circle of

---

[133] Also referring to *Operation Desert Shield* and *Operation Desert Storm* as the early models for the idea of coalitions of the willing, see Haass, *The Reluctant Sheriff*, pp. 93–94.

[134] This should come as no surprise since it was Richard Haass, then the Special Assistant to President George H. W., who put this option on the table, see Richard N. Haass, *War of Necessity, War of Choice: A Memoir of Two Iraq Wars* (New York: Simon & Schuster, 2009), p. 86. Haass was awarded with the Presidential Citizens Medal in 1991 'for his contributions to the development and articulation of U.S. policy during Operations Desert Shield and Desert Storm', see Biography Richard N. Haass, at web.archive.org/web/20060621182405/www.state.gov/outofdate/bios/h/5492.htm.

68   TESTING THE FRAME: THE GENEALOGY OF A CATCHPHRASE

US foreign policy elite. It is, however, in Haass's work where we can find the most articulated version of the coalition of the willing approach, developed over years not only from the desktop of an academic and think-tanker but also as the result of his important trajectory within US administrations.

3.2.2.2   Global Governance by Posse

Motivated by what he saw as missed opportunities due to the reluctance by the Clinton administration to engage more decidedly in foreign affairs, Richard N. Haass wrote the influential book, *The Reluctant Sheriff*, which was first published in 1997.[135] Haass complains there that the USA was losing the opportunity to reaffirm its role as the benevolent superpower, and consequently to shape the international post–Cold War (dis)order according to its values, as well as in the pursuit of international peace and stability. Accordingly, he proposes a mixture of four mutually reinforcing approaches that the USA should apply in the conduct of its foreign policy. It is worth reproducing them *in extenso*:

(a) Resort to *alliances* like NATO, which 'continues to tie the United States to Europe, thereby constituting a valuable bulwark against American isolationism and European parochialism';[136] though he also envisages a differentiated engagement with NATO members according to their willingness and capabilities, but which should draw on the 'organizational assets' of the Alliance;[137]

(b) *Unilateralism* as an exceptional recourse 'when narrow interests are at stake and where the involvement of others is not necessary';[138]

(c) A rather limited reliance on *institutionalism*, which is partly inspired in Madeleine Albright's 'assertive multilateralism', and which recognizes the value of IOs, especially the UN, and importantly emphasizes the need to 'empowering' them; however, Haass is very clear about the limitations of standing institutions in handling by their own 'most of the challenges sure to arise in the post-Cold War world';[139]

(d) Finally, the *coalition of the willing approach*, which emerges as a direct response to the said limitations of alliances and unilateralism,

[135] Haass, *The Reluctant Sheriff*.
[136] Ibid., p. 84.
[137] Ibid., p. 82.
[138] Ibid., p. 87.
[139] Ibid., p. 91.

3.2 THE GENEALOGY OF THE CONCEPT 69

and most importantly to the shortfalls of IOs and organized multi-lateralism more broadly. Accordingly, he suggests to increasingly resort to 'posses' or 'coalitions of the willing', inspired by informal groups of states like those that emerged during the Cold War in the field of arms control, which should be flexible, issue oriented, and assembled and led by the sheriff – i.e., the USA – to deal effectively with global challenges.[140]

It is not difficult to see how the ideas and ideals entailed in the surface and deep frames of the metaphorical concept 'coalition of the willing' are present in the 'posse model' in their full expression: international co-operation is understood in terms of friendship and effectiveness; flexible posses, in order to perform effectively, are freed from the institutional constraints that so often hinder IOs' ability to respond rapidly to urgent global threats. Therefore, coalitions or posses 'are better understood as an activity than an organization'.[141] However, this does not mean that they should not strive, when viable, to a certain form of institutionalization without, however, giving away their flexibility.[142] Although embryonic-ally, Haass puts forward the notion of 'durability' – i.e., that coalitions should have some structure (without mutating into formal institutions) that enables them to interact on a long-term basis with other institutions and schemes of co-operation. This, as I will show in the following chapters, is crucial for differentiating coalitions of the willing from mere ad hoc diplomatic efforts.

The chapter where these four foreign policy tactics are explained is called 'foreign policy by posse'.[143] This denotes not only a clear prefer-ence for the resort to posses as foreign policy tools (the fourth tactic) but also how the coalition of the willing approach, or 'foreign policy by posse' – both expressing the same idea – informs the whole strategy. What the advisor to former President George H. W. Bush proposes in the *Reluctant Sheriff*, as well as in several speeches delivered as the chief of the Policy Planning Staff of former Secretary of State Colin Powell is a multilateral strategy;[144] it is not US unilateralism. Haass's multilateral

---

[140] Ibid., p. 93.

[141] Ibid., p. 95. This became the recurrent slogan for describing the *Proliferation Security Initiative* (PSI), see below Chapter 4, note 21, and accompanying text.

[142] Haas, *The Reluctant Sheriff*, p. 99.

[143] Ibid., Chapter 4, pp. 78–102.

[144] See, *inter alia*, Richard N. Haass, 'From Reluctant to Resolute: American Foreign Policy after September 11', Remarks to the Chicago Council on Foreign Relations (26 June

70   TESTING THE FRAME: THE GENEALOGY OF A CATCHPHRASE

strategy is often equated to the notion of 'multilateralism *à la carte*',[145] coined by him too. *À la carte* multilateralism means that the USA would pick and choose according to its preferences those multilateral undertakings – treaties and also less formal arrangements – in which to participate, as well as its degree of engagement on a case-by-case basis.[146] It is thus a matter of priority setting, which has important and not precisely positive implications for multilateralism as a whole[147] and for international law,[148] as it means that in several cases the most powerful state will remain at the margins, influencing from the outside but not contributing to the overall strength of the treaty regime or institution – something that raised worries in foreign ministries and among international lawyers in the late 1990s and early 2000s.[149]

There is a close relation between coalitions of the willing and multilateralism *à la carte*, as the latter also implies that, at times, informal venues will be preferred over multilateral institutions or that an informal arrangement will be conceived as the better alternative to a multilateral treaty.[150] But multilateralism *à la carte* is not necessarily tied to informality as the preference for treaty making in the field of international

---

2002), at http://2001-2009.state.gov/s/p/rem/11445.htm; and *id.*, 'Planning Policy in Today's World', Remarks at the Kennan Institute Annual Dinner (22 May 2003), at http://2001-2009.state.gov/s/p/rem/2003/20910.htm.

[145] See Thom Shanker, 'White House Says the U.S. Is Not a Loner, Just Choosy', *The New York Times* (31 July 2001), at www.nytimes.com/2001/07/31/world/white-house-says-the-us-is-not-a-loner-just-choosy.html?src=pm&pagewanted=2(quoting Haass).

[146] See Haass, *War of Necessity, War of Choice*, p. 182.

[147] See Shashi Tharoor, 'Saving Humanity from Hell', in Edward Newman, Ramesh Thakur and John Tirman (eds.), *Multilateralism under Challenge? Power, International Order, and Structural Change* (Tokyo: United Nations University Press, 2002), p. 21, at p. 26; Timothy Garton Ash, *Free World: America, Europe, and the Surprising Future of the West*, reprinted edition with a new postscript (London: Penguin, 2005), p. 136; Sarah E. Kreps, *Coalitions of Convenience: United States Interventions after the Cold War* (Oxford: Oxford University Press, 2011) p. 166.

[148] On the implications of this notion for international law, see Edward Kwakwa, 'The International Community, International Law, and the United States: Three in One, Two against One, Or One and the Same', in Byers and Nolte (eds.), *United States Hegemony*, p. 25, at p. 53.

[149] See Nolte, 'Die USA und das Völkerrecht', 119.

[150] Among those who have associated coalitions of the willing with multilateralism *à la carte*, see, Paulus, 'The War against Iraq and the Future of International Law', 30; as well as Cooper, 'Stretching the Model of "Coalitions of the Willing"', p. 269. At times, Haass's own work mixes both notions – see, e.g., Richard N. Haass, *A World in Disarray: American Foreign Policy and the Crisis of the Old Order* (New York: Penguin Press, 2017), pp. 198–200.

3.2 THE GENEALOGY OF THE CONCEPT

trade shows. Although narrower in the sense that it is restricted to the informal realm, the coalition of the willing approach runs deeper, so to speak, through the structure of multilateralism. It crucially encompasses the goal of 'empowering' multilateral institutions and legal frameworks. The US *National Security Strategy 2002* clearly mentions that '[c]oalitions of the willing can *augment* ... permanent institutions'.[151] This relates to coalitions' inter-institutional relations – i.e. the interplays between them and IOs, as well as between coalitions' informal norms and formal international law, which I will describe in further detail in Chapter 5. For now, it should be highlighted that 'empowering' IOs is basically about *shaping* their work through coalitions, thus showing that these are highly interactional and not parallel venues to standing institutions.

The multilateral strategy of which the coalition of the willing approach is an essential component is much more about integration than it is usually acknowledged. But integration should not be understood here in the sense of the universalization of multilateral institutions and treaties and of international law's centrality aspirations as a legal system. For Haass, it is clear: the post–Cold War and post-9/11 world is far too fragmented to be reintegrated through the traditional means of multilateralism. Consensus among old and new powers on the guiding principles that may help navigate this messy world is needed, but it can only be built through a less comprehensive and rather informal multilateralism: with some countries on a certain issue, while relying on others for different matters; in some cases through more classical contact groups and other diplomatic venues, in others by resort to loose and flexible posses.[152] This strategy is, paradoxically as it may seem, one of fragmentation[153] and reintegration at the same time: dividing and reuniting according to the unifying criteria of those who have the power and resources to be at the core of most coalitions and institutions; of those who can best assemble coalitions and shape pre-existing institutions; and, most importantly, of

---

[151] US National Security Strategy 2002 (preface). Emphasis added.

[152] See Richard N. Haass, *The Opportunity: America's Moment to Alter History's Course* (New York: Public Affairs, 2005), pp. 171–182.

[153] I am referring here to fragmentation as a power strategy in the sense of *divide et impera*, which encompasses but goes beyond fragmentation in its legal/technical sense. For an account of the political economy of fragmentation, see Eyal Benvenisti and George W. Downs, 'The Empire's New Clothes: Political Economy and the Fragmentation of International Law' (2007) 60 *Stanford Law Review* 595; see also Alejandro Rodiles, 'La Fragmentación del Derecho Internacional. ¿Riesgos u Oportunidades para México?' (2009) 9 *Anuario Mexicano de Derecho Internacional* 373.

72   TESTING THE FRAME: THE GENEALOGY OF A CATCHPHRASE

those who can *manage complexity and co-ordinate* the many different components.

There is a clear line of continuity from the *Reluctant Sheriff* of 1997 to *The Opportunity* of 2005 through Haass's later writings in *Foreign Affairs*[154] to his latest book *A World in Disarray* of 2017[155] – which are all motivated by the preoccupation of maintaining US predominance in a rapidly changing and uncertain world. Predominance has first to be rearticulated in the face of the post–Cold War era, characterized by uncertainty and deregulation (in the sense of transiting 'from a highly structured world dominated by two or at most a few to a less structured world of the many'[156]). Deregulation is to be contained through the piecemeal and selective coalition of the willing approach that introduces patterns of behaviour, though not through bottom-down or formal hierarchies, but by means of a game played on different sites, formal and informal. In today's 'post–post–Cold War' era, US hegemony (and Western predominance) is increasingly under strain by non-polarity and the unravelling disorder.[157] This challenge must be also confronted via a differentiated and selective approach that moves on a case-by-case basis (the 'pieces of process' he talks about in his latest book[158]), according to what can be done, with whom, when, and how:

> At the global level, the goal of U.S. policy should still be integration, trying to bring others into arrangements to manage global challenges such as

---

[154] Among the most representatives, see Richard N. Haass, 'The Age of Nonpolarity. What Will Follow U.S. Dominance' (May/June 2008) *Foreign Affairs* 44; and *id.*, 'The Unraveling. How to Respond to a Disordered World' (November/December 2014) *Foreign Affairs* 70.

[155] Haass, *A World in Disarray*, note 150.

[156] Haass, *The Reluctant Sheriff*, p. 25.

[157] Non-polarity stands for the augmentation of strength of several states, most of all China but also the rest of the BRICS and others represented in the G20, as well as the relative loss of power by Western states, including the USA. Cf. Haass, 'The Age of Nonpolarity'; and Charles A. Kupchan, *No One's World: The West, The Rising Rest, and the Coming Global Turn* (New York: Oxford University Press, 2012). The term is related to but not equal to multipolarity: whereas the latter is commonly understood as a more ordered redistribution of power among certain major players (the USA, China, Russia, Europe – as far as Europe can be taken as a more or less unified actor in global politics – maybe Japan and India), the former stands for continuously changing power constellations in global affairs beyond those actors and beyond states; non-polarity is thus far less stable, reflecting more 'a world in disarray' (see Haass, *A World in Disarray*, pp. 203–205; see also Rodiles, 'Non-Permanent Members of the United Nations Security Council', 338–339).

[158] Haass, *A World in Disarray*, pp. 195–205.

3.2 THE GENEALOGY OF THE CONCEPT

climate change, terrorism, proliferation, trade, public health, and maintaining a secure and open commons. Where these arrangements can be global, so much the better, but where they cannot, they should be regional or selective, involving those actors with significant interests and capacity and that share some degree of policy consensus.[159]

Haass also talks about 'encouraging a greater degree of global integration' in the context of what he calls 'concerted nonpolarity'.[160] A new doctrine of regulation in which formal institutions and law are 'augmented' by informal means of action and regulation, as well as 'orchestrating nonpolarity', comes quite close to what is described by IR scholars as 'regime complexity'.[161] 'Complexity' may well serve to describe a plural, at times chaotic, environment, but it is also deliberately promoted by those who seek to co-ordinate and manage it. This is a multilayered game Francis Fukuyama calls 'multi-multilateralism':

> A realistic solution to the problem of international action that is both effective and legitimate must therefore lie in the creation of new institutions and the adaptation of existing ones to new circumstances. An appropriate agenda for American foreign policy is to promote the creation of an array of overlapping and sometimes competitive international institutions, a project we may call, for lack of a more sonorous term, *multi-multilateralism*.[162]

And this is the game of global governance[163] – i.e., a 'diversity of institutions to provide governance across a range of issues',[164] with IOs and international law at the end of one spectrum and informal types of

---

[159] Haass, 'The Unraveling', 78.

[160] Haass, 'The Age of Nonpolarity', 56.

[161] See, for example, the contributions to the 'Symposium on The Politics of International Regime Complexity', 7 *Perspectives on Politics* (2009); see further Chapter 5, pp. 151–152, and Chapter 6, Section 6.1.1.

[162] Francis Fukuyama, 'The Paradox of International Action', *The American Interest* (1 March 2006), at www.the-american-interest.com/2006/03/01/the-paradox-of-international-action/. Emphasis added.

[163] Cf. Andrew Hurrell, 'International Law 1989–2010: A Performance Appraisal', in James Crawford and Sarah Nouwen (eds.), *Select Proceedings of the European Society of International Law: Third Volume, International Law 1989–2010: A Performance Appraisal* (Oxford: Hart Publishing, 2012), p. 3, at p. 7 (mentioning that '[l]ooking back it is hard to avoid the conclusion that much of the talk of global governance was a rhetorical façade. The real heavy lifting was to be done by the apparently effective centralization of power around the United States and a liberal Greater West').

[164] Fukuyama, 'The Paradox'.

74 TESTING THE FRAME: THE GENEALOGY OF A CATCHPHRASE

co-operation and flexible rules at the other. To be sure, for Haass, the role of the latter increasingly outweighs the former:

> As a result, we are in an era of multilateralism that will not simply be selective or a la carte [sic] in terms of who signs on to what but also is likely to become much more informal. We're probably in an era in which formal international treaties and conventions and the like are much more the exception than the rule.[165]

In *A World in Disarray*, Richard Haass sets the rhetoric of 'posses assembled by the sheriff' aside, but his thoughts on how to best navigate the unravelled disorder are the corollaries of the previously described arguments. Driven by the same anxiety of re-establishing order in a non-polar world, Haass underlines that order can only be achieved by expanding and adapting it 'to the realities of our interconnected world'.[166] For this, he proposes an idea of global order based on sovereignty but conceived as 'obligations beyond borders' –[167] i.e., as the acknowledgement of responsibilities that states have towards other states, as well as private actors across jurisdictions. 'Sovereign obligation' is the adaptation of the building block of the old international system, or 'World Order 1.0', to an interconnected world where borders are increasingly porous, and the actions of one actor in a given place have consequences on other actors somewhere else. It is about a new global consciousness of co-existence and co-operation that shares the same basic idea underlying Eyal Benvenisti's concept of 'sovereigns as trustees of humanity',[168] though means and ends of 'sovereign obligation' are quite different. For Haass, this consciousness has to be raised through intense and continuous consultations among sovereigns on the public goods and common pool resources most affected by globalization like security, climate, health, or the Internet, as well as on the means to protect these most efficiently. Consultation is thus not to be confused with negotiations leading to solutions contained in formal treaties and other traditional international legal instruments. It is rather about

---

[165] Richard N. Haas (interviewee), Bernard Gwertzman (interviewer), 'The New Informal Multilateral Era' (24 September 2009), at www.cfr.org/international-organizations-and-alliances/new-informal-multilateral-era/p20275.

[166] Haass, *A World in Disarray*, p. 233.

[167] Ibid.

[168] See Eyal Benvenisti, 'Sovereigns as Trustees of Humanity: On the Accountability of States to Foreign Stakeholders' (2013) 107 *The American Journal of International Law* 295.

3.2 THE GENEALOGY OF THE CONCEPT

developing a risk-management mindset that seeks to co-ordinate national policies that have a global impact. Only through the development of such a new global consciousness, 'World Order 2.0' might be achieved. In the construction of World Order 2.0, the coalition of the willing approach is as present as ever before in Haass's thought. 'Multilateralism needs to be rethought and reconfigured if it is to encourage the adoption of sovereign obligation',[169] and this reconfiguration should unfold according to three premises: the best practices approach, pragmatism, and the inclusion of relevant non-state actors. Whereas the latter speaks for itself, let me explain the other two. 'Best practices multilateralism' reflects the idea of consultations as opposed to negotiations – i.e., of reconceiving commitment as non-contractual. It is interesting to note that, for Haass, a prime example of this is the *2015 Paris Agreement on Climate Change*,[170] a a highly unconventional treaty to which I shall return later.[171] 'Pragmatic multilateralism', on its part, is the chosen neologism for *à la carte* multilateralism and the coalition of the willing approach:

> This means bringing together the representatives of those countries (and . . . entities other than countries) that are the most relevant and that are both willing and able to address the particular challenge at hand. It matters not whether this is described as "designer multilateralism" or "multilateralism à la carte"; *what matters is that the bias favors getting things done with those who matter most rather than favoring inclusion for its own sake.* Such coalitions of the willing can become more formal with time, but what matters is that they are forged as needed.[172]

This shows clearly how the coalition of the willing approach has remained unaltered over time, and not only in Haass's writings. His ideas have been highly influential in the design of US grand foreign policy strategy in the post-Cold War world.[173] In the remaining part of

---

[169] Haass, *A World in Disarray*, p. 254.

[170] Ibid.

[171] See Chapter 5, and 6; see also Alejandro Rodiles, 'El Acuerdo de París: un empujoncito hacia la justicia climática', blog contribution, *Nexos* (25 February 2015), at https://eljuegodelacorte.nexos.com.mx/?p=5680.

[172] Haas, *A World in Disarray*, p. 255. Emphasis added.

[173] I understand 'grand foreign policy strategy' as the integral and long-term vision of how a country can best advance its fundamental interests. See further, Terry L. Deibel, *Foreign Affairs Strategy: Logic for American Statecraft* (New York: Cambridge University Press, 2007), pp.13–32. It could be argued that the 'pieces of process' of the coalition of the willing approach is not compatible with long-term and comprehensive perspectives that grand strategy presupposes (cf. Deibel, p. 13). But the key word here is 'process', i.e. the

76 TESTING THE FRAME: THE GENEALOGY OF A CATCHPHRASE

this chapter, I will show to what extent the multilateral strategy – of which Richard Haass is not the only but without a doubt one of the major architects – was not only characteristic of George W. Bush's foreign policy but that it actually remained largely in place under President Barack Obama, all the change in tone and diplomatic forms notwithstanding. As mentioned in the introduction to this book (Chapter 1), it is not clear how this strategy and the coalition of the willing approach in particular will unfold under President Donald Trump. So far, Trump's foreign policy seems to lack a coherent route, not to mention a strategy.[174] For this reason, I will limit my comments on this issue to a few speculative remarks in the conclusion – in the hope that this period of uncertainty and darkness for world affairs will remain a historical hiatus.

3.2.2.3 The Continuity of the Coalition of the Willing Approach: On Spins and Strategy

Coalitions of the willing are most commonly associated with the Iraq War of 2003, an illegal war that occurred in the aftermath of 9/11. That unique historical moment, when the hegemon was at the height of its power and at the same time wounded as never before, facilitated the breach of law and the defiance of organized multilateralism: the turn from hegemony to imperialism.[175] In that historical context, the coalition of the willing approach in general terms – i.e., far beyond *Operation Enduring Freedom* and ad hoc military alliances – was more aggressively framed and advanced as an alternative to standing institutions and international law. The US *National Security Strategy 2006* puts this straightforwardly:

> Existing international institutions have a role to play, but in many cases coalitions of the willing may be able to respond more quickly and creatively[.][176]

piecemeal approach is a doctrine itself of how to cope coherently and in the long run with non-polarity (such as containment was the one for dealing with bipolarity).

[174] Haass himself (once considered a possible choice for deputy secretary of state by Trump) has dubbed the improvisational and erratic foreign policy of Trump's administration 'adhocracy', see Yoni Appelbaum, 'Trump's Foreign Policy "Adhocracy"', *The Atlantic* (27 June 2017), at www.theatlantic.com/international/archive/2017/06/trumps-foreign-policy-adhocracy/531732/.

[175] Cf. Herfried Münkler, *Imperien. Die Logik der Weltherrschaft – Vom alten Rom bis zu den Vereinigten Staaten* (Berlin: Rowohlt, 2005), pp. 70 and 172 (noting that while hegemony implies predominance within a rules-based system, empire is unbound).

[176] *US National Security Strategy 2006*, p. 48.

3.2 THE GENEALOGY OF THE CONCEPT

Although Hasss later distanced himself from that 'war of choice',[177] his experience of the 1991 Gulf War (the 'war of necessity') and his broader ideas on coalition diplomacy clearly informed that instance of coalition building and parts of the discourse that surrounded it. In 2004, the *Proliferation Security Initiative* (PSI) was launched. The PSI clearly follows the model of coalitions of the willing proposed by Haass and has even been called a 'posse'.[178] However, it was designed by people in the Bush administration who did not precisely share the integrationist vision of Haass. This well-known division inside the Bush administration was reflected itself in the way coalitions of the willing were framed at the time. Whilst Colin Powell spoke of 'partnerships', highlighting complementarity and the working *with* institutions,[179] former US Secretary of Defense Donald Rumsfeld and then – Undersecretary for Arms Control at the State Department John Bolton employed a different vocabulary, a discourse of open rivalry and confrontation, of 'with or against us'. But this internal division should not obfuscate the fact that the USA has promoted the creation and use of coalitions of the willing since then and until this very day, regardless of whether they are called 'coalitions', 'partnerships', 'initiatives', or 'platforms'. Actually, Haass was very clear from the beginning about the role of his country as the sheriff who sets the criteria for the posse's composition:

> Call it the 'posse' model, in which *we* assemble 'coalitions of the willing' to deal with the issue at hand.[180]

As I will show in the following chapter, the creation of the PSI and the move from non-proliferation to counter-proliferation of WMDs is emblematic for the rhetoric of confrontation with IOs and international law that prevailed in the aftermath of 9/11. But not only did the 'imperial overstretch'[181] provide many lessons in the sense that even the most powerful state cannot have it all its way down, eventually forcing the second Bush Jr. administration to embark in a different discourse. In fact,

---

[177] See Haass, *War of Necessity, War of Choice*, pp. 233–266.

[178] Former Undersecretary of State for Arms Control in the US DoS, Robert G. Joseph (quoted in Natalie Klein, *Maritime Security and the Law of the Sea* (Oxford: Oxford University Press, 2011), p. 122).

[179] Colin L. Powell, 'A Strategy of Partnerships' (January/February 2004) *Foreign Affairs* 22, at 25–26.

[180] Haass, 'From Reluctant to Resolute'. Emphasis added.

[181] Phrase famously coined by historian Paul Kennedy, though in a different context, see Paul Kennedy, *The Rise and Fall of the Great Powers* (New York: Random House, 1987).

it was the government of George W. Bush the one that began to redesign the grand multilateral strategy of his father, with a focus on adapting international institutions to a rapidly changing world, *inter alia* though coalitions of the willing and the expansion of the concert-style system of the 'Gs';[182] a strategy of integration, not of rivalry. But, the Iraq War of 2003, the pictures of Abu Ghraib, Guantanamo, and rendition practices had imposed negative associations on 'Bush and coalitions of the willing' that became very difficult to disassociate.

When high expectations arose around the world that the end of the Bush Jr. era would bring a much awaited renewal in the course of US foreign policy, turning from (what was perceived as) unilateralism to organized multilateralism, from coalitions of the willing to the UN, and from imperial defiance to a renewed commitment to international law, Timothy J. Lynch and Robert S. Singh published a book that makes the case for continuity in US foreign policy.[183] These authors argue that 'the necessary option of 'coalitions of the willing'[184] will not depend on divisions between Republicans and Democrats, and that

> [t]he central premises and prescriptions of the National Security Strategy (USNSS) documents of 2002 and 2006 will continue to shape American foreign policy in the new administration of 2009–13 and beyond.[185]

Regardless of the sympathies one may or may not have with this, history proved these authors right, at least as far as the strategic conception of Obama's foreign policy is concerned. No doubt, there was a change in tone, and an addition of much talk about a renewed commitment to international law and multilateralism, which has been even described as the 'Obama doctrine'.[186] Moreover, the new tone brought with it a certain acknowledgement of the role of international law and organizations. But this role remained fundamentally instrumentalist, defined in terms of its usefulness for US leadership. In that vein, the utility of the UN and IOs more broadly were recognized in light of their potential to

---

[182] See Daniel W. Drezner, 'The New New World Order' (March/April 2007) *Foreign Affairs* 36.

[183] Timothy J. Lynch and Robert S. Singh, *After Bush: The Case for Continuity in American Foreign Policy* (Cambridge: Cambridge University Press, 2008).

[184] Ibid., p. 8.

[185] Ibid., p. 6.

[186] See Harold H. Koh, 'The Obama Administration and International Law' (keynote address) (2010) 104 *Proceedings of the Annual Meeting (American Society of International Law)* 207.

3.2 THE GENEALOGY OF THE CONCEPT

efficiently co-operate within a variegated space of evolving coalitions, institutions, and other innovative frameworks – i.e., the space of global governance. At this point, I am not evaluating whether this 'role among many' is appropriate, beneficial, or harmful for the idea of an organized international community for which the UN has long stood. What is important now is to make clear that this other idea of organized multi-lateralism (networking is a form of organization) is genealogical to the approach developed in the USA according to which 'existing international institutions have a role to play',[187] a role that 'coalitions of the willing can augment',[188] and which is most efficient if 'enhanced coordination'[189] takes place among them. This paraphrasing of the US National Security Strategies of the George W. Bush and Obama administrations is illustrative in regard to the continuity underlying the coalition of the willing approach.

3.2.2.4 Obama's Framing of Coalitions of the Willing: The 'Hub of Alliances'

That being said, it is important to comment about the way change in rhetoric – i.e. framing – matters most. And this is clearly related to the perceptions of other states, international actors, and observers. Changing perceptions has the potential of affecting the dynamics of coalition building, as well as the broader sensitivities towards coalition diplomacy. Richard Haass has been emphatic on the important role of persuasion for the coalition of the willing approach from the very beginning,[190] and as noted in Chapter 2, the conceptual metaphor 'coalition of the willing' is itself a means of persuasion, a frame put forward for convincing others about the right way of understanding and engaging in international co-operation.

Obama's foreign policy was quite consistent in promoting a discourse of complementarity between informal and formal institutions and mechanisms, as well as other 'frameworks'. The idea of enhancing IOs and international law in order to make them efficient components of global governance is not new, but the Obama administration was more pronounced in highlighting the mutually reinforcing nature of these interactions and integration more broadly, as opposed to rivalry. This has to

---

[187] US National Security Strategy 2006, p. 48.
[188] US National Security Strategy 2002, preface.
[189] US National Security Strategy 2010, p. 46.
[190] See Haass, *The Reluctant Sheriff*, p. 44.

80 TESTING THE FRAME: THE GENEALOGY OF A CATCHPHRASE

do with the fact that increasing non-polarity augments the need to work with others in coalitions as well as institutions: the USA under Obama's leadership did no longer threaten to go it alone, but it showed an increased interest in engaging partners and constructing partnerships of mutual trust.[191] Hence, it was also about building trust along the international community – and to a large extent rebuilding it, due the legacy of the Iraq War and the Bush administration's war on terror rhetoric. It is in this sense that a shift of emphasis from rivalry to complementary took place. It was not a change in conception but a rhetorical change with important practical and strategic consequences: informal coalitions and standing institutions shall co-operate, and the former strengthen the latter in their capacity to 'anticipate and prevent problems from spreading'.[192]

This resonates well with a conception of power present in the writings of leading international relations and law scholars who played an important role in the design of President Obama's foreign policy, like Anne-Marie Slaughter, the head of the Policy Planning Staff of former Secretary of State Hillary R. Clinton. Under this conception, which has been called 'power with' as opposed to 'power over',[193] or indeed 'coalitional power',[194] the skills of building, expanding, and changing connections are regarded as the most valuable asset in today's networked world.[195] In this context, it is important to recall the *Princeton Project on National Security*, which gathered nearly 400 leading individuals in international affairs from academia, think tanks, and government in a bipartisan

---

[191] Making the case for coalition diplomacy in today's non-polar world, see Bruce Jones, *Still Ours to Lead: America, Rising Powers, and the Tension between Rivalry and Restraint* (Washington, D.C.: The Brookings Institution Press, 2014) (mentioning that the 'ability to pull together coalitions for action is perhaps the most enduring feature of American power', at p. 5).

[192] Barack H. Obama, *Remarks by the President at the United States Military Academy Commencement Ceremony* (28 May 2014) [hereafter *West Point Commencement Address* (2014)], at: www.whitehouse.gov/the-press-office/2014/05/28/remarks-presi dent-united-states-military-academy-commencement-ceremony.

[193] See Joseph S. Nye, *The Future of Power* (New York: Public Affairs, 2011), p. xvii, and pp. 10 et seq.

[194] Jones, *Still Ours to Lead*, pp. 92, 201–206.

[195] See Slaughter, *The Chessboard & the Web*. This conception was articulated earlier by the same author in id., 'America's Edge: Power in the Networked Century' (January/February 2009) *Foreign Affairs* 94. This article had an impact on Hillary R. Clinton, who, after reading it, invited Professor Slaughter to be the head of her Policy Planning Staff: see Hillary R. Clinton, *Hard Choices. A Memoir* (New York: Simon & Schuster, 2014), p. 550.

3.2 THE GENEALOGY OF THE CONCEPT 81

manner in order to discuss US national security in the post-9/11 world. The *Final Paper* – presented by the co-directors of the project, Slaughter and John Ikenberry –[196] summarizes the findings with the aim of serving as a basis for the design of US national security and, in general, to delineate the outlines of the future course of action the USA should take in global affairs. Although the word 'coalition' is only used to refer to the PSI, and to 'counter-coalitions' –[197] i.e., those opposed to US interests – the pivotal role of informal groups of states and networks is present throughout the *Final Paper*, the general thread of which is to construct a liberal order in a networked world:

> Building a liberal order does not mean placing our faith in any one institution, such as the United Nations, or even a set of institutions ... commitment to multilateralism can be realized through a *wide range of formal and informal multilateral* tools ... *Finding ways to link these different types of institutions, arrangements, mechanisms, and networks is central to the construction of a liberal order.* They must be linked in ways that avoid centralization and hierarchy and encourage *flexibility and innovation* ... *Formal treaty-based institutions need the eyes and ears that can be provided by issue-based networks of national officials*; those networks, in turn, can often benefit by creating one or more central nodes that provide a secretariat function.[198]

This understanding is in line with the coalition of the willing approach conceived in the early post–Cold War years and maximized after 9/11, no doubt, but it transforms it in that the notion of coalition building is less vertical compared to the idea of 'posses assembled by the sheriff'. Connecting the dots requires force of attraction on a horizontal plane. Thus, there is the recognition within US foreign policy circles that 'relational power' is becoming increasingly useful to face rapidly changing, interconnected global challenges.[199]

In President Obama's words, it is the ability to be 'the hub of alliances'[200] that will ensure the USA to stay unrivalled in world affairs. The

---

[196] G. John Ikenberry and Anne-Marie Slaughter, *Forging a World of Liberty under Law: U.S. National Security in the 21st Century* (Final Paper of the Princeton Project on National Security) (Princeton: The Woodrow Wilson School of Public and International Affairs, 27 September 2006).

[197] Ibid., pp. 16 (on the emergence of 'hostile powers') and 46 (on the PSI).

[198] Ibid., pp. 28–29. Emphasis added.

[199] For a clear description of this, see Nye, *The Future of Power*, pp. 10 et seq. Haass also embraces horizontality and relationality in his latest book, *A World in Disarray*, see above note 150 and accompanying text.

[200] *West Point Commencement Address* (2014).

'hub' has to be reliable, not feared, and for that purpose, the promises of co-ordination through mutual recognition and accommodation have to be articulated. And here, the language of international law and the frames (social and cognitive) provided by IOs are useful again: there is renewed value attached to organized multilateralism. But this very value is transformed by and adjusted to today's circumstances and demands. Accordingly, the UN is to perform as a platform of co-ordination, which will best fulfil its tasks by coalescing with other institutions and informal networks. Strobe Talbott mentions in this regard that:

> the UN needs to be incorporated into an increasingly variegated network of structures and arrangements – some functional in focus, others geographic; some intergovernmental, others based on systematic collaboration with the private sector, civil society, and NGOs. Only if the larger enterprise of global governance has that kind of breadth and depth will it be able to supplement what the UN does well, compensate for what it does badly, and provide capabilities that it lacks.[201]

It is remarkable how close the US *National Security Strategy 2010* comes to the grand strategy conception of the *Princeton Project*, the ideas on global governance articulated earlier by Strobe Talbott, as well as Richard Haass's posse model with its division of labour and the efficiency paradigm underlying it. In its section, 'Strengthen Institutions and Mechanisms for Cooperation', this strategy stresses the need for enhanced coordination among the UN and 'a wide range of frameworks and coalitions',[202] and continues:

> We need to spur and harness a new diversity of instruments, alliances, and institutions in which a division of labor emerges on the basis of effectiveness, competency, and long-term reliability. This requires enhanced coordination among the United Nations, regional organizations, international financial institutions, specialized agencies, and other actors that are better placed or equipped to manage certain threats and challenges.[203]

This, as I will argue in Chapter 6, touches directly upon the increasing role of transnational regime complexes, as well as the growing importance of risk management and resilience in international law, bearing

---

[201] Strobe Talbott, *The Great Experiment: The History of Ancient Empires, Modern States, and the Quest for a Global Nation* (New York: Simon & Schuster, 2008), p. 394.
[202] *US National Security Strategy 2010*, p. 46.
[203] Ibid.

critical consequences for organized multilateralism, and more concretely, for the role of international law in todays multilayered global governance.

3.3 Concluding Remarks on Coalitions of the Willing in a Non-Polar Post-11/8 Global Environment

Defined as ad hoc alliances of like-minded states – as they often are – it could be argued that coalitions of willing and able states existed at least since the Vienna Congress and the 'concert system' set in motion by it.[204] Much later, during the Cold War, several states coalesced around the common goal of establishing an informal nuclear exports control regime, issuing non–legally binding but effective international parameters of conduct regarding non-proliferation of nuclear weapons and dual-use materials. International 'clubs' proliferated, like CoCoM, and the *London Club*, which later became known as the *Nuclear Suppliers Group* (NSG). This informal regime has evolved over the years into a club network covering the control of exports and imports of conventional arms, as well as chemical and biological WMDs. And there are other important historical precedents of coalitions of the willing, even archetypes, such as the 1974 *Basel Committee on Banking Supervision*,[205] and other informal trans-governmental networks.[206]

However, the expression 'coalition of the willing' began to be used as a political catchphrase construed as a conceptual metaphor – or a conceptual metaphor advanced strategically to catch attention in a particular way and pursuing concrete goals – in the early 1990s, primarily by the US government. It soon resonated in international legal scholarship and UN circles, describing multinational forces acting somehow within the collective security system but not precisely according to the black letter law of chapter VII UN Charter. Global networks of NGOs, coalescing at times with friendly governments and IOs in the pursuit of humanitarian goals, have been called coalitions of the willing too. These are

---

[204] On the Vienna Congress as a loose form of legalized hegemony, see Gerry Simpson, *Great Powers and Outlaw States: Unequal Sovereigns in the International Legal Order* (Cambridge: Cambridge University Press, 2006), pp. 91–131.

[205] There is plenty of legal analysis on the Basel Committee, for a general view within the trans-governmental networks literature, see only Slaughter, *A New World Order*, pp. 42–43.

[206] See Keohane and Nye, 'Transgovernmental Relations and International Organizations'; Slaughter, *A New World Order*, pp. 36–64; as well as Raustiala, 'The Architecture of International Cooperation'.

84   TESTING THE FRAME: THE GENEALOGY OF A CATCHPHRASE

manifestations of newer forms of diplomacy that champion human security that have challenged traditional conceptions of multilateralism as well.[207] However, the *Coalition for the International Criminal Court*, the *International Campaign to Ban Landmines*, or the more recent *Humanitarian Initiative* tend to pursue more traditional goals, such as the making of treaties, and lean towards the strengthening of standing institutions and legal regimes. Global campaigns of this sort can be explained as adaptations of coalitions of the willing – as cases where the model has been stretched, to paraphrase Andrew F. Cooper.[208]

In the mid-1990s, the coalition of the willing approach started to be treated as a foreign policy concept by leading US IR scholars and diplomats preoccupied with maintaining the recently won predominance in a rapidly changing world: coalitions of the willing became tactical tools of US foreign policy, and the coalition of the willing approach became a key strategy of global governance in the post–Cold War world, which has been adjusted since then to other tectonic shifts in world order, such as the post-9/11 situation and the emergence of non-polarity. Hence, the genealogy of coalitions of the willing traced in this chapter shows that the strategic usage of this conceptual metaphor, as well as the tactical employment of the actual phenomenon named by it, is tied to the USA and its hegemonic anxieties. Nevertheless, this genealogy would miss a major evolution if it would not refer to the role of other (established or emerging) powers. Neither multilateralism *à la carte* nor the broader coalition of the willing approach is exclusively pursued by the USA. Other states and actors play an active and in some cases leading role in forming coalitions in this or that field of global governance.[209] Importantly, this approach should not be conceived as owned by the West. States from the so-called 'Global South' have learned to play the game too. What seems rather intriguing to me is that many of these states are still anchored in a discourse of a traditional multilateralism, and of

---

[207] See Axworthy, 'Human Security and Global Governance: Putting People First', 20–23.

[208] Cooper, 'Stretching the Model', p. 257. For a critical view on the use of the notion of coalition of the willing, and the resort to these 'informal associations' in relation to R2P and issues involving international moral agency, see Toni Erskine, 'Coalitions of the Willing and Responsibilities to Protect: Informal Associations, Enhanced Capacities, and Shared Moral Burdens' (2014) 28 *Ethics and International Affairs* 115.

[209] Germany, for example, has been particularly outspoken in regard to create '*Koalitionen der Willigen*' in the field of climate change governance, and leads the *Petersberger Climate Dialogue*, see Chapter 5, p. 199.

3.3 CONCLUDING REMARKS ON COALITIONS OF THE WILLING 85

formalism indeed, while their actions take place more and more often in the fluid arena of governance.

The club formed by Brazil, Russia, India, China, and South Africa called 'BRICS' is a case in point. It is the most important non-Western-led informal group of like-minded states, or a 'counter-coalition' indeed, since its main mission has been to counterweight Western predominance. It defines itself as a 'pragmatic platform for cooperation' that has established a 'multilevel process' on various issue areas according to the principle of division of labour, and that is loosely organized through international summitry.[210] Hence, it is driven by the efficiency paradigm, but it entertains an ambivalent attitude towards the formal/informal divide. It seems fascinating to me how the BRICS, on the one hand, reaffirms its commitment to 'the basic norms of the international law ... including sovereign equality and non-interference in other countries' internal affairs', while on the other hand, it endorses co-operation with other coalitions that are not precisely deferential to sovereign equality and non-interference, like the *Financial Action Task Force* (FATF). While the BRICS is prone to reiterate in very formal terms 'the central role' of the UN and international law, it calls for flexible and best practices in the various fields to which it has malleably expanded its scope of action over the years, ranging today from economic co-operation to development to counter-terrorism.[211]

There are many reasons why states (mostly powerful states) from the Global South resort to flexible pragmatism. First, informal mechanisms are becoming the common currency of global governance, and they just wish not to stay behind. Second, for them, too, many global problems are urgent, and traditional means of co-operation appear inappropriate. This common thread of global governance – i.e. the efficiency paradigm – is ubiquitous today: 'networked threats require networked responses' here and there.[212] Finally, the notion of 'counter-coalitions' comes into scene: strengthening ties among those who share the overall goal of countering Western predominance.[213] This is not necessarily the case in each and every instance of South–South co-operation, and many of these coalitions interact with Western-dominated ones in rather pragmatic terms,

---

[210] See 'What is BRICS?', at www.brics2017.org/English/AboutBRICS/BRICS/.

[211] See *BRICS Leaders Xiamen Declaration* (Xiamen, China: 4 September 2017), paras. 6 and 35, at www.brics2017.org/English/Headlines/201709/t20170908_2020.html.

[212] Slaughter, *The Chessboard & the Web*, p. 12; id., *A New World Order*, p. 2.

[213] See note 197 and accompanying text.

86 TESTING THE FRAME: THE GENEALOGY OF A CATCHPHRASE

as mentioned above in the case of the BRICS and the FATF. There are also coalitions in which the unifying criterion is not linked to a North–South or West–rest divide at all. The *Humanitarian Initiative*, for instance, basically assembled non-nuclear states and antinuclear arms networks from around the globe. Yet, the emphasis on coalition building as a matter of promoting a liberal networked order has contributed to the perception of the coalition of the willing approach as a Western mission-ary construct,[214] thus generating a strong impulse in favour of a self-comprehension of South–South partnerships as counter-coalitions.

While it is not difficult to understand why states from the South are building coalitions and thus embracing informality, it is intriguing to see that many of these states remain at the same time attached to formalism in discourse. It is my strong belief that this is a matter of legal and political culture historically rooted in the struggles of several of these countries for equality in international relations. The countries that we are talking about used to be assembled under the label 'Third World' (or 'Second World' in the case of the former communist bloc) before it became fashionable or politically correct to refer to them as the 'Global South' – a problematic term itself that is defined negatively, i.e., as denoting those who are not from the West. In the end, the discursive bond between formalism and the 'South' is part of a 'culture of formal-ism' that, following Koskenniemi, is inherently tied to a struggle for equality through process.[215] Formal notions like sovereign equality have always been more fictions and aims than operational legal principles. However, the ideals of international law have opened up channels of

---

[214] See note 198 and accompanying text.

[215] This concept has provoked a variety of interpretations. To me, it seems rather clear that Koskenniemi talks about a 'culture of resistance to power' that enables those who *lack* (in terms of Ernesto Laclau) 'to articulate this lack, and to do this in universal terms', and that this enabling language is that of legal formalism (the formal argumentative structure that is 'empty' of substantive contents) as understood by Weber and Kelsen, which should not be confused with formal legalism (the 'black letter formalism' Klabbers talks about, see Jan Klabbers, 'Towards a Culture of Formalism? Martti Koskenniemi and the Virtues' (2013) 27 *Temple International & Comparative Law Journal* 417, at 419–420). See Martti Koskenniemi, *The Gentle Civilizer of Nations - The Rise and Fall of International Law 1870-1960* (Cambridge: Cambridge University Press, 2005), pp. 500–506. The emancipatory force of formalism in regard to the ongoing debate that permits the negotiation and renegotiation of social and political agreements is also present in Kelsen's notion of tolerance ('negative' and 'empty' by definition) that informs his theory of justice; see Hans Kelsen, *Was ist Gerechtigkeit?* (Stuttgart: Reclam, 2000).

3.3 CONCLUDING REMARKS ON COALITIONS OF THE WILLING 87

contestation, resistance, and appropriation for even the less powerful.[216] These channels have been basically those of procedural fairness and legal certainty – i.e., rule of law values anchored in law's formal rationality. Law's formal rationality is to be understood in this book in the sense of the intra-juridical criteria for the formation of law, as explained by Max Weber,[217] or according to Kelsen, in the sense that law regulates its own creation.[218] By rejecting law's exogenous determination and instrumentalization, the culture of formalism excels as an emancipatory force that enables ongoing contestation about the universal, hence rebutting missionary mindsets as the Western missionary deep frame. This is what I identified at the beginning of this chapter as the aspiration of international law as a historical universal project (the law of the international community), and this remains a vital goal to pursue if international law is not to stagnate.

It is now important to reflect on whether the oscillation between formality and informality in the Global South is more than about old habitus co-existing in tension with new realities. This may be true in some cases. For example, I doubt that many foreign policy circles in several of these countries are making conscious efforts to relate the two approaches. Marriages of convenience, so to speak, between diplomats and globalized technocrats that speak different languages may be the case more often than not. These marriages survive due to an arrangement that leaves discourse to the former while it gives away the terrain of (economic) action to the latter. But there are other instances in which formality is consciously promoted in discourse (at the UN, and the GA in particular) because it advances a world-view that many states from the South still fully adhere to. Here, less powerful states may not have the resources to insert themselves in many edges, and so they rely on 'World Order 1.0' with the formal structures that are, and that they have achieved to integrate, for instance as a result of decolonization. In order to connect with these fellow audiences, the more powerful players from the South are well advised not to abandon a culture of struggle for equality (even though some of them do not have really to engage in this

---

[216] For an analysis of how the formal criteria of Statehood played a crucial role in the appropriation of international law in Latin America, see Arnulf Becker Lorca, *Mestizo International Law – A Global Intellectual History 1842-1993* (Cambridge: Cambridge University Press, 2016) pp. 337–352.

[217] See Max Weber, *Economy and Society* (edited by Guenther Roth and Claus Wittich) volume one (Berkeley: The University of California Press, 1978), pp. 656–658.

[218] See Kelsen, *Reine Rechtslehre*, p. 239.

88   TESTING THE FRAME: THE GENEALOGY OF A CATCHPHRASE

struggle anymore). Thus, the culture of formalism is also a legitimacy-conferring device for those players from the South with hegemonic ambitions. This legitimacy works beyond the South, as the language of formal international law is still perceived as the most legitimate one in broader UN circles, including wealthy and northern countries. In other words, the culture of formalism is instrumentalized when advanced strategically in tandem with pragmatism, flexibility, and dynamism – i.e., when juxtaposed with a culture of informality. Now, this instrumentalist usage of formalism needs not to be entirely cynical. There may very well be areas and themes in contemporary world affairs that are considered to pertain still to the classical international domain, and thus to formal international law, whereas in others the solutions offered by the classical law of nations appear inadequate. This is the image of *the chessboard and the web* that co-exist in stereo, according to Slaughter's metaphor of contemporary world affairs.[219] In this scenario, it makes sense to talk formalism on issues related to war and peace or the high seas, and, on the other hand, to use the informal vernacular for addressing climate change or the Internet. Of course, the difficulty lies in that in today's globalized world, issues of war and peace and the Internet are as enmeshed as the high seas and climate change. Moreover, this dual approach entails the risk of extracting different international laws: a formal international law of jurisdictional immunities, a semi-formal global law on security, an informal transnational law on the governance of the Internet, etc. In the end, once informality is embraced, albeit only partially, the centrality of international law as a legal system is abandoned, even as an aspiration. One may feel indifferent to international law's systemic problems as a matter of legal theory, but thinking of international law as a legal system is inherently linked to its formal rationality and thus of great geopolitical relevance.

Not long ago, the conclusion to reach from the above was more or less the following. Inasmuch as the Global South embarks in the coalition of the willing approach, it inevitably contributes to render obsolete the culture of formalism to which it feels more attached due to the historical reasons mentioned earlier and in which's defence it has a more acute interest. This may spur particular interests of certain more powerful states from the South in concrete instances, but the overall gain would be for those who invented the game of multilayered global governance

[219] See Slaughter, *The Chessboard & the Web*.

3.3 CONCLUDING REMARKS ON COALITIONS OF THE WILLING 89

performed through the interplays of coalitions and other networks with the traditional structures of international law. The partial retreat of many important southern players from formalism in favour of flexible pragmatism still holds true. However, whether this is a victory of the West, and the USA in particular, is not clear anymore. Donald Trump's administration is not only departing from the multi-multilateral strategy of his predecessors, especially Bush Jr. and Barack Obama, in populist rhetoric, but also in concrete nationalist protectionist actions. There is no reason to think that his government will set aside coalition building as such,[220] and existing US-led coalitions as those I will describe in the ensuing chapters will not cease to exist in the near future.[221] But his government will hardly advance the coalition of the willing approach as a multilateral strategy. The abandonment of two unorthodox treaties the design of which clearly reflects an innovative and informal international legal style that carries US insignia – i.e. the *Transpacific Partnership* (TPP) and the *Paris Agreement on Climate Change* – show that the USA under his leadership feels uncomfortable with the networked order and does not favour any kind of multilateralism, not even *à la carte* in its most minimalist expression. The essential question is whether the 'buffers against turbulence now, at both domestic and international level'[222] will hold strong and make Trump's katechonic protectionism[223] an unfortunate but only temporary trend in US foreign policy that will not make the 'United States lose the ability to afford to sustain order'.[224]

---

[220] In his speech to the GA, Trump referred to 'a coalition of strong and independent nations that embrace their sovereignty to promote security, prosperity, and peace for themselves and for the world'; see *Remarks of President Trump to the 72nd Session of the United Nations General Assembly* (New York, 19 September 2017), at www.whitehouse.gov/the-press-office/2017/09/19/remarks-president-trump-72nd-session-united-nations-general-assembly.

[221] It should be noted that within Trump's administration there are high-ranking officials who strongly favour US-led coalitions of the willing, in particular in the global security realm, such as Secretary of Defence James N. Mattis and National Security Advisor John Bolton; on their role in coalition-building during previous US administrations, see Chapter 4, Sections 4.1. and 4.2.2.

[222] Joseph S. Nye Jr., 'Will the Liberal Order Survive?' (January/February 2017) *Foreign Affairs* 10, at 15.

[223] In Trump's inaugural address, there are several lines that resemble the idea of protection as the power to restrain the anti-Christ, as his words on 'God's people . . . protected by God' denote; see *Remarks of President Donald J. Trump* (as prepared for delivery), *Inaugural Address* (20 January 2017), at www.whitehouse.gov/inaugural-address.

[224] Nye Jr., 'Will the Liberal Order Survive?', 15.

90 TESTING THE FRAME: THE GENEALOGY OF A CATCHPHRASE

It is impossible to answer this as it depends to a great extent on contingent factors such as the time his administration will last. However, the damage to the grand US foreign policy strategy for globalization and non-polarity described in this chapter is already noticeable. Betting for the *katechon*[225] in an interconnected world seems highly problematic if not self-defeating. Even if the USA should sooner than later return to embrace the picture of the world as the web it has so spiritedly promoted in the recent past, Trump has already closed up several spaces and interrupted crucial edges for his country, which are being ceded (almost literally if one considers the abandonment of the TPP) to other major powers, including from the Global South.

The BRICS may serve again to illustrate this. Almost already falling into oblivion after the deceleration of several of its integrating economies, it has experienced an important revival in recent times – i.e., after 11/8. This coalition is performing today as a platform to promote major infrastructure projects beyond its participating states. The initiative to intensify dialogue and build flexible partnerships with other emerging markets and developing countries (EMDCs) is expanding the coalition's reach under the rubric of '*BRICS Plus*'. Aimed at 'interconnected development' through 'market inter-linkages as well as infrastructure and financial integration', this initiative is key to 'the future of the BRICS', according to the *Xiamen Declaration*.[226] BRICS Plus, again, is closely tied to the participation of EMDCs in China's *Belt and Road* initiative.[227] Hence, China is taking the lead within the BRICS and using this 'South–South coalition' as a means to advance its worldwide hegemonic ambitions.

---

[225] On this concept, see only Carl Schmitt, *Der Nomos der Erde im Völkerrecht des Jus Publicum Europaeum*, second edition (Berlin: Dunker & Humboldt, 1974), pp. 28–32.

[226] *BRICS Leaders Xiamen Declaration*, para. 6.

[227] The connection between BRICS Plus and the participation of EMDCs in China's *Belt and Road* initiative is clearly stated in the press releases of the meetings between President Xi Jinping with the Presidents of Egypt and Mexico, both invitees to the Xiamen summit, see *Xi Jinping meets with President Abdel-Fattah al-Sisi of Egypt* (7 September 2017), at www.brics2017.org/English/Headlines/201709/t20170907_2013 .html; and *Xi Jinping meets with President Enrique Peña Nieto of Mexico* (6 September 2017), at www.brics2017.org/English/Headlines/201709/t20170906_1995.html; see also Alejandro Rodiles, 'After TPP is Before TPP: Mexican Politics for Economic Globalization and the Lost Chance for Reflection', in Benedict Kingsbury et al. (eds.), *Megaregulation Contested: Global Economic Ordering After TPP* (Oxford: Oxford University Press, forthcoming).

3.3 CONCLUDING REMARKS ON COALITIONS OF THE WILLING 91

The concrete features of the *Belt and Road* initiative are in the making, difficult to grasp at this moment. However, from what I understand, it is a network of networks aimed at building a series of bilateral and plurilateral partnerships through Chinese-financed infrastructure in what amounts to a world-ordering project:[228] 'a world of networks in which all roads lead to Beijing', in Slaughter's words.[229] This is, in essence, no different from what the USA has pursued through Western-led coalitions and the coalition of the willing approach for much longer than the powers from the South. It is in this sense, too, that the study of coalitions of the willing and international law makes most sense by focusing on the strategic design and implementation carefully put in place by Washington, D.C., over the years, which amounts to a highly interconnected web of coalitions in close interplay with standing institutions.

In the following chapters, I will closely examine how this strategy has been translated into concrete instances of global governance so far. Drawing from coalitions in the security, financial, and climate change realms, I will show that coalitions are not indifferent to international law, all its instrumentalism notwithstanding or precisely because of it. Coalitions of the willing are transforming international law from within through the interplays they strategically entertain with it. At whose service this strategic re-engineering of international law will stand in the end, is a tricky question that only leads to futurism in a non-polar, highly unstable post-11/8 world. Only one thing is clear: it cannot but serve power.

---

[228] This passage owes much to conversations with Benedict Kingsbury in the framework of the *MegaReg* project; for information on this project, see www.iilj.org/megareg/.
[229] Slaughter, *The Chessboard & the Web*, p. 17.

4

Global Security Governance by Posse:
The Proliferation Security Initiative & Co.

In this chapter as well as in the next chapter, I will analyze some specific manifestations of coalitions of the willing. In this sense, both chapters can be read as one. They are interrelated, and some findings in the present one will be confronted with those in the next. Moreover, it is in the very nature of coalitions to be highly relational, so that those analyzed here are connected with the coalitions I will deal with in Chapter 5. This applies to the fields of governance where they operate too. Although the present chapter focuses on counter-proliferation of weapons of mass destruction (WMDs) whereas the following chapter is more about counter-terrorism, these fields are interconnected to such a degree that it is difficult to draw a line between them, and the intensification of this linkage is also due to the work of the coalitions operating in a flexible manner in and between these fields. However, I find it useful to divide the case studies in two chapters not only because of their respective length, but also for the following reason, which is about the book's architecture. The principal aim of this chapter is to show how the ideas that are entailed in the conceptual metaphor 'coalition of the willing' (Chapter 2) have materialized over time, as well as to demonstrate how this relates to the US foreign policy strategy of 'governance by posse' (Chapter 3). In this sense, it can be seen as the corollary of the concept's genealogy. In showing how the ideas behind the catchphrase have been translated into practice, it also deals with the interplay between formality and informality, thus building a bridge to the ensuing chapters that concentrate on the interactions of coalitions with international institutions, as well as on the jurisgenerative character of the formal–informal interplay spurred by coalitions of the willing.

In the following pages, I will analyze the *Proliferation Security Initiative* (PSI) and other closely related coalitions and informal schemes of international co-operation, including at the bilateral level, which together with the former integrate a network of coalitions in counter-proliferation and other related aspects of global security. It is in this sense that I talk of the '*PSI & Co.* '.

The PSI is a well-known example of international co-operation understood and experienced in terms of the willingness and the ability to do the right thing. A closer look into how and why this coalition was created shows how the surface frames of friendship, virtue, and efficiency were present since its very conception, hence denoting the underlying representation of a division between friends and foes – i.e., the 'dynamic of difference'[1] between those who share certain values and are willing to defend them, and the unwilling or unable ones. Furthermore, the evolution of the PSI helps to elucidate the development of the coalition of the willing approach within US foreign policy discourse. It emerged in the aftermath of 9/11 as a rather provocative and competitive alternative to organized multilateralism, which has experienced important shifts towards complementary as global order becomes increasingly non-polar.

The evolution of the PSI is also telling in regard to the amorphous nature of coalitions of the willing, which I have highlighted as one of their persistent characteristics (Chapter 2). *PSI & Co.* is a case in point for a 'fluid'[2] network within a multilayered scheme of global security governance. It goes beyond counter-proliferation, strengthening, on the one hand, US homeland security on the global plane, and, on the other hand, striving to create a grand maritime coalition to secure the global common of the seas.

4.1 The Proliferation Security Initiative

The coalition of the willing approach is no longer exclusively pursued by the USA and its Western allies, but still, the USA has long been the principal promoter of this approach, the international actor with the greatest force of attraction to assemble coalitions, and the one who has advanced this form of international co-operation in the clearest strategic way. Counter-proliferation of WMDs is one of the fields in which the USA has pursued this approach most vehemently and where its disdain for IOs and formal multilateral procedures became most visible in the

---

[1] See Anghie, *Imperialism, Sovereignty and the Making of International Law*, pp. 9, 310 et seq.

[2] Cf. Colin Powell, Interview, *Frontline* (7 June, 2002), at www.pbs.org/wgbh/pages/front line/shows/campaign/interviews/powell.html (using the notion of 'fluid coalition' to indicate the transformations that *Operation Iraqi Freedom* experienced over time).

94   GLOBAL SECURITY GOVERNANCE BY POSSE

post-9/11 environment.[3] In the words of former President George W. Bush:

> To counter proliferation networks, we are working in common cause with like-minded states prepared to make maximum use of their laws and capabilities to deny rogue states, terrorists, and black marketeers access to WMD-related materials and delivery means.[4]

The PSI stands as a paradigmatic case of US-led coalitions of the willing and as a model for the version of multilateralism represented by them.[5] Accordingly, the US *National Security Strategy 2006* foresees the goal of:

> Establishing *results-oriented partnerships on the model of the PSI* to meet new challenges and opportunities. These partnerships emphasize international cooperation, not international bureaucracy. They rely on *voluntary adherence rather than binding treaties*. They are oriented towards action and results rather than legislation and rule-making.[6]

Though not explicitly stated, its creation was already announced in the *National Strategy to Combat Weapons of Mass Destruction of 2002*:

---

[3] See Stewart Patrick, '"The Mission Determines the Coalition": The United States and Multilateral Cooperation after 9/11', in Bruce D. Jones, Shepard Forman and Richard Gowan (eds.), *Cooperating for Peace and Security: Evolving Institutions and Arrangements in a Context of Changing U.S. Security Policy* (New York: Cambridge University Press, 2012), p. 20, at p. 41.

[4] George W. Bush, *President's Statement on the Proliferation Security Initiative* (31 March 2005), at http://2001-2009.state.gov/t/isn/rls/prsrl/47260.htm.

[5] See the several contributions on 'International Coalitions of the Willing' and the debate on 'Weapons of Mass Destruction, International Institutions, and World Order' (especially the remarks by former Assistant Secretary of State, Steve Rademaker in 'International Coalitions of the Willing, Introduction' (2005) 99 *Proceedings of the Annual Meeting (American Society of International Law)*, at 243–255, and 313–323; see also Emma Belcher, 'The Proliferation Security Initiative: Lessons for Using Nonbinding Agreements', *Council on Foreign Relations, Working Paper* (July 2011) 1; Benvenisti, 'Coalitions of the Willing and the Evolution of Informal International Law', p. 7; Michael Byers, 'Policing the High Seas: The Proliferation Security Initiative' (2004) 98 *The American Journal of International Law* 526, at 543–544; Daniel H. Joyner, *International Law and the Proliferation of Weapons of Mass Destruction* (Oxford: Oxford University Press, 2009), p. 303; Maximilian Malirsch and Florian Prill, 'The Proliferation Security Initiative and the 2005 Protocol to the SUA Convention' (2007) 67 *Zeitschrift für ausländisches öffentliches Recht und Völkerrecht* 229; Rodiles, '*Coalitions of the Willing*: Coyuntura, Contexto y Propiedades', 686–687; Baker Spring, 'Harnessing the Power of Nations for Arms Control: The Proliferation Security Initiative and Coalitions of the Willing', *The Heritage Foundation, Backgrounder # 1737* (18 March 2004), at www.heritage.org/research/reports/2004/03/harnessing-the-power-of-nations-for-arms-control-the-proliferation-security-initiative-and-coalitions-of-the-willing.

[6] *US National Security Strategy 2006*, p. 46. Emphasis added.

4.1 THE PROLIFERATION SECURITY INITIATIVE 95

> [WMDs] represent a threat not just to the United States, but also to our friends and allies and the broader international community. For this reason, it is vital that we work closely with like-minded countries on all elements of our comprehensive proliferation strategy [and]
>
> We will hold countries responsible for complying with their commitments. In addition, we will continue to build coalitions to support our efforts[.][7]

This strategy was released on 11 December 2002, only two days after the much-discussed *SoSan* incident, when US officials first requested the Spanish navy to stop and search that vessel on the high seas, which was suspected of carrying WMD-related materials from North Korea to Yemen. After members of the Spanish frigate *Navarra*, which 'was patrolling [the Arabian Sea] as part of Operation Enduring Freedom',[8] found several SCUD missiles, 'hidden under thousands of bags of cement',[9] US authorities had to send a subsequent request to allow the *SoSan* and its cargo to proceed, due to the 'lack of any basis in international law allowing seizure of otherwise legal weapons',[10] according to the White House. This incident is thus commonly viewed as the direct impetus for creating the PSI,[11] although the strategy document on WMDs suggests that the Bush Jr. administration was working on this coalition beforehand.[12] The PSI was launched by President George W. Bush during a G8 meeting in Krakow on 31 May 2003,[13] and it rapidly became one of his most important multilateral undertakings.

---

[7] US *National Strategy to Combat Weapons of Mass Destruction 2002*, pp. 4 and 6, at www.state.gov/documents/organization/16092.pdf.

[8] Douglas Guilfoyle, 'The Proliferation Security Initiative: Interdicting Vessels in International Waters to Prevent the Spread of Weapons of Mass Destruction?' (2005) 29 *Melbourne University Law Review* 733, at 735.

[9] Belcher, 'The Proliferation Security Initiative', p. 3.

[10] Guilfoyle, 'The Proliferation Security Initiative', 736 (referring to a press conference by the former White House Press Secretary Ari Fleischer).

[11] Belcher, 'The Proliferation Security Initiative', p. 3.

[12] John Bolton describes the *SoSan* incident as the event that 'catalyzed and drove the process forward', but recalls that discussions were under way before with the UK 'about enhanced interdiction efforts'. See John Bolton, *Surrender is Not an Option: Defending America at the United Nations and Abroad* (New York: Threshold Editions, 2008), p. 122.

[13] See, for instance, the PSI information website, at www.psi-online.info/. This site is provided by the German Foreign Office but is not part of the website of that ministry. This gives the PSI an Internet presence on its own, which, until recently, it did not have. References to a sort of 'primary source' are made to the web page hosted by the DoS website. Unless otherwise indicated, I will draw the information on the PSI from both the 'German PSI website', and the PSI webpage of the DoS, at www.state.gov/t/isn/c10390.htm.

Today, there is an overwhelming amount of literature on the PSI in international law scholarship.[14] This coalition has become an important part of the study of the law of the sea and of 'non-proliferation law', a term coined by Daniel Joyner that comprises the sources of international law that regulate the proliferation of WMDs.[15] Interestingly, Joyner includes in this category the informal multilateral export control regimes that emerged during the Cold War – like the *Nuclear Suppliers Group*, the *Australia Group*, and others –[16] but he remains sceptical about the PSI, which, together with the Iraq intervention of 2003, he describes as 'the challenges of counterproliferation'.[17]

The PSI is an informal group of states coalesced around the common goal of combating the proliferation of WMDs, their means of delivery, and related materials. It is a mechanism of co-ordination of efforts among competent national authorities of the participating states that seeks to enhance the interdiction at sea, in the air, and on land of the transfer or transport of these weapons and materials 'to and from States and non-State actors of proliferation concern'. In practice, however, the coalition's activities have focused on interdictions of merchant vessels at sea. This may be done 'alone or in concert'. Participating states also commit to share information. These and other commitments are established in the *Statement of Interdiction Principles* (SIP) – i.e., the principal document where the mission of the PSI is described.[18] States become thus PSI participants by endorsing the SIP, and hence are also called 'endorsing states'. It is important to recall that the SIP is not a treaty, nor does it establish any legal obligation; it is a 'political commitment'. The PSI is very keen on this, insisting that endorsing states 'retain the ability to

[14] In addition to the references in notes 5 and 8, see, *inter alia*, Craig H. Allen, *Maritime Counterproliferation Operations and the Rule of Law* (Westport: Praeger Security, 2007); Michael A. Becker, 'The Shifting Public Order of the Oceans: Freedom of Navigation and the Interdiction of Ships at Sea' (2005) 46 *Harvard International Law Journal* 131; Klein, *Maritime Security and the Law of the Sea*, pp. 193–210; John Yoo and Glen Sulmasy, 'The Proliferation Security Initiative: A Model for International Cooperation' (2006) 35 *Hofstra Law Review* 405.

[15] Joyner, *International Law and the Proliferation of Weapons of Mass Destruction*, pp. xiv–xvii.

[16] Ibid., pp. 125–128, 246.

[17] Ibid., pp. 254–332.

[18] See PSI, *Statement of Interdiction Principles* [hereinafter 'SIP'], at www.psi-online.info/Vertretung/psi/en/07-statement/Interdiction-Principes.html. The quotations in this paragraph also refer to these principles. Further information on the PSI composition and its functions will be taken from the PSI web page (www.psi-online.info) unless otherwise indicated.

assess each intervention opportunity on a case by case basis'. In the same vein, it is underlined that the PSI does not create new legal rules, and that it seeks to co-ordinate efforts of participating states 'consistent with national authorities and relevant international law and frameworks', whereby the UN Security Council (SC) and its resolution 1540 (2004) is underlined.

It is important to mention that in the framework of this coalition, its leading member, the USA, pursues the signing of so-called 'PSI agreements' – i.e., bilateral ship-boarding treaties with specific participating states that usually represent the largest shipping registries and flags of convenience countries.[19] Finally, regarding its organizational structure, this is rudimentary, lacking a secretariat whatsoever. But this is not perceived as a deficit by the participants and advocates of this coalition, but rather as one of its strengths. The principal architect of the PSI, former Undersecretary for Arms Control at the US Department of State (DoS), later US Permanent Representative to the UN, and National Security Advisor in the Trump administration, John Bolton, explained that one of the advantages of initiatives launched by the USA of the sort of the PSI (i.e., coalitions of the willing) lies in that they circumvent 'cumbersome treaty-based bureaucracies'.[20] The PSI was designed from the very beginning as 'an activity not an organization',[21] a catchphrase that signals the disdain for the UN, which, according to Bolton, is 'an organization, not an activity'.[22] There are only two flexible structures recognizable in the PSI: the High-Level Political Meetings (HLPM), which convene on the anniversaries of the PSI, and the Operational Experts Group (OEG). Both were incorporated to the PSI in 2004, partly as a response to criticisms about the PSI's two-tiered composition, reflected in the differentiation between the 'core group' and the rest. Actually, the composition of the PSI and its evolution is a case in point for highlighting the ideas that underlie this coalition of the willing and

---

[19] See, for instance, Douglas Guilfoyle, 'Maritime Interdiction of Weapons of Mass Destruction' (2007) 12 *Journal of Conflict & Security Law* 1, at 21–28. PSI ship-boarding agreements in force can be consulted at www.state.gov/t/isn/trty/index.htm.

[20] John R. Bolton, 'An All-Out War on Proliferation', *Financial Times* (7 September 2004), at http://2001-2009.state.gov/t/us/rm/36035.htm.

[21] Bolton, *Surrender is Not an Option*, p. 128 (quoting a British diplomat who participated in the negotiation process of the coalition's principles). However, this catchphrase goes back to Richard N. Haass, who used it to describe coalitions of the willing in general; see Haass, *The Reluctant Sheriff*, p. 95.

[22] Bolton, *Surrender is Not an Option*, p. 128.

98   GLOBAL SECURITY GOVERNANCE BY POSSE

correspond to the frames of friendship and efficiency as explained in Chapter 2.

4.1.1   The Dynamic of Difference Inside and Outside the PSI

As of November 2017, the PSI is composed of 105 participating states.[23] At first sight, the broad participation of the international community in this coalition would undermine one of the recurrent and most important criticisms it has received, namely that it is a selective club, or, in other words, a coalition of like-minded states based on exclusion rather than inclusion, and, as I have argued, informed by a deeply rooted notion of self-evident values that justify this exclusion in light of the higher mission of the coalition – i.e. the *Western missionary deep frame*.[24] But the high number of states participating in the PSI should not obfuscate the dynamic of difference that informs the PSI, both in its internal compos-ition and towards non-participating states. These aspects are two sides of the same coin. The PSI remains informal and outside the UN also because it wants to keep potential 'spoilers' – i.e., unwilling or unable states – as far away as possible from its core. Spoilers come in many shades of grey, just as not every state is equally able or willing. In this sense, there are those who are welcome to lend their support but are supposed to stay at the margins, at least as long as their capabilities are being built – capacity building is a central objective of the PSI. And there are those who are not desired to be incorporated at all, at least as long as their degree of unwillingness continues to show that they are at odds with the very mission of the coalition of the willing. These are the complete outsiders – the 'outlaw', 'evil', or 'rogue states'. In the vocabulary of the PSI, these are 'states of proliferation concern'. But before turning to this more evident manifestation of exclusion, it is important to show that the very same logic of division according to the frames of friendship and effectiveness is inherent also to the inner composition of the PSI.

4.1.1.1   PSI's Composition: The Coalition of the Willing within the Coalition of the Willing

As explained in the previous chapter, selectiveness and exclusion are part and parcel of the coalition of the willing approach: in order to respond

---

[23] See U.S. Department of State, *Proliferation Security Initiative Participants*, at www.state.gov/t/isn/c27732.htm.
[24] See Chapter 3, Section 3.1.

quickly and effectively to dynamically evolving global challenges, only the most willing and able states, according to the issues at hand, should coalesce. Inclusion based on equality would only reproduce the same vices coalitions are supposed to overcome in the very first place, especially prolonged and burdensome consensus-seeking procedures. Instead, effective decision making and action-driven co-ordination are preferred, and this is much more likely to happen among a few like-minded countries than in multilateral fora of a wider membership. This has been referred to as 'minilateralism', a term which indeed captures quite accurately the older idea and phenomenon of selective international co-operation among friends.[25]

But however minilateral networks tend to be in their composition and *modi operandi*, they usually try to reach out as broadly as possible – outreach activities are another central objective of the PSI. This is especially true in the case of ad hoc coalitions of states trying to solve or manage global risks. The PSI is a clear example of a coalition that was created and maintains – the Obama's administration change in rhetoric notwithstanding – a minilateral approach while, at the same time, trying to embrace as many supporters as it can: 'every State concerned about the proliferation of WMDs should be encouraged to endorse the Statement of Interdiction Principles'.[26] This reaffirms that every 'willing' state is invited to join the coalition, even if unable, since unable but willing countries can be turned able through, *inter alia*, capacity building, or by resorting to their differentiated capabilities, even if these are restricted to political support. This is so because of legitimacy concerns, but also because risk-management calculations indicating that a high number of

---

[25] The term 'minilateralism' owes much to its current popularity to Moisés Naím, 'Minilateralism: The Magic Number to Get Real International Action', (July/August 2009) *Foreign Policy* 136. It has been used to describe the resort to parallel venues to the UN in the field of climate change, see Kati Kulovesi, 'Addressing Sectoral Emissions outside the United Nations Framework Convention on Climate Change: What Roles for Multilateralism, Minilateralism and Unilateralism?' (2012) 21 *Review of European Community & International Environmental Law* 193; for a critical assessment, see Jeffrey Scott McGee, 'Exclusive Minilateralism: An Emerging Discourse within International Climate Change Governance?' (2011) 8 *Portal Journal of Multidisciplinary International Studies* 1. For an interesting account of the uses of minilateralism and its role in an increasing multipolar world, see Chris Brummer, *Minilateralism: How Trade Alliances, Soft Law and Financial Engineering Are Redefining Economic Statecraft* (New York: Cambridge University Press, 2014).

[26] *Chairman's Summary of the PSI Tenth Anniversary High Level Political Meeting (HLPM)*, Krakow, 28 May 2013, at https://2009-2017.state.gov/t/isn/2013/211495.htm.

100   GLOBAL SECURITY GOVERNANCE BY POSSE

participants – in their very different actual capacities – has a bigger deterrent effect on potential proliferators, and specifically on terrorists who wish to acquire WMDs.[27] As one Japanese official said, PSI exercises are aimed at showing that authorities around the world 'are ready as one'.[28] To cope with these apparently contradictory goals – i.e., exclusion and inclusion – the PSI has reproduced within its internal structures the same division on which it operates towards non-participants. Before taking a closer look into PSI's genesis and composition, it is useful to recall Richard N. Haass's words on the 'posse model':

> Call it the "posse" model, in which we assemble "coalitions of the willing" to deal with the issue at hand. In building and leading such coalitions, we [i.e., the US, AR] should not expect every nation to make the same commitment to every coalition. Differences in capabilities, location, foreign policy outlook, and domestic concerns make this impracticable. Instead, we should expect our coalitions to be dynamic and embrace the benefits of division of labor.[29]

It was a selective group of eleven states, referred to as the 'core members', who negotiated the SIP during several informal and closed meetings in the summer of 2003. Based on a paper prepared and circulated by the US Department of Defense (DoD) called the 'rules of the road',[30] Australia, France, Germany, Italy, Japan, the Netherlands, Poland, Portugal, Spain, the UK, and the USA adopted the SIP during a meeting, in Paris, on 4 September 2003. Members of the Bush Jr. administration talked openly about the advantages of negotiating the core elements of the PSI with only a small group of like-minded states,[31] although the coalition was intended from the outset to have a much broader, though differentiated, participation. After six other states subsequently joined the PSI, the core

---

[27] On the PSI, the FATF, and the private International Air-Transport Association (IATA) as paramount instances of an 'emerging global risk governance architecture', see Yee-Kuang Heng and Kenneth McDonagh, *Risk, Global Governance and Security* (London/New York: Routledge, 2009).

[28] See the video in *The Guardian* online: *Japanese Troops Simulate Anti-terrorist Operation*, at www.theguardian.com/world/video/2012/jul/04/japanese-simulate-terrorist-video.

[29] Haass, 'From Reluctant to Resolute'.

[30] See Bolton, *Surrender Is Not an Option*, p. 123.

[31] Referring to the negotiation process of the SIP, Bolton clearly mentions that 'one reason Russia and China were not in the core group to begin with was that we wanted to get something going that was not wishy-washy or watered down, and then bring others on board'; Bolton, *Surrender Is Not an Option*, p. 126.

4.1 THE PROLIFERATION SECURITY INITIATIVE   101

group was expanded to fifteen, to include Canada, Norway, Russia, and Singapore;[32] the other two, Denmark and Turkey, stayed outside the core.[33] With the SIP and the contours of the PSI defined, the role of the expanded core group basically consisted of trying to augment the support for the coalition – i.e. in outreach activities. The core was dismantled in 2005, which some attribute to the fact that the mission of the PSI was already defined after the adoption of the SIP,[34] and others to India's criticism that the coalition did not only represent a select group of states but that it also discriminated among its own members.[35] Given that considerable effort has been made to integrate India to the PSI,[36] the second explanation seems more accurate.

India's criticism about the discrimination among PSI participants is relevant indeed. Notions like 'core' and 'extended core members', without any clear criteria for each category, contribute to an impression that there are first- and second-class members according to the preferences of the leading state and its closest allies. The friendship frame is clearly present. In this case, it may not denote a division between friends and foes, but certainly between friends and best friends, so to speak. In addition, the lack of clear criteria makes more room for an explanation based on the efficiency paradigm: the core is integrated by the ones who are considered more able than others, be it because of naval capacity, international political stance, geostrategic position, or geopolitical role capable of attracting others to join the club. Here, we can see how the distinction between willing and able states, on the one hand, and the rest, on the other, is also present *within* coalitions of the willing. Based on interviews with officials of the Bush Jr. administration, Stewart Patrick explains that '[o]nce a core group of critical nations had signed on the narrow agenda and scope of activities, the United States would lead a global campaign to

---

[32] It is rather doubtful whether Russia and Singapore were considered entirely like-minded by the original core group. However, their incorporation was crucial, in the first case, due to Russia's naval capacities and its role as a key player in the global war on terror and, in the second, due to the need to reach out to other states in Asia, a region which has shown much skepticism towards the PSI.

[33] Denmark and Turkey also joined subsequently but were not considered part of the core, see Sharon Squassoni, 'Proliferation Security Initiative (PSI)', *CRS, Report for Congress* (Washington, D.C., 14 September 2006).

[34] See Klein, *Maritime Security*, p. 196 (with further references).

[35] Squassoni, 'Proliferation Security Initiative'.

[36] See Vinod Kumar, *India and the Nuclear Non-Proliferation Regime: The Perennial Outlier* (New Delhi: Cambridge University Press, 2014), pp. 144 et seq.

102   GLOBAL SECURITY GOVERNANCE BY POSSE

get the others to join, on its own terms'.[37] This is coalition building, top-down at its best, and one of the clearest examples of the sheriff-assembling posses to deal with the issues at hand.[38] Robert G. Joseph, who succeeded John Bolton as Undersecretary of State for Arms Control in the DoS, and, according to the latter, 'did much of the conceptual thinking'[39] that led to the creation of the PSI, illustratively described the division of labour within this coalition as 'a deputized posse'.[40]

Beyond the division within the PSI, these unclear categories have caused some confusion about the very question of who is part of the club – i.e., for outside observers, it has not always been clear who the participants of this initiative are. Denmark and Turkey, who joined at an early stage but were not considered part of the core, were at times referred to as 'to have participated in meetings'.[41] Mostly during its early years, there was much talk about 'partners' or 'participants', on the one hand, and those who 'supported' the PSI or 'committed' to its principles, on the other.[42] As Mark Valencia notes, in 2006 it was still not clear what defined a 'supporting state', a category that sometimes seemed to suggest that states that did not publicly endorse the principles were nonetheless supporting the coalition.[43] The favourite slogan used by John Bolton and other officials of the core states to describe the initiative as 'an activity, not an organization' is itself an expression of this unclear line between members, or participants, and supporters, and it goes indeed back to the very conception of the posse model: 'They [i.e., coalitions of the willing] are better understood as an activity than an organization'.[44]

Shortly before it was dismantled, the core group met in Lisbon in March 2004, where it agreed upon several criteria for determining PSI involvement, which include: a formal commitment and public endorsement of the PSI and the SIP; the review of 'national legal authorities' (i.e.,

---

[37] Patrick, 'The Mission Determines the Coalition', p. 42.

[38] Cf. Haass, *The Reluctant Sheriff*, p. 94.

[39] Bolton, *Surrender Is Not an Option*, p. 122.

[40] Quoted in Klein, *Maritime Security*, p. 196.

[41] Guilfoyle, 'The Proliferation Security Initiative', at 737 (referring to a press release of 17 December 2003 by John Bolton).

[42] See the speech by former Foreign Minister of Australia Alexander Downer, *The Threat of Proliferation: Global Resolve and Australian Action* (23 February 2004), at www.foreignminister.gov.au/speeches/2004/040223_lowy.html.

[43] See Mark Valencia, 'Is the PSI Really a Cornerstone of a New International Norm?' (2006) 59 *Naval War College Review* 123, at 125. See also Squassoni, 'Proliferation Security Initiative'; as well as Becker, 'The Shifting Public Order of the Oceans', at note 14.

[44] Haass, *The Reluctant Sheriff*, p. 95.

domestic laws and regulations) to undertake interdictions at sea, in the air, as well as on land; the identification of national assets in the fields of intelligence sharing, military and/or law enforcement co-operation; the designation of points of contact for interdiction requests and other operational activities; the establishment of internal government processes to co-ordinate PSI response efforts; the willingness to participate in interdiction training exercises and actual operations; as well as the willingness to consider signing relevant agreements (e.g., ship-boarding agreements), or to otherwise establish a concrete basis for co-operation (e.g., memoranda of understanding on overflight denial).[45]

This list of criteria, which states are 'encouraged to consider' as 'practical steps that *can* establish the basis for involvement in PSI activities' does not seem to be exhaustive and does not really clarify that much.[46] Although nothing indicates that all of them have to be met, it is not clear which of them would be necessary to undertake in order to be counted as a full participating state, which would rather indicate by their own only an ad hoc participation, or whether there is a sufficient condition at all. The German PSI website mentions that 'States become PSI participants by endorsing the PSI Statement of Interdiction Principles',[47] and subsequently speaks of 'endorsing States', referring to the same states that are listed as 'participants' in the PSI web page of the DoS.[48] So, it seems that SIP endorsing states are participants, whereas those who meet some of the other criteria but not the first one would still be some sort of 'supporters'. At the same time, it is not clear if endorsing the SIP really suffices in order to be counted as a full participant, or whether other additional practical steps or all of them need to be satisfied. Hence, the uncertainties in regard to PSI's composition and degrees of participants remain. And this uncertainty is not only problematic in terms of transparency and equality, but it also bears important consequences for the eventual formation of customary international law in the framework of the PSI.

It is fair to mention that subsequently to the dismantlement of the core group, the HLPM was set up, which is open to all PSI participating states,

---

[45] PSI, *Chairman's Statement at the Fifth Meeting*, Lisbon, 5 March 2004.
[46] Ibid. Emphasis added.
[47] See PSI's Information Website, 'PSI Endorsement', at www.psi-online.info/Vertretung/psi/en/01-about-psi/0-about-us.html.
[48] See US Department of State, 'Proliferation Security Initiative Participants', at www.state.gov/t/isn/c27732.htm.

104   GLOBAL SECURITY GOVERNANCE BY POSSE

apparently including supporting states. The first HLPM was held only a few months after the last core group meeting, on the occasion of PSI's first anniversary, in Krakow, from 31 May to 1 June 2004. This inclusive structure may suggest that the PSI has abandoned the internal logic of division explained above. However, a closer look at PSI's current organization reveals that although changes have occurred, the same logic is still very present. First, the HLPM has only met four times since its creation (in 2004, 2006, 2008, and 2013; the next meeting is scheduled for 2018 in Paris – a 'mid-level political meeting' took place in Washington, D.C., in 2016, which served as a sort of preparatory meeting for the next HLPM). Compared to the five meetings held by the core group in less than one year, this could be interpreted as a sign for a decreasing interest in the PSI, but a parallel structural evolution suggests a different reading. Also in 2004, the OEG was put in place, which gathers quite frequently, sometimes holding several meetings a year. It is composed of twenty-one participating states, including the former members of the core group, and six additional countries, which were selected according to their naval capacities, their importance for the international shipping industry, as well as regional distribution,[49] though it seems that the determining factor is not so much a traditional sense of a balanced regional representation as known in the UN, but rather the countries' outreach potential within their regions. This group emerged from a working group within the core group, the Operational Experts Working Group (OEWG),[50] and divides its activities in subgroups, also called working groups, which deal with further specific issues, including legal matters. It is not clear whether these subgroups are open to all twenty-one members of the OEG, but given the division of labour within the PSI, as well as that in other related coalitions, this is doubtful.

One such related coalition is the *Global Initiative to Combat Nuclear Terrorism* (GICNT), launched by Presidents Bush and Putin during a G8 meeting in St. Petersburg, in 2006, as a US –Russian–led forum to coordinate efforts among partner nations, international initiatives, and organizations in order to prevent, detect, and respond to eventual nuclear

---

[49] These are Argentina, Denmark, Greece, New Zealand, the Republic of Korea, and Turkey. On the *Operational Expert Group* (OEG), see Jacek Durkalec, 'The Proliferation Security Initiative: Evolution and Future Prospects', *EU Non-Proliferation Consortium*, Non-Proliferation Papers No. 16 (June 2012), 6–8, at www.sipri.org/research/disarmament/eu-consortium/publications/nonproliferation-paper-16.

[50] See Durkalec, 'The Proliferation Security Initiative', 7.

terrorist activities.[51] One of the leading minds in the creation of this coalition was former Undersecretary for Arms Control at the DoS, Robert G. Joseph, who, as previously mentioned, also played a leading role in the conception of the PSI.[52] Regarding its structure, the GICNT has a plenary body in which all 'endorsing states'[53] are represented, similar to the HLPM, though it meets more frequently. The GICNT has established a 'working arm', the so-called Implementation and Assessment Group (IAG), which, like the OEG, has a limited participation and performs some of the coalition's crucial tasks, such as the compilation of best practices and the issuance of guidelines – which are not publicly available. The IAG is comprised of three working groups on (1) nuclear detection, (2) nuclear forensics, and (3) the response and mitigation working group, which are again of further limited participation. It is thus not difficult to see how the main objectives of the GICNT and certainly the most substantive outcomes in terms of legal relevance are not the product of deliberations among the eighty-eight partner nations, but of more 'streamlined'[54] discussions of a limited group within the club. It must be said, however, that in contrast to the PSI, the GICNT is more transparent about its working methods. Importantly, the outcomes of the IAG and its working groups – i.e., the guidelines and compilations of best practices, are endorsed, by consensus, in plenary meetings.

The information about the OEG and its working methods is far more opaque, but its overall importance within the PSI can hardly be overstated. According to the German Ministry of Foreign Affairs, the original circle of eleven active participants (i.e., the original core group) has been actually expanded to the twenty-one countries that integrate the OEG.[55] There is little information available on the work and

---

[51] See GICNT Information Website, at www.gicnt.org/; see also Rodiles, '*Coalitions of the Willing*: Coyuntura, Contexto y Propiedades', 688.

[52] See note 39 and accompanying text.

[53] Similar to the PSI's SIP, the GICNT has its Statement of Principles (SOP) – i.e., a non-binding set of political commitments, 'consistent with national legal authorities and obligations ... under relevant international legal frameworks', see GICNT, SOP, pre-amble, at www.gicnt.org/documents/Statement_of_Principles.pdf.

[54] See note 57 and accompanying text.

[55] See Federal Foreign Office, *Proliferation Security Initiative*, at www.auswaertiges-amt .de/DE/Aussenpolitik/Themen/Abruestung/NukleareAbruestung/GremienPj-PSI_node .html.

106 GLOBAL SECURITY GOVERNANCE BY POSSE

outcomes of the OEG. According to some papers issued by the *Stockholm International Peace Research Institute* (SIPRI), which are based on interviews with officials from OEG countries, the few available informal summaries by the countries that have hosted OEG meetings and some leaked cables from the DoS,[56] the OEG functions as a steering committee that gives the impulses to be followed by the rest of the participating states. In one DoS-leaked cable, for example, it is said that the participation in the OEG 'is limited to hold streamlined discussions, [but] the work of these meetings is undertaken on behalf of all PSI participants'.[57] The OEG defines the parameters for capacity-building activities destined for the rest of the participating states. It is the main body in charge of outreach activities, including with non-participating states, something that it performs through Regional Operational Experts Groups (ROEG), and makes decisions (by consensus) concerning organizational matters. One such decision is the appointment of the USA as the PSI Focal Point,[58] which in a way 'formalizes' the leading role of this country in this coalition. It is thus not difficult to see why the German PSI website mentions that this group plays 'a leading role in the initiative', including on its further development.[59] It is the OEG, and not the HLPM, that represents today the initiative's core. In other words, all the talk about the restructuration of the PSI notwithstanding, even today, there is still a *coalition of the willing within the coalition of the willing*.

This internal dynamic of difference brings to mind those well-known patterns of international co-operation present in several international and regional organizations, which is often referred to as the concentric circles approach. It is thus not surprising that proposals on European integration according to 'different speeds', with a 'core Europe' and a more 'basic Union', have been associated with the coalition of the willing

---

[56] See Durkalec, 'The Proliferation Security Initiative', 6–8, as well as Aaron Dunne, 'The Proliferation Security Initiative: Legal Considerations and Operation Realities', SIPRI Policy Paper 36 (May 2013).

[57] Cable: 08STATE31946_a: PSI: Talking Points for February 2008 London, Operational Experts Group (OEG) Meeting (27 March 2008), at www.wikileaks.org/plusd/cables/08STATE31953_a.html.

[58] This decision was taken during an OEG meeting in 2009; see Dunne, 'The Proliferation Security Initiative', 41.

[59] See the German PSI website: www.psi-online.info/Vertretung/psi/en/04-Operational-Experts-Group/0-operational-experts-group.html.

frame.[60] Such proposals have been criticized for implying 'some arrogance, distinction, separation' and for having adversarial consequences for the cohesion of the integration process based on inclusion and solidarity.[61]

Finally, it is necessary to mention the circumstance that some participating states outside the core of the PSI (or the OEG) seem to feel quite comfortable with the different degrees of participation that allow them to engage in accordance with their actual resources and as far as their domestic legal and political restraints allow.[62] This could be seen as a factor undermining the critique of uneven treatment within the PSI, as well as other coalitions. Following the 'free-rider' argument,[63] it could be said that smaller states do actually benefit from this uneven participation: being part of the club and taking advantage of a more robust maritime safety environment but without having to co-operate with the same intensity as others. The problem with the free-rider argument in the present context, as well as in relation to other coalitions structured in a similar way, is that it does not give sufficient consideration to the fact that each and every endorsement is an important contribution for the very

---

[60] See 'Charlemagne: Coalitions for the Willing: "Multi-speed Europe" is Making a Comeback, along with the Constitution', *The Economist* (1 February 2007). Originally attributed to Jacques Delors and related to the different levels of integration member states were willing to accept, the idea of a European Union (EU) of concentric circles has experienced a new turn with the Euro crisis and the core group around Germany managing it; particularly relevant in this context is the so-called '*Groupe de Francfort*' or 'F-Team': '[c]onsisting of the leaders of Germany, France, the Eurogroup of finance ministers, the European Central Bank, the European Commission and the International Monetary Fund, the F-team has quickly established itself as the cluster managing the euro's crisis. It has no legal structure or secretariat, but it is now the core within Europe's core', see '*Charlemagne*: A Crisis? Call the F-Team', *The Economist* (4 November 2011).

[61] See Ingolf Pernice, 'Coalitions of the Willing and European Integration: Different Speed? A Core Europe?', in Calliess, Nolte, Stoll (eds.), *Coalitions of the Willing: Avantgarde or Threat?*, p. 89, at pp. 97–98.

[62] This has been reflected in the *Chairman's Summary of the PSI Tenth Anniversary Meeting* (HLPM), Warsaw, 27–29 May 2013, at www.psi.msz.gov.pl/resource/06f9eba4-3715-415c-bbd9-d1170e5216a8:JCR.

[63] The 'free rider argument' emerged in economic theory of public goods and is applied today to several issues related to multilateral diplomacy and international law, especially in the environmental field, see, for instance, Krisch, 'The Decay of Consent', 3–4 and 12–16; Scott Barrett and Robert Stavins, 'Increasing Participation and Compliance in International Climate Change Agreements' (2003) 3 *International Environmental Agreements: Politics, Law and Economics* 349. It also figures in studies related to US-led coalition building in the frame of international security, see Jennifer D. P. Moroney et al., *Building Partner Capabilities for Coalition Operations* (Pittsburgh: RAND Corporation, 2007), 10.

108 GLOBAL SECURITY GOVERNANCE BY POSSE

thin legitimacy of the coalition. Secondly, regardless of the actual threat that individual states face from the proliferation of WMDs, there is considerable political pressure to take part in it. Less powerful states that most likely need to redirect their scarce resources otherwise cannot easily afford to be labelled as 'unconcerned states'[64] in regard to such a serious threat to international peace and security as the proliferation of WMDs.[65]

4.1.1.2   PSI's Targets: The External Dynamic of Difference

Turning to those outside the club – i.e., those that by exclusion determine the meaning of 'willing' in this case – it is clear that apart from non-state actors pursuing to acquire WMDs for illegal and illegitimate purposes, especially terrorists, the PSI is aimed also against 'outlaw', 'evil', or 'rogue states', called by this coalition 'States of proliferation concern'.[66] This term emerged in US foreign policy discourse and is now widely used among diplomats, especially from Western countries. It should be recalled that it was the Clinton administration that introduced the term 'state of concern' as a replacement for the more offensive metaphor 'rogue state'.[67] In June 2000, the *New York Times* reported that

> the Clinton administration abruptly declared today that 'rogue nations' no longer exist. There are, instead, 'states of concern'. They are the very same states as before – no less dangerous or unpredictable – but possibly more easily swayed by gentler American terms, officials said.[68]

The Clinton administration was very worried about North Korea's nuclear policies, and understood the notion 'state of concern' precisely,

---

[64] The chapeau of the SIP calls 'on all states concerned with this threat to international peace and security to join'; see SIP, preambular paragraph.

[65] The SC first agreed to identify the proliferation of WMD as a threat to international peace and security in 1992, in a 'note of the President', following a meeting at the level of heads of States and governments; see UN Document S/23500 (31 January 1992), p. 4. Subsequent resolutions and presidential statements have reaffirmed this identification, most clearly: SC Res. 1540 (28 April 2004), preambular paragraph (pp) 1; SC Res. 1977 (20 April 2011), p. 2; UN Doc. S/PRST/2014/7 (7 May 2014), para. 1.

[66] SIP, I.

[67] On this terminological evolution and its significance for US foreign policy strategy, see Alex Miles, *US Foreign Policy and the Rogue State Doctrine* (New York: Routledge, 2013), pp. 65 et seq.

[68] Christopher Marquis, 'US Declares "Rogue Nations" are now "States of Concern"', *The New York Times*, (20 June 2000), at www.nytimes.com/2000/06/20/world/us-declares-rogue-nations-are-now-states-of-concern.html.

though not exclusively, in relation to the proliferation threat posed by the regime in Pyongyang, as well as by those in such countries as Cuba (mostly in relation to biological weapons), Iran, Iraq, Syria, and Sudan; all states that have been officially listed by the DoS as 'sponsors of terrorism'.[69] Thus, there is a clear lineage in the usage of the terms 'rogue states', 'states of concern', 'axis of evil', and 'states of proliferation concern' in official US foreign policy discourse. President George W. Bush declared Iran, Iraq, and North Korea, together with 'their terrorist allies', as comprising an 'axis of evil, arming to threaten the peace of the world'.[70] Based on the same criteria of proliferation concern, a few months later, his undersecretary of state John Bolton expanded the axis of evil to include Libya, Syria, and Cuba.[71]

With the probable exceptions of Iraq, once Saddam Hussein was ousted, and Cuba after the re-establishment of diplomatic relations with the USA under the Obama administration, there has been little change as to the perception of which countries represent a 'proliferation concern' – Gaddafi's Libya was said to have changed its proliferation activities as a consequence of one of the few successful PSI operations publicly known, i.e., the interdiction of the *BBC China*, a German owned ship, which was carrying nuclear-related materials to Libya.[72] The PSI was clearly created with the intention to impede the acquisition of WMDs by non-state actors and to counter possible proliferation activities from and to some particular states. US officials have referred to Iran, North Korea, and

---

[69] According to the DoS, states that are 'determined by the Secretary of State to have repeatedly provided support for acts of international terrorism are designated pursuant to three laws: section 6(j) of the Export Administration Act, section 40 of the Arms Export Control Act, and section 620A of the Foreign Assistance Act'. As of November 2017, the listed states are Iran (since 1984), North Korea (since 2017), Sudan (since 1993), and Syria (since 1979). See DoS, *State Sponsors of Terrorism*, at www.state.gov/j/ct/list/c14151.htm.

[70] George W. Bush, *President Delivers State of Union Address* (29 January 2002), at http://georgewbush-whitehouse.archives.gov/news/releases/2002/01/20020129-11.html.

[71] John R. Bolton, 'Beyond the Axis of Evil: Additional Threats to Weapons of Mass Destruction', *The Heritage Foundation, Lecture No. 743 on Missile Defense* (6 May 2002), at www.heritage.org/research/lecture/beyond-the-axis-of-evil.

[72] See Bolton, 'An All-Out War on Proliferation'. According to US officials there have been a series of successful PSI operations (for a useful summary of these official statements, see Mary Beth Nikitin, 'Proliferation Security Initiative (PSI)', *Congressional Research Service* (CRS), Report for Congress (Washington D.C., 15 July 2012). However, publicly known cases remain scarce. The secrecy under which the PSI operates makes any objective assessment as to the actual success of its interdictions very difficult.

110   GLOBAL SECURITY GOVERNANCE BY POSSE

Syria as 'states of proliferation concern',[73] and John Bolton openly acknowledged that the coalition was not concerned with India, Israel, and Pakistan 'as these States possess WMDs "legitimately"'.[74] However, the informal *US-Indian Civil Nuclear Cooperation Initiative of 2006* show that even among these states, some possess WMDs more 'legitimately' than others – like Pakistan, which was denied a similar deal.[75] More important in the present context is that in one of the few documents produced by one of the only two recognizable PSI structures, i.e. the chair's statement of the second high level meeting (of the core group), the coalition has explicitly referred to Iran and North Korea as states of proliferation concern, something which it supported on the basis of a prior statement of the G8, and a joint EU–US declaration.[76]

It is in this sense that the PSI has been criticized for an 'uneven approach' whereby specific states are 'targets' of the coalition.[77] This approach is clearly based on one of the basic frames that inform the

---

[73] Klein, *Maritime Security*, p. 197 (with further references).

[74] Bolton, 'An All-Out War on Proliferation'.

[75] Another manifestation of unequal treatment through informality, the *US-Indian Civil Nuclear Cooperation Initiative* is a bilateral partnership launched in 2006, through which India commits to separate its civil and military nuclear facilities and materials through a series of measures at the national and international plane, including co-operation with the International Atomic Energy Agency (IAEA). The USA, in turn, commits to amend its national legal framework in order to supply India with nuclear materials and technology, which was prohibited before, due to India's status as a non-party to the *Treaty on the Non Proliferation of Nuclear Weapons* (NPT). As a follow-up measure, in 2008, the USA and India signed a formal agreement on peaceful nuclear co-operation (the so-called '123 Agreement'). However, the informal initiative of 2006, based on a joint statement of 18 July 2005 by former President Bush and then Indian Prime Minister Manmohan Singh, introduced a recognition by the USA of India as a special nuclear power – i.e., 'not as a Nuclear Weapon State according to the NPT, but as a great power with a certain right to possess nuclear weapons'; see Christopher Daase, 'Coercion and the Informalization of Arms Control', in Oliver Meier and Christopher Daase (eds.), *Arms Control in the 21st Century: Between Coercion and Cooperation* (New York: Routledge, 2013), p. 67, at p. 72. This has not remained without consequences, as the subsequent admission of India to the *Nuclear Suppliers Group* (NSG) shows (see ibid.). And although it is not clear that the initiative violates the NPT, it has caused irritations among non-nuclear weapon states (NNWS) of the NPT, especially among those which resigned to their nuclear weapons in order to enter the NPT and be part of the global non-proliferation regime. Thus, it has been rightly characterized as a measure that introduces an 'informal international hierarchy' (Daase, ibid.), thereby 'significantly weaken[ing] the NPT system' (Joyner, *International Law and the Proliferation of WMD*, p. 40).

[76] PSI, *Chairman's Statement at the Second Meeting* (Brisbane, Australia, 10 June 2003), at https://2001-2009.state.gov/t/isn/rls/other/25377.htm.

[77] See, among others, Becker, 'The Shifting Public Order of the Oceans', 159 et seq.; Klein, *Maritime Security*, p. 197.

4.1 THE PROLIFERATION SECURITY INITIATIVE   111

coalition of the willing approach – i.e., the friendship frame and its correlate idea of a division between friends and foes (willing versus unwilling). As such, the PSI's concept of states of proliferation concern is an expression of the *dynamic of difference* I have highlighted – following the concept developed by Anthony Anghie – as a benchmark of coalitions of the willing. The poor guidance provided in the SIP concerning the designation of a 'state or non-state actor of proliferation concern' is telling:

> 'States or non-state actors of proliferation concern' generally refers to those countries or entities that the PSI participants involved establish should be subject to interdiction activities because they are engaged in proliferation through: (1) efforts to develop or acquire chemical, biological, or nuclear weapons and associated delivery systems; or (2) transfers (either selling, receiving, or facilitating) of WMD, their delivery systems, or related materials.[78]

This is a rather redundant definition, which can be rephrased as follows: *PSI participants determine that there are states and non-state actors of proliferation concern whenever they determine that countries or entities have been involved in activities of proliferation concern.* The definition established in the SIP has been rightly criticized by legal scholars because it fails to provide clear criteria for designating targets and leaves the question of the evidence required for such a designation, which carries very important consequences for those designated, unanswered.[79] This indeterminacy, accompanied by the circumstance that political discourse and statements by officials from leading participating states strongly associate this category to the usual suspects pinpointed by the USA and its closest allies, further contributes to the perception that the PSI is a US- and Western-driven coalition of the willing.[80]

How strong this perception actually is can be seen in the section on *questions and answers* (Q&A) on the PSI 'German website':

Q3. Is the PSI an international coalition against specific countries?
– No. The PSI does not target specific situations or specific countries[.][81]

---

[78] SIP, Principle I.

[79] See Becker, 'The Shifting Public Order of the Oceans', 161; see also Klein, *Maritime Security*, p. 197.

[80] See also Yee-Kuang Heng and Kenneth McDonagh, *Risk, Global Governance and Security*, pp. 100–101.

[81] *Q&A on the PSI*, at www.psi-online.info/contentblob/3687934/Daten/2715572/QandA.pdf.

112   GLOBAL SECURITY GOVERNANCE BY POSSE

Some of the states that have so far rejected to participate in the PSI – which include, among others, China, India, Indonesia, and Pakistan in Asia; Brazil and Mexico in Latin America; and Egypt and South Africa in Africa –[82] have alluded to this dynamic of difference. China has been most outspoken, mentioning in its official posture on non-proliferation policy and measures of 2010 that

> either the improvement of the existing [non-proliferation] regime or the establishment of a new regime should be based on the universal participation of all countries and on their decisions made through a democratic process. Unilateralism and double standards must be abandoned, and great importance should be attached and full play given to the role of the United Nations.[83]

In addition, China has highlighted during SC open debates on non-proliferation, in 2004 and 2014, its preference to deal with proliferation issues through dialogue and diplomatic means, mentioning that 'multilateralism must be respected' and that 'full play' must be given to the role of the 'existing non-proliferation machinery' – i.e., 'the United Nations and other international organizations'.[84] This is related to a concrete

---

[82] The reasons for the non-participation of these states are of course diverse and often correspond to concrete national interests and perceptions, which are not necessarily connected with questions of international order. Mexico's reluctance, for instance, is closely related to the traditional position of this country not to enter ship-boarding agreements with the USA in the field of counter-narcotics, after which the PSI agreements are modelled. At the same time, however, concerns have been raised that the PSI might shift the non-proliferation regime towards counter-proliferation, weakening the disarmament component of the former. The rivalries between India and Pakistan probably play an important role in the decision of these two non-NPT countries not to participate in this initiative, and India's attitude towards informal initiatives in the non-proliferation field is ambivalent, to say the least, as we saw in regard to the 2006 US–Indian Civil Nuclear Cooperation Initiative (see note 75). Sovereignty concerns over the Strait of Malacca by Indonesia have been associated with this country's non-participation, in addition to the statements of this country regarding the incompatibility of the PSI with UNCLOS (see note 137 and accompanying text).

[83] *China's Non-Proliferation Policy and Measures* (27 May 2010), at www.fmprc.gov.cn/mfa_eng/wjb_663304/zzjg_663340/jks_665232/kjlc_665236/fkswt_665240/t410729. shtml. China has stated this view since its *2003 White Paper on Non-Proliferation* (see www.fmprc.gov.cn/ce/cgvienna/eng/dbtyw/fks/t127666.htm) and pronounced itself in the same vein during the UN Security Council's open debate on non-proliferation of WMDs that was held during the negotiations that led to SC resolution 1540 (2004), see UN Doc. S/PV.4950 (22 April 2004), p. 6. For an overview of China's position on the PSI, see Jinyuan Su, 'The Proliferation Security Initiative (PSI) and the Interdiction at Sea: A Chinese Perspective' (2012) 43 *Ocean Development and International Law* 96, at 98–99.

[84] See UN Doc. S/PV.4950 (22 April 2004), p. 6, and UN Doc. S/PV.7169 (7 May 2014), p. 8.

worry that the PSI might further alienate the regime in Pyongyang, obstructing diplomatic solutions. But it is also a broader reaffirmation of organized multilateralism as a process that facilitates dialogue through inclusion, and hence a criticism of the ad hocism inherent to the informal regime. Similar concerns have been raised by India (which has sought clarification on the states perceived as of proliferation concern),[85] Indonesia, and Brazil.[86]

4.1.1.3 Concluding Remarks on the PSI's Dynamic of Difference and the Principle of Sovereign Equality

By describing the PSI's structure and aims in terms of the division between those who are willing and able, states that are willing but unable, and finally the unwilling nations, as well as by critically assessing the dynamic of difference that this implies, I am neither putting into question nor uncritically affirming that certain political regimes may have engaged in proliferation activities that represent a serious threat to international peace and security. I am questioning neither the legal bases for actions by the SC and other competent IOs, targeting North Korea and until recently Iran[87] nor whether these actions may lay the ground for implementation measures performed by some states in the framework of the PSI. The preceding pages are aimed at showing that even in the presence of founded and legitimate concerns regarding the proliferation activities of some states, the coalition of the willing approach in the realm of counter-proliferation, which many regard as a new model of effective multilateralism,[88] is viewed, for important reasons, not only with suspicion by others, including several states from the so-called Global South, but also as potentially pernicious for constructing lasting solutions to international political crises, questioning thus the very same efficiency paradigm that serves as a justification for this approach.

---

[85] Kumar, *India and the Nuclear Non-Proliferation Regime*, p. 128.

[86] On the concerns raised by Asian States, see Valencia, 'Is the PSI Really the Cornerstone of a New International Norm', 124; and Kumar, *India and the Nuclear Non-Proliferation Regime*, pp. 139 et seq. On Brazil's position, see Ibrahim Abdul Hak Neto, *Armas de Destruição em Massa no Século XXI: Novas Regras para um Velho Jogo. O Paradigma da Iniciativa de Segurança contra a Proliferação* (Brasilia: FUNAG, 2011), pp. 143 et seq.

[87] For a critical analysis, see Daniel H. Joyner, 'The Security Council as Legal Hegemon' (2012) 43 *Georgetown Journal of International Law* 225.

[88] Emblematic in this respect, 'The New Multilateralism', *Wall Street Journal* (8 January 2004, A22); see also Yoo and Sulmasy, 'The Proliferation Security Initiative'.

The analysis of the internal logic of division that informs the design of the PSI has revealed that there are considerable costs for less powerful states 'who are invited to join coalitions at a later stage, if at all'.[89] It has also thrown further evidence that the core of coalitions of the willing usually corresponds to the most industrialized Western states, which brings the 'like-mindedness' of their broader participation into question.[90] This challenges the 'cosmopolitan inclusion' of the PSI[91] and calls for taking characterizations of this initiative as a 'model [that] would allow the United States to determine the agenda for collective action' quite seriously.[92]

The external dynamic of difference that characterizes the PSI's approach towards states of proliferation concern is highly problematic regarding a cornerstone of international law, namely the principle of sovereign equality. This has been highlighted by Chinese international legal scholars in specific relation to the PSI[93] and by others regarding coalitions of the willing in general.[94] But there is a counter-argument to this critique that cannot be ignored. Responding to those questioning the legality of the PSI, Robert G. Joseph underscored that PSI's participants 'are free to engage in selective enforcement' due to the voluntary nature of the activity, 'which is not governed by treaty mandates', as long as they 'operate within the bounds of existing domestic and international law'.[95] Some consider this assertion to be correct, arguing that as long as PSI activities are consistent with international law, the problem with sovereign equality loses relevance.[96] Here, we are reminded of the *Lotus presumption* as articulated by the Permanent Court of International Justice (PCIJ) in 1927, according to which restrictions upon states' freedom of action – their 'independence', in the words of the PCIJ – cannot be presumed in the absence of existing restrictions under

---

[89] Benvenisti, 'Coalitions of the Willing', p. 16.

[90] See Rodiles, *'Coalitions of the Willing*: Coyuntura, Contexto y Propiedades', 689.

[91] See Heng and McDonagh, *Risk, Global Governance and Security*, pp. 100–101 and 142.

[92] Patrick, 'The Mission Determines the Coalition', p. 41.

[93] As described in Su, 'The Proliferation Security Initiative', 112 (referring to G. Gu and Q. Zhao).

[94] For a powerful argument of how coalitions of the willing pose a threat to this fundamental principle, see Krieger, 'Coalitions of the Willing – A Résumé', pp. 46–47; see also Rodiles, *'Coalitions of the Willing*: Coyuntura, Contexto y Propiedades', 700.

[95] Quoted in Klein, *Maritime Security*, p. 197.

[96] See Su, 'The Proliferation Security Initiative', 112.

positive international law.[97] It is therefore important to assess the ways in which the PSI, or more precisely the activities that participating states have committed to perform in their framework, affect international law, if they affect it at all.

4.1.2 The PSI and International Law: A Question of Legality?

Various authors have commented on the legality of the PSI, especially in regard to the law of the sea as enshrined in the *1982 United Nations Convention on the Law of the Sea* (UNCLOS),[98] which largely reflects customary international law and is thus insofar binding on all states, importantly including the USA in the present context, which is not a party to the 'Constitution of the Oceans'. For most of these scholars, the PSI is consistent with international law, though some are sceptical about the implications the initiative might have for the law of the sea regime.[99]

For those assessing the legality of the PSI *tout court*,[100] the line of argument is quite similar to that of Joseph, and this is indeed plausible, at first sight, given that the SIPs are based on flag state consent in regard to interdiction activities on the high seas,[101] thus conforming to the principle of the exclusive jurisdiction of the flag state.[102] Moreover, debates about the lawful exceptions to this principle, as listed in Art. 110 UNCLOS, which do not include reasonable ground for suspecting that the ship is engaging in the transport of WMDs as a basis for the right of visit,[103] also become irrelevant as far as PSI-related interdictions are carried out with the consent of states on a case-by-case basis. The

---

[97] *Case of the S.S. Lotus*, PCIJ Ser. A No. 10 (1927), 18.

[98] *1982 United Nations Convention on the Law of the Sea*, 1833 UNTS 3.

[99] In this sense, see Guilfoyle, 'The Proliferation Security Initiative', 739; and *id.*, 'Maritime Interdiction', 13; Joyner, *International Law and the Proliferation of WMD*, pp. 315 et seq.; see also Klein, *Maritime Security*, p. 203.

[100] In this sense, see Byers, 'Policing the High Seas', 529, as well as Yoo and Sulmasy, 'The Proliferation Security Initiative', 410.

[101] See SIP, IV (3).

[102] UNCLOS, Art. 92 (1). This principle was already recognized by the PICJ in the *Lotus* case, see *Case of the S.S. Lotus*, 25.

[103] The right of visit may be carried out if there is reasonable ground for suspecting that the vessel is '(a) engaged in piracy; (b) in slave trade; (c) in unauthorized broadcasting; or that the ship (d) is without nationality; or (e) though flying a foreign flag or refusing to show its flag, the ship is, in reality, of the same nationality as the warship'. UNCLOS, Art. 110 (1).

116   GLOBAL SECURITY GOVERNANCE BY POSSE

same applies to the contested scope of the right of visit.[104] As Douglas Guilfoyle explains, boarding and searching, on the one hand, and arrest of persons and/or seizure of cargo, on the other, are two different phases of interdiction, and consent to exercise the right of visit does not automatically include 'permission to seize'.[105] But here again, the SIPs are worded so that participating states commit to 'seriously consider providing consent ... to the boarding and searching of its own flag vessels by other states, and to the seizure of such WMD-related cargoes'.[106]

Another reason of concern has been the bilateral PSI ship boarding agreements, which have been signed so far between the USA and some of the world's largest shipping registry countries.[107] These considerably expand the interdiction framework of the PSI by, *inter alia*, conferring broad law enforcement powers upon the requesting state (usually the USA) and by establishing the tacit consent procedure through which in cases where no objection has been raised by the flag state within a given time frame (ranging between two and four hours), the requesting state is 'deemed to have been authorized' to board and search the vessel.[108] This recourse to bilateralism can be criticized for a variety of reasons of legal policy and political economy. That the bargaining power of smaller states, which happen to be the largest ship registries in the world, diminishes dramatically on a bilateral plane *vis-à-vis* the USA, does not need further explanation. This is a well-acknowledged hegemonic technique,[109] whereby powerful states seek to impose their interests, which

---

[104] See Becker, 'The Shifting Public Order of the Oceans', 184–185; as well as Joyner, *International Law and the Proliferation of WMD*, p. 317.

[105] Guilefoyle, 'Maritime Interdiction', 4–5.

[106] SIP, IV (3).

[107] PSI ship-boarding agreements are modelled after bilateral 'ship-rider agreements' usually signed between the USA and states of Latin America and the Caribbean in the field of counter-narcotics. So far, the USA has concluded PSI agreements with Antigua and Barbuda, Bahamas, Belize, Croatia, Cyprus, Liberia, Malta, Marshall Islands, Mongolia, Panama, and St. Vincent and the Grenadines. This list and the agreements can be consulted at https://2001-2009.state.gov/t/isn/c12386.htm.

[108] See, e.g., the *Agreement between the Government of the United States of America and the Government of Antigua and Barbuda Concerning Cooperation to Suppress the Proliferation of Weapons of Mass Destruction, Their Delivery Systems, and Related Materials by Sea* (St. John's, Antigua, on 26 April 2010), Art. 4 (3) (d), at www.state.gov/documents/organization/154075.pdf. It must be said that not each of these agreements contemplate the tacit consent procedure, and where it is contemplated, it varies from case to case. On these agreements see further Guilfoyle, 'Maritime Interdicition', 21–28.

[109] See Nico Krisch, 'International Law in Times of Hegemony: Unequal Power and the Shaping of the International Legal Order' (2005) 16 *European Journal of International*

4.1 THE PROLIFERATION SECURITY INITIATIVE 117

on a multilateral plane tend to encounter greater resistance. Mexico, for example, has so far refused to enter a so-called 'ship-rider agreement' in the area of counter-narcotics with the USA – on which PSI agreements are modelled – for exactly these reasons. However, from a strict legal perspective, PSI bilateral agreements can be regarded as 'acts of interference derive[d] from powers conferred by treaty', contemplated in UNCLOS Art. 110 as a further exception to the exclusive jurisdiction of the flag state,[110] thus they would not pose serious problems regarding PSI's legality.

So far, it is difficult to say that the SIP contravenes the principle of exclusive jurisdiction of the flag state, or Art. 110 UNCLOS for that matter. Notwithstanding, and as previously mentioned, for some authors who have written extensively on the PSI, this initiative raises serious doubts that go beyond the law of the sea regime – including the use of force and international law-making. These concerns are not self-evident, and further explanation is required.

Natalie Klein, who, after engaging in a careful examination of the PSI *vis-à-vis* the law of the sea, concludes that the 'the *prima facie* consistency of the PSI with existing international law, as drawn from the Statement of Interdiction Principles, is maintained'.[111] Importantly, she then goes on to analyze the 'law-making nature of the PSI' and the possible deviances of these law-making activities in relation to the coalition's stated purposes. Guilfoyle, on his part, does not consider the commitments contained in the SIP to be in and by themselves contrary to international law, but points to their vagueness, and regards them as representing 'minimum commitments'.[112] Therefore, he goes on to examine possible legal bases for interdictions not based on flag state consent, in an early article in the frame of naval law,[113] and in a later article in regard to the expanded interdiction framework within which the PSI operates,[114] and

---

Law 369, at 389–390 (exemplifying this, *inter alia*, with the use of bilateral agreements by the British Empire in the 19th century in order to 'establish a maritime police against the slave trade'); see also Benvenisti and Downs, 'The Empire's New Clothes', 610–611 (commenting on the impact of what the authors term 'serial bilateralism' as a fragmentation strategy in the service of power, with especial reference to bilateral investment treaties).

[110] UNCLOS, Art. 110 (1).
[111] Klein, *Maritime Security*, p. 203.
[112] Guilfoyle, 'The Proliferation Security Initiative', 739.
[113] Ibid.
[114] Guilfoyle, 'Maritime Interdiction'.

118   GLOBAL SECURITY GOVERNANCE BY POSSE

that comprises, along PSI bilateral agreements, the International Maritime Organization's (IMO) *2005 Protocol to the 1988 Convention for the Suppression of Unlawful Acts against the Safety of Maritime Navigation* (hereinafter the '2005 SUA Protocol'),[115] as well as SC resolution 1540. Daniel Joyner – the most critical of the three – also deems it necessary to go beyond an analysis of the conformity of the SIP with the law of the sea during peacetime by examining the PSI in light of the law on the use of force but arriving at different conclusions than Guilfoyle. Whilst for the former, 'the PSI is at its essence a counterproliferation-oriented pre-emptive use of force, analogous thereby at a base level with the 2003 Iraq intervention',[116] the latter distinguishes different scenarios under which interdictions on the high seas without flag state consent could take place and, though equally rejecting the lawfulness of pre-emptive self-defence, considers that the existence of a continuing armed conflict between the USA and its allies, on the one hand, and Al-Qaida, on the other, together with a reasonable suspicion of WMD cargo destined for the adversaries, would render such interdictions lawful according to the law of contraband.[117]

What these three authors hold in common, which I find significant for present purposes, is that they build upon the premise that the SIP alone tells very little about the actual relationship of the PSI with international law. Joyner is particularly clear on this when he points at the lack of clarity regarding the 'scope and character of the actions contemplated to be included in the PSI framework' and acknowledges that the examination of the principles of the initiative has to take into account 'the Statement of Interdiction Principles released by the United States *and in other statements by officials involved in the PSI*'.[118] This should not be confused with international law's usual method of interpreting the meaning and scope of a treaty in its context and taking into account any subsequent practice of the parties regarding its interpretation,[119] of which statements by (state) officials involved could be a manifestation. The SIP is not a treaty and does not possess legal force, at least not in the traditional sense. To what Joyner points is to what the SIP and the PSI generally might actually be about; it is, indeed, the 'paranoia' that,

---

[115] Protocol of 2005 to the Convention for the Suppression of Unlawful Acts against the Safety of Maritime Navigation [hereinafter '2005 SUA Protocol'], IMO Doc. LEG/CONF.15/21 (1 November 2005).

[116] Joyner, *International Law and the Proliferation of WMD*, p. 332.

[117] Guilfoyle, 'The Proliferation Security Initiative', 760–764.

[118] Joyner, *International Law and the Proliferation of WMD*, p. 315. Emphasis added.

[119] *1969 Vienna Convention on the Law of Treaties* (VCLT), Art. 31 (3) (b), 1115 UNTS 331.

4.1 THE PROLIFERATION SECURITY INITIATIVE 119

according to Joseph, all of the critics of the PSI share, 'based more on how PSI may evolve rather than a realistic interpretation of the present-day PSI'.[120] If the PSI 'never specifically asserts that the procedures are conducted in self-defense',[121] why then engaging in analyses concerning the nature of interdictions on the high seas as possible manifestations of a dubious doctrine of pre-emptive self-defence? Or, for that matter, what is the relevance of naval law and the rules of contraband for an activity that simply tries to co-ordinate efforts among like-minded countries, based on flag state consent, and their jurisdictional prerogatives in territorial seas and internal waters and at ports? And why bother about the law-making nature of 'an activity', which does not aim at creating anything legal? All of these questions are concrete expressions of the broader interrogation one often faces when dealing with coalitions of the willing from a legal perspective, and until not long ago, with informal international law-making more broadly: why should we (international lawyers) even bother? This may be termed the *non-issue issue of coalitions of the willing*. PSI's relation with international law, which goes beyond the mere legality of the SIP, is a case in point for explaining why we should actually care.

4.1.2.1 PSI's Relation with International Law and the 'Non-Issue Issue' of Coalitions of the Willing

As Klein observes, the 'paranoia is not completely without merit',[122] and it is shared not only by some of the international legal scholars most engaged in the study of the PSI, and of maritime interdiction of WMDs in general, but also by some states, most remarkably China, as we will subsequently see.

One problem with the line of argumentation articulated by Joseph and others is that it is very difficult to assess if activities performed in the framework of the PSI violate international legal norms or not. This is firstly related to the secrecy of PSI operations and the lack of transparency that characterizes this coalition, but also due to the vagueness of the SIP. As Guilfoyle observes, principle IV (the operational one), which calls

---

[120] Quoted in Klein, *Maritime Security*, p. 198.

[121] Yoo and Sulmasy, 'The Proliferation Security Initiative', 416 (responding to the criticisms by Joyner; however, subsequently adding that 'if it did [conduct in self-defense], the PSI could be justified upon a self-defense argument—not through a strict reading of Article 51 but rather by the evolving customary application of self-defense in the world today', which is precisely what Joyner criticizes).

[122] Klein, *Maritime Security*, p. 198.

on participating states to '[t]ake specific actions in support of interdiction efforts ... to the extent their national legal authorities permit and consistent with their obligations under international law and frameworks',[123] seems to establish 'minimum commitments, and not necessarily an exhaustive statement of available measures'.[124] In relation to this indeterminacy, the same author refers to remarks of officials from PSI participating states, which have indicated a willingness to conduct interdictions beyond the minimum commitments and the consent of the flag state involved (Australia) and, at times, suggested the right to self-defence as the legal basis for such interdictions (USA).[125] The same preoccupation is shared in very similar terms by Joyner, who comments that 'in light of statements by some PSI participant state officials, and unassisted by the secrecy surrounding the prosecution of the PSI, it is not known whether PSI-related high seas interdictions are being carried out'.[126] Guilfoyle furthermore refers to a series of 'statements of political intent' on counter-proliferation and maritime enforcement,[127] which, in combination with instruments of a legal nature like SC presidential statements and resolutions, augment the possibilities of constructing legal bases for interdictions on the high seas without due regard to the principle of flag state jurisdiction.

Following these authors, it is important to emphasize that the SIP has to be read in correlation with other statements of political intent on counter-proliferation, like the *Kananaskis Principles* through which another counter-proliferation coalition was created, namely the *G8 Global Partnership against the Spread of WMD*. Here, the G8 states have agreed on developing and maintaining 'effective border controls, law enforcement efforts and international co-operation to detect, deter and interdict in cases of illicit trafficking in such items'.[128] Counter-proliferation strategy documents of key players also call for enhanced international co-ordination in order to conduct effective interdictions. For example, the *European Union Strategy against the Proliferation of WMD* mentions that where political dialogue and diplomatic measures

---

[123] SIP, IV.
[124] Guilfoyle, 'The Proliferation Security Initiative', 739.
[125] Ibid.
[126] Joyner, *International Law and the Proliferation of WMD*, p. 329.
[127] Guilfoyle, 'Maritime Interdiction', 10 et seq.
[128] Statement by G8 Leaders, *The G8 Global Partnership against the Spread of Weapons and Materials of Mass Destruction* (Kananaskis, Canada, 27 June, 2002), at www.g8.utoronto.ca/summit/2002kananaskis/arms.html.

4.1 THE PROLIFERATION SECURITY INITIATIVE

have failed, 'coercive measures under Chapter VII of the UN Charter and international law' such as 'interceptions of shipments and, as appropriate, the use of force ... could be envisioned'.[129] And US commanders 'must be ready' to conduct military interdictions during hostilities and during peacetime to stop the transit of WMDs, delivery systems, and associated materials and technologies between 'States of concern and between State and non-State actors', 'in both non-permissive and permissive environments and coordinate efforts with other U.S. Government agencies and partner/allied States, as directed'.[130] It must be added, though, that PSI operations are highlighted in this US military strategy in the frame of interdictions conducted in a 'permissive environment', meaning an 'operational environment in which host country military and law enforcement agencies have control as well as the intent and capability to assist operations that a [US] unit intends to conduct'.[131] This can be interpreted as a reference to willing and able flag states participating in the PSI – i.e., interdictions conducted on the basis of consent. Nonetheless, taken together, these declarations of political intent by groups of states, the statements pronounced by their officials and the official security postures of some of the very same states point at a clear trend towards more intrusive counter-proliferation measures and related interdiction practices. In the end, and recalling not only the genesis of the PSI but also the Chair's Statement of the second PSI high-level meeting (where express reference to Iran and North Korea as 'States of proliferation concern' is made),[132] it is indeed difficult to believe that

> where a PSI member, knowing that a WMD cargo bound for a state or non-state actor 'of concern' was travelling through international waters on a vessel not covered by a PSI bilateral treaty or flagged by a PSI member, on a route not passing through any PSI member's territorial jurisdiction, would choose to do nothing.[133]

These doubts are further augmented by the PSI's risk-management approach. Indeed, the PSI – as many other coalitions of the willing and

---

[129] *EU Strategy against the Proliferation of Weapons of Mass Destruction (2003)*, Council of the European Union, EU Doc. 15895/03 (8 December 2003).

[130] *US National Military Strategy to Combat Weapons of Mass Destruction*, Chairman of the Joint Chiefs of Staff, Washington, DC 20318 (13 February 2006), p. 24.

[131] Ibid., p. 30.

[132] PSI, *Chairman's Statement at the Second Meeting* (Brisbane, Australia, 10 June 2003).

[133] Guilfoyle, 'The Proliferation Security Initiative', 739.

122 GLOBAL SECURITY GOVERNANCE BY POSSE

clearly those examined in the present book – operates on the basis of assessing and managing risks; it is a global risk-management activity.[134] Proliferation of WMDs is conceived, above all, as a global security risk that needs be addressed by trying to mitigate it through preventative strategies.[135] Following risk-management approaches, including in the legal field,[136] there are unacceptable risks – i.e., those that if they occurred would have such disastrous consequences that although their probability is extremely low, everything must be done to prevent them from happening. Nuclear security as understood today – and as we will see in the next chapter in the case of the *Nuclear Security Summit* (NSS) – is based on precisely this fundamental premise: nuclear terrorists need to be successful only once to achieve their goals, while the community of managers – i.e., the nations concerned and their private partners – needs to be successful all of the time in order to avoid a major catastrophe. The risk-management approach to global security is having a profound impact on the structures of international law, and it would require a whole separate study to analyze this trend properly. Here, suffice it to mention that the priority setting it presupposes is unlikely to favour a binary rationale of legal/illegal, or consent/non-consent, in the decision-making processes that define if an interdiction to suppress the proliferation of WMDs will take place or not.

This might explain why China, as opposed to other states that have claimed violations of concrete legal rules by the PSI, like the right of innocent passage established in Art. 17 UNCLOS,[137] has expressed its concern

> about the possibility that the interdiction activities taken by PSI participants might go *beyond* international law.[138]

---

[134] See Heng and McDonagh, *Risk, Global Governance and Security*, pp. 79–107.

[135] See Craig H. Allen, 'The Limits of Intelligence in Maritime Counterproliferation Operations' (2007) 60 *Naval War College Review* 35, at 40 et seq.

[136] See Richard A. Posner, *Catastrophe: Risk and Response* (New York: Oxford University Press, 2004).

[137] See Su, 'The Proliferation Security Initiative', 109 (referring to an article by the then Secretary of Defence of Indonesia, Juwono Sudarsono, published in the *Jakarta Post*, 10 June 2006).

[138] Ministry of Foreign Affairs of the People's Republic of China, The Department of Arms Control, *Positions on Non-Proliferation Issues: The Proliferation Security Initiative* (7 April 2011), at www.fmprc.gov.cn/mfa_eng/wjb_663304/zzjg_663340/jks_665232/kjlc_665236/fkswt_665240/t410725.shtml. Emphasis added.

4.1 THE PROLIFERATION SECURITY INITIATIVE   123

If nothing important was lost in translation, it is really remarkable that China's Ministry of Foreign Affairs uses the word 'beyond', and not 'contrary to' or an equivalent. It would indeed point at the *non-issue issue*: the PSI may not be illegal, but it is affecting the common understanding of important rules and principles of international law in ways that do not easily fit into the usual canons of the discipline.

Another problem with Joseph's counter-argument is the following. Different consequences follow from the absence of legal breaches by 'selective enforcement', on the one hand, and from the avoidance of constraints by groups of states in order to selectively enforce international law, on the other. In the first case, concepts like sovereign equality are indeed not at the forefront of the debate. The second issue, in turn, has everything to do with sovereign equality as it relates to the evasion of constraints on hegemony by turning away from institutions and organized multilateralism and by fading out formal principles of international law, as Heike Krieger argues pointedly.[139]

As can be seen, there are broader and rather fundamental problems posed by coalitions of the willing like the PSI to the rule of international law, which clearly go beyond the question of whether specific legal obligations are infringed by their activities. These problems relate to the role of international law in global governance and whether coalitions strengthen or weaken it through selective enforcement, for example. Furthermore, an enquiry into the structural relationship of coalitions of the willing with international law has to address the question of whether they really perform in parallel to that body of law. In the next chapter, I will further demonstrate that the interactions of coalitions with legal institutions and fields of international law suggest otherwise, and that this interplay between formality and informality is too significant for coalitions of the willing to benefit from the non-legal waiver – i.e., to be considered extra-legal activities that do not interfere with international law.[140] In Chapters 6 and 7, I will come

---

[139] See Krieger, 'Coalitions of the Willing – A Résumé', pp. 45–48.

[140] For a strong articulation of how that what is usually considered non-legal (i.e., il-, extra-, pre-,post-, supra-, and infra-legalities), is more often than not extremely relevant for international law's structure and actual work, see Fleur Johns, *Non-Legality in International Law – Unruly Law* (Cambridge: Cambridge University Press, 2013). In these pages, I am referring mostly to the 'extra-legality' of the PSI – i.e., 'the legal construction of that which is understood to lie outside the province of international law' (Johns, *Non-Legality in International Law*, p. 10), as put forward by Robert G. Joseph, and which I argue is nonetheless highly relevant for international law.

124   GLOBAL SECURITY GOVERNANCE BY POSSE

back to these issues by proposing that we are actually in presence of an *anti-law law*.[141]

4.2   The PSI at the Intersection of US Border Security and Global Maritime Security

So far, I have shown how the PSI emerged as a paradigmatic case of a coalition of the willing in the post-9/11 environment; and although it has undergone some organizational changes, it retains its basic structure, and its logic still corresponds to the frames of friendship and efficiency – i.e. the dynamic of difference. Having said this, it is undeniable that a change in rhetoric related to the PSI took place under President Obama's administration. This is part of a larger change of Obama's international communication strategy in relation to his predecessor, as explained in the preceding chapter. It is not a change of conception, but a change of rhetoric. But it is nonetheless significant as it relates to the perceptions of other states, actors, and observers, and hence has the potential of affecting the dynamics of coalition building, as well as the broader sensitivities towards coalition diplomacy. This variation of frames in regard to the PSI is also worth commenting on since it reveals much of the nature of the interplay between formality and informality that coalitions of the willing entertain.

At the beginning of the Obama administration, there was much talk in diplomatic circles about the PSI transforming into a formal international institution. These expectations arose mainly from two sources. The first was the internationally much-esteemed 'Prague speech' of President Obama of April 2009, where he addressed several global security issues, including non-proliferation, in a very different way from his predecessor, highlighting international co-operation. There he mentioned that because the threat of proliferation of WMDs

> will be lasting, we should come together to turn efforts such as the Proliferation Security Initiative and the Global Initiative to Combat Nuclear Terrorism into durable international *institutions*. And we should start by having a Global Summit on Nuclear Security that the United States will host within the next year.[142]

---

[141] Particularly in the Conclusion, I will argue that this notion is related but not identical to Fleur Johns' 'non-legality'; see Chapter 7.

[142] Barack H. Obama, *Remarks by President Barack Obama, Hradcany Square Prague, Czech Republic* (4 April 2009), at https://obamawhitehouse.archives.gov/the-press-office/remarks-president-barack-obama-prague-delivered [hereinafter 'Obama, *Prague*

4.2 US BORDER SECURITY AND GLOBAL MARITIME SECURITY 125

And the only Security Strategy document of his administration, released in May 2010, announced that

> To detect and intercept nuclear materials in transit, and to stop the illicit trade in these technologies, we will work to turn programs such as the Proliferation Security Initiative and the Global Initiative to Combat Nuclear Terrorism into durable international *efforts*.[143]

But these expectations were never met under his presidency, and there are good reasons to think that Obama never intended to transform these coalitions into IOs. According to information obtained from leaked DoS cables, a commentator has observed in regard to the PSI that the USA did not propose to establish 'a secretariat or another bureaucratic structure, but rather wanted to "secure multilateral buy-in" [for which], in May 2009, [it] proposed and took the role of PSI Focal Point'.[144] This is reaffirmed by a response by the German government to a parliamentary request of clarification by the parliamentary faction of the *Social Democratic Party* (SPD). Here, the German government was asked about the progress made in relation to President Obama's announcement to 'institutionalize the PSI', and if so, whether Germany's government supported such plans. The government's answer refers to the appointment by the PSI's OEG of the USA as the focal point, which would provide 'institutional support to member States' and clearly adds that there were no further plans regarding the PSI's institutionalization. Regarding Germany's position, reference is made to the initiative's nature as a 'cooperative activity of like-minded States', consistent with international and national law, and that therefore, the *'juridification of the initiative is not an issue'*.[145]

During the preparatory meetings that led to the first *Nuclear Security Summit* (NSS), held in Washington, D.C., in April 2010, the issue never appeared on the agenda, although some delegations expected this, precisely due to Obama's Prague speech. Related inquiries were not

---

Speech']. Emphasis added. See also the US DoD, *Nuclear Posture Review Report* (April 2010), pp. 10, 12, at www.defense.gov/Portals/1/features/defenseReviews/NPR/2010_Nuclear_Posture_Review_Report.pdf.

[143] US *National Security Strategy 2010* (May 2010), at http://nssarchive.us/NSSR/2010.pdf, p. 24. Emphasis added.

[144] Durkalec, 'The Proliferation Security Initiative', 8.

[145] Deutscher Bundestag, 17. Wahlperiode, *Antwort der Bundesregierung auf die Große Anfrage der Abgeordneten Uta Zapf, Dr. h.c. Gernot Erler, Petra Ernstberger, weiterer Abgeordneter der Fraktion der SPD* (Drucksache 17/7226, 29 February 2012), p. 21. Emphasis added.

126 GLOBAL SECURITY GOVERNANCE BY POSSE

addressed further. As I will show in the next chapter, what seemed to become an interesting case of formalization of an informal coalition turned out to be a not less interesting, but quite different, instance of a larger, US-driven strategy of regime change, involving the NSS as a new and crucial informal body for nuclear security governance. At this point, however, the important thing is that the change in words regarding the PSI did not translate into deeds, at least not in the sense expected by several states and other observers. The PSI and the GICNT remain US-led coalitions of the willing until the very day – i.e., under President Trump. Finally, it is important to observe how the PSI is related to other transnational efforts of the USA to protect its borders and to police the global commons. This will show to what extent US-led coalitions of the willing are interrelated within a broader network strategy to defend the national interest in a networked world full of dynamically evolving and interacted transnational threats.

4.2.1 US Border Security by Means of Informal Serial Bilateralism: The Container Security Initiative

The PSI is interlinked with several other coalitions. One of these is the *Container Security Initiative* (CSI), which, also according to the DoS, complements the PSI.[146] Before turning to their relationship, it is important to describe the less-noticed CSI in some detail, since it displays many interesting features of the sort of transnational executive action pursued and promoted by the coalition of the willing approach, but it is undertaken primarily on a bilateral basis. This is important for the purposes of this book. It is true that the said approach in US foreign policy, and beyond, is far more usual in the multilateral realm and it forms actually part of a multi-multilateral strategy, as reflected in the notion of 'multilateralism *à la carte*'.[147] However, as PSI ship-boarding agreements already suggested, coalitions' goals can be pursued bilaterally. There, the multilateral undertaking is supplemented by means of bilateral treaties. Here, CSI's objective of creating an informal international port security regime is primarily pursued through a series of bilateral

---

[146] See DoS, Bureau of International Security and Nonproliferation, *Proliferation Security Initiative Frequently Asked Question, Fact Sheet* (22 May 2008), at http://2001-2009 .state.gov/t/isn/rls/fs/105213.htm.

[147] See Chapter 3, pp. 70–76.

4.2 US BORDER SECURITY AND GLOBAL MARITIME SECURITY 127

arrangements, which together integrate a plurilateral posse of several partner nations, assembled and led by the USA.

The CSI was created as an 'anti-terror coalition', a few months after 9/11,[148] thus preceding the PSI. According to the Customs and Border Protection (CBP) of the US Department of Homeland Security (DHS) – i.e. the government agency in front of this global programme – its principal goal is to identify high-risk containers that could be used for terrorist purposes, including the transport of WMDs and related materials. The identification of containers that are destined to the USA is done at the ports of departure. In order to do this, containers are prescreened before shipped, using technology 'to ensure that screening can be done rapidly without slowing down the movement of trade. This technology includes large-scale X-ray and gamma ray machines and radiation detection devices.'[149] The use of this expensive technology is obviously favoured by this risk-management initiative, thus involving considerable economic interests.[150]

From the perspective of international law, the most interesting feature of the CSI is that it is aimed at stationing US customs officials in foreign ports in order to help carrying out the previously mentioned tasks *in situ*; in particular to decide, together with local officials, which containers to prescreen.[151] Participating states are offered the same prerogative, but only a few have placed customs officers in US ports so far.[152] Moreover, the reciprocity underlying this scheme has been questioned, with one commentator noting that 'the implementation of the CSI has been heavily skewed in favour of U.S. interests'.[153] This unequal relationship is mirrored in the *Declaration of Principles* signed between the USA and

---

[148] To be precise, in January 2002. For an overview of CSI's history and early days, see Ashley Roach, 'Container and Port Security: A Bilateral Perspective' (2003) 18 *The International Journal of Marine and Coastal Law* 341, at 343 et seq.

[149] Information at www.cbp.gov/border-security/ports-entry/cargo-security/csi/csi-brief.

[150] The appeal and duration of any risk-management strategy rest on the strength of the risk perception. Thus, the industry involved in this initiative may play a role too in nurturing this sensitivity.

[151] See Roach, 'Container and Port Security', 346 (noting that US customs officials 'in foreign ports will not have any enforcement powers').

[152] As far as it is known, only Canada and Japan have stationed customs officers at US ports; see Gregory W. Bowman, 'Thinking Outside the Border: Homeland Security and the Forward Deployment of the U.S. Border' (2007) 44 *Houston Law Review* 189, at 223; see also Rodiles, '*Coalitions of the Willing*: Coyuntura, Contexto y Propiedades', at note 43.

[153] Bowman, 'Thinking Outside the Border', 205; and Klein, *Maritime Security*, pp. 165–166.

128   GLOBAL SECURITY GOVERNANCE BY POSSE

Honduras, according to which '[o]fficers of the CBP *are to be stationed*' in Honduran ports, whereas '[a]t the request of the Republic of Honduras, Honduras Customs officers *may be stationed* in the United States'.[154] The real incentive to participate in this initiative seems rather to lie in the expectation of obtaining economic benefits, since pre-screened cargo is likely to be more expediently processed at US ports, and, in general terms, 'CSI ports' are considered more reliable, allegedly reducing insurance costs.[155] Although these economic expectations are not uncontroversial,[156] the 'carrot-and-stick' approach attached to this initiative is quite clear.[157] About thirty-two states participate in the CSI, counting fifty-eight 'CSI ports' throughout the world, which amounts to about 85 per cent of containers bound to the USA.

4.2.1.1 Construing Global Port Security through Informal Bilateral Arrangements: The Disadvantages of Legal Obligation

It is commonly said that participating states provide their consent on the stationing of foreign customs officers through bilateral agreements.[158] Although it is true that they give their consent on a bilateral basis, this does not happen through an 'international agreement ... governed by international law' in the sense of the *1969 Vienna Convention on the Law of Treaties* (VCLT)[159] but rather through informal bilateral arrangements

---

[154] *Declaration of Principles among United States Customs and Border Protection, the Department of Energy of the United States of America, and the Ministry of State, Office of Finance, of the Republic of Honduras Concerning Cooperation to Enhance the Security of Container Cargo*, signed in Tegucigalpa, Honduras, 15 December 2005, at http://energy.gov/sites/prod/files/pi_iec_local/098b7ef980056548.pdf. Emphasis added.

[155] See Roach, 'Container and Port Security', 353–354.

[156] See Klein, *Maritime Security*, p. 166 (noting that 'examination costs have been shifted from the US importer to the foreign shipper [and that] [t]here are concerns that costs will then be passed to the consumer'). Citations omitted.

[157] Cf. Bowman, 'Thinking Outside the Border', 214–216 (though not expressly referring to the CSI, but to similar and related initiatives, like C-TPAT and *Free and Secure Trade* (FAST), a trilateral border security programme operating among the USA, Canada, and Mexico.

[158] See Bowman, 'Thinking Outside the Border', 205; Klein, *Maritime Security*, p. 165; Jessica Romero, 'Prevention of Maritime Terrorism: The Container Security Initiative' (2003) 4 *Chicago Journal of International Law* 597, at 600–601, and note 21 (though noting that the fact that these 'completely reciprocal' agreements are not subject to ratification by the US Senate 'severely limit[s] congressional oversight').

[159] *1969 Vienna Convention on the Law of Treaties*, 1155 UNTS 331, Art. 2(1)(a). As Anthony Aust has observed, the crucial distinction that can be derived from the *Commentaries of the International Law Commission*, as well as from the position of states, lies in that agreements 'governed by international law' are those 'instruments

4.2 US BORDER SECURITY AND GLOBAL MARITIME SECURITY 129

called 'declarations of principles'. These are not submitted to internal approval procedures and are usually signed between the US agencies involved – i.e. the CBP and the Department of Energy – and their foreign counterparts. More importantly, these inter-institutional co-operative arrangements are not formulated in a prescriptive language;[160] rather, they represent 'understandings' and, at least in one case, explicitly state that it does 'not constitute a legally binding agreement',[161] following thus the *DoS Guidance on Non-Binding Documents*.[162]

It is interesting to observe that when prior bilateral agreements on co-operation and mutual assistance in customs matters between the USA and other states are in place, CSI arrangements are often said to intensify the former and to be adopted within their framework.[163] This seems to suggest that the new measures that are to be carried out according to the CSI have their legal basis in those prior treaties, something that would lend the CSI internal political legitimacy, since those treaties usually have been approved according to the constitutional procedures of the participating states. But it is doubtful whether the stationing of US customs officials in foreign ports, even 'on a pilot basis',[164] can be seen as just a measure that intensifies the existing treaty by way of, for example, a subsequent agreement between the parties regarding the interpretation or application of the treaty.[165] The following example shows some of the difficulties and problems underlying this proposition.

---

which the parties intended to be legally binding'; see Anthony Aust, 'The Theory and Practice of Informal International Instruments' (1986) 35 *International and Comparative Law Quarterly* 787, at 795. Also in this sense, see Oscar Schachter, 'The Twilight Existence of Nonbinding International Agreements' (1977) 71 *The American Journal of International Law* 296, at 301.

[160] Cf. Aust, 'The Theory and Practice', 795, 800; as well as Schachter, 'The Twilight Existence', 296 et seq.

[161] See note 154.

[162] See Chapter 1, note 12.

[163] Press releases of the US government announcing the signing of 'Declaration of Principles' often refer to this complementary function; see, e.g., US Customs Service, Press Release, *Italy Signs Declaration of Principles to Join U.S. Customs Container Security Initiative, Strengthening Anti-Terror Coalition La Spezia and Genoa Ports to Pre-Screen U.S.-Bound Cargo Containers* (7 November 2002).

[164] CSI arrangements on the stationing of US customs officials in foreign ports are made first for an initial pilot phase, which is then usually extended. But it is not clear for how long and on what basis these extensions are made.

[165] See VCLT, Art. 31(3)(a); see also the work of the ILC's Special Rapporteur, Georg Nolte, on subsequent agreements and subsequent practice, in particular ILC, *Report on the Work of Its Sixty-Fifth Session (6 May to 7 June and 8 July to 9 August 2013)*, UN Doc.

130   GLOBAL SECURITY GOVERNANCE BY POSSE

On the occasion of a parliamentary request for clarification on activities carried out by the DHS in EU ports and airports made by members of the German parliament from the party *Die Linke*, the German government answered that the *Declaration of Principles* in 'support of the CSI' between US and German customs authorities of 1 August 2002, was made 'in the framework of the 1973 Customs Mutual Assistance Agreement' between the two countries.[166] But it is very difficult to discern from the 1973 Agreement any provision that could be interpreted as potentially allowing such a broadening of the co-operation envisaged in its text, as the stationing of foreign customs officials at either side certainly is. Actually, the treaty clearly establishes that special surveillance of conveyances and goods are to be carried out, at the request of either party, by the customs services of the port country 'to the extent of its ability [and] within its jurisdiction'.[167] Thus, if the new measures go clearly beyond what the parties once agreed upon – as they do in this case – a new treaty amending or supplementing the 'framework treaty' – however called (usually a 'protocol') – would be the expected way of procedure under international law. This holds especially true if the proposition that CSI declarations of principle are adopted within the framework of those treaties is to be taken seriously. But CSI bilateral arrangements, including the *Declaration of Principles* with Germany (*Grundsatzerklärung*) of August 2002, are clearly not formulated as protocols amending or supplementing the former mutual assistance treaties, something that is already clear in that the internal approval procedures that accompany the ratification process of protocols are systematically eschewed by CSI arrangements. The fact that these arrangements are not intended to

---

A/68/10, Supplement No. 10 (2013), Chapter IV (*Subsequent Agreements and Subsequent Practice in Relation to the Interpretation of Treaties*), p. 9, at pp. 31 et seq.

[166] Deutscher Bundestag, 17. Wahlperiode, *Antwort der Bundesregierung auf die Kleine Anfrage der Abgeordneten Andrej Hunko, Jan van Aken, Christine Buchholz, weiterer Abgeordneter und der Fraktion Die Linke, Aktivitäten des US-Departments of Homeland Security an Flug- und Seehäfen der Europäischen Union* (Drucksache 17/6654, 21 June 2011). On the content of the *Declaration of Principles* of August 2002, see Julia Pfeil, 'Völkerrechtliche Praxis der Bundesrepublik Deutschland in den Jahren 2000 bis 2002 (3. Teil Friedenssicherung)'(2004) 64 *Zeitschrift für ausländisches öffentliches Recht und Völkerrecht* 1105, at 1127–1128.

[167] *Gesetz zu dem Vertrag vom 23. August 1973 zwieschen der Bundesrepublik Deutschland und den Vereinigten Staaten von Amerika über die gegenseitige Unterstützung ihrer Zollverwaltungen*, Art. 5, 1975 Bundesgesetzblatt (Nr. 24) 445. Translation by the author.

create legal obligations could undermine those criticisms that argue that the mutual assistance treaties are actually modified without following the normal way of procedure according to the law of treaties. If no new obligations are created, no pre-existing ones can be formally altered. But even if this argument should be correct – which it is in strict formal terms – the criticism still holds true because under this line of argument, the proposition that CSI declarations of principle are adopted within the framework of pre-existing international treaties would not make much sense anymore. So, why insist on the legal relationship between formal mutual assistance treaties on custom matters and informal CSI arrangements, when the latter are said to be and are formulated as extra-legal, bilateral political commitments?

This is of the utmost importance. One of the very reasons to flee into informal arrangements, bilateral or multilateral, is the desire of governments to avoid domestic constraints,[168] especially regarding the approval of treaties and their formal amendments. In this sense, governments show themselves as willing to renounce the advantages of treaties, and of international legal obligation altogether: breaches of CSI commitments will hardly give rise to legal consequences under the law of state responsibility. However, participating governments usually follow these commitments, also due to the economic incentives attached to them. In other words, from the perspective of those promoting the CSI and like initiatives through informal 'serial bilateralism',[169] the risk of losing the advantages of legal obligation is worth taking. At the same time, however, this informal approach is attached to the formal, legal language of treaties, giving rise to speculations about the precise legal nature of such arrangements, which do not pretend to create legal obligations but are said to be adopted within the framework of existing legal obligations and to strengthen legal frameworks. This seemingly paradoxical attitude towards law is at the core of the coalition of the willing approach. Coalitions constantly reject the creation of legal obligations but claim to foster existing legal frameworks, as the case of the PSI already revealed; they neglect international law's formality but borrow the formal language of international law to frame their goals and activities. I will return to this

---

[168] Making this point in relation to international trade law, see also Frieder Roessler, 'Law, De Facto Agreements and Declarations of Principle in International Economic Relations' (1978) 21 *German Yearbook of International Law* 27, at 45–50.

[169] See note 191 and accompanying text.

132   GLOBAL SECURITY GOVERNANCE BY POSSE

crucial point in Chapter 6. For now, it suffices to underline what became already apparent in the preceding lines: the usage of a legal vocabulary to describe extra-legal activities also has to do with the search for legitimacy. But the closer examination of CSI arrangements shows that the legitimacy obtained in such a way is highly questionable; in fact, it could be argued that it renders the CSI even more problematic because the reference to formal treaties sounds more a like a disguise for pure transnational executive action.

Already in the late 1970s, Frieder Roessler very accurately described that another reason to renounce the advantages of treaties and to resort to informal arrangements is 'to avoid formalizing differences in status'.[170] It is not only true that the very nature and existence of this US official programme with global outreach reflects asymmetries in world affairs and that the factual reciprocity of CSI arrangements is absent in the vast majority of cases, but it is also true that, at least in one case, the asymmetric relationship is clearly stipulated in the text of the Declaration.[171] Now, note that not dissimilar to Honduras, the EU has recognized that

> expansion of CSI should occur as quickly as possible for all ports within the European Community where the exchange of sea-container traffic with the United States of America is more than *de minimis*.[172]

There is no equivalent clause regarding US ports. It is true that this is the text of a formal agreement – the only one so far – but the reasons for adopting this treaty were related to worries within the EU that potential unfair competitive advantages for those EU countries with CSI arrangements in place may have violated EU law.[173] The agreement, which takes 'due account' of the bilateral declarations of principles in place, actually serves the purpose of achieving that those EU countries that have not done so enter such declarations with the USA, as stated in Art. 3 (1), whereby the parties agree to

---

[170] Roessler, 'Law, De Facto Agreements and Declarations of Principle', 53.
[171] See note 154 and accompanying text.
[172] *Agreement between the European Community and the United States of America on Intensifying and Broadening the Agreement on Customs Cooperation and Mutual Assistance in Customs Matters to Include Cooperation on Container Security and Related Matters* (Brussels, 28 April 2004), preamble; annexed to Council Decision (2004/634/EC), Official Journal of the European Union, L304/32 (30 September 2004).
[173] See Klein, *Maritime Security*, p. 165.

> supporting the prompt and successful expansion of the CSI to all ports in
> the European Community that meet relevant requirements, and promoting comparable standards in the relevant US ports.[174]

This agreement contains additional elements of co-ordination, like the establishment of a mixed working group in charge, *inter alia*, of formulating recommendations to the pre-existing EU–US Joint Customs Cooperation Committee on how to better implement the CSI. This shows, on the one hand, that EU–US customs co-operation is institutionally and legally structured, which may reduce asymmetries. On the other hand, it is a quite revealing case of formal–informal norm interaction, and of the shaping of norms through such interaction.

4.2.1.2 PSI-CSI Complementarity

The CSI contributes to the efforts of the PSI in that it enhances the policing functions of the latter at the earliest stage of the transportation cycle.[175] This has the practical advantage that the searching of suspected cargo is much easier in the ports of PSI participating states, both for operational and legal reasons. States enjoy the greatest authority to board, search, and seize cargo prohibited under their domestic law, with only a few limitations, the most important of which is the immunity afforded to warships and governmental vessels.[176] Through the SIP, endorsing states commit themselves 'to take appropriate actions to . . . enforce conditions on vessels entering or leaving their ports, internal waters or territorial seas that are reasonably suspected of carrying [WMDs, their delivery systems, and related materials]'.[177] The SIP also expect from endorsing states that they '[r]eview and work to strengthen their relevant national legal authorities where necessary to accomplish these objectives'.[178] Accordingly, if a PSI participating state does not already have legislation in place prohibiting the cargo of WMDs, delivery systems, and related materials, at the time of endorsement of the SIP, they are committed by

---

[174] See note 172.
[175] See DoS, *Proliferation Security Initiative Frequently Asked Question*; see also Klein, *Maritime Security*, p. 119; Heng and McDonagh, *Risk, Global Governance and Security*, p. 94.
[176] See UNCLOS, Art. 32.
[177] SIP, IV (4)(2).
[178] SIP, III.

them to adopt such internal measures. It is reasonable to think that the CSI would complement the PSI in cases where such internal legal reform is still pending. CSI arrangements do not require any legislation from participating states, and although this initiative does not refer to the boarding and seizing of cargo, prescreening activities are a means of searching and identifying high-risk cargo. This would only apply to cargo destined for the USA and not to the rest of transportation activities covered by the PSI. However, one could assume that for a state that has already committed to the prescreening of cargo for counter-terrorism and counter-proliferation purposes on a bilateral basis, and then joins the broader multilateral related effort, the pull for greater compliance with both US-led initiatives would be stronger. Be that as it may, where such internal laws are in place, the activities carried out under CSI would facilitate and accelerate the boarding, searching, and eventual seizing of prohibited cargo that is bound from the ports of PSI participating states to US ports.

Another way in which the CSI complements the PSI is simply numerical. It is interesting to observe that states, which have so far refused to participate in the latter, do participate in the former. These are Brazil, China, Egypt, Jamaica, Pakistan, and South Africa. Many of these states are known for their strong embracement of organized multilateralism, particularly of the UN. As we have seen, most of all China has been very outspoken regarding its reservations to the PSI, which are driven out of concerns that this initiative might go 'beyond' international law, as well as that it could sidestep the UN. It is thus interesting to see how some states show themselves as reluctant to engage in a multilateral counter-proliferation undertaking that operates outside formal legal frameworks and international institutions but willing to participate on a bilateral basis in activities that pursue similar objectives through equally informal channels. Of course, a basic difference between the two initiatives is that CSI activities are circumscribed to the search and identification (screening) of suspected cargo at ports, leaving aside complicated issues of interdictions of vessels at sea. However, this alone does not explain how states that have serious legal and political concerns in joining the PSI have a different attitude towards a closely related initiative, which is perhaps even more problematic from a sovereigntist point of view. Even if particular CSI arrangements should be perfectly in accordance with the internal law of participating states, politically speaking, sovereignty concerns regarding the presence of foreign customs officials in national ports would probably not easily vanish. It might well be that non-PSI states

4.2 US BORDER SECURITY AND GLOBAL MARITIME SECURITY 135

have decided to join the less-known CSI primarily because of the economic incentives that come along with it.[179] But it might have to do also with the different attitude states often have towards bilateral and multilateral issues.

4.2.1.3 CSI, PSI, and the Multilayered Approach to US Homeland Security

CSI and PSI are not only linked to each other, but they actually form an integral part of US national maritime security strategy,[180] together with other global initiatives and programmes such as *Megaports*,[181] the *Secure Freight Initiative*,[182] and the *Customs Trade Partnership against*

---

[179] In the case of China, it should be added that although its several CSI ports (Chiwan, Hong Kong, Shanghai, Shenzhen) account for the highest volume of cargo destined to the USA, other ports which are said to be of crucial importance for curtailing proliferation to North Korea, like the port of Dailan, remain outside the initiative in spite of efforts by the USA to integrate them; see Benjamin Hautecouverture, 'The Container Security Initiative', ONP. 83, *Centre d'Etudes de Sécurité Internationale et des Maîtrise des armements* (CESIM) (2012).

[180] See *The National Strategy for Maritime Security* (September 2005), p. 14, at www.hsdl.org/?view&did=456414.

[181] An initiative of the US Department of Energy's National Nuclear Security Administration (NNSA), which operates on a bilateral basis through the signing of memoranda of understandings and 'helps partner countries equip major international seaports with radiation detection equipment and alarm communication systems. In addition, [it] provides comprehensive training for foreign personnel, short-term maintenance coverage, and technical support to ensure the long-term sustainment and viability of installed radiation detection systems'. The costs of these detection systems are shared on a case-by-case basis, whereby the host government and terminal operator usually pay for the equipment and its installation, and the NNSA provides maintenance and training for its use for a period of three years. After this 'sustainability transition period', the initiative seeks to establish 'operational megaports'. *Megaports* partners commit also to information sharing, which is facilitated through periodical workshops among participants; see NNSA, *Megaports Initiative,* at http://nnsa.energy.gov/aboutus/ourprograms/nonproliferation/programoffices/inter nationalmaterialprotectionandcooperation/-5.

[182] The DHS describes the Secure Freight Initiative as 'part of the Department's layered approach to port and container security'. During the initial phase of this initiative, which began in early 2007, 'a combination of existing technology and proven nuclear detection devices' were deployed to six foreign ports in order to scan containers 'for radiation and information risk factors before being allowed to depart for the United States. In the event of a detection alarm, both homeland security personnel and host country officials will simultaneously receive an alert'; see DHS, *Secure Freight Initiative,* at www.dhs.gov/secure-freight-initiative#3.

Terrorism (C-TPAT).[183] Port security is, in turn, closely related to transportation security, which is again part of the overall homeland security strategy. This also explains why the DHS plays the leading role among the US government departments and agencies involved in many of these initiatives. It is also important to mention that these initiatives keep mushrooming. From almost every one of the programmes, several others emerge, complementing and sometimes overlapping: *Megaports* and the *Secure Freight Initiative* are both about establishing high-tech detection and alarm systems for radiological and nuclear materials at ports of departure, and, as we have seen, the CSI also contemplates the use of large-scale X-ray and gamma ray machines and radiation detection devices. This overlap may cause co-ordination problems, but it is not an error of design. States that do not participate in one or several of these initiatives may be willing to be part of another that pursues practically the same objectives. Mexico, for instance, has long resisted participation in the PSI and the CSI, but is part of *Megaports* and supports C-TPAT through the informal bilateral border security initiative called the *21st Century Border*, which is an integral component of the equally informal but much broader *Mérida Initiative* established in the framework of the failed 'war on drugs and crime'.[184]

---

[183] An international voluntary public–private partnership (PPP) led by the US Customs and Border Protection (CBP) that functions through agreements between companies that export to the USA, which are signed online. C-TPAT partner companies commit to identifying security risks following established criteria and improving the protection of the supply chain by implementing best practices and specific measures consistent with C-TPAT security criteria. They are also required to develop a periodic self-assessment procedure. Upon acceptance, review, and/or certification, the CBP provides technical assistance and recommendations to improve the importer's supply chain security; provides trade incentives, including expedited processing of cargos; and assigns a supply chain specialist as CBP liaison for communication, validation, procedural updates, and training; see CBP, *CTPAT: Customs Trade Partnership Against Terrorism*, at www.cbp.gov/border-security/ports-entry/cargo-security/ctpat.

[184] *Declaration by the Government of the United States of America and the Government of the United Mexican States Concerning Twenty-First Century Border Management* (19 May 2010) at https://obamawhitehouse.archives.gov/the-press-office/declaration-government-united-states-america-and-government-united-mexican-states-c. See also Alejandro Rodiles, 'The Tensions Between Local Resilience-Building and Transnational Action – US-Mexican Cooperation in Crime Affected Communities in Northern Mexico, And What This Tells About Global Urban Governance', in Helmut P. Aust and Anél du Plessis (eds.), *The Globalisation of Urban Governance – Legal Perspectives on Sustainable Development Goal 11* (Routledge, forthcoming).

This shows that although 'technically separate ... [these initiatives] are expressly intended to interact with and be complementary of one another'.[185] Accordingly, the DHS speaks of a multilayered, risk-based approach to port security. CSI and the like are US official programmes, formally established under US law,[186] but their global reach is part and parcel of their very nature. It should thus come as no surprise that specific agencies within the DHS have their own global offices, such as the Office of Global Strategies (OGS) of the Transportation and Security Administration (TSA), the function of which is to assess 'vulnerabilities at international locations to determine risk, evaluate risk impacts to determine mitigation activities and execute mitigation activities to reduce those risks to the United States. When a new threat or vulnerability emerges, OGS coordinates with foreign governments, airlines and international organizations to implement responses that will effectively mitigate the likelihood of a successful attack'.[187] One commentator rightly describes this approach as 'the forward deployment of the U.S. Border'.[188] In the words of former Commissioner of CBP Robert C. Bonner, initiatives like the CSI are efforts to 'push the border outwards' and 'expand our perimeter of security away from our national boundaries and towards foreign points of departure'.[189] Thus, there is a clear extraterritorial component to these transnational initiatives.[190] However, this extraterritoriality has acquired a new, more sophisticated guise through what might be termed, following Eyal Benvenisti and George Downs, *informal serial bilateralism*.[191]

---

[185] Bowman, 'Thinking Outside the Border', 203.

[186] See US Government Printing Office (GPO), H.R. 4954 (enrolled) (109th): *Act to improve maritime and cargo security through enhanced layered defenses, and for other purposes* (SAFE Port Act) (13 October 2006), Pub.L. 109–347.

[187] See DHS, Transportation Security Administration, *Global Strategies*, at https://www.tsa .gov/about/tsa-leadership.

[188] Bowman, 'Thinking Outside the Border', 189.

[189] Quoted in ibid., 192.

[190] Former Secretary of Foreign Affairs of India Shyam Saran described the PSI and CSI as a combination of 'national and transnational efforts', opposing them to the global community's response, as reflected in SC resolution 1540. Quoted in Kumar, *India and the Nuclear Non-Proliferation Regime*, p. 146. It must be recalled that India neither participates in the CSI, PSI nor in *Megaports*.

[191] Cf. Benvenisti and Downs, 'The Empire's New Clothes', 610–611 (defining 'serial bilateralism' as 'the negotiation of separate bilateral agreements, with different states all dealing with the same issue when multilateral negotiations threaten to get out of control').

As already mentioned, bilateralism is an old hegemonic tactic.[192] Powerful states have clear bargaining advantages over a single, less powerful one, so they seek to avoid multilateral negotiations where less powerful states can coalesce and make their claims stronger. Benvenisti and Downs include this tactic within a wider fragmentation strategy in the sense of *divide et impera*.[193] According to these authors, this strategy consists of many tactics, of which the negotiation tactic of dividing a potential mass of bargaining partners into a series of single negotiating counterparts is only one. I would argue that serial bilateralism is also part of this strategy through the tactic of fragmenting the international agenda by dividing perceptions, i.e., by artificially separating what is perceived as a multilateral issue or a matter of concern of the wider international community into a series of bilateral issues. Being a matter of perception, it is difficult to quantify and demonstrate. But it makes much sense if due regard is taken to the way foreign policy communities are organized around the globe.

According to a common understanding among foreign policy officials, the bilateral and multilateral realms are sharply divided, affording the former much greater flexibility, which in a certain sense is considered as only natural since governments have to solve problems with their peers very pragmatically all of the time. Bilateral affairs are much more strongly associated with the day-to-day business and operational part of foreign affairs within foreign ministries, including the legal departments, as opposed to the longer-term nature of multilateral affairs where the construction of shared values and objectives through established processes and open dialogue is not only regarded as the common way of procedure but as a goal in and by itself (dialogue as an international rule of law value). Although, in theory, a diplomat has to be a 'generalist', the actual professional division between 'multilateralists' and 'bilateralists' is common currency in many diplomatic services: multilateral negotiations require not only different skills as compared to bilateral relations, but also different personalities and world-views, which have to do with how diplomats see international law, or more accurately, what role they attribute to law in international affairs. This does also, in part, explain why states often have different attitudes towards the same issues

---

[192] It is of course much more than that. On bilateralism as a major organizing principle for international law, see Helmut Aust, *Complicity and the Law of State Responsibility*, chapter 2.

[193] See Benvenisti and Downs, 'The Empire's New Clothes', 611.

(counter-proliferation, e.g.) and practices (informality), depending on where they are located, i.e., on their bilateral or multilateral agendas. Related to this perceptional issue, there is another that I believe to be very important for understanding the success of serial bilateralism within the coalition of the willing approach. It has to do with a lack of, or poor consciousness about, the close relationship between bilateralism, plurilateralism, and multilateralism. In other words, the crucial question of to what extent the classical bifurcation of the multilateral and bilateral realms stays unaltered in times of increasing coalitional diplomacy and networked global governance has not received sufficient attention in diplomatic circles or international legal scholarship.

IR literature, in its part, has long observed how US diplomacy has engaged in 'transgovernmental policy co-ordination' among subunits of the US government and their direct peers in foreign administrations, building coalitions, mostly on a bilateral basis, sometimes coupled with the aim of bringing actors from other governments 'to improve their chances of success'.[194] Robert Keohane and Joseph Nye referred to this as a tactic 'to penetrate weaker governments',[195] and Samuel Huntington even mentioned that 'the expansion of the United States into the world in large part took the form of the creation and development of U.S. agencies designed not just to deal with other governments, but to operate within other societies',[196] something in which US aid and development agencies took the lead already in the 1950s and 1960s.[197] This happens by circumventing central channels, mostly foreign ministries. Thus, the 'disaggregation of the State'[198] is not only a logical development of an increasingly technocratic world, but it can also serve strategic purposes of more powerful players. 'Penetrating weaker governments' is easier when pursued bilaterally and from agency-to-agency. In Mexico, for example, this diplomatic tactic has been referred to as *knocking on several doors at the same time*, and until recently, it was widely discouraged by the Ministry of Foreign Relations, which usually has the broader picture of international affairs, i.e., of how an apparent purely technical matter between two agencies from two countries may alter broader

---

[194] Keohane and Nye, 'Transgovernmental Relations and International Organizations', 46–47.
[195] Ibid., 47.
[196] Samuel P. Huntington, 'Transnational Organizations in World Politics' (1973) 25 *World Politics* 333, at p. 348.
[197] Ibid.
[198] See Slaughter, *A New World Order*, pp. 12–15.

(e.g., multilateral) commitments or obligations and as such have important consequences for the state's foreign policy.

Following these insights from IR scholarship, Anne-Marie Slaughter has drawn the attention to how bilateral networks often evolve into schemes of plurilateral co-operation.[199] Slaughter seems to use the term 'plurilateral' in quantitative terms – i.e., referring to an arrangement with several participants but still too limited to talk about a multilateral one.[200] This would seem to imply a series of bilateral relationships among all the participants involved, which, as long as CSI bilateral arrangements are concluded solely between the USA and other countries, would not be the case. However, inasmuch as the CSI complements a multilateral framework like the PSI and is complemented by several other bilateral and plurilateral undertakings, it is possible to conceive of it as part of broader informal multilateral enterprise. In any case, 'CSI is an excellent illustration of contemporary evolving preventative legal strategies in the international arena',[201] integrated into a multilayered scheme of classical trans-governmental co-operation, coalitions of the willing, public–private partnerships (PPPs), and global regulatory practices of IOs: a paradigmatic case of global security governance understood as a complex system of rule that addresses global security challenges through the interplay between multiple forms of international and transnational action and regulation – including formal and informal fora, as well as intergovernmental, hybrid, and private mechanisms. The fact that the USA plays a central role in connecting the dots in this scheme of networked governance has to do with many factors, some of the them quite obvious, like the agenda-setting power it has, which allows it to play a leading role in determining what are the global risks in the first place and which, not surprisingly, correspond to its national interests and those of its major constituencies. This is only logical, and these interests may very well match those of many other states, their constituencies, as well as increasingly those of transnational stakeholders that cannot be allocated here or there. In some cases, these interests will correspond not only to the West but also to the wider international community. But it is important to be

---

[199] See Slaughter, 'Governing the Global Economy through Government Networks', p. 189.

[200] In the sense of the standard definition of a 'plurilateral agreement' as 'a treaty negotiated between a limited number of states with a particular interest in the subject matter'; see Anthony Aust, *Modern Treaty Law and Practice*, third edition (Cambridge: Cambridge University Press, 2013), p. 125.

[201] Romero, 'Prevention of Maritime Terrorism', 597.

4.2 US BORDER SECURITY AND GLOBAL MARITIME SECURITY 141

clear about the central, and indeed defining, role of the USA, which, at least until recently, has set the goal to be the 'hub of alliances'[202] and has the know-how to do this. If this is good or bad for global order is a very broad question that I will briefly address in Chapter 6. But it is not a stretch to describe this multilayered scheme of global maritime security governance as a hegemonic strategy, and, accordingly, the evolving legal strategies though which it is constructed (an informal maritime security law) as an instance of hegemonic law.

4.2.2   A Thousand Ships to Command the Commons

The *SoSan* incident, which is considered as the one that gave the impetus for launching the PSI, was an operation carried out under the *Combined Task Force-150* (CTF-150), i.e. a naval coalition that emerged in the framework of *Operation Enduring Freedom* (OEF). Today, the CTF-150 forms part of the *Combined Maritime Forces* (CMF), together with two other multinational naval coalitions – i.e., the CTF-151 and the CTF-152. The CMF is an informal naval partnership of thirty states under the joint leadership of the US and the UK navies, which seeks to contribute to an overall 'safe maritime environment'.[203] While the CTF-151 was specifically created to combat piracy and armed robbery at sea,[204] as one of the major players involved in the implementation of SC resolutions on the matter, the CTF-150 is in charge of maritime security, including countering terrorism and 'related illegal activities, which terrorists use to fund or conceal their movements'.[205] This comprises the transport of WMDs.

Although there is no available evidence regarding the interaction of the CTF-150 and the PSI, their overlapping 'mandates' suggest that both complement each other. While the area of operation of the CTF-150 encompasses the Red Sea, Gulf of Aden, Indian Ocean, and Gulf of Oman, maritime security in the Persian Gulf falls under the responsibility of the CTF-152. Accordingly, one commentator has mentioned that in the absence of political support for the PSI from regional powers,

---

[202] Obama, *West Point Commencement Address* (2014).
[203] On the CMF, see http://combinedmaritimeforces.com/.
[204] See CMF, *CTF-151: Counter-piracy,* at http://combinedmaritimeforces.com/ctf-151-counter-piracy/.
[205] See CMF, *CTF 150: Maritime Security,* at http://combinedmaritimeforces.com/ctf-150-maritime-security/.

interdictions related to proliferation activities from and towards Iran 'would be relatively straightforward to implement'.[206]

There is also a series of regional coalitions in the field of maritime security, promoted and led by the USA, like the *Regional Maritime Security Initiative* (RMSI). Destined to improve maritime security in the Western Pacific and East Asian seas, particularly in the Strait of Malacca, this US Pacific Command (PACOM)–led partnership of willing nations engages in capacity building and the identification, monitoring, and interception of vessels suspected to be involved in piracy, armed robbery at sea, and terrorist and related activities. RMSI is often associated with the PSI and is said to complement other initiatives, like the CSI.[207] Though related to the so-called 'war on drugs', international maritime partnerships operating in Central America and the Caribbean also comprise the collection of US-led coalitions of the willing in the field of maritime security – such as the *Joint Interagency Task Force South* (JITFS) created under the Clinton administration, or the US Southern Command (SOUTHCOM)–led *Operation Martillo* – including partners from Europe and the Americas. These coalitions conduct 'multinational detection, monitoring and interdiction operations' to counter the trafficking of illicit drugs, precursor chemicals, weapons, and bulk cash along the Central American isthmus.[208]

There is also a series of multinational joint naval operations, often referred to as coalitions as well,[209] which gather informally but for very concrete purposes, and tend to disappear once these are fulfilled. These are cases of ad hoc international co-operation in a more traditional sense,

---

[206] Richard Bond, 'The Proliferation Security Initiative: Targeting Iran and North Korea?', *British American Security Information Council* (BASIC), Paper No. 53 (January 2007), 8 (referring to the CTF-150, however, given the area of operation, the CTF-152 would be the appropriate one).

[207] On the RMSI, see Yann-huei Song, 'Security in the Strait of Malacca and the Regional Maritime Security Initiative: Responses to the US Proposal', in Michael D. Carsten (ed.), *Global Legal Challenges: Command of the Commons, Strategic Communications and Natural Disasters*, International Law Studies vol. 83 (Newport: Naval War College, 2007), p. 97; as well as Xu Ke, 'Myth and Reality: The Rise and Fall of Contemporary Maritime Piracy in the South China Sea', in Shicun Wu and Keyuan Zou (eds.), *Maritime Security in the South China Sea: Regional Implications and International Cooperation* (Burlington: Ashgate, 2007), p. 81, at p. 92.

[208] See US Defense Security Cooperation Agency, *Operation Martillo*, at www.dsca.mil/tags/operation-martillo, and JITFS, *Information Website*, at www.jiatfs.southcom.mil.

[209] See Admiral Jonathan Greenert and Rear Admiral James M. Foggo III (US Navy), 'Forging a Global Network of Navies' (2014) 140 *Proceedings* 335 (the following examples are taken from this article).

and they do not necessarily imply the creation of alternative venues to international institutions or formal legal structures. Examples include international search-and-rescue operations (SAR), like the search for the missing Malaysia Airlines Flight MH370 in March 2014, as well as instances of multinational aid and assistance in the event of natural disasters, like the *Typhoon Haiyan Response Group*, in November 2013. Within this kind of operations, the joint efforts by Norway, Denmark, Italy, Germany, China, Russia, and the USA for destroying Syria's arsenal of chemical weapons, and thus helping to implement SC resolution 2118 (2013),[210] is mentioned too. And so is the *International Mine Counter-measures Exercise* (IMCMEX), whereby a task force of ships from twenty-nine countries trained together in the Persian Gulf in 2013, aiming not only to strengthen their operational capabilities of cleaning sea lanes from mines but also, or perhaps even primarily, to send Iran a strong message regarding its activities of 'proliferation concern'.[211]

However, even in those cases that seem to be part of the ordinary day-to-day business of international military affairs, a clear line between ad hoc international co-operation and coalitions of the willing is not always easy to draw. This is so mainly because of two reasons. First, the political discourse underneath these operations is quite similar to that which informs the coalition of the willing approach: be it the case of willing and able states that stand beside the SC in the exercise of collective security, responding 'together on behalf of the international community',[212] or that of a posse of able navies showing the limits to the 'outlaw', also in the name of world peace. Here, the words of US Secretary of Defense General James Mattis, in his former capacity as commander of the US Central Command, are illustrative:

> We didn't make an anti-Iranian exercise, we made an anti-mine exercise ... the Iranians looked at it and realized they were actually creating an international coalition against them that was brought forward by the only navy in the world that could have done it.[213]

The second reason is that some of these multinational exercises tend to morph into durable activities – i.e. long-lasting informal means of

---

[210] See SC Res. 2118 (27 September 2013), in particular op. 10.

[211] IMCMEX had two phases: the first consisted of a seminar of high ranking military officials from participating nations, in 2012, and the second, the actual exercise conducted by 35 ships of these states; see Greenert and Foggo III, 'Forging a Global Network of Navies'.

[212] Ibid.

[213] Quoted in ibid.

co-ordinated international action. This seems to be the case of IMCMEX, 'a serial-driven exercise consisting of multiple mine countermeasures (MCM), maritime security operations (MSO) and maritime infrastructure protection (MIP) events planned to be conducted in the Arabian Gulf, Sea of Oman, Gulf of Aden and Red Sea [in which] [p]artner nations are invited to participate'.[214] For such purposes, the International Maritime Exercise Force (IMEF) within IMCMEX has been created.[215] Resembling the PSI, IMCMEX is an 'activity' that has lasted for several years, acquiring some flexible structures for sustained co-ordination, and perhaps even turning into a 'durable effort', but remaining informal through and through. In addition to the function of cleaning sea-lanes from mines, IMCMEX engages today in many other activities, including the so-called MSO – i.e., 'international forces working with industry representatives to protect and defend shipping while it is transiting through global commerce lanes'.[216] The continuous evolution of their self-proclaimed 'mandates' is a key feature of coalitions' fluid nature, or amorphousness, as we shall see in more detail with the *Financial Action Task Force* (FATF), in the next chapter.

All these international and regional partnerships, the multinational initiatives on a bilateral basis, as well as the previously mentioned ad hoc operations, are not only linked to each other in some varying and not always easily determined degrees. A broader, literally all-encompassing effort is aimed at integrating them into a grand maritime coalition of coalitions, a 'global network of navies',[217] initially referred to as the '1000 Ship Navy', [218] which later became known as the *Global*

---

[214] See US Naval Forces Central Command, CMF US 5th Fleet, *IMCMEX*, at www.cusnc.navy.mil/IMCMEX/.

[215] Ibid.

[216] Ibid.

[217] Greenert and Foggo III, 'Forging a Global Network of Navies'.

[218] The title of this section is taken from the term coined by US Navy Admiral Mike Mullen, '1000-Ships Navy' (see note 221) and from a banner displayed at the Pentagon in 2006, which stated, *Command of the Commons: Command of the Commons is the key military enabler of the United States*, as reproduced by Craig H. Allen, 'Command of the Commons Boasts: An Invitation to Lawfare?', in Michael D. Carsten (ed.), *Global Legal Challenges: Command of the Commons, Strategic Communications and Natural Disasters*, p. 21, at p. 39. In this article, Allen discourages the use of the catchphrase 'the command of the commons' in order to avoid lawfare strategies against the USA, and noting that the 'concept of lawfare might provide one means to deny, or at least to limit, a hegemon's use of the sea'. Thus, in choosing this title, I am reframing the 'Global Maritime Partnership' concept by recalling those initial slogans that designated the very same concept but were more clearly associated with hegemonic strategies.

Maritime Partnership (GMP).[219] This is a coalition of the willing *in fieri* for global maritime security, modelled on the PSI. The intellectual father of this initiative, former Joint Chief of Staff (2007–2011) and Chief of Naval Operations (2005–2007) Admiral Mike G. Mullen, explained his idea in some detail in several speeches during 2005, including a proposed list of 'first principles' that are clearly inspired from the SIP of the PSI.[220] In one of these speeches, Mullen refers to the need for designing new security arrangements capable of responding efficiently to the global risks that affect the security of the vast commons that are the oceans, mentioning that

> acting in national and thereby global interests is more than just words. It requires both a maritime capability and the political will – something that not all countries share equally. Sometimes a nation has one, but not the other; sometimes it has neither. But I believe there is a solution. I'm thinking about a global network that focuses on making the maritime domain safer for everyone's use ... I think that a model for the future of maritime relationships and security can also be seen today in programs like the *Proliferation Security Initiative* ... I envision a 1,000-ship Navy – a fleet-in-being, if you will, made up of the best capabilities of all freedom-loving navies of the world.[221]

The GMP was incorporated into the US *Cooperative Strategy for the 21st Century Sea Power* (2007), a joint strategy paper of the Navy and the Coast Guard. This Strategy refers to the GMP as an informal arrangement that would promote the international rule of law by fighting 'piracy, terrorism, weapons proliferation, drug trafficking, and other illicit activities'.[222] The implementation of this grand maritime coalition has encountered some resistance within the USA,[223] and the new US

---

[219] On the evolution of this initiative, see Chris Rahman, 'The Global Maritime Partnership Initiative: Implications for the Royal Australian Navy', *Papers in Australian Maritime Affairs No. 24* (Canberra: Sea Power Centre Australia, 2008).

[220] Ibid, p. 6.

[221] Admiral Mike Mullen, *Remarks as delivered for the 17th International Seapower Symposium* (21 September 2005), at www.navy.mil/navydata/cno/mullen/speeches/mullen050921.txt. Emphasis added.

[222] Department of the Navy, United States Marine Corps, Department of the Navy, USA, United States Coast Guard, *A Cooperative Strategy for the 21st Century Seapower* (October 2007), at www.hsdl.org/?view&did=479900.

[223] See Robert Farley, 'Managing the United States' Global Naval Partnerships: The U.S. Navy has decisions to make on cooperation with other global navies. Will it make the right ones?', *The Diplomat* (10 July 2014), at http://thediplomat.com/2014/07/managing-the-united-states-global-naval-partnerships/?allpages=yes&print=yes.

Cooperative Strategy for the 21st Century Sea Power (2015) does not mention the GMP as such anymore. However, the ideas underlying the GMP still inform one of the main goals of US maritime security strategy:

> [N]aval forces are stronger when we operate jointly and together with allies and partners. Merging our individual capabilities and capacity produces a combined naval effect that is greater than the sum of its parts. By working together in formal and informal networks, we can address the threats to our mutual maritime security interests. Maximizing the robust capacity of this *global network of navies concept*, we are all better postured to face new and emerging challenges.[224]

4.3   Concluding Remarks on the *PSI & Co.*: The Amorphous Nature of Coalitions of the Willing

The fluidity that characterizes coalitions of the willing makes them difficult to grasp. Establishing typologies may have brought some clarity at the beginning, but those would have soon revealed that they represent little more than *a priori* comprehensions, superseded by the day-to-day evolution of these groupings, which morph into whatever the issues at hand demand. Multilateral activities are complemented by bilateral arrangements and vice versa, putting the classical bifurcation of the multilateral and bilateral realms into question in today's networked global governance. Coalitions also bring together key fields of international security with core areas of US homeland security, and merge them back into global enterprises.

The amorphous nature of coalitions is also driven by what can be called the *uncertainty assumption* that drives much of today's international threat response – i.e., a notion of risks based on the worst-case scenario of the unknowns that might happen: the 'unknown unknowns'[225] of former US Secretary of Defense Donald Rumsfeld. These are potentially of such a devastating nature that responsive measures need to be ready, and preventative action has to be taken. Since the nature of the threats is not always known or set once and for all, coalitions are designed as highly flexible mechanisms that can swiftly

---

[224] US Navy, Marine Corps and Coast Guard, *A Cooperative Strategy for the 21st Century Seapower* (March 2015), p. 2, at www.navy.mil/local/maritime/150227-CS21R-Final.pdf. Emphasis added.

[225] US DoD, Press Operation, *Secretary Rumsfeld and Gen. Myers, Transcript* (12 February 2002), at http://archive.defense.gov/Transcripts/Transcript.aspx?TranscriptID=2636.

4.3 CONCLUDING REMARKS ON THE *PSI & CO.* 147

adapt to evolving threats – that is, to morph into whatever the circumstances at hand demand. In this sense, coalitions denote a bouncing-forward resilience, since they reorganize dynamically according to changing risks.[226] The uncertainty assumption is followed by the perception of a strong interconnectedness of these threats. Accordingly, challenges and threats to international peace and security are not only constantly evolving, as acknowledged by the UN Security Council (SC);[227] they are also increasingly connected with each other.[228] And this calls for coalitions' ability to relate to each other in multiple and flexible ways, especially if they are to continue to perform as voluntary enforcers of collective security.

In the preceding pages, I have explained how challenges to global maritime security are considered to be increasingly interlinked and evolving so that international responses must also be woven into a fast-growing and continuously moving global web of maritime, port, and border security, which actually involves analogous international initiatives on air security. I have not dealt with the latter, nor have I referred in any detail to the increasing collaboration of many of these coalitions with the private sector, as this would stretch into other open horizons. I hope to have shown, nonetheless, that coalitions of the willing like the PSI, the GICNT, and the CSI are embedded into a highly complex network system and are constantly reshaped by the exigencies of the times. Coalitions are remodelled to a considerable extent through their own interactions: there is a clear chain of mimesis processes, as the internal structures of the PSI and the GICNT demonstrate. But this is only an instance of the larger chain.

In the next chapters, I will look more closely at some of these interactions among coalitions, showing that overlapping mandates is not an error of design but part of the complexity that is sought and achieved through this mimesis. More importantly, I will analyze the ways in which coalitions interact with institutions, in particular with the SC. This will allow for a better understanding of the jurisgenerative interplay between formality and informality.

---

[226] On the different meanings attributed to the concept of resilience, see Peter Rogers, 'The Etymology and Genealogy of a Contested Concept', in David Chandler and Jon Coaffee (eds.), *The Routledge Handbook of International Resilience* (Abingdon/New York: Routledge, 2017), p. 13.

[227] In this sense, the SC has acknowledged the 'evolving challenges and threats to international peace and security', see UN Doc. S/PRST/2012/16 (April 25, 2012).

[228] UN Doc. S/PRST/2012/17 (4 May 2012); UN Doc. S/PRST/2010/19 (27 September 2012).

5

Coalitions of the Willing in Context: The Interplay between Formality and Informality

As seen in the previous chapter, coalitions' amorphousness – and the open texture of the concept underlying this phenomenon – relates to their extreme adaptability to evolving circumstances. This resilience is made possible through their informal structures and flexible 'mandates', allowing them to co-operate in operational terms more easily. Furthermore, they complement each other by pursuing some of the very same goals through different strategies (e.g., multilateral or bilateral). Just as the absence of international bureaucratic structures is considered one of their major assets, so are overlapping functions construed as an advantage in reaching shared aims more efficiently: clearly defined and delimited legal powers, so cherished in juristic thought, would be at odds with the efficiency paradigm.

Coalitions work closely together and constantly learn from each other. These processes of mutual learning are quite typical for coalitions of the willing; actually, their 'institutional' evolution takes place to a great extent through mimesis. Therefore, a closer look at such processes is crucial for better understanding the phenomenon. It will show, for example, how the informality that characterizes these entities is a fluctuant process too, according to which 'activities' tend to morph into 'durable efforts', task forces constantly add new tasks to their functions, and summit diplomacy turns into something like 'institutionalized summitry'.[1] These *quasi-formalization* processes show that coalitions represent alternative (sometimes complementary, sometimes competing, but never parallel)

---

[1] Borrowing the expression from Richard Feinberg, 'Institutionalized Summitry', in Andrew F. Cooper, Jorge Heine, and Ramish Thakur (eds.), *The Oxford Handbook of Modern Diplomacy* (Oxford: Oxford University Press, 2013), p. 303. However, I use the expression here circumscribed to informal fora – i.e., to summits that take place on a regular basis without being attached to formal institutions or treaties, like the *Nuclear Security Summit* (NSS).

COALITIONS OF THE WILLING IN CONTEXT 149

venues to pre-existing formal institutions,[2] and not just cases of ad hoc diplomatic co-operation; coalitions of the willing are much more than business as usual.

But coalitions not only interact with each other, they do this with formal institutions as well, and quite intensively so. Following the theses of James N. Rosenau, global governance is best understood as a system of rule that addresses global risks through the interplay between multiple forms of international and transnational action and regulation, including those that emerge from formal and informal fora, as well as intergovernmental, hybrid, and private mechanisms.[3] The multilayered approach to maritime security discussed in the previous chapter already revealed some of these features. Here, I will deepen these observations by focusing on the interplay between coalitions of the willing and IOs, especially in those cases in which the former play a leading role. This is very clear in the fields of counter-proliferation and counter-terrorism, which, also due to this interplay, are increasingly merged and constitute today one of the most active fields of global security governance. The leading IO in this area is still the UN and, within its institutional structure, the Security Council (SC) in particular. Today, the Council functions to a great extent as a platform for many of these interactions, also involving other formal institutions. Accordingly, special attention will be paid to the relations between the SC and some of the most important coalitions dealing with these issues, like the *Proliferation Security Initiative* (PSI), the *Financial Action Task Force* (FATF), the *Nuclear Security Summit* (NSS), and the *Global Counterterrorism Forum* (GCTF). These coalitions interact with other IOs in the said fields as well, like the International Maritime Organization (IMO), in the case of the PSI, or the International Atomic Energy Agency (IAEA), in that of the NSS. Thus, some of these relations will be considered too. The multilayered approach to global security governance will become visible in these cases, and references to other

---

[2] See Raustiala, 'The Architecture of International Cooperation', 90 (predicting in 2002 that '[i]nteraction between the different cooperative architectures [i.e., networks and traditional tools of international law and organization] will likely be commonplace'); see also Slaughter, *A New World Order*, pp. 152–165 (though she uses the term 'parallel', she also notes that '[t]he informal sector of government networks coexists with the formal sector of traditional international organizations in a number of ways', at p. 164).

[3] See James N. Rosenau, 'Governance, Order, and Change in World Politics', in James N. Rosenau and Ernst-Otto Czempiel (eds.), *Governance without Government: Order and Change in World Politics* (Cambridge: Cambridge University Press, 1992), p. 1, at p. 4.

150   COALITIONS OF THE WILLING IN CONTEXT

informal bodies, such as the *Global Initiative to Combat Nuclear Terrorism* (GICNT), will be made. Although this chapter – as well as the previous one – focuses on global security, I will also draw on some examples from the field of climate change governance in order to show that the coalition of the willing approach is not exclusive to security matters but applicable to every field of global governance. Moreover, the *2015 Paris Agreement on Climate Change* represents a paradigmatic case of the penetration of informal governance techniques into the formal realm of treaty law.

The themes and questions that have been identified within the literature on 'regime interaction' and 'inter-institutional relations' are of the utmost importance for the present chapter; both encompass 'formal and informal institutions'. This notion stems from institutionalism in IR theory, which adopts a broad definition of 'institutions', equating formal and informal ones.[4] However, there is something counter-intuitive about calling coalitions of the willing 'institutions', since the latter concept is strongly associated with formal – i.e., legally established structures. In the best introductory book to the study of law known to me, the Argentinean legal and political philosopher Carlos S. Nino (building upon Herbert Hart and Hans Kelsen) construes his analytical jurisprudence around the notion of law's 'institutionalized character', meaning that a necessary condition of any legal system is that its norms are operated by established and competent organs.[5] In the same vein but from the angle of political science, Rosenau calls for caution when using a broader meaning of institutions in the realm of global governance, since '[i]nstitutions connote the presence of authoritative principles, norms, rules, and procedures, thereby running the risk of obscuring the informal, non-authoritative dimensions that are so essential to the functioning of international orders and regimes'.[6] Moreover, when international law scholars began to pay attention to the tendency of turning to informal fora, it was rightly commented that 'a move away *from institutions* nearly

---

[4] According to institutionalism in IR theory, institutions are defined (and identified with regimes) as 'sets of implicit or explicit principles, norms, rules, and decision-making procedures around which actors' expectations converge in a given area of international relations' (Stephen D. Krasner, 'Structural Causes and Regime Consequences: Regimes as Intervening Variables' (1982) 36 *International Organization* 185, at 186).

[5] Carlos S. Nino, *Introducción al Análisis del Derecho*, second edition, twelfth reprint (Buenos Aires: Astrea, 2013), pp. 105 et seq.

[6] Rosenau, 'Governance, Order, and Change in World Politics', p. 9.

COALITIONS OF THE WILLING IN CONTEXT 151

as serious as the 20th century's move towards them'[7] was taking place. For these reasons, I will not refer to coalitions as 'institutions'. Having clarified this, I will occasionally use the notion 'inter-institutional relations' as encompassing the interplays between informal coalitions and networks, on the one hand, and 'formal' institutions on the other.

Inter-institutional relations have been studied by IR scholars in the framework of regime theory, especially under the rubric of 'regime complexity'.[8] International legal scholarship has started to pay attention to them too,[9] mostly motivated by the fragmentation of international law.[10] The approach that I will follow here is a very promising research project that emerged within the larger global administrative law project (GAL). During its first years of existence, GAL concentrated on 'regime specific' analyses of global regulation instances.[11] Then, a further step in its research agenda was taken: a project that focuses on the interactions among multiple institutions – including formal and informal, international and national, hybrid and private – as they happen within the global administrative space.[12] Since the latter represents a variegated realm of action and regulation, which, among several other

---

[7] José Alvarez, 'The Move from Institutions: Introductory Remarks' (2006) 100 *Proceedings of the Annual Meeting (American Society of International Law)* 287 (referring to the seminal article by David Kennedy, 'The Move to Institutions' (1987) 8 *Cardozo Law Review* 841, which describes the opposite tendency by that time). Emphasis added. Already referring to the move *from* institutions, see Jan Klabbers, 'Institutional Ambivalence by Design: Soft Organizations in International Law' (2001) 70 *Nordic Journal of International Law* 403, at 406.

[8] See, for example, the contributions to 'Symposium on the Politics of International Regime Complexity'; see also Julia C. Morse and Robert O. Keohane, 'Contested Multilateralism' (2014) 9 *The Review of International Organizations* 385.

[9] But see already Slaughter, A *New World Order*, pp. 152–165.

[10] See Margaret A. Young, *Regime Interaction in International Law: Facing Fragmentation* (Cambridge: Cambridge University Press, 2012); but see already Laurence R. Helfer, 'Regime Shifting: The TRIPs Agreement and New Dynamics of International Intellectual Property Lawmaking' (2004) 29 *Yale Journal of International Law* 1 (building upon IR regime theory, the author analyzes the use of different fora for international intellectual property law-making as a strategy for shifting this legal regime). A different though related fragmentation strategy – i.e., the switch of institutions, or the exit from institutions to informal venues in order to achieve certain outcomes – has been studied by Benvenisti and Downs, 'The Empire's New Clothes', 614 et seq.; see also Rodiles, 'La Fragmentación del Derecho Internacional', 403.

[11] Jeffrey L. Dunoff, 'A New Approach to Regime Interaction', in Young, *Regime Interaction in International Law*, p. 136, at p. 159.

[12] The inter-institutional relations project has, however, not been further pursued in recent time; for a brief description of its aims, see Institute for International Law and Justice (IILJ), *Inter-Institutional Relations*, at www.iilj.org/inter-institutional-relations/.

manifestations, is 'increasingly occupied by … informal inter-state bodies with no treaty basis (including 'coalitions of the willing'), and formal interstate institutions (such as those of the United Nations)',[13] GAL's inter-institutional relations project offers an adequate frame of reference for analyzing the themes and problems that emerge from the interplay I am interested in. Within that project, four major questions have been identified: How are the different dynamics among institutions managed? Do these interactions promote institutional change, and if so, how do they affect institutions? What are their major normative effects, and how do they alter distributions of power? And what are the possible consequences of these relations for law?[14] While all of these questions touch upon cross-cutting issues, I will concentrate on institutional change and the consequences for law.

It is important to clarify that both types of consequences that stem from inter-institutional relations – i.e., legal and institutional – are closely related to each other. It is not difficult to see how a change in the law of a given field will affect the institutions that are in charge of that area and vice versa. For instance, if the NSS successfully 'improves' the legal framework on nuclear security, this will not be without consequences for the functioning of the IAEA, and the expectations states place on it. Under IR theory on regime complexity, the differentiation probably would not even make much sense. But it is important to analyze these interconnected but not identical issues separately, let alone for the purpose of better assessing their impact on international legal rules, and law-making more broadly. Therefore, I will follow the approach of GAL's inter-institutional project, which addresses the effects of these relations on institutional change and their consequences for law separately, without denying the mutually affecting dynamics in play.

In a first step, I will describe some of the alterations of institutional design that occur by mimesis and basically among coalitions; this with

---

[13] Benedict Kingsbury, 'The Concept of "Law" in Global Administrative Law' (2009) 20 *European Journal of International Law* 23, at 25. In this sense, the global administrative space shares descriptive characteristics with Rosenau's 'spheres of authority'. This should come as no surprise since both are informed by a similar understanding of global governance; see Rosenau, 'Governing the Ungovernable'. I have elsewhere situated coalitions of the willing within the global administrative space, see Rodiles, '*Coalitions of the Willing: Coyuntura, Contexto y Propiedades*', 695–696.

[14] See, IILJ, New York University School of Law, *Analyzing and Shaping Inter-Institutional Relations in Global Governance: Conference Report* (16 April 2012), at www.iilj.org/wp-content/uploads/2017/08/Aprilreport.pdf.

5.1 COALITIONS' EVOLUTION BY MIMESIS   153

the principal aim of showing that we are dealing with informal fora, not just 'activities', which function alongside formal institutions. Following this, the legal effects of some particularly telling instances of informal–formal rule interaction will be assessed, which will demonstrate that even if coalitions did not produce anything legal, as they claim, they do affect international law significantly. And finally, on the basis of these findings, the broader aspects of institutional change as produced by interplays between coalitions and IOs will be analyzed, demonstrating that the former are powerful means for producing changes in the functioning of the latter, without having to resort to formal institutional modifications (i.e., amendment procedures).

5.1 Coalitions' Evolution by Mimesis: More Than Just 'Activities'

Mimesis often produces changes of institutional design – i.e., modifications within an institution's structures and procedures resulting from informal interplays with other institutions. I will focus on such changes as they occur among and within coalitions of the willing. The modification of coalitions' institutional design usually takes place through mutual learning of how to best improve efficiency. This is another characteristic feature of coalitions' amorphousness.

5.1.1 Extending Coalitions' Reach through Working Groups and Regional Bodies

I have already drawn the attention to how the PSI and the GICNT have established similar structures that enable them to sustain an internal dynamic of difference in order to proceed efficiently according to the division of labour inherent to the 'posse model', while at the same time trying to respond to criticisms regarding their two-layered composition.[15] This should come as no surprise, since the PSI and the GICNT are closely related: they both combat nuclear terrorism and were created by the same governmental departments – and people – in the US government.[16]

A similar development can be observed in the case of the NSS, one of the main multilateral undertakings of the Obama administration. Unlike the other coalitions analyzed in this book, which are all active, the NSS

---

[15] See Chapter 4, pp. 100–102.
[16] See Chapter 4, notes 39 and 52, and accompanying text.

ceased to exist in 2016. Yet it lasted for six years, developed a sophisticated structure, created highly innovative ruling techniques, and was crucial in shaping an entire legal regime though the interplay it entertained with IOs. For all these reasons, I regard the NSS as an illustrative case of a coalition of the willing and not as mere summit diplomacy. An informal coalition of fifty-three participating states and four IOs (the UN, the IAEA, INTERPOL, and the EU) invited as observers, the main purpose of the NSS was to streamline and enhance a global nuclear security regime, focusing on the prevention of nuclear terrorism. Within the NSS, a Working Group on Transport Security of Nuclear and Radiological Materials was established, which comprised only five participating countries, namely France, the Republic of Korea, Japan, the UK, and the USA, as well as the four IOs mentioned above. The Working Group strived at furthering the commitment to enhanced security of these materials while in domestic and international transport. This 'commitment' was adopted by the heads of state and government at the second NSS, held in Seoul, in March 2012.[17] The Working Group was meant to implement and develop this rather vague 'commitment' by, *inter alia*, sharing best practices, conducting joint exercises, strengthening trans-governmental co-operation (i.e., from agency to agency), and assisting other states in the implementation of the *Convention on the Physical Protection of Nuclear Material* and its 2005 amendments,[18] which entered into force on 8 May 2016. The date of entry into force of these amendments is relevant since this means that efforts were made to apply them provisionally before their entering into force, and their entry into force was due, to a large degree, to the pressure exercised from within the NSS.[19]

Working groups that, on the one hand, deepen the coalitions' commitments among a smaller group of participating states and, at the same time, engage in capacity-building activities with coalition partners that

---

[17] *Seoul Communiqué: 2012 Seoul Nuclear Security Summit* (Seoul, 26–27 March 2012), para. 8; the text of the *Communiqué* can be found at www.mofa.go.jp/policy/un/disarma ment/arms/nuclear_security/2012/pdfs/communique.pdf.

[18] *1980 Convention on the Physical Protection of Nuclear Material*, 1456 UNTS 125.

[19] For information on the amendments, see IAEA, *Convention on Physical Protection of Nuclear Material (CPPNM) and Amendment thereto*, at www-ns.iaea.org/conventions/physical-protection.asp?l=42; for the NSS Working Group, see the *Joint Statement of France, Japan, the Republic of Korea, the UK and the US on Transport Security* (24 March 2014), at https://obamawhitehouse.archives.gov/the-press-office/2012/03/27/joint-state ment-transport-security.

have limited capacities in a certain field can also be found in the case of the GCTF. This 'informal, a-political, multilateral counterterrorism (CT) platform',[20] was launched in September 2011 by the USA and Turkey with the aim of streamlining positions and actions on counter-terrorism that are too politically contested to advance rapidly inside the UN. This platform focuses its efforts on three broader themes – i.e., 'criminal justice and the rule of law', 'countering violent extremism', and 'foreign terrorist fighters'. For such purposes, it has established a thematic working group on each of these subjects, as well as two (formerly three) regional working groups focused on capacity building in East and West Africa. 'Detention and reintegration' is another main topic pursued by the GCTF, though its specific working group on that has ceased to exist, and the theme has been reallocated within the scope of the other three thematic working groups.[21] This structure confirms that the division of labour inherent to the 'posse model' is in fact present in several coalitions, and the specific means to carry it out are often copied from one coalition to the other.

The logic behind regional working groups established within coalitions has an additional component. These groups are not just aimed at furthering specific commitments within the participants of the different regions represented in a given coalition, they also – and very importantly – function as a vehicle for transmitting the coalitions' goals to those outside the posse. This begins with pure 'outreach activities' whereby the benefits of the coalition are disseminated, often with the aim of gaining new partners for the initiative. But the objective is at times more ambitious, and regional groups are tasked with engaging non-participants with the coalition's mission. This may be done through ad hoc cooperation. Many comments on the PSI, for example, suggest that non-participants, including some of the states most critical of the initiative, take part in its operations on a purely ad hoc basis, without publicly acknowledging it, be it due to internal political constraints, or due to a somewhat cynical, but not uncommon, attitude among states of taking part in certain conduct the legitimacy and sometimes even legality of which they are not willing to recognize – I call this only 'somewhat' cynical because it may have important consequences for the formation, or non-formation, of customary international law.

---

[20] See the website of the Global Counterterrorism Forum (GCTF), at www.thegctf.org/About-us/Background-and-Mission.
[21] See GCTF, *Structure*, at www.thegctf.org/Working-Groups/Structure.

156 COALITIONS OF THE WILLING IN CONTEXT

Engaging non-participants is done also by means of 'capacity building'. This technique is on the rise, not least as a result of the work of coalitions of the willing and other networks such as public–private partnerships (PPP), as well as IOs, which either engage themselves in capacity building (like the United Nations Office on Drugs and Crime – UNODC) or function as platforms for bringing these efforts, including by informal entities, to their member states.[22] Thus, capacity building is often performed through the interplay of several institutions, universal and regional, and of informal coalitions and networks. It remains largely understudied by international lawyers, although through it, states are more and more brought in line with international legal rules and informal standards. It is a tool of global governance.[23]

The two main tasks of the Regional Operational Experts Groups (ROEGs) of the PSI are outreach activities and capacity building for non-participants in the respective regions,[24] whereby those outside the coalition are taught the importance of the coalition's mission and how to accomplish it (this is *paideia's* new normative force in the global realm). The same can be observed among the regional working groups of the GCTF. Actually, in this case, the chairs of the thematic groups may invite non-participants to take part in their activities, which also include capacity building on their respective themes.[25] Outreach activities and capacity building towards non-participants were first conducted by the FATF and its eight FATF-style regional bodies (FSRBs), an evolution that has certainly influenced the PSI, the GCTF, and other coalitions.

---

[22] A prime example is the SC Committee established pursuant resolution 1373 (2001) concerning Counter-Terrorism (CTC), which, especially through its body of experts, i.e., the Counter-Terrorism Executive Directorate (CTED), helps to ensure that capacity-building measures and technical assistance offered by partner organizations, are brought to UN member States.

[23] It may also be seen as a technique of governmentality – i.e., of conducting conduct in the sense of Michel Foucault. For a powerful analysis of the CTC in terms of Foucault's disciplinary thesis, see Isobel Roele, 'Disciplinary Power and the UN Security Council Counter Terrorism Committee' (2014) 19 *Journal of Conflict & Security Law* 49.

[24] As a result of the High Level Political Meeting (HLPM), held on occasion of PSI's fifth anniversary, in Washington, D.C., on 28 May 2008, PSI participating states agreed 'to strengthen their operational cooperation, with special emphasis on the regional dimension ... to distribute general information on PSI and capacity-building knowledge', see DoS, Office of the Spokesman, *Washington Declaration for the PSI 5th Anniversary Senior-Level Meeting* (28 May 2008), at http://2001-2009.state.gov/r/pa/prs/ps/2008/may/105268.htm.

[25] See GCTF, *Partners and Outreach*, at www.thegctf.org/About-us/Partners-and-Outreach.

5.1 COALITIONS' EVOLUTION BY MIMESIS

However, the FATF's regional ramifications hold important differences in comparison to the two other cases, regarding their legal nature, their place within the coalition, and their functions. First, FSRBs have a formal or quasi-formal nature, created by regional organizations and being organs of the former,[26] or constituted by semi-formal agreements as inter-governmental regional bodies;[27] although they are clearly modelled after the FATF, some of them have legal personality on their own. Second, FSRBs are associated members of the FATF, integrated thus into the FATF system but not strictly part of it, unlike the regional workings groups of the GCTF and PSI, which are part of their structures. FSRBs integrate 'an affiliated global network to combat money laundering and the financing of terrorism around the globe'.[28] Thus, FSRBs are more than just working groups of the coalition; at the same time, they are clearly at the service of it. And they serve the FATF not only through the outreach and capacity-building activities described above, but also by engaging in straightforward implementation activities of FATF standards with non-FATF members – i.e., they bring the standards and practices adopted only by a few to the many, using a multilayered strategy that proceeds separately from region to region but adds up to the whole in what can be described as the universalization of the very particular.

Each FSRB has the mandate to ensure the adoption, implementation, and enforcement of the FATF recommendations in the domestic sphere of their members, which, in sum, go clearly beyond membership in the FATF. It is a case in point for transnational law-making resulting from a close interplay between informal, semi-formal, and formal institutions integrated into a global network centred on a politically powerful coalition of finance officials from the largest economies around the world.

---

[26] This is the case, e.g., of the *Inter-Governmental Action Group against Money Laundering in West Africa* (GIABA), created in 1999 by the Economic Community of West African States (ECOWAS), see www.giaba.org; the *Committee of Experts on the Evaluation of Anti-Money Laundering Measures and the Financing of Terrorism* (MONEYVAL), was established by the Committee of Ministers of the Council of Europe (CoE), in 1997. However, this pre-existing monitoring body was entrusted with the implementation of the legal framework of the CoE, and integrated fully into the FATF system only until 2006, information at CoE, *MONEYVAL,* at www.coe.int/en/web/moneyval/home.

[27] The FSRB for Latin America, GAFILAT (formerly GAFISUD), e.g., is an intergovernmental organization based in Buenos Aires, which was created by a memorandum of understanding, signed in Cartagena, Colombia, on 8 December 2000; information at www.gafilat.org/.

[28] This description is taken from the website of the *Asia/Pacific Group on Money Laundering,* see www.apgml.org/about-us/page.aspx?p=52e840ea-0599-4c85-9424-1abd272ba9f3.

158   COALITIONS OF THE WILLING IN CONTEXT

This is done mainly through two techniques. First, a sort of enhanced capacity building – i.e., technical assistance and training (TA&T) – which includes 'awareness raising' with national parliaments and other authorities in charge of regulation and enforcement, and, very importantly, assistance in the drafting of national legislation;[29] the other technique is 'mutual evaluation' – i.e., peer review among the domestic authorities of the member states of the respective FSRB – with the assistance of the secretariat or central administrator of the latter. Mutual evaluation has been directly imported by the FRSBs from the FATF.

5.1.2 Transforming Activities into Durable Efforts: Coalitions' Fluctuant Informality

The FATF is not only a case in point for how the activities and the regulatory impact of coalitions of the willing are expanded beyond their membership; it is also a paramount example of an originally ad hoc body that has turned into a long-lasting effort. In order to achieve this, an elaborated infrastructure has been developed, which deserves further attention.

An informal trans-governmental network *par excellence*,[30] the FATF was created in June 1989 by the G7, in Paris, in order to combat money laundering, primarily derived from the international illegal narcotic business, which had become a serious economic problem by that time. For that purpose, a network of finance ministers and high-ranking financial officials from the most industrialized nations (the G7, eight other countries, and the European Commission) was established, representing a paradigmatic case of a selective, Western-driven 'international club'.[31] At the time of writing, thirty-five states, including the whole

---

[29] Assistance in legal drafting is also facilitated by the CTC regarding national implementation of SC Resolution 1373.

[30] See Slaughter, *A New World Order*, pp. 6 and 54. On trans-governmental networks and international law generally, see also Raustiala, 'Transgovernmental Networks and the Future of International Law'; on trans-governmental relations, see Keohane and Nye, 'Transgovernmental Relations and International Organizations'.

[31] On the nature of the FATF as an 'international club', see Daniel W. Drezner, *All Politics Is Global: Explaining International Regulatory Regimes* (Princeton: Princeton University Press, 2007), pp. 67–68, and pp. 142 et seq.; see also Krisch, 'The Decay of Consent', 23; on the 'club model' in international affairs, see Robert O. Keohane and Joseph S. Nye Jr., 'Between Centralization and Fragmentation: The Club Model of Multilateral Cooperation and Problems of Democratic Legitimacy', *KSG Working Paper No. 01–004* (February 2001) (commenting that from the Bretton Woods conference on, 'key regimes for

BRICS, and two regional organizations are members of the FATF, so that its Western-centred character may be questioned. It must be mentioned also that the task force receives important political guidance from the G20 nowadays. However, in this case, too, the basic rules of the game were defined by a small group of mostly Western countries with the USA taking the lead. Moreover, the FATF's membership policy is as far away from universal inclusiveness as it can be, relying instead on strategic criteria such as the size of the gross domestic product (GDP), the size of the banking, insurance and security sectors, and that of the population.[32] At the same time, the FATF pursues universal adherence to its standards for which it carries out an aggressive strategy towards non-members: 'non-cooperative jurisdictions', members and non-members alike, are subject to a series of actions, from 'naming and shaming' to economic 'counter-measures'; the latter have been applied in recent times against Iran and North Korea.[33]

By 1990, FATF participants had agreed on forty recommendations on how to face the problem of money laundering, including proposals to change national criminal and financial legislations. These global standards are non-binding, but have proved to have a high degree of efficacy as they are implemented at the transnational plane through their incorporation into national laws and regulations.[34]

As mentioned above, the increasing perception of the augmenting inter-connectedness of global risks and challenges helps the coalitions' fluid nature to flourish. The FATF is a role model in this regard; its recommendations are up-dated and revised from time to time in order to better respond to evolving risks to the international financial system. Over the years, new tasks have been added to the FATF's 'mandate', which clarifies that it 'is not intended to create any legal

---

governance operated like clubs. Cabinet ministers or the equivalent, working in the same issue-area, initially from a relatively small number of relatively rich countries, got together to make the rules').

[32] See FATF, *FATF Members and Observers,* at www.fatf-gafi.org/pages/aboutus/member sandobservers/fatfmembershippolicy.html.

[33] 'Counter-measures' against Iran were 'suspended' in June 2016, but Iran remains catalogued as a 'high risk and non-cooperative jurisdiction'; see FATF, *High-risk and noncooperative jurisdictions,* at www.fatf-gafi.org/topics/high-riskandnon-cooperativejurisdictions/.

[34] See Rodiles, *'Coalitions of the Willing: Coyuntura, Contexto y Propiedades'*, 697–699 (with special reference to the impact of FATF recommendations on Mexico's penal and financial laws).

rights or obligations'.[35] A month after 9/11, the special recommendations on the financing of terrorism were adopted,[36] following the trend in the US administration to merge anti–money laundering and counter-terrorism financing.[37] In 2008, a recommendation on non-proliferation of WMD was further added to the list.[38] And in 2012, a major revision led to the current version of the recommendations, which are no longer divided into the '40 + 9' formula, but represent a coherent whole of forty recommendations, most of which have 'interpretive notes', 'which should be read in conjunction with the recommendation'.[39] The FATF describes its recommendations as 'international standards on combating money-laundering and the financing of terrorism and proliferation'.[40] However, through its guidelines and compilations of best practices regarding the implementation of these recommendations, as well as through the typologies developed in order to assess the methods and trends involved in 'money laundering, terrorist financing *and other threats to the integrity of the financial system*',[41] the FATF keeps expanding its scope of action and is today also engaged in the international fight against corruption,[42] and it plays an increasingly important role in

---

[35] See *Financial Action Task Force Mandate (2012–2020)* (20 April 2012) [hereinafter '*FATF Mandate (2012–2020)*'], para. 48, at http://www.fatf-gafi.org/media/fatf/documents/FINAL%20FATF%20MANDATE%202012-2020.pdf.

[36] Originally eight, the ninth special recommendation on terrorist financing was added in October 2004; information at www.fatf-gafi.org/pages/aboutus/historyofthefatf/.

[37] On this merging, see Bruce Zagaris, 'The merging of the Anti-Money Laundering and Counter-Terrorism Financial Enforcement Regimes after September 11, 2001' (2004) 22 *Berkeley Journal of International Law* 123.

[38] Adopted in order to assist states in the implementation of targeted financial sanctions in the framework of the North Korea and former Iran UN sanctions regimes, i.e. SC Res. 1718 (14 October 2006), and SC Res. 1737 (27 December 2006), and subsequent resolutions.

[39] See FATF, *International Standards on Combating Money Laundering and the Financing of Terrorism and Proliferation: The FATF Recommendations* (October 2016), p. 5, at www.fatf-gafi.org/media/fatf/documents/recommendations/pdfs/FATF_Recommendations.pdf [hereinafter '*FATF Recommendations*'].

[40] Ibid.

[41] *FATF Mandate (2012–2020)*, para. 3 (a). Emphasis added.

[42] See, for instance, the FATF typology *Laundering the Proceeds of Corruption* (July 2011), whereby the links between corruption and money-laundering were assessed, and the *Best Practices Paper: The Use of the FATF Recommendations to Combat Corruption* (October 2013), both at FATF, *Corruption*, at www.fatf-gafi.org/topics/corruption/.

5.1 COALITIONS' EVOLUTION BY MIMESIS   161

the international efforts on 'financial inclusion' – i.e., efforts to mitigate the informal economy sector.[43]

As suggested by its name, this task force was created for a limited time period, but its mandate has been renewed several times since then, most recently on 20 April 2012, and until 31 December 2020.[44] With almost thirty years of existence, it has developed a quite sophisticated structure that consists of the plenary, the president and vice president, the Steering Committee, and, in contrast to the PSI and other coalitions, even a secretariat, which, as well as the offices, is provided by the Organization for Economic Cooperation and Development (OECD).[45] The plenary is the governing body; all decisions on the task force's mandate, budgetary issues, as well as the substantive matters concerning the recommendations, guidelines, and other reports are taken therein by consensus. In contrast to the PSI and GICNT, for example, FATF documents are publicly available on its website. A noteworthy feature of the FATF is that it makes a systematic usage of a legal vocabulary ('mandate', 'counter-measures', and 'jurisdictions'; 'members' as opposed to 'participants'; 'monitoring', 'implementation', and 'recommendations'), and its documents, like the *Mandate 2012–2020*, are formulated in a way that resembles documents of traditional IOs. All these elements push the classification of the FATF as an informal coalition to its limits. Eyal Benvenisti, who treats the FATF together with the PSI as typical coalitions of the willing, has nonetheless referred to them as 'formal but non-legally binding institutions'.[46]

However, in the end, the question depends on what is meant by 'informal', or as the case may be, 'formal'. The FATF has certainly undergone a formalization process, in the sense that it has developed a clear and organized structure; it has a recognizable form. But, as mentioned earlier, a 'formal' institution – or just an institution – is related to

---

[43] See FATF, *Revised Guidance on Anti-Money Laundering and Terrorist Financing Measures and Financial Inclusion* (February 2013), at www.fatf-gafi.org/media/fatf/documents/reports/AML_CFT_Measures_and_Financial_Inclusion_2013.pdf.

[44] *FATF Mandate (2012–2020)*, para. 49.

[45] It is important to make clear that although FATF borrows organs from the OECD, it is not an agency of the latter as sometimes described.

[46] See Benvenisti, 'Coalitions of the Willing and the Evolution of Informal International Law', p. 4; Benvenisti and Downs, 'The Empire's New Clothes', 618. However, more recently, he has used the rubric 'informal inter-governmental agreements', which seems more accurate; see Eyal Benvenisti, 'Towards a Typology of Informal International Lawmaking Mechanisms and Their Distinct Accountability Gaps', in Pauwelyn, Wessel, and Wouters (eds.), *Informal International Lawmaking*, pp. 299–301.

legally established structures. The point is not that an entity would have to enact binding measures in order to be considered a formal organization. As it is well known, the amount of legally binding norms represents only a small part of the universe of decisions taken within IOs, a tendency that will most probably continue since these organizations rely more and more often not only on traditional soft law but also on compilations of best practices and all sorts of indicators. The reason why the FATF is not a formal institution despite its elaborated structure and highly organized functioning is its non-legal nature. It is an 'entity [that remains] outside the realm of law':[47] its authority rests on no legal basis whatsoever, it has no legal personality, and its mandate explicitly denies the intention of creating legal rights and obligations. One of the most important motivations for remaining outside the law is that for the FATF, as for any other coalition, retaining its built-in flexibility is an imperative strictly related to the efficiency paradigm. As rightly noted by one commentator, '[t]he informality of the FATF is the key feature providing this flexibility'.[48]

Hence, the FATF shows that the ad hoc nature of coalitions of the willing, understood as a temporal element, is not accurate. Coalitions are ad hoc in the sense that they are created for solving or managing specific problems; they are strictly issue-oriented international task forces, initiatives, or platforms, not fora created for enabling deliberation among states, and, accordingly, process is always subordinated to results. Their mandates are prolonged as long as the case demands, and flexibly adapted as the menaces they face evolve. As long as terrorism poses a serious threat to international peace and security, the coalitions that have emerged or been adapted to counter it, like the FATF, will most probably continue to exist, evolving quickly as terrorism evolves, and flexibly expanding their mandates as the risk activities that are considered to be linked to terrorism continue to proliferate. Since terrorism is a global threat, responses to it need to have a global outreach too, but their design and adoption cannot afford to go through the cumbersome and protracted processes common to IOs and traditional multilateral decision-making. In order to achieve these not easily reconcilable goals – i.e. built-in flexibility and durability,

---

[47] Klabbers, 'Institutional Ambivalence by Design', 408 (refering to soft institutionalism more broadly).

[48] Kenneth S. Blazejewski, 'The FATF and Its Institutional Partners: Improving the Effectiveness and Accountability of Transgovernmental Networks' (2008) 22 *Temple International Law and Comparative Law Journal* 1, at 10–11.

efficiency in decision-making and efficacy in their implementation- they have to develop their organization and remain fluid at the same time. A certain formalization of structures and processes is thus required, which enables coalitions' existence over time and endows them with a certain legitimacy by facilitating a better recognition of their organization and functions to those outside their core and to non-participants. But this formalization has to be a limited one, since coalitions have to remain sufficiently informal in order to retain the high degree of responsiveness that the dark sides of globalization demand, or so the narrative goes.

Coalitions' fluctuant informality – i.e., the constant shifts from informality to formality, and back again – seems to have emerged as a viable solution to this tension. The FATF epitomizes this fluctuant form of organization, and the tendency initiated by the government of George W. Bush and promoted by the Obama administration, to turn activities into 'durable efforts', as we saw in the cases of the PSI, the GICNT, and even some military multinational exercises like IMCMEX confirms this.[49] It should be recalled that the US *National Security Strategy 2010* rectified President Obama's promise to turn the PSI and the GICNT into 'durable international *institutions*', using instead the term 'durable international *efforts*'.[50] This is significant. The rectification followed the expectations that his Prague speech promise awoke among diplomatic circles in the sense that these initiatives would indeed be transformed into full-fledged IOs, with a constitutive treaty, rules of procedure, and possibly embedded into the UN system. But, as mentioned, his government probably never intended this to happen since this would have put the built-in flexibility of the PSI and the GICNT in jeopardy. Many speculations on the real motivations behind Obama's words have been articulated, one of the most recurrent being that they were intended to give these coalitions new political momentum, which seemed in peril due to the perceived flaws of legitimacy that prevailed among members of the international community, especially after the abuses of the Bush Jr. administration regarding the coalition rhetoric. This is very plausible indeed. However, paying due regard to the fact that the government of George W. Bush already envisioned this durability for the PSI, it is not difficult to see that the term 'durable effort' captures far more accurately the nature of coalitions of the willing as international fora that are created to function alongside formal institutions over prolonged periods of time without having to

---

[49] See Chapter 4, note 215, and accompanying text.
[50] See Chapter 4, note 143, and accompanying text.

sacrifice what are considered their major assets in terms of efficiency. And what has happened to the PSI and the GICNT since Obama's Prague speech is that they have begun to mimic the fluctuant informality that has made the FATF a successful model of a durable and far-reaching coalition.

In the same vein, the NSS was convened in 2009 by President Obama and turned into a six-year effort.[51] The main purpose of the NSS was to streamline and enhance a coherent global nuclear security regime, for which it promoted interactions among several IOs and informal coalitions related to the subject. Now, the fact that the NSS lasted 'only' six years could put into question its nature as a durable effort. One could be inclined to think of it as another instance of the contemporary international *Concert*, characteristic of the several 'Gs'. The dynamic of work of the NSS, which consisted of preparatory meetings at the levels of *sherpas* and *sous-sherpas*, in which *communiqués* were negotiated before they were adopted by the heads of state and government at the summits, points precisely in that direction.

I will not engage here in a thorough analysis of the nature of the Gs and its differences and commonalities with coalitions of the willing. There are some elements that, in my view, permit to separate both phenomena, which certainly hold many things in common but are not the same. The differences are of degree but very important ones, which allow speaking about the Gs as a 'permanent Concert' that sets in motion as many durable efforts (coalitions and networks) as necessary. One of these differences in degree is certainly not met by the NSS, namely the political level of participation. A coalition of the willing in the sense of a durable effort requires a lesser political clout in order to get the technical job done. Coalitions are rather technocratic creatures. So one may be

---

[51] When convened by letters from President Obama to the heads of states and governments of the invited states, it was not clear at all for many of the invitees which shape the summit was supposed to take – nor exactly why the focus was again on nuclear security issues, like counter-terrorism, counter-proliferation, and physical protection, and not on disarmament as many had hoped after the Prague speech. During first meetings at the *sous-sherpa* level, delegates commented bilaterally on the impression that another coalition of the willing was just being created when promises had been made to transform coalitions into institutions. During later preparatory sessions to the Washington Summit 2010, a couple of representatives even warned that the documents (the Washington Communiqué and the Work Plan) had to be carefully drafted in order to avoid the impression among non-participants that the NSS was another coalition of the willing (this is based on the recollections of the present author as *sous-sherpa* of the Mexican government to the NSS, from October 2009 to March 2011).

tempted to say that the NSS was the 'G53 for nuclear security'. But this would be too narrow a field for a 'Concert'.[52] Richard Feinberg and others use the term 'institutionalized summitry' for describing the reiterated gatherings of heads of states and government in the several Gs and other summits, which 'once established ... often generate their own inertia'.[53] Although there are several and relevant differences between the NSS and the Gs, the notion of 'institutionalized summitry' is helpful for describing the NSS process. Most of all, it captures the fluctuant informality described earlier: the NSS was much more than just an ad hoc diplomatic channel to address a crisis, but at the same time it did not amount to an IO. Moreover, the NSS developed remarkable features, which go more in the direction of non-legally binding rule-making by coalitions, or informal law-making indeed, than the broader political principles adopted by the Gs do. Some of these regulatory features have been mimicked by the PSI and are now also increasingly to be found within formal institutions. However, as this touches directly upon the jurisgenerative role of coalitions of the willing, I will deal with it in Section 2 of this chapter.

When the last summit of the NSS was approaching, in 2016, policy papers of think tanks and academic institutions in the USA made the proposal to transform the NSS into a forum below the summit but high-level enough 'to maintain the impetus for nuclear security'.[54] At first sight, these plans did not succeed. Yet a closer look at the decisions taken during the last NSS Washington summit of March–April 2016 reveals a different and quite fascinating story.

During that summit, five 'Action Plans' were adopted so that the work of the NSS can be continued within three IOs (the UN, the IAEA, and Interpol), and two other coalitions (the GICNT and the Global Partnership against the Spread of WMD).[55] In other words, NSS participating

---

[52] Cf. Risto E. J. Penttilä, *The Role of the G8 in International Peace and Security* (Oxford: Oxford University Press/International Institute for Strategic Studies, 2003), pp. 17–31 (describing the G8 as a 'Concert' and comparing it to the Concert of Europe, while differentiating it from contact groups and the Security Council, which he calls 'concerts').

[53] Richard Feinberg, 'Institutionalized Summitry', p. 305.

[54] Matthew Bunn et al., *Advancing Nuclear Security: Evaluating Progress and Setting New Goals* (Harvard Kennedy School, Belfer Center for Science and International Affairs, March 2014), p. 76; see also Michelle Cann, Kelsey Davenport and Sarah Williams, *The Nuclear Security Summit: Assessment of Joint Statements* (Arms Control Association/ Partnership for Global Security, March 2014), p. 26.

[55] See Arms Control Association, *Nuclear Security Summit at a Glance* (August 2017), at www.armscontrol.org/factsheets/NuclearSecuritySummit.

states – with the exception of Russia, which did not attend the 2016 Washington summit –[56] agreed to continue co-ordinating their efforts beyond 2016 in order to accomplish the goals of the NSS. These agreed actions include efforts to adopt GA resolutions for reviewing the implementation of legal instruments (i.e., the *International Convention on the Suppression of Acts of Nuclear Terrorism*),[57] submitting voluntary reports to subsidiary organs of the SC (i.e., the 1540 Committee on non-proliferation), conducting outreach activities within UN fora in order to continue mobilizing support among the broader international community for the objectives identified during the NSS process, advocating for the development of guidance by the IAEA (i.e., the adoption of guiding principles or best practices), promoting capacity-building activities within the GICNT, etc. (Former) NSS participating states with a capacity to do so should also provide technical assistance to requesting states for the implementation of their international legal obligations in nuclear security matters, including in the drafting of national legislation.[58] Moreover, a group of forty particularly willing states emerged from the NSS with the explicit goal of continuing the efforts to construct a comprehensive global nuclear security regime – that is, the *raison d'être* of the NSS.[59] This is the *Nuclear Security Contact Group* (NSCG), which has adopted a statement of principles that practically reflects the objectives of the said action plans.[60] The NSCG can very well be described as the successor coalition of the NSS, and thus the aforementioned plans of certain US think tanks and academic institutions actually materialized. However, I believe that the NSCG should be contemplated together with the action plans, as well as with some NSS initiatives that are still very much alive, like the *Strengthening Nuclear Security Initiative*.[61] These are all mutually reinforcing daughter initiatives of the NSS that were created in order to turn this effort very durable. We are actually in presence of the *NSS 2.0*, a

---

[56] See note 226 and accompanying text.

[57] *2005 International Convention on the Suppression of Acts of Nuclear Terrorism*, 2245 UNTS 89.

[58] This information is taken from the five *NSS 2016 Action Plans*, available at www.nss2016.org/2016-action-plans/.

[59] See NSS 2016, *Joint Statement on Sustaining Action to Strengthen Global Nuclear Architecture* (5 April 2016), at www.nss2016.org/document-center-docs/2016/4/4/joint-statement-on-sustaining-action-to-strengthen-global-nuclear-security-architecture.

[60] The NSCG Statement of Principles has been circulated by the Canadian Mission to the IAEA (in its role as co-ordinator of the NSCG); see IAEA, INFCIR/899 (2 November 2016).

[61] See note 186 and accompanying text.

sort of meta-coalition created through a highly innovative technique that extends the activities of the posse in time beyond its nominal existence: the total absence of form of the coalition is achieved while it continues to perform.

5.1.3   Concluding Remarks on Durable Efforts

The flexibility of coalitions of the willing facilitates mutual learning processes that lead to the changes of institutional design that are needed for accomplishing the mission. In this sense, too, it is 'the mission [that] must determine the coalition',[62] and not the other way around. As such, these changes are motivated by the efficiency paradigm, and legitimacy concerns form part of the equation. Sophisticated structures, like those developed by the FATF, not only help to deliver results more efficiently; these contribute also to a better recognizable organization, which improves transparency and helps to face legitimacy concerns. This, in turn, enhances effectiveness, since an entity that is perceived as being more legitimate has better chances to get their standards accepted by the many, and especially by those on the outside. But it takes much more than just an improved perception derived from a better-articulated organization in structures and processes and from more information available on their websites. Adding layers to the system is a lesson learned in global governance. Highly complex global networks are then again less transparent, but their authority is dislocated to such a degree that global standards begin to be internalized as regional measures. The FATF is a role model in this regard, and other counter-terrorism and counter-proliferation coalitions are following suit by establishing their own regional ramifications, which, however, differ in certain aspects, as we have seen.

Quasi-formalization processes are also key for turning activities into durable efforts, which is a crucial feature in differentiating coalitions from pure ad hoc diplomatic channels. The FATF with its almost thirty years of existence and the evolution of its mandate, which has been adapted to evolving global security risks in a highly flexibly way, is again a paradigmatic case that shows where the limits to formalization have to be put in order to conserve a fluctuant, amenable informality. Another way of turning activities into durable efforts is through the abandonment

---

[62] Rumsfeld, 'Transforming the Military', 31.

of form altogether once the activities have been sufficiently defined and the actors streamlined within some shape of organization. This is fluctuant informality at its best: like-minded actors are assembled in a flexible setting, which acquires a certain structure over time without hardening too much, and once these structures are not considered necessary anymore or are deemed inconvenient for whatever (political) reason, the structure is dismantled altogether, but co-ordinated actions of coalesced states are still carried out. This is what the NSS 2.0 is about. Rather than a limit case between a coalition and international diplomatic summitry, it can actually be described as the purest model of coalitions of the willing, a completely 'amorphous'[63] 'coordination of efforts of 'like-minded States',[64] something that is 'better understood as an activity than an organization'.[65]

As durable efforts, coalitions coexist with formal institutions in a multilayered complex, where transnational regulation emerges more easily and swiftly, and international law and its institutions are being constantly reshaped. It is precisely the *raison d'être* of durable efforts to cohabit the global administrative space in order to change it. In the following section, I will elaborate on the changes to international law as they result from the interplay between formality and informality.

5.2 Coalitions' Jurisgenerative Capacity Arising from the Interplay with (Formal) Institutions

The interactions that occur among informal coalitions and formal organizations are not limited to co-operation between coalition y and IO z, for instance, in the sense that y helps z to enforce what the latter decides. This is the sort of relationship that has long existed between coalitions of willing and able states and the SC: the multinational forces that emerged out of the necessity to make up for the UN Charter's *manqué* collective security system.[66] In contrast to other informal groups of states with which the Council has worked together since the 1970s, coalitions of the willing such as the PSI, the NSS, the FATF, or the GCTF are issue oriented and of a long-term nature – i.e., durable efforts. Accordingly, their interactions with the SC occur on a more technical, day-to-day

---

[63] Rodiles, '*Coalitions of the Willing: Coyuntura, Contexto y Propiedades*', 693–695.
[64] Benvenisti, 'Coalitions of the Willing', p. 1.
[65] Haass, *The Reluctant Sheriff*, p. 95.
[66] See Chapter 3, Sections 3.2.1.2 and 3.2.1.3.

5.2 COALITIONS' JURISGENERATIVE CAPACITY 169

basis, as opposed to the political nature of the dynamics between the Council and 'contact groups', for instance.[67]

The interplay between coalitions and formal institutions today occurs also at the normative level, importantly comprising norm evolution. Coalitions not only enforce formal law, but they also have a say in defining how international law should be implemented. Likewise, these normative interactions are not just the result of the usual process, whereby political negotiations path the way for the adoption of legal rules, determining the content of the latter. Indeed, nothing new would be proven by telling how SC resolutions, e.g., are often the result of the outcomes of informal groups of states like contact groups, groups of friends of the Secretary General, and the like.[68] There is a significant difference between the interactions among institutions and more traditional informal groups of states like multinational forces and contact groups, on the one hand, and the interplay between IOs and the coalitions of the willing I am dealing with here, on the other. In the first case, non-legal facts first precede the law and then help to determine its efficacy by showing if and how it *is* implemented; in the second, non-legal norms affect how the law *should be* created and implemented. The jurisgenerative potential of coalitions of the willing can be appreciated best by looking at how institutions react to their work and how they actually work together.

For this, I have chosen three examples, each one involving one of the coalitions I have dealt with so far in this book. First, I will turn back to the PSI and look at how the interplay among this initiative, the SC, and the IMO have shaped crucial aspects of the international law of the sea as established in the *1982 United Nations Convention on the Law of the Sea* (UNCLOS), without the need to embark in cumbersome amendments or in the long and uncertain route towards new rules of customary international law. The second case involves the FATF and its interaction with the SC, especially with its subsidiary organs on counter-terrorism. The purpose here is to show that the former's recommendations, guidelines, and compilations of best practices on the combat of the financing of

---

[67] See Jochen Prantl, *The UN Security Council and Informal Groups of States: Complementing or Competing for Governance?* (New York: Oxford University Press, 2006). It should be noted that contact groups are evolving too; the *Contact Group on Piracy off the Coast of Somalia* is a case in point, which in terms of its functions comes closer to a coalition of the willing but, at the same time, is institutionally linked to the SC.

[68] See Prantl, *The UN Security Council and Informal Groups of States*, pp. 91 et seq.

170 COALITIONS OF THE WILLING IN CONTEXT

terrorism contribute to the specification of SC resolutions on the matter, which are practically to be read together with these informal documents. Finally, the so-called 'gift basket' of the NSS will be examined. The point will be made that this is an innovative instance in non-binding trans-national regulation, which is being reproduced by coalitions and IOs, and that has the potential of transforming international soft law emanating from the IAEA into hard, legal obligations. Moreover, I will show – and thereby go beyond global security issues – to what extent this instance of regulation has been mimicked in the framework of the UN process on climate change and inserted into the Paris Agreement of 2015.

5.2.1 Shaping the Law of the Sea through the Dynamics between the PSI, the SC, and the IMO

The fact that over 100 states participate in the PSI has raised questions to what extent this initiative may affect the international law of the sea, with some commentators arguing that a new norm of customary international law is crystalizing regarding the right to interdict merchant vessels at the high seas in cases of proliferation concern, without the flag state's consent.[69] But this assertion is problematic. First, it is not clear how many and which PSI participants regularly take part in such interdic-tions. PSI's secrecy and the differentiated levels of participation involved in this coalition make it extremely difficult to prove whether a sufficiently widespread practice exists. Secondly, PSI core states have been keen on clarifying that the PSI does not create new legal obligations, as empha-sized by the US *National Security Strategy 2006*: 'partnerships on the model of the PSI are oriented towards action and results rather than legislation or rule-making'.[70] It is thus difficult to assert the existence of a general practice, and the element of *opinio iuris* is seriously questioned. States participate in coalitions like the PSI under the stated assumption that they are not creating legal norms.

---

[69] See Joel Doolin, 'The Proliferation Security Initiative: Cornerstone of a New International Norm' (2006) 59 *Naval War College Review* 29; for a critique, see Mark Valencia, 'Is the PSI really the Cornerstone of a New International Norm?' (2006) 59 *Naval War College* 123. For a nuanced and differentiated argument, but pointing at the same direction, see Timothy C. Perry, 'Blurring the Oceans Zones: The Effect of the Proliferation Security Initiative on the Customary International Law of the Sea' (2006) 37 *Ocean Development & International Law* 33. *Contra*, see Klein, *Maritime Security and the Law of the Sea*, p. 205, at fn. 367.

[70] *US National Security Strategy 2006*, p. 46.

5.2 COALITIONS' JURISGENERATIVE CAPACITY   171

The emergence within the PSI of 'a general practice accepted as law'[71] is thus questionable, but this does not mean that the conduct of states within this coalition does not affect international law. As Benvenisti observes, 'these coordinated policies [do not] necessitate making novel assertions about customary international law'.[72] And it is the same author who also pointed out in a previous article, which is the first comprehensive legal essay on coalitions of the willing, that by following PSI standards, states set the standard 'indirectly but efficiently' for what the SC considers 'appropriate' or 'effective' in regard to measures to counter the proliferation of WMD.[73] SC resolution 1540 (2004) contains several references to 'appropriate' and 'effective' measures where the activities of the PSI and other related frameworks of co-ordinated state action, such as the *Container Security Initiative* (CSI), are relevant. These include measures on border and trans-shipment controls, for example.[74] Most important in this context is op. 10, which calls upon states 'to take cooperative action to prevent illicit trafficking in nuclear, chemical or biological weapons, their means of delivery, and related materials'.[75] The USA and other delegations that negotiated this resolution sought to include an express reference to the PSI in this context, but this failed due to China's resistance.[76] Today, however, there is little doubt that this 'cooperative action' takes place primarily within the PSI and according to the parameters defined by the PSI's *Statement of Interdiction Principles* (SIP).[77] In other words, the 'cooperative action' the Council refers to in this context most likely comprises information sharing on proliferation activities,[78] joint interdiction exercises, and a general willingness on behalf of states to *consider giving consent* to interdict merchant vessels flying their flags when there is proliferation concern. This co-operative action is about enhanced collaboration to be carried out towards or against non-state actors who wish to acquire WMD, as clearly addressed in resolution 1540, *and* against states of 'proliferation concern', as the PSI

---

[71] *1945 Statute of the International Court of Justice*, Art. 38 (1) (b), 1 UNTS 993.
[72] Benvenisti, 'Towards a Typology', p. 300.
[73] See Benvenisti, 'Coalitions of the Willing', pp. 18–19.
[74] See SC Res. 1540, op. 3 (c) and (d).
[75] Ibid., op 10.
[76] See, e.g., Belcher, 'The Proliferation Security Initiative', 12.
[77] See Chapter 4, note 18, and accompanying text.
[78] SIP, II.

172   COALITIONS OF THE WILLING IN CONTEXT

understands them, that are not addressed in that resolution.[79] This indicates that beyond being a pure mechanism of implementation of international obligations, the PSI plays an important role in determining meaning and scope of existing legal rules through the co-ordinated practice of their members. This is related to the thin line that exists between the implementation and the creation of international law and coalitions of the willing tend to take advantage of it; nothing more, but nothing less.

The multilayered approach does not stop there. Co-ordinated efforts among like-minded states within coalitions like the PSI are also aimed at enhancing 'legal frameworks' – i.e., shaping legal regimes.[80] According to the SIP, participants will 'work to strengthen when necessary relevant international law and frameworks in appropriate ways to support these [the PSI's] commitments'.[81] And, as documented by Natalie Klein, officials from core participants have emphasized this function, most remarkably the former National Security Advisor of the USA, Condoleezza Rice, who mentioned in regard to the PSI that the USA is 'also seeking ways to expand those [national and international legal] authorities'.[82]

As it is widely acknowledged,[83] a major contribution of the PSI in strengthening international law was the 2005 adoption of the *Protocol to the 1988 Convention for the Suppression of Unlawful Acts Against the Safety of Maritime Navigation*, also known as the 2005 SUA Protocol.[84]

---

[79] Although proliferation to and from Iran and North Korea have been addressed in several resolutions within the respective sanction regimes; see SC Res. 1737 (2006), and SC Res. 1718 (2006), and subsequent resolutions, respectively.

[80] I use the term 'legal regime' in this context in one of the three understandings of the term 'special regime' identified by the International Law Commission (ILC), namely as 'formed by a set of special rules, including rights and obligations, relating to a special subject matter. Such rules may concern a geographical area (e.g., a treaty on the protection of a particular river) or some substantive matter (e.g., a treaty on the regulation of the uses of a particular weapon). Such a special regime may emerge on the basis of a single treaty, several treaties, or treaty and treaties plus non-treaty developments (subsequent practice and custom)'. See ILC, *Report on the Work of its Fifty-Eighth Session (1 May–9 June and 3 July–11 August 2006)*, UN Doc. A/61/10 (2006), Chapter XII (*Conclusions of the Work of the Study Group on the Fragmentation of International Law: Difficulties arising from the Diversification and Expansion of International Law*), p. 400, at p. 411.

[81] SIP, III.

[82] Quoted in Klein, *Maritime Security*, p. 205.

[83] See Maximiliam Malirsch and Florian Prill, 'The Proliferation Security Initiative and the 2005 Protocol to the SUA Convention' (2007) 67 *Zeitschrift für ausländisches öffentliches Recht und Völkerrecht* 229, at 236 et seq. Commenting on the negotiations and anticipating the outcome, see Byers, 'Policing the High Seas', 530.

[84] See Chapter 4, note 115.

5.2 COALITIONS' JURISGENERATIVE CAPACITY   173

In that case, PSI endorsing states, led by the USA, took an active part in the negotiations of the Protocol, which introduces the criminalization of WMD transport by merchant vessels on the high seas and provides procedures for boarding suspected vessels on the high seas with the flag state's consent.[85] No doubt this is another instance of informal standards accelerating developments in the law, this time through a co-ordinated bargaining effort that took place in London, supported and guided by what was already agreed upon informally by a considerable number of states. In a way, it could be said that for those states parties to the 2005 SUA Protocol and participants of the PSI, the customary rule embodied in Article 110 UNCLOS[86] has been supplemented in the sense that, in cases of proliferation concern, flag states should *seriously consider giving* their consent to other parties (to the SUA Protocol) and participants (of the PSI) for interdicting their merchant vessels: 'participating States parties' is a notion used in the framework of some coalitions – the NSS, e.g. – which gives account of the juxtaposing nature of legal obligations and non-legal commitments that result from such cross-regime interactions (between formal and informal regimes). The informal PSI principle and the formal SUA rules hence become mutually reinforcing in their application – i.e., in their efficacy.

While most concerns on the legality of the PSI have been raised in relation to interdiction activities on the high seas, some states[87] have questioned the interdiction commitments contained in the SIP that affect participating states' ports, internal, and territorial waters.[88] Special attention deserves the commitment to stop, search, and seize foreign vessels, which are 'reasonably suspected of carrying [WMD and related] cargoes to or from states and non-state actors of proliferation concern'[89] in the territorial seas of PSI participants, since this could eventually contradict

---

[85] See 2005 SUA Protocol, Arts. 3bis and 8bis, as well as Malirsch and Prill, 237–238.

[86] See Chapter 4, note 98.

[87] This is the case of Indonesia and Mexico, for example. On Indonesia, see above Chapter 4, notes 82 and 137, and accompanying text; on Mexico, see the interview with Ambassador Juan Manuel Gómez Robledo, former Undersecretary for Human Rights and Multilateral Affairs of the Mexican Ministry of Foreign Relations, *Stockholm International Peace Research Institute* (SIPRI) (10 October 2012), at www.youtube.com/watch?v=-ffqY1xlmVc (when asked about Mexico's possible future participation in the PSI, Ambassador Gómez Robledo mentioned that his country has an issue with interdiction powers in territorial seas conferred to PSI participants, which, in Mexico's view, causes troubles in regard to UNCLOS).

[88] See SIP, IV (4).

[89] Ibid.

174 COALITIONS OF THE WILLING IN CONTEXT

the right of innocent passage, which, according to Article 17 UNCLOS, all states, whether coastal or landlocked, enjoy through the territorial sea of other states.[90] This right is not absolute, and Article 25 UNCLOS establishes rights of protection for the coastal state in those cases where the passage is not innocent. So, the question is whether the transport of WMD, their delivery systems, and related materials to or from 'states or non-state actor of proliferation concern', whatever that means, amount to non-innocent passage according to the relevant UNCLOS provisions, which here again reflect customary international law.[91]

Article 19 UNCLOS defines 'innocent passage' as that which is 'not prejudicial to the peace, good order or security *of the coastal State*'.[92] At the same time, it should be added, Article 19 (2) (a) mentions that passage of a ship shall be considered prejudicial to the coastal state's peace, security or good order, if it engages in 'any threat or use of force against the sovereignty, territorial integrity or political independence of the coastal State, *or in any other manner in violation of the principles of international law embodied in the Charter of the United Nations*'.[93] This has been interpreted as not restricting eventual threats posed by the transport of WMD to the peace, security, or good order of the coastal state alone.[94] However, even among those who regard this provision as 'wide enough to encompass threats directed against States others than the coastal State',[95] this reading is made with caution and reference is made

---

[90] UNCLOS, Art. 17.

[91] See The *'ARA Libertad' (Argentina v. Ghana), Provisional Measures (Order)*, ITLOS Case No. 20 (15 December 2012), paras. 40–42; ICJ Reports (2001) *Maritime Delimitation and Territorial Questions between Qatar and Bahrain (Qatar v. Bahrain), Merits, Judgement* (16 March 2001), p. 40, at para. 223 and 252 (2) (b); ICJ Reports (1986) *Military and Paramilitary Activities In and Against Nicaragua (Nicaragua v. United States of America), Merits, Judgment* (27 June 1986), p. 14, at para. 214; ICJ Reports (1949) *Corfu Channel Case (United Kingdom of Great Britain and Northern Ireland v. Albania), Judgment* (9 April 1949), p. 4, at pp. 28, 30–31, 35; see also International Tribunal for the Law of the Sea (ITLOS), Statement by the President of the Tribunal, Rüdiger Wolfrum, *Freedom of Navigation: New Challenges* (2008), p. 8, at www.itlos.org/fileadmin/itlos/documents/statements_of_president/wolfrum/freedom_navigation_080108_eng.pdf.

[92] UNCLOS, Art. 19 (1). Emphasis added.

[93] UNCLOS, Art. 19 (2) (a). Emphasis added.

[94] See Joyner, *International Law and the Proliferation of Weapons of Mass Destruction*, p. 317; cf. Klein, *Maritime Security*, p. 201 (referring to Joyner and seemingly subscribing the same position, but, in any case, preferring a wider interpretation in favour of 'the entitlement of the coastal State to take steps').

[95] R. R. Churchill and A.-V. Lowe, *The Law of the Sea*, third edition, (Manchester: Manchester University Press, 1999), p. 85.

5.2 COALITIONS' JURISGENERATIVE CAPACITY 175

subsequently to state practice that has favoured a narrower reading of Article 19.[96] It should be underlined that the chapeau of Article 19 (2) UNCLOS clearly refers to activities 'prejudicial to the coastal State'. Accordingly, the former president of the International Tribunal for the Law of the Sea (ITLOS), Rüdiger Wolfrum, has stated in that capacity that according to Article 19, the coastal state 'may act in its own interest only'.[97] Others follow a similar interpretation and highlight that as long as there are no intentions to carry out activities directed against the coastal state, a foreign vessel carrying WMD, their delivery systems, or related materials that passes through the territorial sea of another state would not represent a non-innocent passage and thus be entitled to that right, even if these weapons or materials constituted a threat for a third state.[98]

Yet other commentators have suggested that in order to perform interdiction activities in their territorial waters against foreign merchant vessels, PSI participating states would have to enact relevant legislation criminalizing WMD transport.[99] The SIP calls participants to 'review and work to strengthen their relevant national legal authorities where necessary to accomplish' the PSI's objectives.[100] Thus, this would seem to be a pertinent means for bringing the said objectives in conformity with the right of innocent passage. This argument is raised in connection with Articles 21 and 27 UNCLOS, since the former permits the coastal state to adopt laws and regulations in relation to the right of innocent passage and the latter establishes the bases for exercising criminal jurisdiction on board of a foreign vessel passing through its territorial sea.

According to Wolfrum, the issues that may be regulated in terms of Article 21 do not cover 'the mere transit' of WMD, and in the case of Article 27, 'again, either the coastal State's action has to be taken in defence of its own interests or it has to be taken at the request of the

---

[96] Ibid., pp. 85–87.

[97] Wolfrum, 'Freedom of Navigation', p. 9.

[98] Cf. Klein, *Maritime Security*, pp. 200–201 (referring, among others, to Natalio Ronzitti); see also Guilfoyle, 'Maritime Interdiction of Weapons of Mass Destruction', 16–17 (highlighting that Art. 19 refers to external acts of the ships, and that it is difficult to see how 'a latent threat in the vessel's hold, destined elsewhere, has any 'external' manifestation capable of affecting the character of passage'; however, Guilfoyle finds a basis for such jurisdiction on different grounds, see note 105).

[99] See Valencia, 'Is the PSI Really the Cornerstone of a New International Norm?', 125 (with further references).

[100] PSI, SIP, III.

master of the ship or of the flag State or for suppression of illicit traffic in narcotic drugs or psychotropic substances'.[101] Thus, according to this reading, there are important restrictions on the coastal state's criminal jurisdiction over foreign vessels on lateral passage, which would render interdictions on foreign vessels in the territorial seas of PSI participants problematic, even if appropriate legislation were in place. It is in this sense that the former president of ITLOS has referred to the respective paragraph of the SIP (IV (4)) as the 'most problematic' measure of the PSI in regard to the principle of *mare liberum*.[102]

But other commentators have pointed to the fact that Article 27 (1) UNCLOS mentions that the coastal state's criminal jurisdiction '*should not* be exercised ... save only' in the cases there provided. This strongly suggests that the exercise of such jurisdiction is 'not strictly prohibited in other cases'.[103] Douglas Guilfoyle emphasizes that other prohibitions on national legislation in the same Section of UNCLOS are phrased in mandatory language ('shall not' as opposed to 'should not'). For him, in combination with SC resolution 1540, which mentions that states 'shall adopt and enforce appropriate effective laws which prohibit any non-State actor to ... transport' WMD,[104] this capacity to act in the territorial sea becomes an *obligation*.[105] Of course, this obligation would only concern the transport to and from non-state actors, as resolution 1540 does not address states of proliferation concern as the PSI Principles do. But this, in turn, would mean also that states *can* supplement the exceptions to the prohibition on criminal jurisdiction on territorial waters established in Article 27 UNCLOS in the sense of PSI's fourth interdiction principle.

What these examples on PSI's practice and principles show is that without the need of formally amending Article 110, or Article 27 (1) UNCLOS, or of engaging in a long and uncertain route towards the generation of new customary rules, there are other means derived from the interplay among informal and formal regimes that are very efficient at shaping the law, which does not mean to break it, as the example on the right of innocent passage shows.

---

[101] Wolfrum, 'Freedom of Navigation', p. 9 (references in brackets omitted).

[102] Wolfrum, 'Freedom of Navigation', p. 8.

[103] Yoshifumi Tanaka, *The International Law of the Sea* (Cambridge: Cambridge University Press, 2012), p. 95; see also Guilfoyle, 'Maritime Interdiction', 17.

[104] UN Doc., S/RES/1540 (2004), op. 2.

[105] Guilfoyle, 'Maritime Interdiction', 17. Emphasis added.

5.2.2 Specifying and Developing SC Resolutions: The FATF

The FATF holds a close relationship with the SC,[106] in particular with its two most important subsidiary organs in charge of counter-terrorism – i.e., the Counter-Terrorism Committee (CTC) and the ISIL (Da'esh)/Al-Qaida Sanctions Committee. Since the FATF expanded its mandate to include the financing of proliferation of WMD in 2008, this relationship also comprises the subsidiary organs of the Council dealing with counter-proliferation – i.e., the 1540 Committee as well as the sanctions committee on North Korea. The work of this task force is so deeply rooted into that of the counter-terrorism, counter-proliferation, and sanctions committees that we can fairly speak of the FATF as an informal arm of the SC. In contrast to the PSI, which has not been explicitly recognized in a SC resolution, especially due to China's resistance, which dates back to the drafting history of resolution 1540 (2004),[107] the FATF has enjoyed explicit recognition by the SC since 2005.[108]

The FATF and the FSRBs regularly brief the CTC and the ISIL (Da'esh)/Al-Qaida Sanctions Committee. The purpose of these briefings is to inform on the concrete measures taken by the FATF in the framework of its co-operation with the Council, particularly regarding its involvement in technical assistance to UN member states. Open briefings to the wider UN membership have been organized by all the committees mentioned above with the participation of FATF's highest-ranking officials. In those meetings, FATF representatives raise awareness about the benefits of the FATF recommendations and guidelines in assisting all countries to effectively implement SC counter-terrorism and counter-proliferation obligations.[109] In addition, the FATF and the

---

[106] The interactions of the FATF with formal institutions in relation to counter-terrorism activities go far beyond the SC, involving the General Assembly's UN Global Counter-Terrorism Strategy, particularly its Counter-Terrorism Implementation Task Force (CTITF) and relevant agencies of the UN system, such as the Vienna based UN Office on Drugs and Crime (UNODC) and particularly its Terrorism Prevention Branch. The co-operation of the FATF with the World Bank and the International Monetary Fund (IMF) is quite intense too. However, the interplay with the SC remains the most active and important one, especially in light of its mutually reinforcing character – i.e., the FATF's role in advancing the implementation of SC resolutions, and the SC's role in promoting the observance of FATF recommendations.

[107] See note 76.

[108] See SC Res.1617 (29 July 2005), op. 7.

[109] See, for instance, Vladimir Nechaev, *Remarks of FATF President at the Open Briefing by the 1267 (Al Qaïda), 1373 (Counter-Terrorism), 1540 (Non-proliferation), 1718 (DPKR), 1737 (Iran) AND 1988 (Taliban) Security Council Sanctions Committees and the FATF*

178   COALITIONS OF THE WILLING IN CONTEXT

FSRBs take active part in workshops on capacity building, which take place under the auspices of these SC committees, especially the CTC and its influential experts' group, the Counter-Terrorism Executive Directorate (CTED). These activities often involve the General Assembly's Counter-Terrorism Implementation Task Force (CTITF), UNODC, as well as INTERPOL.

Moreover, the FATF has participated in country visits conducted by CTED.[110] This is remarkable because these visits are aimed at assessing the respective member states' implementation status of SC resolutions on counter-terrorism. Once a CTED-led country visit takes place, an implementation-monitoring procedure is set in motion: CTED produces a country visit report, identifying the successes and shortfalls and issuing recommendations. Visited states can comment on the report, which is discussed and eventually – usually – adopted by the CTC and then sent back, as a Council document, to the visited state, which in turn has 120 days to inform the CTC on how it has responded to the recommendations.[111] The participation of the FATF in these country visits thus suggests the involvement of this informal network in the monitoring of UN member states' compliance with SC obligations, including those counter-terrorism treaties that the SC calls on states to implement.[112] It must be said that CTED-conducted country visits require the respective states' consent. However, considerable pressure is exercised by CTED's officers, who frequently approach states' representatives, and states tend to succumb to this pressure, also in order to demonstrate their willingness to engage actively in the international fight against terrorism. Incentives are attached to these visits too, as states tend to benefit from the

---

(18 November 2013), at www.fatf-gafi.org/topics/fatfrecommendations/documents/unscs-nov-13.html; see also Je-Yoon Shin, *Keynote speech by FATF President at the Joint UN/FATF open briefing on depriving terrorist groups of sources of funding* (14 April 2016), at www.fatf-gafi.org/publications/fatfgeneral/documents/keynote-un-fatf-open-briefing-apr-2016.html.

[110] There is documentation on FATF participation in CTED-conducted country visits regarding Azerbaijan, India and Morocco, see Cable: 09USUNNEWYORK693_a: Financial Action Task Force President Briefs CTC (29 October 2009), at https://wikileaks.org/plusd/cables/09USUNNEWYORK963_a.html.

[111] See the *Guidelines of the Counter-Terrorism Committee for Post-Visit Follow-Up* (adopted by the CTC on 11 December 2012), at www.un.org/sc/ctc/wp-content/uploads/2016/09/2012-12-11_CTC_guidelines_post-visit.pdf.

[112] See SC Res. 1373 (28 September 2001), op. 3 (e).

5.2 COALITIONS' JURISGENERATIVE CAPACITY 179

'seal', so to speak, obtained from having undergone such a review of their counter-terrorism capabilities, as well as from receiving capacity building, which is offered in the framework of such visits.[113]

The identification of gaps in implementation legislation and institutional capacities is CTED's main job[114] and ultimately the principal objective of the CTC as a monitoring body.[115] However, as important as the identification of gaps is the facilitation of co-operation between these countries and donors delivering technical assistance. Although the FATF is not included in the roster of donors administered by CTED, this list is not exhaustive,[116] and the FATF, in particularly through its global network of regional bodies, is one of the main donors of technical assistance to UN member states regarding the combat against the financing of terrorism, proliferation, and related issues. This includes assistance in the drafting of national legislation, law-enforcement measures, and issues regarding the strengthening of national institutions' counter-terrorism capabilities.

Recommendations of the SC subsidiary organs on how to best implement the obligations contained in the respective resolutions, particularly regarding the financial sanctions – i.e. the assets freeze – often refer to the FATF recommendations, their interpretative notes, and other documents.[117] These guidelines of the subsidiary organs are usually prepared

---

[113] This becomes relevant, for example, in the view of candidatures presented by states or their cities for organizing major international sports or cultural events, though here the capacity-building measures offered by the FATF are less relevant than those offered – e.g., by the United Nations Interregional Crime and Research Institute (UNICRI) with its expertise on urban security.

[114] On CTED's mandate, see SC Res. 1535 (26 March 2004).

[115] Besides country-visit reports, CTED also produces the so-called Overview of Implementation Assessment (OIA) and the Detailed Implementation Assessment (DIS). OIAs consist of general conclusions drawn from the DIS – i.e. from the detailed data on a country's implementation status of resolutions 1373 and 1624. The OIA is discussed and eventually approved by the CTC, and shared with the respective state in order to initiate the 'dialogue' on how to improve implementation; DIS is an internal working document of the CTC which is not shared with the respective state in order to avoid prolonged contestation (see *Revised procedures for the Counter-Terrorism Committee's Stocktaking of Member States' Implementation of Security Council Resolutions 1373 (2001) and 1624 (2005)* (adopted by the CTC on 11 March 2013), at www.un.org/sc/ctc/wp-content/uploads/2016/09/2013-03-11-stocktaking_revised_procedures.pdf.

[116] Available at CTC, *List of Donors Working with CTED to Provide Technical Assistance*, at https://www.un.org/sc/ctc/resources/technical-assistance/.

[117] See, for example, the *CTC Directory of International Best Practices, Codes and Standards Relevant to the Implementation of Security Council Resolution 1373 (2001)* [hereinafter

180   COALITIONS OF THE WILLING IN CONTEXT

by their expert bodies and endorsed by the committees, and are non-binding.[118] However, since they stem from organs of the SC, these recommendations have an authoritative imprint. This is particularly visible in the case of CTC's recommendations to UN member states to follow the FATF's recommendations, interpretative notes, compilations of best practices, and other documents, including documents from the FSRBs,[119] in order to achieve better implementation of operative paragraph (op.) 1 of SC resolution 1373, which addresses the prevention and suppression of the financing of terrorism.[120] One can almost randomly open a country report pursuant to op. 6 of that resolution and find detailed information about the respective state's implementation measures on the FATF '40 + 9' recommendations, as well as of their overall co-operation with this informal body.[121] Moreover, a state's mutual evaluation assessment under the FATF is often reported as an indicator that helps to assess that state's compliance with SC resolution 1373.[122] The peer review process countries undertake in the framework of the FATF has become a highly valuable tool for the work of the CTC, so much so that today the SC 'encourages CTED to work closely with the FATF, including in the FATF's mutual evaluation process, focusing on effective implementation of counter terrorist financing recommendations'.[123]

It is thus not difficult to see how the interplay between the CTC and FATF has become vital in furthering compliance with SC resolution

---

'CTC, *Directory of Best Practices (1373)*'], at www.un.org/sc/ctc/resources/databases/recommended-international-practices-codes-and-standards/united-nations-security-council-resolution-1373-2001/.

[118] CTED, *Technical Guide to the Implementation of Security Council Resolution 1373 (2001) and Other Relevant Resolutions* (New York: compiled by CTED in 2017) [hereinafter 'CTED, *Technical Guide (1373)*'], p. 5.

[119] See CTC, *Directory of Best Practices (1373)*.

[120] See SC Res. 1373, op. 1.

[121] Country Reports regarding the implementation of SC resolution 1373 are publicly available only until 2006 (that is why they refer to the '40+9' recommendations); see CTC, *Reports by Member States*, at www.un.org/sc/ctc/resources/assessments/.

[122] See, *inter alia*, the reports by Mexico (*Fifth Report of Mexico to the Counter-Terrorism Committee Established Pursuant to United Nations Security Council Resolution 1373 (2001), Submitted in Response to the Request by the Chairman of the Committee in Her Note of 3 March 2006 (S/AC.40/2006/OC.62)*, enclosed in UN Doc. S/RES/2006/447 (30 June 2006), p. 11; the Russian Federation (*Reply of the Russian Federation to the Letter Dated 21 October 2005 from the Counter-Terrorism Committee Chairman, Ms. Ellen Margrethe Løj*, enclosed in UN Doc. S/2006/98 (13 February 2006), p. 20); and Spain (*Report Submitted pursuant paragraph 6 of Security Council Resolution 1373 (2001) of 28 September 2001*, enclosed in UN Doc. S/2004/523 (29 June 2004), p. 6).

[123] SC Res. 2129 (17 December 2013), op. 17.

5.2 COALITIONS' JURISGENERATIVE CAPACITY 181

1373. At the same time, the recognition by the Council of the 'comprehensive international standards embodied in the FATF's revised Forty Recommendations',[124] and the constant call by the CTC and CTED to observe them, exercises a significant compliance pull towards these formally non-binding standards and the rest of the work produced by the task force. The FATF mentions that although its standards are

> not binding instruments under international law; however, when combined with other FATF processes and mechanisms, there has been an increasing pressure for all countries to implement them.[125]

This increasing pressure is not exercised by the FATF and the FSRBs alone, but by formal institutions as well – most remarkably by the SC, through processes and mechanisms that are increasingly linked to those of the FATF. This mutually enforcing dynamic is further evidenced by the participation of CTED in the peer review process of the FATF, and of the latter, at least occasionally, in the country visits that are carried out under the auspices of the CTC. 'Awareness-raising' activities and the key role that the FATF plays – mainly through its regional bodies – in technical assistance delivered to UN member states for purposes of implementing the obligations imposed on them by the SC are other efficient tools of this approach to countering the financing of terrorism and related activities, in which formal and informal norms overlap, not because of deficiencies in rule-making such as unintended norm redundancies, but by design. Repetition plays a key role in strengthening the rules' efficacy and the regime's overall efficiency.

However, the FATF not only contributes to the effective implementation of SC resolutions by augmenting the pressure on states and adding layers to the monitoring mechanism. Guidance on the implementation of rules – binding or non-binding, formal or informal – is almost necessarily linked to the interpretation, and, at times, the evolution of these rules. Telling how a rule is best applied is also pronouncing on what the rule actually means in this or that respect. For instance, the chapeau of op. 1 of resolution 1373, which only mentions that states 'shall prevent and suppress the financing of terrorist acts', has been subject to far-reaching interpretations by the CTC and CTED concerning the concrete institutional measures states are supposed to adopt in this regard, including

---

[124] Ibid.
[125] See FATF, *20 Years of the FAFT Recommendations (1990–2010)*, pp. 4–5, at www.cbr.ru/StaticHtml/File/36801/20_years.pdf.

182   COALITIONS OF THE WILLING IN CONTEXT

on cross-border control of cash couriers and the regulation of informal remittance systems, like the *hawala*.[126] Among these institutional measures, states are called by CTC's *Directory of International Best Practices, Codes and Standards Relevant to the Implementation of Security Council Resolution 1373 (2001)*, as well as by CTED's *Technical Guide to the Implementation of Security Council Resolution 1373 (2001)*, to establish, or to enhance existing Financial Intelligence Units (FIUs) within their ministries of finance, following the standards and best practices on these units as developed by the FATF.[127] The establishment of FIUs has long been requested by the task force, and is now contemplated in its recommendation 29. According to this recommendation, FIUs should serve 'as a national centre for the receipt and analysis of: (a) suspicious transaction reports and (b) other information relevant to money laundering, associated predicate offences and terrorist financing, and for the dissemination of the results of that analysis'.[128]

Another example is the criminalization of the financing of terrorism. Resolution 1373 establishes that states shall criminalize the financing of terrorist acts, but does not cover the funding of terrorist organizations:

> Criminalize the wilful provision or collection, by any means, directly or indirectly, of funds by their nationals or in their territories with the intention that the funds should be used, or in the knowledge that they are to be used, in order to carry out terrorist acts;[129]

The *1999 International Convention for the Suppression of the Financing of Terrorism*, which resolution 1373 calls upon UN member states to ratify and fully implement, mentions the financing of terrorist organizations only in the preamble, but focuses on the financing of terrorist acts in its Article 2.[130] In contrast, FATF' recommendation 5 explicitly requires the criminalization of this sort of funding:

---

[126] The *hawala* is an ancient system of money transfer that plays a significant role in the economies of several states in the Middle East, North Africa, and the Horn of Africa, as well as in the Indian subcontinent. According to some authors, the measures taken by the FATF against the *hawala* have caused serious damage to the economy in Somalia; see, for example, Heng and McDonagh, *Risk, Global Governance and Security*, pp. 140–141 (with further references).

[127] See CTED, *Technical Guide (1373)*, p. 10; as well as CTC, *Directory of Best Practices (1373)*.

[128] *FATF Recommendations*, recommendation 29, p. 24.

[129] SC Res. 1373, op. 1 (b).

[130] *1999 International Convention for the Suppression of the Financing of Terrorism*, 2178 UNTS 197 (the sixth paragraph of the preamble recalls 'General Assembly

5.2 COALITIONS' JURISGENERATIVE CAPACITY 183

> Countries should criminalise terrorist financing on the basis of the Terrorist Financing Convention, and should criminalise not only the financing of terrorist acts but also the financing of terrorist organisations and individual terrorists even in the absence of a link to a specific terrorist act or acts. Countries should ensure that such offences are designated as money laundering predicate offences.[131]

One could regard this recommendation just as a stand-alone informal standard that contributes, on a voluntary basis, to the international combat against the financing of terrorism. This would already be significant given the reach of FATF recommendations that goes beyond its members. But it is questionable to what extent states have a realistic option not to follow these standards. In the face of the whole compliance mechanism that backs them, ranging from peer review and naming and shaming procedures to the so-called 'counter-measures' to which non-cooperative jurisdictions, including non-FATF members, are exposed,[132] the lack of a formal legal authority emitting these standards does not seem to make a difference in terms of their efficacy, and the perception of states as *having an obligation* to follow them.[133] I will return to this issue in the next chapter since it is closely related to the concept of international law and the ways informal law is affecting it. For now, suffice it to mention that, in practical terms, FATF recommendations and the interpretations of them made by that network through its interpretative notes, guidelines, and other documents, add to the universe of rules to be followed by states in the international fight against terrorism, constituting an important element of that normative regime. In practice, there can be little doubt that FATF recommendation 5, *inter alia*, has become an integral part of resolution 1373, op. 1. This is a clear example of how informal norms have considerable effects on legal rules, specifying their meaning, or even adding meaning to them. But how can we cope with it in legal terms?

---

resolution 51/210 of 17 December 1996, paragraph 3, subparagraph (f), in which the Assembly called upon all States to take steps to prevent and counteract, through appropriate domestic measures, the financing of terrorists and terrorist organizations').

[131] *FATF Recommendations*, recommendation 5, p. 13.

[132] For an analysis of these 'counter-measures', see Chapter 6, Section 6.1.2.2.

[133] For Hart, the distinction between *having an obligation* and *being obliged* is crucial for the concept of law as it strictly relates to the internal point of view and, hence, to the rule of recognition, see H. L. A. Hart, *The Concept of Law*, second edition (Oxford: Clarendon Press, 1997), pp. 6, 82–91.

184 COALITIONS OF THE WILLING IN CONTEXT

The Council's recognition of these informal norms as the 'comprehensive international standards'[134] on the subject matter, and the way that the CTC integrates them as appropriate measures that states should follow in order to comply with their international obligations on the prevention and suppression of terrorism, hints towards an interpretation of resolution 1373, and subsequent ones. In the end, states are asked by the Council to criminalize both the funding of terrorist acts and of terrorist organizations, as well as associated money laundering, while implementing resolution 1373, op. 1 (a). This is shown by the *Technical Guide to the Implementation of Security Resolution 1373 (2001)*, in which CTED qualifies FATF recommendation 5 as the international standard and good practice that guides the '[a]nalysis of Member States' implementation of those measures'.[135] 'Best' or 'good practices' reflect standards followed by many states that may assist others in complying with their SC obligations. It is therefore even more significant that the Council, through the CTC, monitors that the proscription of the financing of terrorist acts *and* organizations is incorporated into national penal and financial codes, as well as that these offences are both stand-alone and predicate offences to money laundering. In doing this, the SC acts as if the recommendation of the FATF was to be read into its resolution.

Hence, we are in presence of a far-reaching interpretation of resolution 1373 and subsequent ones, through the practice of the CTC, which actually modifies the main obligation by adding the connection of the financing of terrorism to money laundering. In his seminal article on the interpretation of SC resolutions, Michael Wood notes that 'Sanctions Committees in effect interpret their respective [SC resolutions] whenever they apply them'.[136] The same holds true, no doubt, for other subsidiary organs like the CTC. Wood also asks if these interpretations have the same status as those that the SC makes in subsequent resolutions or presidential statements, for example, and that may amount to subsequent agreements of the members of the Council regarding the interpretation of previous resolutions. As recognized in doctrine and by the ICJ, the rules of treaty interpretation contained in Articles 31–32 of the *1969 Vienna*

---

[134] See, *inter alia*, SC Res. 2129, op. 17.
[135] CTED, *Technical Guide (1373)*, p. 7.
[136] Michael C. Wood, 'The Interpretation of Security Council Resolutions', in Jochen A. Frowein and Rüdiger Wolfrum (eds.), *Max Planck Yearbook of United Nations Law*, volume 2 (1998), p. 73, at p. 84.

5.2 COALITIONS' JURISGENERATIVE CAPACITY 185

Convention on the Law of Treaties,[137] are auxiliary in interpreting SC resolutions.[138] This is relevant in the present context since subsequent agreements and practice of the Council on its resolutions constitute authentic interpretations of the latter.[139] An authentic interpretation, without being binding *per se* or necessarily conclusive, carries more weight than other, non-authentic means of interpretation, because it reflects an objective element of the conduct of the member states of the SC, which itself reflects a common understanding of these members as to the meaning of the resolution.[140] Other means of interpretation of subsidiary organs are still relevant, and 'may, depending on the circumstances, be highly persuasive',[141] but they would hardly support evolutive interpretations of SC resolutions, which in some cases are very difficult to distinguish from actual modifications. The criminalization of the funding of terrorist organizations in addition to the funding of terrorist acts is a case in point for this thin line between interpretation and modification.

---

[137] *1969 Vienna Convention on the Law of Treaties*, 1155 UNTS 332 [hereinafter VCLT].

[138] In the words of the ICJ, the Vienna rules 'may provide guidance' in the interpretation of SC resolutions; see ICJ Reports (2010) *Accordance with International Law of the Unilateral Declaration of Independence in Respect of Kosovo*, Advisory Opinion (22 July 2010), p. 403, at p. 442; see also, Wood, 'The Interpretation', p. 85.

[139] See Wood, 'The Interpretation', p. 82 (referring to the *Jaworzina* advisory opinion of the Permanent Court of International Justice (PCIJ)), in which the PCIJ reaffirmed the principle that the right to interpret authoritatively a legal rule belongs to the body who has the power to modify that rule, see PCIJ, *Jaworzina Advisory Opinion* (6 December 1932); PCIJ Series B, No. 8, 37). Although the usage of the terms 'authoritative interpretation' and 'authentic interpretation' is confusing, it can safely be said in this context (as in many others) that both refer to an interpretation of an authoritative character but that is not binding *per se*.

[140] Here, I follow (*mutatis mutandis*) the work of the ILC on subsequent agreement and subsequent practice in relation to the interpretation of treaties, see ILC, *Report on the Work of Its Sixty-Eight Session (2 May–10 June and 4 July–12 August 2016)*, UN Doc. A/71/10 (2016), *Chapter IV* [hereinafter 'ILC, *Report on the Work of its Sixty-Eight Session*, Chapter IV'], pp. 132–134. It must be said, however, that the ILC distinguishes between 'authentic interpretation' and 'authentic means of interpretation', arguing that the former suggests a necessarily conclusive or binding interpretation, whereas the latter does not. In this sense, draft conclusion 3, adopted on first reading in 2016, speaks of 'authentic means', since subsequent practice and agreements are not binding *per se*. I think this is confusing. All interpretations – authentic or not – are the product of the application of certain means of interpretations (methods). Accordingly, subsequent practice and agreements are means of interpretation that, because of the authors of the interpretation they presuppose (i.e., states parties or, in our case, the members of the organ), give rise to authentic interpretations. This reading is in line with the *Jaworzina Advisory Opinion* (see above note 139), as well as with Wood, 'The Interpretation', p. 137, and Kelsen, *Reine Rechtslehre*, pp. 346–354.

[141] Wood, 'The Interpretation', p. 84.

186 COALITIONS OF THE WILLING IN CONTEXT

As Wood convincingly argues, a SC subsidiary organ may undertake authentic interpretations of SC resolutions, whenever the Council authorizes it to do so.[142] So, the crucial question here is whether the CTC is authorized by the SC to interpret these resolutions? Although the Council has not given an express mandate to the CTC for interpreting its resolutions, it constantly refers to the role of this organ in implementation activities, which cannot be divorced from interpretations. For instance, the *Declaration on the Global Effort to Combat Terrorism*, adopted at the level of foreign ministers, calls on the CTC to 'explore ways in which States may be assisted' in the implementation of resolution 1373, such as 'the promotion of best-practices in the areas covered by resolution 1373 (2001), including the preparation of model laws as appropriate'.[143] Other resolutions request the Committee 'to develop a set of best practices to assist states in implementing the provisions of Resolution 1373 (2001) related to the financing of terrorism'.[144] Thus, there are elements supporting the view that the SC has entrusted the CTC with the task of interpreting these resolutions. If this is correct, the Council would not need to endorse each reading of the CTC, and the latter's subsequent practice in the application of resolutions 1373 and 1624 would arguably reflect an agreement of the Council regarding their interpretation. This would not make such interpretations binding or necessarily conclusive, but they would have to be taken into account.[145]

This, of course, does not hinder the SC from expressly reaffirming the interpretations made by the CTC. For instance, in a presidential statement (PRST) of 2013, the SC, while acknowledging the 'important work' of the FATF, underlies the 'continued need to prevent and suppress the financing of terrorism *and terrorist organizations*'.[146] This PRST has a similar effect as a subsequent agreement in terms of Article 31 (3) (a) VCLT.[147] It is a rather clear evidence of the

---

[142] See ibid., p. 91.

[143] SC Res. 1377 (12 November 2001), para. 13

[144] SC Res. 1566 (8 October 2004), op. 7.

[145] Cf. ILC, *Report on the Work of Its Sixty-Eight Session*, Chapter IV, pp. 133–134.

[146] UN Doc. S/PRST/2013/1 (15 January 2013), para. 13.

[147] On the role of PRSTs as subsequent agreements to resolutions, see Wood, 'The Interpretation', p. 91 (mentioning that the equivalent of Art. 31 (3) (a) VCLT would be 'a subsequent resolution . . . or other formal act by the Council regarding the interpretation or application of a resolution'); see also Stefan Talmon, 'The Statements by the President of the Security Council' (2003) 2 *Chinese Journal of International Law* 419, at 455 (commenting that 'presidential statements may be used as a means of interpretation in

5.2 COALITIONS' JURISGENERATIVE CAPACITY 187

agreement of the members of the SC regarding the interpretation of Resolution 1373 op. 1 (a), which confirms the understanding established through the subsequent practice of the CTC in the application of this norm.

There is quite a lot happening in terms of normative evolution of SC resolutions through the interpretative work of subsidiary organs; so much so that we can speak of resolutions 1373 and 1624 as 'framework international laws' that are further developed through the regulatory work of the CTC. In addition, the SC '[u]nderscores the essential role of CTED within the United Nations to assess issues and trends relating to the implementation of resolutions 1373 (2001) and 1624 (2005)', and directs this special political mission under the auspices of the CTC 'to identify emerging issues, trends and developments related' to the implementation of said resolutions.[148] The 'assessment of issues and trends', which CTED is required to perform, deserves further attention since these evaluations can often be regarded as evolutive interpretations of the respective SC resolutions.[149] This functions through the dissemination of expert knowledge. For instance, the constant repetition by CTED – strongly supported by the Analytical Support and Sanctions Monitoring Team of the ISIL (Da'esh)/Al-Qaida Committee (Monitoring Team) – of the narrative that informal or 'alternative' remittance systems like the *hawala* represent major risks for the financing of terrorism has led to the adoption of this assessment by the CTC as an important element states have to consider while preventing and suppressing terrorism. There can be little doubt that today the regulation of and the restrictions upon this traditional and culturally anchored system of money transfer are part and parcel of the measures states are required to take in accordance with resolution 1373, op. 1.[150] These risk assessments are often directly taken from the diverse studies on

---

the sense of Article 31, paragraphs 2 (a) and 3 (a) of the *Vienna Convention on the Law of Treaties* to establish the context of the resolution').

[148] SC Res. 2129, op. 4 and 5.

[149] Elsewhere, I have examined this instance of interplay in relation to its repercussions on targeted sanctions, see Alejandro Rodiles, 'The Design of UN Sanctions through the Interplay with Informal Arrangements', in Larissa van den Herik (ed.), *Research Handbook on UN Sanctions and International Law* (Cheltenham/Northhampton: Edward Elgar, 2017), p. 177, at pp. 187–189.

[150] See CTC, *Directory of Best Practices (1373)*, and CTED, *Technical Guide (1373)*, p. 10.

188   COALITIONS OF THE WILLING IN CONTEXT

'methods and trends' of the FATF, a risk-based network through and through.[151]

In assessing risks, the FATF establishes typologies and indicators of the conducts that are to be countered. These are rapid responses based on risk analysis – i.e., expert knowledge rather than politically contested, cumbersome rule-making – but they rule, and the more so if constantly reproduced by different global security bodies – formal and informal – and ultimately integrated into what is read into SC resolutions adopted under Chapter VII UN Charter. As can be observed in the FATF report on the *hawala*,[152] certain Treasury Departments and Financial Ministries, usually of the same Western countries that have always constituted the core of the FATF, all above the USA, take the lead in establishing the practices that the FATF later recognizes as 'best practices'. This should come as no surprise since we are talking in part of the very same people sitting in those governmental departments as national officials, and in the FATF as transnational regulators.[153] The whole risk-management approach so dominant today in the prevention and suppression of terrorist financing and related activities promoted by the FATF and mimicked by the SC has been favoured by the US government, at least since it proved to be an efficient response in the aftermath of 9/11.[154]

The next example taken from the ISIL (Da'esh)/Al-Qaida Sanctions Committee shows that the informal standards of the FATF are at times directly included in SC resolutions.[155] In the frame of this Committee, the SC has long relied much more straightforwardly on the work of this trans-governmental network. Already in resolution 1617 (2005), it

---

[151] See Heng and McDonagh, *Risk, Global Governance and Security*, pp. 51 et seq.; as well as *FATF Recommendations*, recommendation 1, p. 11.

[152] See FATF, *Report: The Role of Hawala and Other Similar Service Providers in Money Laundering and Terrorist Financing* (October 2013), p. 57, at www.fatf-gafi.org/media/fatf/documents/reports/Role-of-hawala-and-similar-in-ml-tf.pdf.

[153] Cf. Richard Stewart, 'The Global Regulatory Challenge to US Administrative Law' (2005) 37 *New York University Journal of International Law and Politics* 695, at 704 (noting that governmental officials participate at the global level in trans-governmental networks where they adopt the very same norms they are called to implement at the national level).

[154] See Heng and McDonagh, *Risk, Global Governance and Security*, p. 61 (also referring to declarations of the former Director of the US Treasury Financial Crime Centre, William J. Fox).

[155] See also Rodiles, 'The Design of UN Sanctions', pp. 189–190.

5.2 COALITIONS' JURISGENERATIVE CAPACITY 189

'strongly urges' UN member States to implement the FATF '40+9 recommendations'.[156] This tendency has only increased in recent years. In its *Fifteenth Report*, issued in January 2014, the Monitoring Team expresses that the proper implementation of the assets freeze imposed by the SC on individuals and entities listed by the Committee,[157] 'remains an area of difficulty for a number of States',[158] and further mentions that in its efforts to face these difficulties, it has continued to work with the FATF and the FSRBs, and that, together with CTED, it has extensively commented on FATF's report on international best practices on targeted financial sanctions –[159] i.e., the compilation of best practices on the implementation of FATF recommendation 6, which in turn deals with the implementation of SC resolution 1267, and subsequent ones. Reports of the Monitoring Team are thoroughly discussed within the Committee, signalling issues that need to be addressed by the subsidiary organ, and, in certain cases, by the SC itself in subsequent resolutions. The resolution that followed the *Fifteenth Report*, resolution 2161 (2014) practically incorporates FATF recommendation 6 with its interpretative note, the report on best practices, as well as other relevant documents of the task force, and urges member states to implement and apply them.[160]

This has been reiterated in the subsequent resolutions that renew the mandate of the Monitoring Team and the Office of the Ombudsperson, first in resolution 2253 (2015),[161] and more recently in resolution 2368 (2017),[162] which expands the mandate of these organs until December 2021. Moreover, these resolutions incorporate also FATF recommendation 5 on the criminalization of terrorism.[163]

---

[156] SC Res. 1617 (29 July 2005), op. 7.

[157] SC Res. 1267 (15 October 1999), and subsequent resolutions.

[158] *Fifteenth Report of the Analytical Support and Sanctions Monitoring Team submitted pursuant Resolution 2083 (2012) concerning Al-Qaida and Associated Individuals and Entities*, contained in UN Doc. S/2014/41 (23 January 2014), para. 32.

[159] Ibid., para. 33. The referred document being: FATF, *International Best Practices: Targeted Financial Sanctions Related to Terrorism and Terrorist Financing (Recommendation 6)* (June 2013) [hereinafter 'FATF, *International Best Practices (Recommendation 6)*'], at www.fatf-gafi.org/media/fatf/documents/recommendations/bpp-fin-sanctions-tf-r6.pdf.

[160] SC Res. 2161 (17 June 2014), op. 11.

[161] See SC Res. 2253 (17 December 2015), op. 10.

[162] See SC Res. 2368 (20 July 2017), op. 17.

[163] SC Res. 2368, op. 18. As mentioned above, FATF's recommendation 5 has long been highly influential for the interpretation of SC resolution 1373, and thus indirectly relevant for targeted sanctions under the 1267/1989/2253 regime (see above note 131, and accompanying text); now, this is directly incorporated into the latter.

It is true that these 'urgent calls' are not binding – i.e. they are not worded in mandatory language – but there is at least a duty to consider them by virtue of the general obligation of co-operation in good faith in the achievement of the obligations assumed in accordance with the Charter (Article 2 (2)), and more concretely because of the duty of member states to assist the UN, under Article 2 (5) UN Charter.[164] As such, this broad endorsement of FATF documents has important consequences for the interpretation of certain aspects of resolution 1267 and subsequent ones, and for the whole sanctions regime.

For instance, the sanctions committee has dealt for quite some time with the improvement of domestic enforcement agencies of the sanctions list. This also comprises the capacity of such authorities to identify and initiate proposals for the incorporation of new entries into the sanctions list. The possibility of proposing a model law has been discussed, and the Monitoring Team has visited states with the aim of assisting them on the issue. Now, the recent resolutions reproduce significant parts of the FATF's interpretative note to its recommendation 6 regarding the appropriate domestic authorities that should be in place in order to enforce SC-targeted sanctions, mentioning 'the need to have appropriate legal authorities and procedures to apply and enforce targeted financial sanctions that are not conditional upon the existence of criminal proceedings'.[165] Moreover, the SC, directly following the interpretative note to recommendation 6,[166] calls on these national legal authorities 'to apply an evidentiary standard of proof of "reasonable grounds" or "reasonable basis"'.[167] This is no minor thing. As I have mentioned elsewhere, in doing this, 'the Council adopts the evidentiary standard of proof followed by the FATF ... which contrasts with the standard of proof followed by the Ombudsperson ... namely that of 'reasonableness *and* credibility".[168] The reason why the Ombudsperson opts for that standard of proof is not only to bring the requirements for listing closer to the rule of law; it is also an acknowledgement of the difficult balance the sanctions regime needs to strike between the presumptive preventive

---

[164] *Charter of the United Nations*, 1 UNTS (1946) xvi.
[165] SC Res. 2368, op. 17.
[166] *FATF Recommendations*, interpretive note to recommendation 6, p. 39, pp. 41–45.
[167] SC Res. 2368, op. 17.
[168] Rodiles, 'The Design of UN Sanctions', pp. 189–190.

5.2 COALITIONS' JURISGENERATIVE CAPACITY 191

nature of the targeted sanction, and the fact that these measures, no matter how non-punitive they are presumed to be, suspend specific and fundamental rights of concrete individuals:

> it is a standard which recognizes a lower threshold appropriate to preventative measures, but sets a sufficient level of protection for the rights of individuals and entities in this context.[169]

Taken together, recommendation 6, its interpretative note, and the document on best practices constitute a detailed guideline for states to adjust their legal systems and institutional apparatuses to the need of more efficiently enforce the sanctions regime, and the Council explicitly urges states to do this according to the terms of the FATF. This seems to be more than just normal co-operation between the FATF and the SC.

These examples demonstrate that the interactions among the FATF and the subsidiary organs of the SC on counter-terrorism have acquired such a density that they amount to global regulation in this field. 'Commitments' that are non-legally binding but efficiently backed by a strong compliance pull add to the already-heavy burden that states have in regard to the series of counter-terrorism obligations that arise within the SC counter-terrorism regulatory machinery, contributing thus to what Kevin Davis and Benedict Kingsbury pointedly describe as 'obligation overload'.[170] As a result of these interactions, the meaning of rather vague obligations contained in SC resolutions are specified, and further developed, by recourse to informal standards adopted within a club of the most industrialized states, which has adapted its mandate as the risks of global security evolve. The introduction of the financing of terrorism right after 9/11, and of the financing of proliferation of WMD in the height of the crisis with Iran's nuclear programme, show further that the USA and its closest allies play an instrumental role in the design and functioning of the FATF, which has, in turn, become instrumental in the work of the SC in these areas.

---

[169] Office of the Ombudsperson to the ISIL(Da'esh)/Al-Qaida Sanctions Committee, *Approach and Standard*, at www.un.org/sc/suborg/en/ombudsperson/approach-and-standard.

[170] See Kevin Davis and Benedict Kingsbury, 'Obligation Overload: Adjusting the Obligations of Fragile or Failed States', preliminary, unpublished paper, New York University, School of Law (2010), at www.iilj.org/wp-content/uploads/2016/11/Davis-et-al-Obligation-Overload-2010.pdf (see particularly pp. 4–5 on the CTC and the FATF).

5.2.3 Turning International Soft Law into Transnational Hard Law: Following the Nuclear Security Summit's Example

As mentioned, the main purpose of the NSS was – and is, if we contemplate the efforts carried out until today under the 'NSS 2.0' – to streamline and enhance a coherent global nuclear security regime, for which it promoted interactions among several IOs and informal coalitions related to the subject, such as the UN, particularly the SC, and, most importantly, the IAEA, as well as the GICNT, and the *G8 Global Partnership against the Spread of WMD*, among others. This included normative interactions among international rules – soft and hard, informal and formal – related to nuclear security. The NSS used its considerable political weight, which derived from the fact that it gathered all states with nuclear weapons, except for North Korea,[171] for galvanizing these interactions. But apart from giving this political drive, the NSS developed quite sophisticated global regulatory devices through which its participants committed to undertake concrete and significant steps towards the improvement of their internal nuclear security, and the overall global regime in the making. As in the case of other coalitions, bilateral agreements pursuing similar goals were promoted and signed within its framework, and participant states' conduct within IOs such as the IAEA was co-ordinated through this informal platform. Although the NSS ceased to exist as a setting in which participants gather from time to time, through the five *Action Plans* it invented an interesting arrangement in order to continue much of this work until the very day.[172]

In an interesting case of provisional application of treaties,[173] NSS participants who were at the same time parties to the *Convention on Physical Protection of Nuclear Material*,[174] and who were accordingly

---

[171] The five nuclear powers who are parties to the NPT (China, France, Russia, the UK and the US), those non-NPT members with declared nuclear arsenals (India and Pakistan), and those with undeclared nuclear weapons (Israel), and countries which have given up their nuclear arms (such as Argentina, Brazil, South Africa, and several former Soviet Republics) were all participating states of the NSS.

[172] See note 58 and accompanying text.

[173] See VCLT, Art. 25. See also the consideration of the topic by the ILC, for which Ambassador Juan Manuel Gómez Robledo has been appointed Special Rapporteur: ILC, *Report on the Work of Its Sixty-Ninth Session (1 May–2 June and 3 July–4 August 2017)*, UN Doc. A/72/10 (2017), Chapter V.

[174] *1980 Convention on the Physical Protection of Nuclear Material*, 1456 UNTS 125.

5.2 COALITIONS' JURISGENERATIVE CAPACITY 193

called 'participating states parties'[175] to that treaty, decided to act in accordance with the object and purpose of a major amendment to the Convention of 2005,[176] which had not entered into force by that time, and called upon all other states parties to do the same, as well as to assist them in doing this.[177] Moreover, the NSS created a mechanism through which commitments that were not ready for adoption by all participants were undertaken nevertheless by the more willing and able participants, replicating the division of labour inherent to the posse model. It is worth looking at this mechanism more closely.

During each of the four summits that were held from 2010 to 2016 (Washington, D.C., 2010, Seoul 2012, The Hague 2014, and Washington, D.C., 2016), the heads of state and government of this co-operative effort convened by President Obama adopted a *communiqué*, which gives political guidance on matters concerning nuclear security. These documents contain broad commitments to secure vulnerable nuclear and radiological materials. Although non-binding and of a general nature, *communiqués* have the capacity to set in motion intense international co-operation schemes, create coalitions and networks, and sometimes give birth to a whole regulatory framework. The *2010 Washington Communiqué* did this by calling on participants to undertake 'continuous national efforts facilitated by international co-operation and ... on a voluntary basis', and by issuing a 'Work Plan as guidance for national and international action including through co-operation within the context of relevant international fora and organizations'.[178] In other words, the general declarations of the *communiqués* as well as the more concrete commitments of the *Washington Work Plan* are developed, until the very day, through continuous national efforts and co-ordinated action in formal and informal fora.

A means of doing this is through the 'gifts' participating states were encouraged to bring to each summit meeting, whereby they, either alone or in concert with other participants, commit further on specific aspects

---

[175] *Work Plan of the Washington Nuclear Security Summit* (13 April 2010) [hereinafter 'Washington Work Plan (2010)'], chapeau 2 (1), (2) and (3), at www.mofa.go.jp/policy/un/disarmament/arms/nuclear_security/2010/pdfs/workplan.pdf.

[176] It was to a great extent due the pressure exercised by the NSS that these amendments entered into force on 8 May 2016; see above note 19, and accompanying text.

[177] See *Washington Work Plan* (2010).

[178] *Communiqué of the Washington Nuclear Security Summit* (13 April 2013) [hereinafter 'Washington Communiqué (2010)'], at https://photos.state.gov/libraries/libya/19452/public/NSS%20-%20Communique%20With%20Logo%20040710.pdf.

of nuclear security derived from the *communiqués* or the *Washington Work Plan*. These gifts are publicly available as pledges or joint statements in the NSS 'gift basket'.[179] We have already seen an example of this regarding the commitment of five participating states to specific measures on transport security of nuclear and radiological materials, specifying a rather broad call to work on this issue of the *Seoul Communiqué*.[180] Those five states thereby also created a working group of the NSS on transport security, which was aimed at the progressive development of these measures, and at giving feedback to the NSS as a whole.

By means of pledges, states committed to specific actions and measures in the framework of the *communiqués* and the *Washington Work Plan* (2010). For instance, several states voluntarily agreed to remove from their territory or reduce to a minimum highly enriched uranium or separated plutonium used for peaceful purposes (medical purposes, for instance) and to substitute it with low-enriched materials, which pose a lesser risk.[181] These 'gifts' can be considered implementation measures of paragraph 3 of the *2010 Washington Communiqué* (2010), and of chapeau 9 of the *Washington Work Plan*.

The lesson from this is quite clear: it is not necessary to engage in difficult multilateral negotiations with the aim of amending treaties or creating a new one that would ban these materials or pose considerable hurdles for states using them, since states can be mobilized (managed) through persuasion and incentives to commit voluntarily to remove these materials from their territory. It is even possible to pick and choose those who represent the greatest risk given their reduced capabilities of physical protection, or just because of their internal security situation, or both.

---

[179] See NSS, *2016 Gift Baskets*, at www.nss2016.org/2016-gift-baskets/; *2014 Gift Baskets*, at www.nss2016.org/2014/giftbaskets; and *2012 Joint Statements*, at www.nss2016.org/2012/jointstatements, respectively.

[180] See note 17.

[181] See the Joint Statement delivered by Chile, Czech Republic, Denmark, Georgia, Hungary, Mexico, Republic of Korea, Romania, Sweden, Turkey, Ukraine, and Vietnam on countries free of highly enriched uranium (HEU), delivered to the gift basket of the NSS of The Hague, of March 2014; information available at https://obamawhitehouse.archives.gov/the-press-office/2014/03/24/joint-statement-countries-free-highly-enriched-uranium-heu. It is also pertinent to mention that reduction or removal of HEU was usually facilitated by the USA or other highly industrialized states, sometimes providing the substitute material. For such purposes, bilateral agreements or arrangements were adopted, the bases of which were at times negotiated on a bilateral basis at the corridors or side rooms of the *sherpa* and *sous-sherpa* meetings (information based on the recollections of the present author as the *sous-sherpa* of Mexico, from October 2009 to March 2011).

5.2 COALITIONS' JURISGENERATIVE CAPACITY   195

Bargaining costs are drastically reduced by this tactic, especially if we consider that traditional multilateral negotiations on this issue would have probably raised difficult and highly emotional debates on what this would mean for the right to develop and use nuclear energy for peaceful purposes, considered a fundamental right of all states under the *Treaty on the Non-Proliferation of Nuclear Weapons* (NPT).[182] Last but not least, implementation is much more readily achieved through this means.

Another remarkable example of the gift basket is the *Joint Statement on Strengthening Nuclear Security Implementation*, subscribed by thirty-five states that thereby commit to incorporate soft-law instruments from the IAEA into binding national law.[183] We are talking of the recommendations known as 'Nuclear Security Series', in particular No. 13, on physical protection of nuclear materials; No. 14, on safety and security of radioactive material and associated facilities, including the Code of Conduct on the Safety and Security of Radioactive Sources; No. 15, on the security of nuclear and radioactive material out of regulatory control; and No. 20, establishing fundamental principles on nuclear security.[184] It is important to mention that these non-binding IAEA guidelines already appear throughout the *2010 Washington Work Plan*. There, for example, the importance of NSS13 in respect to the implementation of SC resolution 1540, op. 3 (a) (b) on physical protection of WMD and related material, is recognized.[185] However, at that time, and despite the efforts by the US team and others to make stronger reference to these guidelines, this was not possible precisely due to their nature as non-binding recommendations. The solution for those pushing for a stronger commitment by the participants came thus in the form of another 'gift', not from all but from two-thirds of the summit's attendants. According to this

---

[182] *1968 Treaty on the Non-Proliferation of Nuclear Weapons* [hereinafter 'NPT'], 729 UNTS 161, Art. IV (the treaty text uses the expression 'inalienable right'). On the conceptualization of fundamental rights of states based precisely on the right to use and develop nuclear energy, see Daniel H. Joyner, 'Fundamental Rights of States in International Law and the Right to Peaceful Nuclear Energy' (2014) 4 *Cambridge International Law Journal* 661.

[183] See NSS, *Strengthening Nuclear Security Implementation* (25 March 2014), at https://2009-2017.state.gov/documents/organization/235508.pdf.

[184] These recommendations, technical guidance papers, and implementation guidelines to treaties such as the *Convention on Physical Protection of Nuclear Materials*, the *International Convention for the Suppression of Acts of Nuclear Terrorism*, as well as to SC resolutions 1373 (2001) and 1540 (2004), can be consulted at IAEA, *Nuclear Security Series Publication*, www-ns.iaea.org/security/nss-publications.asp.

[185] See *Washington Work Plan* (2010), chapeau 3 (5).

present, 'subscribing States' commit to enact national laws and regulations to incorporate the guiding principles and recommendations contained in the IAEA nuclear security series, to conduct self-assessments, and to participate, after the model of the FATF, in a periodical peer-review process, as well as to act upon the recommendations that follow from that process. This joint statement mutated into an ongoing initiative of its own, opened to other IAEA member states that did not participate in the NSS process. In October 2014, the Joint Statement was circulated as an IAEA document, attached to a note verbale by the Mission of the Netherlands to the IAEA, encouraging *non-participant NSS-IAEA member states* to subscribe the *Strengthening Nuclear Security Initiative*. This option remains on the table within the IAEA.[186] Accordingly, the Nuclear Security Governance Expert Group (NSGEG), a multi-sector coalition of experts that works closely together with NSS participating states, describes it as follows:

> This initiative moves signatories beyond the voluntary implementation of the IAEA's guidance, a significant step forward in building a unified international nuclear security regime ... With respect to norm-development, [it] takes legally non-binding instruments (the fundamentals and recommendations of the IAEA Nuclear Security Series) and, while not changing the legal nature of the instruments, requires subscribing states to reflect them in their domestic systems. In this way, applicable provisions of the instruments will become law, or regulations, at the national level. As more states make the explicit pledge to reflect these fundamentals and recommendations in national regimes, their role as the accepted standards of conduct will be reinforced.[187]

Hence, the NSS gift basket can be described as a compendium of long-term commitments adopted throughout the NSS process that serve implementing and developing the general guidelines agreed by the heads of states and government at each of the four summits. This shows already that the NSS created a framework for co-ordinated action that clearly goes beyond, in time and substance, the 'normal' scope of diplomatic summitry. Through the *Strengthening Nuclear Security Implementation Initiative*, which has become a sort of ginger group within the IAEA, as

---

[186] IAEA, INFCIRC/869 (22 October 2014).

[187] Bart Dal, Jonathan Herbach, and Kenneth N. Luongo, *The Strengthening Nuclear Security Implementation Initiative: Evolution, Status and Next Steps* (NSGEG, October 2015) pp. 1, 6.

well as through the NSCG described above,[188] the gift basket remains in place as part of what I have termed *NSS 2.0*.

Furthermore, the NSS gift basket is a highly innovative instance of informal global regulation, which acquires its full significance through the interplay with formal law, be it in the form of bilateral agreements or national legislation. In sum, all these measures represent a coherent exercise in transnational law-making through informal means at the global level. Its reliance on differentiated, 'voluntary' commitments – there is, of course, abundant political pressure – of the participants, according to their individual capabilities and willingness, does also resemble the division of labour inherent to the posse model. But it presents this in a completely new conceptual frame, one that gives participants and observers the impression that it is respectful of equality, and hence not anchored in a discriminatory dynamic of difference; a purely voluntary and efficiency-driven division of functions, where each single participant consents to contribute: what can be more based on states' consent than voluntary contributions? It is probably because of this appealing new frame that other coalitions are mimicking the gift basket.

During the HLPM held in Warsaw, in May 2013, the PSI introduced the NSS model, resorting thus to a friendlier and highly efficient frame of the internal dynamic of difference. Four joint statements were adopted by several PSI participants, which, according to the US DoS, represent

> concrete steps to further the Initiative in the years ahead, which includes deterring proliferators through more regular and robust PSI exercises; promoting legally binding international treaties to criminalize international WMD-related trafficking by commercial ships and aircraft; sharing expertise and resources to build critical interdiction capabilities and practices; and expanding the influence of the PSI globally through outreach to new states and the public.[189]

5.2.4 Coalitions As Exporters of Ruling Techniques: Pledges Everywhere

The model of the NSS gift basket is resonating beyond other informal networks and coalitions of the willing, thus becoming an important

---

[188] See note 60 and accompanying text.

[189] See DoS, *2013 High Level Political Meetings*, at https://2009-2017.state.gov/t/isn/meeting/index.htm; the four PSI joint statements can be consulted at Krakow Initiative PSI, *PSI Tenth Anniversary – Warsaw, 27–29 May 2013*, at www.psi.msz.gov.pl/en/.

model of global regulation. This regulatory device is being imported nowadays by IOs as well, such as in the case of the 'voluntary pledging' by UN member states on the rule of law, according to General Assembly resolution 67/1 (2012),[190] and where even a guideline on pledging has been issued by the UN Rule of Law Unit.[191] This might indicate changing patterns regarding the creation of soft law or that further layers are being added to international law's relative normativity.[192] Be that as it may, what cannot be ignored is that governance techniques are infiltrating international institutions and law. The fabric of international law has already been merged with that of global governance, and this merger cannot but affect the ways the former functions – i.e., how law-making occurs today – including in such traditional fields as the law of treaties.

During the nineteenth Conference of the States Parties (COP19) to the *United Nations Framework Convention on Climate Change* (UNFCCC),[193] held in Warsaw in 2013, a decision was adopted regarding the so-called 'intended nationally determined contributions' (INDCs). These are pledges on mitigation that states parties were invited to present, without prejudice to the legal nature of the contributions', with the view of the adoption of the post-Kyoto agreement, be it 'a protocol, another legal instrument or an agreed outcome with legal force'.[194] Thus, the INDCs were primarily thought as inputs for the negotiation process that led to the *Paris Agreement on Climate Change*.[195] The notion of non-binding, nationally determined policies or pledges like those of the NSS gift basket, indeed, had been already promoted by other coalitions, in particular by the *Major Economies Process on Energy Security and Climate Change*, launched by President George W. Bush in 2007, which became known as the *Major Economies Meeting* (MEM) and later on, under Obama's administration, as the

---

[190] See UN Doc. A/RES/67/1 (30 November 2012), op. 42.

[191] See UN Rule of Law Unit, *Explanatory Note/Guidelines on Voluntary Pledges by Member States*, at www.un.org/ruleoflaw/make-a-pledge/; the pledges are available at www.un.org/ruleoflaw/pledging-database/.

[192] Cf. Prosper Weil, 'Towards Relative Normativity in International Law?' (1977) 77 *The American Journal of International Law* 413.

[193] *1992 United Nations Framework Convention on Climate Change* [UNFCCC], 1771 UNTS 107.

[194] See UN Doc. FCCC/CP/2013/10/Add.1 (31 January 2014), Decision 1/CP.19, op. 2 (b).

[195] *2015 Paris Agreement on Climate Change* [Paris Agreement], UNTS No. 54113.

5.2 COALITIONS' JURISGENERATIVE CAPACITY 199

Major Economies Forum on Climate Change (MEF).[196] Although at the beginning, this coalition was viewed with suspicion by many non-participants, as well as by hesitant participating states from the EU who feared it could be used to sidestep the UN process,[197] the idea that national pledges could be incorporated as such into the post-Kyoto protocol slowly but surely took hold. As the COP21 approached, this proposal received vital impetus from the more than thirty states gathered in the *Petersberger Climate Dialogue,*[198] another climate change coalition of the willing, but this time led by Germany, one of the leading nations within the UN process and which enjoys large credibility in the field. States represented at the *Petersberger Dialogue* considered that individual and collective INDCs (i.e., individual and joint pledges) would conform in their aggregate to the general objective of the UNFCCC as interpreted by the Cancún Agreements – i.e., the goal of maintaining the temperature increase 'below 2°C above pre-industrial levels'.[199] In the end, this formula was agreeable to everyone (i.e., to those that could not accept legal obligations, as well as to those for which a lower commitment than that contained in the subsequent agreement of Cancún was out of question), and so became the essence of the Paris Agreement.

---

[196] For information on the MEM, see http://2001-2009.state.gov/g/oes/climate/mem/; see also Rodiles, 'La Fragmentación del Derecho Internacional', 403–404. For its mutation into the MEF, see Chapter 6, pp. 232–233. On the idea of nationally determined pledges already expressed in the MEM, see The White House, *Major Economies Meeting on Energy Security and Climate Change, Fact Sheet* (27 September 2007) at https://2001-2009.state.gov/g/oes/rls/fs/2007/92904.htm (agreeing, *inter alia*, to 'consider national goals and strategies over the mid-term, reflecting each nation's own mix of energy sources, future energy needs, and development priorities'); see also Antto Vihma, 'Friendly Neighbor or Trojan Horse? Assessing the Interaction of Soft Law Initiatives and the UN Climate Regime' (2009) 9 *International Environmental Agreements: Politics, Law and Economics* 239, at 243.

[197] See Rodiles, 'La Fragmentación del Derecho Internacional', 404.

[198] The proposal is not expressly formulated in the outcome of the *Petersberger Dialogue* meeting, held in Berlin, from 13 to 15 July 2014, though some passages point in that direction, and media reports on the meeting have indicated so, see *Petersberger Climate Dialogue, Co-Chairs Conclusions* (15 July 2014), at www.bmub.bund.de/fileadmin/ Daten_BMU/Download_PDF/Klimaschutz/petersberg5_conclusions_bf.pdf; and Markus Balser, 'Frischer Wind in Petersberg', *Süddeutsche Zeitung* (15 July 2014).

[199] UNFCCC, Art. 2; UN Doc. FCCC/CP/2010/7/Add.1 (15 March 2011), Decision 1/ CP.16, op. 4. Adopted by the parties to the Convention in the framework of the COP16. This part of the Cancun agreements constitutes a subsequent agreement regarding the interpretation of Art. 2 UNFCCC, in the sense of Ar. 31 (3) (a) VCLT.

200   COALITIONS OF THE WILLING IN CONTEXT

This protocol to the UNFCCC incorporates a series of governance techniques,[200] from experimentalist governance[201] to resilience to nudging tactics,[202] including what Kenneth W. Abbott describes as 'managing and bypassing recalcitrant States' through a multilayered scheme provided by transnational regime complexes.[203] I shall come back to this in the next chapter. What is important to highlight at this point is how Articles 3 and 4 of the Paris Agreement imported the gift basket model: the now 'national determined contributions' (NDCs) are the basic means through which states parties pledge to undertake efforts 'with the view to achieving the purpose of this Agreement as set out in Article 2'.[204] This format has caused some perplexity among international lawyers.

It has been argued that NDCs could be treated as unilateral acts of states,[205] something pretty doubtful since 'the intention ... to become bound according to its terms'[206] on behalf of the author of the declaration seems rather absent in the case of the voluntary nature of the NDCs.[207] More convincing at first sight is the argument that these could amount in the long run to subsequent practice of the parties.[208] This is possible and legally plausible, but very unlikely. It is true that the practice in the application of the treaty does not need to be the same among those applying it – not even 'concordant, common and consistent', as mentioned by the WTO Appellate Body.[209] However, the agreement

[200] In general terms, see Anne-Marie Slaughter, 'The Paris Approach to Global Governance', *Project Syndicate* (28 December 2015), at www.project-syndicate.org/commen tary/paris-agreement-model-for-global-governance-by-anne-marie-slaughter-2015-12? barrier=accessreg.
[201] See Charles F. Sabel and David G. Victor, 'Making the Paris Process more Effective: A New Approach to Policy Coordination on Global Climate Change', *Policy Analysis Brief* (The Stanley Foundation, February 2016).
[202] See Rodiles, 'El Acuerdo de París: Un Empujoncito hacia la Justicia Climática'.
[203] Kenneth W. Abbott, 'Strengthening the Transnational Regime Complex for Climate Change' (2014) 3 *Transnational Environmental Law* 57, at 67–68.
[204] Paris Agreement, Art. 3.
[205] See Jorge E. Viñuales, 'The Paris Agreement: An Initial Examination (Part II of III)', blog contribution, *EJIL Talk!* (8 Febraury 2016), at www.ejiltalk.org/the-paris-climate-agree ment-an-initial-examination-part-ii-of-iii/.
[206] ICJ Reports (1974) *Nuclear Tests (Australia vs. France)* Judgment (20 December 1974), p. 267, at para. 43.
[207] See Annalisa Savaresi, 'The Paris Agreement: A Rejoinder', blog contribution, *EJIL Talk!* (16 February 2016), at www.ejiltalk.org/the-paris-agreement-a-rejoinder/.
[208] Ibid.
[209] See WTO Appellate Body Report, *Japan – Alcoholic Beverages II*, WT/DS8/AB/R, WT/ DS10/AB/R and WT/DS11/AB/R, adopted on 1 November 1996, sect. E, pp. 12–13;

5.2 COALITIONS' JURISGENERATIVE CAPACITY 201

regarding the interpretation of the treaty needs to reflect a common understanding of the parties.[210] The very nature of the NDCs is that each state party determines for itself the means of applying the treaty, and this cannot be divorced from how the treaty is interpreted. This means that a 'correct' way of applying the treaty is practically foreclosed from the design of the treaty system, unless parties agree that one or a few NDCs are more accurate than others, or national legislation in 170 countries reflects this agreement due to its overall consistency. The latter case is highly improbable – unless very low common denominators are concerned – the former is counter-intuitive *vis-à-vis* what the NDCs are there for.

NDCs are compatible with the principle of common but differentiated responsibilities (Article 3 (1) UNFCCC), and international environmental agreements typically contain 'soft obligations'.[211] This is not new. However, it seems to be one thing to stipulate that parties shall do whatever is within their reach, another that they should strive to do what they can, and yet quite a different one when they commit to determine what they can do in order to try to achieve the objectives of the treaty. In the first case, we are in presence of obligations of conduct, due diligence standards well accepted in international law; in the second, the kind of 'soft obligations' quite usual in environmental treaties come to mind; yet, in the case of the Paris Agreement, the wide margin of manoeuvre pushes soft law to its limits, reminding of the kind of 'non-contractual commitments' that Richard N. Haass talks about when he proposes 'best practices multilateralism' as a way ahead in a world in disarray:

> The goal should be to get governments to commit to adopting certain best practices at home in areas that inevitably affect global efforts to deal with common challenges.[212]

This seems to me the most accurate description of the NDCs, even though we are not talking in terms of established legal criteria – but these are mental representations, and reality escapes them all of the time.

---

establishing that this classification would carry 'the risk of being misconceived as overly prescriptive', see ILC *Report on the Work of Its Sixty-Eight Session, Chapter IV*, p. 191.

[210] See ILC, *Report on the Work of Its Sixty-Eight Session, Chapter IV*, p. 193.

[211] See Alberto Székely, 'Non-Binding Commitments: A Commentary on the Softening of International Law Evidenced in the Environmental Field', in ILC (ed.), *International Law on the Eve of the Twenty-First Century: Views from the International Law Commission* (New York: United Nations Press, 1997), p. 173.

[212] See Haass, *A World in Disarray*, p. 254; see also Chapter 3, p. 75 et seq.

NDCs are much more like the kind of co-ordinated voluntary efforts that I have been dealing with in this book. NDCs amount thus to a sort of collection of pledges, like the NSS gift basket, through which states parties engage in a series of differentiated commitments: a compilation of national public polices called treaty.

5.3 Concluding Remarks on the Interplay among Coalitions of the Willing and Institutions: Outside Orchestration

The NSS 'gift basket' is one of the most innovative global regulatory schemes, and it shows that framing can make significant difference regarding the ways global governance is perceived; it is something that is crucial for its effectiveness. By means of that intelligent spin, the dynamic of difference underlying the coalition of the willing approach is transmitted as a purely efficiency-oriented division of labour, which claims to be respectful of states' consent, and accordingly of sovereign equality, but without resigning the advantages of informal rule-making with its sense for expediency in the face of urging global risks. No formal processes aiming at adopting new multilateral treaties or reforming existing ones are needed, hence avoiding the political contestation inherent to such cumbersome processes, as well as internal constitutional control mechanisms. Remaining differences between the participating states – potential spoilers are left aside anyway – are broken down by this scheme of concentric circles: if a state has a problem with a particular issue, it has the option of not contributing to that 'basket'. The old diplomatic negotiation maxim that says that 'nothing is agreed until everything is agreed' does not function within this fragmented scheme: it is about continued consultation not negotiation, as Haass puts it.[213] If several states nonetheless assemble a bloc (re)presenting a fundamental difference, they can create their own basket of discomfort, expressing a lament on what they perceive, for instance, to be a shifting away from nuclear non-proliferation and disarmament to proliferation security management and counter-terrorism. There are many reasons supporting this perception, but the Brazilian-led *Joint Statement on a Comprehensive Approach to Nuclear Security* presented by NSS participating states mostly from the Global South does not contain anything that could stop that regime shifting from happening. In contrast to most other joint

---

[213] Ibid.

5.3 CONCLUDING REMARKS ON OUTSIDE ORCHESTRATION   203

statements and initiatives of the NSS, it contains no commitment at all. It is basically a declaration of political positions that may pacify their domestic constituencies and friends outside the coalition, but not much more.[214]

The latter point is of the utmost importance. Coalitions of the willing are created to change an existing international regime – i.e., the institutions and norms that address a certain issue area. The NSS process (until the very day through what I have described as 'NSS 2.0') enhances the IAEA's role as the nuclear security watchdog. Of course, this is already part of the function of this IO, but the increased focus on security may come at the expense of paying less attention to the other main goals of the agency, especially the promotion of peaceful uses, which is actually its prime objective according to its statute.[215] The efforts of the NSS and NSS 2.0 are not isolated. The PSI has been acknowledged by Daniel Joyner to be a means of transiting from the non-proliferation regime to a counter-proliferation one.[216] And this reading is strongly supported by the main architect of the PSI, John Bolton, who bluntly said:

> The Bush administration is reinventing the nonproliferation regime it inherited, crafting policies to fill gaping holes, reinforcing earlier patchwork fixes, assembling allies, creating precedents and changing perceived realities and stilted legal thinking. The frontlines in our nonproliferation strategy must extend beyond the well-known rogue states to the trade routes and entities engaged in supplying proliferant countries. This can properly be described not as "nonproliferation," but as "counterproliferation."[217]

Whereas counter-proliferation is usually understood as a more aggressive set of international measures for combating the spread of WMD, with an emphasis on the non-acquisition of these weapons by terrorists, the non-proliferation regime refers to the legal framework derived from the NPT, and related international norms, of a customary or of a complementary

---

[214] See NSS, Joint Statement by Algeria, Argentina, Brazil, Chile, Egypt, Indonesia, Kazakhstan, Malaysia, Mexico, New Zealand, Philippines, Singapore, South Africa, Ukraine and Vietnam, *In Larger Security: A Comprehensive Approach to Nuclear Security* (2014), at www.nss2016.org/document-center-docs/2016/4/1/gift-basket-from-brazil (stating that nuclear security must be articulated within the international community's broader efforts to promote the interrelated goals of nuclear disarmament, non-proliferation, and the advancement of the peaceful uses of nuclear energy).

[215] *1956 Statute of the International Atomic Energy Agency*, 276 UNTS 3, Art. II.

[216] See Joyner, *International Law and the Proliferation of WMD*, chapters 6 (on the move to counter-proliferation) and 8 (on the PSI as a challenge of counter-proliferation).

[217] Bolton, 'An All-Out War on Proliferation'.

204   COALITIONS OF THE WILLING IN CONTEXT

nature as in the case of decisions of the respective conferences of the states parties to these treaties. This legal regime owes much of its stability to the balancing between two fundamental aims: the non-acquisition of WMD by non-nuclear states (non-proliferation), and the gradual dismantlement of nuclear weapons by nuclear powers (disarmament).[218] This delicate balance has been eroding in the last ten years through an emphasis shift promoted by the USA and other nuclear powers towards more intrusive counter-proliferation. Already during the open briefing of the SC, held in connection with the drafting of resolution 1540, several states, including some of the same that delivered the *Joint Statement on a Comprehensive Approach to Nuclear Security* at the NSS, claimed that this emphasis shift was detrimental to the objective of disarmament.[219] Since counter-proliferation focuses on hindering terrorists' access to WMD, it is to a great extent part and parcel of counter-terrorism; it is very difficult to keep both fields apart as the closely interconnected work of the SC subsidiary organs and informal coalitions on these fields show. The PSI, the FATF, and the NSS 2.0 all contribute, through their interplays with the SC and other institutions such as the IAEA and the IMO, to continue with this trend towards a robust regime of nuclear security, which does not aim at gradual disarmament but at managing the risk of nuclear terrorism.[220]

In IR scholarship, these evolutions are often described as 'exit strategies' by the USA and its closest allies from universal institutions.[221] This is true, but it is only part of the story. Especially at the beginning, the PSI was conceptually framed as a competing venue to standing institutions, an opting-out mechanism. At the same time, however, it was also designed from the outset as an additional, not parallel but complementary venue to the SC and the IMO. Through close interplays with these

---

[218] See NPT, Art. VI.

[219] See UN Doc. S/PV.4950, and S/PV.4950 (resumption) (22 April 2004), particularly Spain, Chile, Pakistan, Peru, South Africa, India, Iran, Malaysia, Jordan and Namibia. Chile, South Africa and Malaysia also signed the *Joint Statement*. Mexico, another signatory of the *Joint Statement* has also raised concerns regarding the weakening of the disarmament component as a result from the shifts towards counter-proliferation through the PSI. See Chapter 4, note 82.

[220] This passage owes much to Heng's and McDonagh's important book on risk management and global security governance, where they note that the PSI represents a shift from non-proliferation to a regime of 'proliferation security', in which the risk of proliferation of WMD is *managed*. See Heng and McDonagh, *Risk, Global Governance and Security*, pp. 80–82.

[221] On the PSI, see Stewart Patrick, 'The Mission Determines the Coalition', pp. 41 et seq.

5.3 CONCLUDING REMARKS ON OUTSIDE ORCHESTRATION   205

institutions, important shifts in the non-proliferation and the law of the sea regimes were envisioned and occurred. The co-operation with the UN and the IAEA, in the case of the NSS, was, in contrast, openly promoted from the beginning as one of the assets of this co-operative, complementary effort. But this was a lesson learned by the Obama administration from the excessive emphasis on the dynamic of difference underlying the discourse on coalitions of the willing by the Bush Jr. administration. With the change in frames, the methods have become more sophisticated too – something which also has been enabled through the better know-how the many coalitions have assembled over the years, and which they very easily mimic from each other, due to their informality.

Julia Morse and Robert Keohane speak of 'competitive regime creation',[222] according to which a coalition of dissatisfied states creates new 'informal institutions', like the PSI (that is one of their examples, but the same applies to the NSS, for instance), to shape existing international law and IOs in a way that fits their interests. Earlier in the chapter, I have mentioned why I do not regard coalitions of the willing as 'institutions'; and I see the PSI, the NSS 2.0, and the FATF as acting coalitions of the willing, not just as a result from coalition diplomacy. These variances reflect different perspectives on the same phenomena, which are most likely motivated by the different disciplines from which we stem. It is quite 'natural' that a lawyer has a more restrictive view on what defines an 'institution' than an IR scholar. But beyond this, the reason for regarding these activities as coalitions of the willing has to do with the circumstance that I see them as continuous efforts, determined by a core of just a few states, with the USA usually at the front, which are constantly embarking in the shaping of legal regimes, and they do this more through co-operation than conflict:[223] coalitions are here to stay.[224] They add additional layers to the multilayered approach to global

---

[222] See Morse and Keohane, 'Contested Multilateralism', 398 et seq.

[223] Morse and Keohane mention that one of the criteria of contested multilateralism is 'conflict' with the rules and praxis of *status quo* institutions ('Contested Multilateralism', 388). Although conflict is not narrowly understood by them, in the case of the PSI and the other coalitions analyzed in the course of this chapter, the situation seems to suggest something else.

[224] See Haass, 'The Age of Nonpolarity', 56 (mentioning that 'multilateralism à la carte is likely to be the order of the day'). In a similar vein, but referring to informal multilateralism more emphatically, see Haas (interviewee)/ Gwertzman (interviewer), 'The New Informal Multilateral Era'.

governance promoted most vehemently in Washington, D.C. – unless until very recently – which keeps adjusting international law through multiple interplays across several legal regimes and informal norms: the informal regimes of counter-proliferation and nuclear security with non-proliferation law, the law of the sea, air law, and counter-terrorism law, for instance.

This might be called, borrowing the expression from Kenneth Abbott and Duncan Snidal, 'orchestrated complexity'.[225] With this I mean that groups of states, led by powerful actors, operate through coalitions of the willing with the aim of adjusting legal regimes to their interests. Coalitions of the willing help to orchestrate from the outside, so to speak, for instance, when they develop standards that would have taken too long to be adopted within formal fora due to the political differences therein and the rigid procedures by which the latter operate. These standards are then incorporated into the work of IOs by several means, from 'noting' them and 'acknowledging' their importance to the creation of ginger groups within IOs that streamline the work of the latter – i.e., in their day-to-day business. These ginger groups stem from coalitions and acquire the quality of *participating-member states* – i.e., their participation in the coalition and membership in the IO is merged into a new category that illustrates the concentric circles logic of multilayered global governance.

Outside orchestration can be quite efficient, but it raises several legitimacy concerns, mainly because the institutional redesign it facilitates represents the interests of a few within a broader membership. Even if the former represents large numbers, there will most likely always remain those who are being 'bypassed' by circumventing the formal amendment procedures, or even avoiding less rigid modification mechanisms like subsequent practice or the practice of the organs of the IO as part of the rules of the organization. The latter cases leave some room for indirect

---

[225] It is important to note that these authors are rather optimistic regarding this phenomenon and focus on how the performance of IOs has increasingly 'improved' through the interactions with other actors, most of all from the private sector. See Kenneth W. Abbott and Duncan Snidal, 'International Regulation without International Government: Improving IO Performance through Orchestration' (2010) 5 *The Review of International Organizations* (2010) 315. Elsewhere, Abbott refers to a strengthened regime complex for climate change through the co-ordination and interplays among several transnational institutions, in which he includes formal intergovernmental organizations, global NGOs, business groups, and informal coalitions and networks, including of cities, like the *C40 Cities Climate Leadership Group*. See Abbott, 'Strengthening the Transnational Regime Complex for Climate Change'.

5.3 CONCLUDING REMARKS ON OUTSIDE ORCHESTRATION 207

evolution, but in the end, they are captured according to rules of procedural fairness like the agreement of the parties on any given interpretation, be it solely in the form of acquiescence. Outside orchestration is not concerned with procedural fairness. In this sense, it is worth recalling Russia's retreat from the great orchestrating project that the NSS and NSS 2.0 represent and the reasons delivered by the Ministry of Foreign Affairs of the Russian Federation on that occasion:

> while preparing for the 2016 NSS summit the organisers drastically altered the event's concept. They have suggested that certain 'guidelines' for the International Atomic Energy Agency (IAEA), the Global Initiative to Combat Nuclear Terrorism, the UN, Interpol and the Global Partnership be issued. Obviously, these recommendations, regardless of their formal status, would become an attempt to impose the opinion of a limited group of states on the above-mentioned international organisations and initiatives in circumvention of their own political decision-making mechanisms. We consider the creation of a precedent for *outside interference in the planning of the work of international organisations,* one which possess significant expert status and which rely on democratic procedures, to be unacceptable. And for this reason President Vladimir Putin has decided to call off Russia's involvement in preparing for the 2016 NSS summit.[226]

The main reasons of this departure were probably political, including the well-known personal differences that existed between President Vladimir Putin and former president as well as personal leader of the NSS, Barack Obama. Nonetheless, Russia's official explanation for leaving this initiative expresses the very legitimate concern I explained above, and it should be taken seriously. In the end, this is a case in point of the sort of ambivalent attitude of several non-Western powers towards the culture of formalism, I described in Chapter 3.[227] Russia remains a key player and principal promoter of other coalitions that display very similar patterns as the ones criticized in its statement regarding the NSS, but its discursive attachment to organized multilateralism and formal international law is part of its international legal consciousness.

Another interesting case I want to comment on in this context is that of the GCTF. This informal, action-oriented, and flexible platform was

---

[226] The Ministry of Foreign Affairs of the Russian Federation, *Foreign Ministry Spokesperson Maria Zakharova's Reply to a Media Question on Russian Assessments of the Upcoming Fourth Nuclear Security Summit in Washington (March 31–April 1, 2016)* (5 April 2016), at www.mid.ru/en/foreign_policy/news/-/asset_publisher/cKNonkJE02Bw/content/id/2010701. Emphasis added.

[227] See Chapter 3, Section 3.3.

208   COALITIONS OF THE WILLING IN CONTEXT

launched, following the model of the FATF,[228] with the aim of streamlining positions and actions on counter-terrorism that are too politically contested to advance rapidly inside the UN.[229] The SC refers frequently to the standards developed inside this coalition, especially regarding its framework documents and best practices on kidnapping for ransoms in the context of terrorism financing, which are now said to 'complement the work of the relevant United Nations counter-terrorism entities'.[230] Due to the threat posed by IS, the work of the GCTF has been increasingly and rapidly incorporated into that of the SC, especially in regard to measures designed to counter the growth of violent extremist ideologies and the so called 'foreign terrorist fighters' phenomenon (FTF). It is important to note that on 23 September 2014, at the Fifth Ministerial Meeting of the GCTF in New York, the Forum adopted *The Hague-Marrakesh Memorandum on Good Practices for a More Effective Response to the FTF Phenomenon.*[231] The very next day, the SC adopted resolution 2178, which soon became known as the 'foreign fighters resolution',[232] a far-reaching, quasi-legislative act of the SC that has been criticized for committing similar mistakes as those that followed 9/11, particularly with the adoption of resolution 1373 (2001).[233] In resolution

---

[228] This also according to Anne-Marie Slaughter, who witnessed the creation of the GCTF as head of Hillary R. Clinton's Policy Planning Staff at the US Department of State (DoS), see Anne-Marie Slaughter, 'International Law and International Relations Theory: Twenty Years Later', in Jeffrey L. Dunoff and Mark A. Pollack (eds.), *Interdisciplinary Perspectives on International Law and International Relations: The State of the Art* (New York: Cambridge University Press, 2013), p. 613, at pp. 616–617.

[229] Eric Rosand had been advocating for 'durable, effective and flexible mechanisms' to complement the UN counter-terrorism machinery and help alleviate its deficits, which he knows very well as one of the most experienced US diplomats in the field. His proposals come quite close to the 'outside orchestration' I am referring to here, and the GCTF is clearly influenced by his thoughts; see, e.g., Eric Rosand, 'The UN-Led Multilateral Institutional Response to Jihadist Terrorism: Is a Global Counterterrorism Body Needed?', (2006) 11 *Journal of Conflict & Security Law* 399.

[230] SC Res. 2133 (27 January 2014), p. 7; see also SC Res. 2178 (24 September 2014), p. 17.

[231] See GCTF, *The Hague-Marrakesh Memorandum on Good Practices for a More Effective Response to the Foreign Terrorist Fighters (FTF) Phenomenon*, at www.thegctf.org/documents/10162/140201/14Sept19_The+Hague-Marrakech+FTF+Memorandum.pdf.

[232] SC Res. 2178.

[233] See Martin Scheinin, 'Back to Post 9/11 Panic? Security Council Resolution on Foreign Terrorist Fighters', blog contribution, *Just Security* (23 September 2014), at http://justsecurity.org/15407/post-911-panic-security-council-resolution-foreign-terrorist-fighters-scheinin/; and Alejandro Rodiles, 'La Guerra contra el Estado Islámico y el Legado Bush', blog contribution, *nexos* (2 October 2014), at http://eljuegodelacorte.nexos.com.mx/?p=4111.

5.3 CONCLUDING REMARKS ON OUTSIDE ORCHESTRATION 209

2178, the SC takes note of this compilation of best practices, other documents of the GCTF, as well as of its work in assisting 'interested States with the practical implementation of the United Nations counter-terrorism legal and policy framework and to complement the work of the relevant United Nations counter-terrorism entities'.[234] This resolution and *The Hague-Marrakesh Memorandum* are complementary instruments on central issues such as the measures that states are called upon to adopt for countering violent extremism ideologies, as well as on international co-operation on traveller data sharing, and the sharing of best practices to improve identification of travel patterns.

Coalitions orchestrate legal regimes also by boosting those aspects of an existing field of international law in which they have a special interest. This happens by means of interactions at the normative level – i.e., between informal norms and formal law. Through the enhanced implementation mechanisms that coalitions have developed over the years, they contribute to international law's efficacy, but they do so in a selective way. And quite similarly, by means of their informal standards and the reception these obtain from certain bodies within IOs, which are largely controlled by the same countries that are present at the core of the respective coalitions, they contribute to the specification and evolution of legal obligations. At times, coalitions' ruling devices are mimicked directly by IOs and within formal processes, becoming thus new law-making techniques, as the Paris Agreement reveals. All this suggests that, in the end, coalitions of the willing are 'durable, effective and flexible mechanisms'[235] that accompany standing institutions in a multilayered scheme of global governance, where flexible and multiple interplays have become more important than clearly defined legal powers. This is detrimental for legal security and predictability, but it is regarded as necessary in times of rapidly changing global risks.

---

[234] SC Res. 2178, p. 17.
[235] Rosand, 'The UN-Led Multilateral Institutional Response to Jihadist Terrorism', 399.

6

Coalitions of the Willing and the Role of Law in the Deformalized Global Complex

The case studies undertaken in Chapters 4 and 5 showed that coalitions of the willing are alternative venues to standing, formal organizations, and thus part of a broader move from institutions[1] that began somewhere at the end of the past century, when the 'globalization paradox' –[2] i.e., the need for more global ruling without global government – made room for the burgeoning presence of trans-governmental networks,[3] coalitions of the willing, and other informal arrangements. Today, they keep mushrooming and are an integral component of global governance with its multilayered scheme of action and regulation – that is, of a *global complex* that is not entirely informal, but to a large extent deformalized since it assemblages formal and informal mechanisms of rule that interplay constantly and define and redefine each other along the way.

Two opposite implications for international law arise from the increasing role of coalitions of the willing in global affairs: the promotion of law's efficacy, on the one hand, and the weakening of some of the values and structures on which this legal system *qua* system – or, more accurately, aspiration thereof –rests, on the other. It is not difficult to see how the rule of law is in tension here. Fostering implementation through innovative frameworks, enhancing enforcement via co-ordinated state action, and contributing to the dynamic evolution of international legal rules by means of an interactive process of multiple venues can be regarded as the promotion of the rule of international law – i.e., the strengthening of this body of law. At the same time, however, we are not only in presence of a quite selective promotion of international legal rules by some powerful states, according to their preferences, but also of a

---

[1] See above Chapter 1, note 7. Referring to the move from institutions in relation to what he terms 'soft organizations', see Klabbers, 'Institutional Ambivalence by Design', 406 et seq.

[2] Slaughter, *A New World Order*, p. 8 (referring to the writings of Renaud Dehousse regarding the European Union (EU), and of Robert Keohane on international affairs).

[3] Ibid., pp. 36 et seq.

highly instrumentalist version of international law, which, as Pierre d'Argent eloquently puts it, 'challenges implicitly our post-modern conception of the common good being the result of a procedural deliberation'.[4] As seen in the previous chapters, the means for achieving efficiency that coalitions employ are often at odds with foundational principles of international law, and with some of the basic ideas that are closely associated with the rule of law at the international level. To begin with, the basic notion of this political ideal, namely that law should constrain the exercise of sheer power, is seriously jeopardized by coalitions' efficiency paradigm. Rule of law tensions permeate the relationship of coalitions of the willing with international law since they touch upon the very role that the law is supposed to play in today's global complex: is it being strengthened, or weakened, or even substituted[5] by coalitions of the willing and the multilayered approach to global governance?

In order to address these questions, in this chapter, I will critically evaluate the interplay in which coalitions typically engage (Section 6.1). This interplay intensifies the global complex as a system of rule, so that in a first step, some of the salient characteristics of regime complexity will be assessed and problematized (Section 6.1.1). As shown in Chapters 4 and 5, the formal–informal interplay has concrete consequences for international law as we know it. In a second step, I will elaborate those findings further (Section 6.1.2). Building on some of the theses of the informal international law-making project,[6] I will argue that we are witnessing the emergence of an *anti-law law* as a consequence of this interplay (Section 6.2). In the next and concluding chapter, I will make some tentative remarks on how to cope with this.

6.1 The Interplay between Formality and Informality: Promoting Informal Hierarchies

It is tempting to describe coalitions of the willing as parallel venues to standing (formal) institutions and traditional diplomatic conferences. It is insofar plausible as it denotes that we are in the presence of alternatives, which at times compete with those institutions and more classical

---

[4] Pierre d'Argent, 'Coalitions of the Willing: Why, How and What?', in Calliess, Nolte, and Stoll (eds.), *Coalitions of the Willing: Avantgarde or Threat?*, p. 25, at p. 28.

[5] Eyal Benvenisti, 'The Move from Institutions: Substituting International Law' (2006) 100 *Proceedings of the Annual Meeting (American Society of International Law)*, 289.

[6] See Pauwelyn, Wessel, and Wouters (eds.), *Informal International Lawmaking*.

212 COALITIONS OF THE WILLING AND THE ROLE OF LAW

multilateral fora. However, most of the time, coalitions interact with international organizations (IOs), and quite intensively so. Hence, it is more appropriate to describe them as interactional schemes of global governance, which form part of a multilayered approach to international and transnational action and regulation. Through these interplays, coalitions contribute to promoting and furthering a semi-formal global complex. This bears important consequences for the aspiration of autonomy of international law as a normative system, and thus on the role of law in global governance. Not unrelated, the interplay between formality and informality reflects power calculations and establishes informal – and less obvious – hierarchies.

6.1.1 Regime Complexity as a Deformalization Process

As seen in the previous chapter, in certain cases, the interactions of coalitions of the willing and formal institutions acquire such a density that we can fairly speak of the former as 'informal arms' of the latter, as evidenced, for instance, by the relationship between the *Financial Action Task Force* (FATF) and the UN Security Council (SC), particularly with its subsidiary organs in charge of counter-terrorism and counter-proliferation of weapons of mass destruction (WMDs). The same applies to the relation between the *Global Counterterrorism Forum* (GCTF) and the SC, which has intensified remarkably due to the rise of the Islamic State (IS), and the need to forcefully counter this kind of terrorism threat. But these relations are no one-way street, so to speak: coalitions not only serve as enforcers of formal law and drivers of their normative evolutions; they establish their own standards, to which implementation IOs often contribute too. In this sense, the SC, for example, may also be viewed as another layer – or a 'framework', as it is called by the *Proliferation Security Initiative* (PSI) –[7] which, together with the FATF and other actors, takes part in the global regulation that combats the financing of terrorism and the proliferation of WMDs, or which adds its voice and measures to those of the GCTF in the countering of violent extremism ideologies and foreign terrorist fighters (FTF).[8] More concretely, the calls of the Council to UN member states to implement the non-binding

---

[7] The PSI *Statement of Interdiction Principles* (SIP) mentions in its chapeau 'relevant international law and frameworks, including the UN Security Council', at www.psi-online .info/Vertretung/psi/en/07-statement/Interdiction-Principes.html.

[8] See Chapter 5, p. 208.

6.1 THE INTERPLAY BETWEEN FORMALITY AND INFORMALITY 213

instruments of the FATF, or the GCTF, can be viewed also as a coadjutant strategy to the work of these informal bodies. Even if these urgent
calls are not binding by themselves, there is a duty to consider them
under international law, and the compliance pull is significant. Particularly in the case of the FATF, with its own strong compliance mechanism,
including through its global network of regional bodies, the peer review
process, and the so-called 'countermeasures', the relevant actions taken
by the SC add up to the already very efficacious global standards, which
in part overlap with Council resolutions. As I have argued, overlapping
functions and contents are considered an asset in multilayered global
governance; they are not an error of design: repetition has become a
specific ruling technique within the broader *techne* of education as a
normative enterprise – i.e. the normative function of *paideia* at the global
level. And the same can be observed in regard to similar evolutions
concerning the PSI and the International Maritime Organization
(IMO), as well as the interplay of the *Nuclear Security Summit* (NSS)
and its continuation under what I have called the *NSS 2.0*,[9] with the
International Atomic Energy Agency (IAEA), where the SC and other
formal and informal entities are involved too, adding their strengths in
this multilayered and selective 'implementation game'.[10]

Considering the above, it becomes clear why coalitions of the willing
are not parallel venues. This description fails to capture the dynamics of
their interplay with (formal) institutions, and law. We are rather in the
presence of complementary means of rule and action – of correlations
and correspondences that are mutually reinforcing and define each other
in a continuous symbiotic relation. In other words, the meaning and
scope of many of the measures that are taken today to face global risks
are the product of dynamic interactions over time. The global community of risk (or 'world risk society', to use Ulrich Beck's words)[11]

---

[9] See above Chapter 5, pp. 166–167.

[10] Borrowing the expression from Carolyn Deere, *The Implementation Game: The TRIPS
Agreement and the Global Politics of Intellectual Property Reform in Developing Countries*
(Oxford: Oxford University Press, 2011) (showing how the implementation of the
Agreement on Trade-Related Aspects of Intellectual Property Rights (TRIPS) is conducted
through a multilayered approach encompassing political alliances, transnational NGOs,
and trade organizations, as well trans-governmental networks and IOs, and how this has
resulted in a game between developed and developing countries, whereby the former
advance enhanced compliance with higher standards than those demanded by TRIPS,
while the latter try to counter this trend). I thank Paola Karam for drawing my attention
to this.

[11] See Ulrich Beck, *Weltrisikogesellschaft* (Frankfurt a.M.: Suhrkamp, 2007).

214   COALITIONS OF THE WILLING AND THE ROLE OF LAW

demands rapid and efficient responses to protect the global public goods, and protect us from the global public 'evils', like terrorism, proliferation of WMDs, or climate change. The efficient dynamism required in an era of *at-risk global public goods* is best assured through interactional schemes, such as the flexible and productive interplay between formality and informality explored in this book.[12]

This brings us back to the understanding of global governance as a system of rule that addresses global challenges through the interplay of multiple forms of international and transnational action and regulation, including formal and informal fora, as well as intergovernmental, hybrid, and private mechanisms.[13] This notion is derived from the writings of James N. Rosenau on global governance at the beginning of the 1990s. Later on, the same author developed the concept of 'spheres of authority' to denote that in contemporary world affairs, authority is exercised by several actors, ranging from states and IOs to transnational corporations and advocacy networks. His notion of global authority is a fluid one that captures the multi-layered approach quite clearly:

> governance will emerge from the interaction of overlapping spheres of authority; regulation will be achieved not through centralized authority but through the spread of norms, informal rules, and regimes.[14]

It is significant to note that for Rosenau, global governance is not only about the disaggregation of the state, but also – and primarily – about the disaggregation of authority in the global realm: 'The disaggregation of authority on a global scale is a quintessential instance of a complex adaptive system'.[15] However difficult the concept of international authority is to define in international relations (IR) theory, what matters here is that this proposition relates directly to what we have observed all the way throughout the present book, namely that IOs with their constitutive treaties and international legal powers more broadly, which are rooted in a general system of law, are watered down into regimes of governance,

---

[12] Thus, the literature on global public goods and international law has noted that the effective international action required to protect them often leads to the perceived need to deploy informal and flexible mechanisms in disregard of state consent (see Krisch, 'The Decay of Consent', 3–7), and that in the expansive definition of and recourse to global public goods, policy-makers pursue broader global governance projects (see Shaffer, 'International Law and Global Public Goods', 674). See also Chapter 3, pp. 42–43.

[13] See Rosenau, 'Governance, Order, and Change in World Politics', p. 4.

[14] Rosenau, 'Governing the Ungovernable'.

[15] Ibid., 95.

6.1 THE INTERPLAY BETWEEN FORMALITY AND INFORMALITY 215

where several spheres of action and regulation – i.e., authority – co-exist. This matches the standard definition of 'international regimes' provided by institutionalism in IR theory, concretely provided here by Stephen D. Krasner:

> sets of implicit or explicit principles, norms, rules, and decision-making procedures around which actors' expectations converge in a given area of international relations.[16]

This includes institutions and norms, both formal and informal. Following this, the legal principles, rules, and procedures on a given issue area would constitute a subset of the regime; the 'legal regime'[17] would thus be an important, yet just another component of the whole. From a given point of view, Krasner's definition is perfectly plausible: all these expectations within an issue area define pretty much how that area works. The role of legal advisors of foreign ministries and other governmental departments seems to confirm this, as it precisely consists in bringing (and elucidating) the legal factors into the equation, which are then pondered *vis-à-vis* other expectations (political and economical). So, is it perhaps an overreaction to say, as Koskenniemi does, that deformalization occurs already when 'the law retreats solely to the provision of procedures or broadly formulated directives to experts and decision-makers for the purpose of administering international problems by means of functionally effective solutions and "balancing interests"'?[18]

In the moment the legal advisor in a foreign ministry balances her legal arguments *vis-à-vis* political or economic considerations, she becomes a political advisor and a negotiator who will probably rely more on legal standards than other factors – but as a persuasion tactic, not as an end in itself. And this, of course, happens all the time. But one should not confound the dual role of the delegate to the Sixth Committee of the UN General Assembly, for instance, or that of other legal experts from governments, IOs, and NGOs engaged in international negotiations, with the main function of the legal advisor who is to explain what the law says (precisely because this is usually not that clear). In other words, when relevant legal rules leave no room to manoeuvre – when the rigidity of

---

[16] Krasner, 'Structural Causes and Regime Consequences', 186.
[17] See above Chapter 5, note 80.
[18] Martti Koskenniemi, 'Constitutionalism as Mindset: Reflections on Kantian Themes about International Law and Globalization' (2007) 8 *Theoretical Inquires in Law* 9, at 13.

216   COALITIONS OF THE WILLING AND THE ROLE OF LAW

the law manifests itself with its legal/illegal dichotomy – in that moment, the autonomy of the law cannot be compromised any longer without giving away its character as law. Regarding and treating international law as just another subset of parameters that inform the actors' expectations while losing sight of this rigid border-line would deprive the law of its aspirations to be an autonomous normative system, and this is precisely what is meant in this context by deformalization. It is, as explained in Chapter 3, the exogenous determination of law, and hence its instrumentalization, which is rejected by formalism in terms of Weber, Kelsen, and Koskenniemi indeed.[19] And then one should ask: what could possibly be the purpose of law if its rules are pondered along other normative expectations, all of the time and without differentiation of pedigree? The *acquis* of the legal profession would probably be reduced to bringing some insight into procedural matters, enriching argumentation, and helping to articulate legitimacy expectations. It would end up being *politics of fairness*. From an IR perspective, international order could possibly not be contemplated much differently. However, it is crucial to remain aware that this is only one perspective.

It could then again be argued that precisely due to this difference in perspective, international lawyers should stick to their discipline and let the world according to IR theory be that of IR scholars; that the dangers of compromising the autonomy of the law begin with the embracement of interdisciplinarity by international lawyers themselves.[20] The 'dual agenda' of IR and international law[21] has indeed a programmatic function, one that, in the end, tends to subsume legal canons under the rationale of IR theory: 'accountability' instead of 'responsibility', 'commitment' in the place of 'obligation', 'universally accepted standard' for 'valid rule', or 'legitimacy' in lieu of 'legality', etc. It is hence itself a significant attempt at deformalization.

---

[19] See above Chapter 3, pp. 86–88.

[20] See Jan Klabbers, 'The Relative Autonomy of International Law or The Forgotten Politics of Interdisciplinarity' (2004–2005) 1 *Journal of International Law and International Relations* 35, at 41–42.

[21] See already Kenneth W. Abbott, 'Modern International Relations Theory: A Prospectus for International Lawyers' (1989) 14 *Yale Journal of International Law* 335; Anne-Marie Slaughter, 'International Law and International Relations Theory: A Dual Agenda' (1993) 87 *The American Journal of International Law* 205; and Slaughter, 'International Law and International Relations Theory', p. 613 (mentioning that she remains committed to the dual agenda, however noticing that in contrast to her 1993 seminal article, she is now 'less starry-eyed about the intellectual hegemony of IR scholarship [and has] a greater appreciation for the role of international law', at p. 624).

6.1 THE INTERPLAY BETWEEN FORMALITY AND INFORMALITY 217

However, the notion of world (dis)order described by Rosenau and many others – i.e., the complex system of rule that is global governance – is a reality that is impossible to ignore. On the one hand, means of global regulation that do not fit within the doctrine of sources of international law according to Article 38 of the Statute of the ICJ are nonetheless ruling the world,[22] most of all at the transnational level. These may be non-binding in the traditional sense, but efficiently compel states around the globe to act in certain ways, as well as to introduce changes to their domestic legal systems. At the same time, the institutional and normative interplay described in the previous chapter, which is but a snapshot of the bigger picture, affects international legal rules and has direct repercussions on the aspiration of international law *qua* legal system. So, can international lawyers ignore these evolutions, which are not new but keep growing exponentially? Can the '*relative* autonomy of international law'[23] be safeguarded by resisting the voices of IR scholars and the interdisciplinary agenda – which has not ceased after 9/11,[24] but rather reappeared more forcefully within the conceptual frame of complexity management?[25]

Deformalization can, of course, mean different things.[26] However, while different meanings are assigned to the term, the loss – or risk of loss – of law's autonomy is always present. Elsewhere, Koskenniemi refers to deformalization as one of the three developments (together with

---

[22] Cf. Benedict Kingsbury, 'The Concept of "Law" in Global Administrative Law' (2009) 20 *European Journal of International Law* 23, at 26 (noting that the 'normative practices addressed under the GAL moniker in the current literature go beyond the recognized sources of 'international law").

[23] Klabbers, 'The Relative Autonomy of International Law', 35. Emphasis added.

[24] See Martti Koskenniemi, 'Law, Teleology and International Relations: An Essay in Counterdisciplinarity' (2011) 26 *International Relations* 3, at 16 (mentioning that both the 'dual agenda' and the liberal elite which espoused it 'collapsed together in September 2001').

[25] It is no coincidence that the pioneer of the 'dual agenda' is now a leading voice on 'regime complexity'; see, e.g., Abbott, 'Strengthening the Transnational Regime Complex for Climate Change'.

[26] One of the classical conceptions of the term goes back to Max Weber, according to whom the materialization of law – i.e., the increasing introduction of substantive contents according to ethical postulates – weakens law's formal rationality, which guarantees predictability and equality before the law; see Weber, *Economy and Society*, pp. 882 et seq. In relation to recent developments in international law, see, e.g., Jean d'Aspremont, *Formalism and the Sources of International Law: A Theory of the Ascertainment of Legal Rules* (Oxford: Oxford University Press, 2013), pp. 118–136 (referring to the different meanings and agendas behind the deformalization of law ascertainment).

218   COALITIONS OF THE WILLING AND THE ROLE OF LAW

fragmentation and empire) that undermine the idea that the 'world can – or should – be governed through a single international law like the domestic',[27] and defines the phenomenon as:

> the increasing management of the world's affairs by flexible and informal, non-territorial networks within which decisions can be made rapidly and effectively.[28]

This is very similar to the situation I described in the previous chapters. Although I focused on informal intergovernmental coalitions, these are increasingly connected to private and hybrid networks. The crucial point to add to Koskenniemi's observation in relation to the present study is that deformalization primarily takes place through the institutional and normative interplay of informal means of governance with the formal ones. The latter are neither disappearing nor losing relevance, but they are being reshaped in light of the efficiency paradigm and, hence, being increasingly deformalized; just think of the growing role of the UN as a 'platform of coordination', the rise of soft law–type norms within IOs and the move away from treaty making, or the resort to ruling devices that are arguably softer than soft law, such as the pledges states make in order to trying to achieve the objectives of a treaty to which they are parties, like the national determined contributions (NDCs) of the *2015 Paris Agreement on Climate Change.*[29]

When one acknowledges this, it becomes impossible – or at least extremely difficult – not to use the language of the IR scholar, who, perhaps due to the circumstance of not feeling constrained to think of ruling in formal terms (of legal powers), has noticed earlier in how many different ways the world is actually being ruled in the era of governance. But, again, this perspective may be wider in some ways but then narrower in others. Conceiving 'ruling' without any reference to the 'power of command'[30] carries the risk of losing authority out of sight.[31] The lawyer

---

[27] Martti Koskenniemi, 'Global Governance and Public International Law' (2004) 37 *Kritische Justiz* 241, at 243 (mentioning that the employed notion of deformalization follows Max Weber).

[28] Ibid. (including private and hybrid mechanisms, as well as trans-governmental informal entities).

[29] See above Chapter 5, pp. 200–202.

[30] Weber, *Economy and Society*, p. 948.

[31] On the difficulties regarding the allocation of authority in international law in an era of fragmentation, see the various contributions in Tomer Broude and Yuval Shany (eds.), *The Shifting Allocation of Authority in International Law: Considering Sovereignty, Supremacy and Subsidiarity, Essays in Honour of Professor Ruth Lapidoth* (Oxford: Hart,

6.1 THE INTERPLAY BETWEEN FORMALITY AND INFORMALITY 219

clearly identifies this risk in terms of the negative effects for the eventual attribution of responsibilities, the lack of a framework of legal competences that may open the doors for anyone with enough resources to impose their own standards, and ultimately the loss of a norm-generating process based on states' consent, which at least limits to some extent inequalities in the international community.[32] In short, the attempt to constrain sheer power through the pursue of the rule of law ideal of equality before the law. These are political values too, not dissimilar from 'accountability', 'transparency' and 'fairness', words the IR scholar and the global technocrat are more likely to employ. But, most importantly, the ideas and ideals that inform the rule of law are the product of historical political struggles, the aim of which has been to make them enduring and demandable through law – i.e., through law's formal rationality and its conception as a legal system.[33] If, and only if, norms are part of a system, they enjoy objective predictability, which is another expression for procedural fairness; rule of law ideals make little sense in relation with loose collections of prescriptions. By jeopardizing the protection that the law affords to these ideals, however imperfect in international law this may be, deformalization represents a serious challenge to rule of law aspirations at the global level. So, before questioning whether formal law can address this challenge in our pluralistic world, it is not an exaggeration but rather a necessity to raise awareness about the perils that the governance-driven deformalization processes pose to the political ideals that nurture the idea of a global rule of law.

6.1.1.1 Regime Complexity as Power Game: Fragmentation Revisited

The co-existence among the different spheres of authority involved in global governance regimes is not always harmonious but sometimes

---

2008); particularly relevant is the analysis by Dirk Pulkowski on the shifting allocation of power in face of the 'heterarchical paradigm' derived from network-governance structures; see Dirk Pulkowski, 'Structural Paradigms of International Law', p. 51, at pp. 72–76.

[32] Cf. Kingsbury, 'Sovereignty and Inequality' (particularly on the challenges posed by 'globalization and the changes in international rule-making' to an order based on sovereign equality, and the implications derived from these challenges for the limits on inequality, at 616 et seq.); see also Krisch, 'International Law in Times of Hegemony', 399 (mentioning in relation to the FATF and other trans-governmental networks that '[i]nformality allows the strictures of sovereign equality to be circumvented in the formal law-making process, and it thus is far a more suitable tool for hierarchy').

[33] See also Eyal Benvenisti, 'The Conception of International Law as a Legal System' (2007) *German Yearbook of International Law* 393.

defined by conflict, especially about the different spheres seeking compliance with its own authority.[34] This sounds pretty similar to the fragmentation debate in international law and its underlying theme of collisions of normative authorities. But Rosenau's approach to global authority differs in that it regards global disaggregation, or fragmentation, not as chaos but as 'patterned', where the different spheres of authority, 'despite their number and variety ... coevolve through time, thereby becoming increasingly adaptive to each other and, in so doing, achieving a measure of coordination that may be increasingly subject to regulation'.[35]

This is what Kenneth W. Abbott and others characterize as 'orchestration', according to which fields of regulation are strengthened through co-operative linkages among the several spheres involved – formal and informal, state-centred, hybrid, and private.[36] Orchestration implies co-ordination among the different spheres of authority, and this suggests that a sort of inter-institutional regulation is in place, or *in fieri*. Abbott proposes some means to strengthen the ties in 'the transnational regime complex for climate change', means that are aimed at making the multi-level, transnational approach to environmental governance more efficient, including by 'managing' and 'bypassing' 'recalcitrant' actors, mainly states.[37]

A look at the means delineated by Abbott reveals that some of the very same are already in place in the interplays described in the previous chapter. I would therefore argue that *patterns of co-ordination* among the different layers involved in global governance regimes are emerging spontaneously in practice.[38]

Before describing these patterns, it is important to clarify that I am not thinking of legal categories or in systemic terms in the sense of legal techniques for overcoming collisions of legal norms. This toolkit

---

[34] See Rosenau, 'Governing the Ungovernable', 94.

[35] Ibid., 95.

[36] See Abbott and Snidal, 'International Regulation without International Government'; and Abbott, 'Strengthening the Transnational Regime Complex'.

[37] Abbott, 'Strengthening the Transnational Regime Complex', 78–81 (these are information sharing and mutual learning; co-operation and co-ordination in order to bypass recalcitrant states; and information strategies, including 'cognitive framing' to manage states).

[38] Although mainly concerned with customary international law, the role of spontaneity in the making of 'unwritten international law' as developed recently by Peter Staubach, is relevant for understanding emerging patterns of conduct in the contemporary global complex; see Peter Staubach, *The Rule of Unwritten International Law – Customary Law, General Principles, and World Order* (London: Routledge, 2018).

6.1 THE INTERPLAY BETWEEN FORMALITY AND INFORMALITY 221

provided by general international law and particularly by the law of treaties, in the clarification of which the UN International Law Commission (ILC) has assumed a strong leadership,[39] plays a pivotal role for resolving classical legal disputes before tribunals. But the instances of interplays between formal and informal, state-centred and non-state-centred fora, that make their way to litigation are not representative. As Jeffrey L. Dunoff argues, international litigation involves a 'highly atypical form of regime interaction'.[40] Moreover, since this toolkit is designed for fixing contradictions between legal norms, it operates from within the legal system – though across different legal regimes. *Lex specialis* and other maxims, as well as the rules of interpretation are well suited for addressing tensions among norms of different legal regimes – environmental law *vis-à-vis* investment protection law, e.g. – but they are unable to address conflicts between legal rules and ruling devices that lack the legal pedigree (i.e., informal norms) because the latter are not part of the system and actually are not intended to be part of it. The patterns of co-ordination I am talking about are consequently strictly pragmatic, informed by a proactive and experimentalist (in the sense of trial and error) risk-management logic, rather than by systemic legal thinking. These are:

- *mimesis* – i.e., mutual learning and emulation of institutional design, outreach activities, and regulatory devices, in order to maximize efficiency and streamline co-operation;
- *information-sharing*, including through joint exercises, outreach and awareness-raising activities, as a means of strengthening co-ordination;

---

[39] See ILC, *Report on the Work of its Fifty-Eighth Session*, chapter XII. In addition to the fragmentation report, the current work of the Commission on subsequent practice and treaty interpretation is also relevant in this regard, since the legal techniques involved in Art. 31 (3) (a) & (b), as well as Art. 32, have the potential of harmonizing normative interactions across legal regimes, if, for instance, states parties to a treaty agree to interpret a provision of that treaty in terms of another treaty, or of a subsequent evolution of the latter; or if their practice in the application of the former is carried out in a way compatible with another treaty, and establishes the agreement regarding the interpretation of the former. For a similar view, see Nele Matz-Lück, 'Norm Interpretation across International Regimes: Competence and Legitimacy', in Margaret A. Young (ed.), *Regime Interaction in International Law: Facing Fragmentation* (Cambridge: Cambridge University Press, 2012), p. 201, at p. 213, and pp. 218–224; see also ILC, *Report on the Work of its Sixty-Eight Session*, chapter IV; and see the various contributions and the Reports of the Study Group on the subject-matter, in Georg Nolte (ed.), *Treaties and Subsequent Practice* (Oxford: Oxford University Press, 2013).

[40] Dunoff, 'A New Approach to Regime Interaction', p. 137.

222 COALITIONS OF THE WILLING AND THE ROLE OF LAW

- *cross-participation* of the different entities in each other's processes, including, where possible, compliance mechanisms, in order to facilitate mutual learning and enhance co-ordination and efficacy;
- *cross-references* to each other's practices and guidelines to facilitate mutual recognition of best practices also via repetition; and
- *self-comprehension* of each forum *as a platform* that facilitates awareness raising of each other's activities and the integrated performance of other institutions, coalitions, and networks according to the capacities of each to deal with particular issues within the field.

This is a non-exhaustive list. Moreover, since these patterns are informed by the logic mentioned above, they are dynamic. If one of traditional international law's main goals is often to strike a balance between stability and change,[41] in the *setting of global law*,[42] where the international, trans-national, and post-national converge around the efficiency paradigm, change is the priority, and thus change-enabling devices are preferred. These patterns of co-ordination are of this sort, and themselves highly adaptive to change: they embody a new kind of *resilience-normativity* that facilitates an ongoing game between several actors. The rules of this game (including who the players may be) are not pre-defined, but spontaneous and responsive to change. They enable the interplay between formality and informality, and are re-determined by the interplay as it unfolds over time.

Patterns of co-ordination are not designed to determine jurisdiction, nor jurisdiction-like questions, the applicable law, nor criteria for deference to *a* normative solution: they are not inspired in private international law, *ius gentium*, cannon law, or the medieval *glossae* of the

---

[41] For a pointed articulation of this issue in relation to the law of treaties, see Georg Nolte, 'Treaties over Time in Particular: Subsequent Agreement and Practice', in *Yearbook of the International Law Commission (2008), Volume 2, Part II* (New York and Geneva, 2015), Anex 1, p. 152.

[42] I refer to the introductory chapter of Klabber's international law textbook (see Jan Klabbers, *International Law*, second edition (Cambridge: Cambridge University Press, 2017), pp. 3 –23). I (and many of my students) find the metaphor of the 'setting of international law' most useful for understanding where international law operates and why it is needed; in short, for understanding the living conditions of the discipline. The 'setting of global law' is not the same, but the challenge is, of course, that both overlap. That is also why international lawyers have indeed to learn '*seeing in stereo*', as mentioned by Anne-Marie Slaughter in her most recent book (see Slaughter, *The Chessboard & the Web*, pp. 66–75).

6.1 THE INTERPLAY BETWEEN FORMALITY AND INFORMALITY 223

Code of Justinian.[43] In this sense, they are different from the global conflict of laws, like the '*Kollisionsrecht*' of Andreas Fischer-Lescano and Gunther Teubner,[44] or 'the construction of interface norms' proposed by Nico Krisch.[45] Enabling interplay is not about accommodating different normative regimes within a pluralistic order: there are no primary and secondary levels. It is the 'lack of an agreed ordering relationship between legal orders, or "disorder of normative orders" [which is] the salient circumstance to which global law responds'.[46] I understand this salient feature of global law that Neil Walker so eloquently brings to the point –i.e., the absence of a meta-ordering principle – as the result of deliberate moves to add spheres of authority to a complex system of rule. There is an underlying narrative of regime complexity that praises juxtaposition, intricacy, and density, whereby each of the spheres involved acquire their normative efficacy through a mutually reinforcing game that only needs to be managed. If it were to be structured, this would bring the complex back to a system of law (or aspiration of it) with all the controls and constraints that legal validity affords through the certainty of process –[47] which is what secondary rules offer, even in the rudimentary form of conflict rules. I firmly believe that

---

[43] The origins of conflict of laws are usually situated in the Bologna School of Law of the late eleventh and twelfth centuries, in which the 'statutists' derived from the sources of Roman law (mainly the Code of Justinian) conflict-of-law rules for enabling the civil and commercial relations among Italian cities – a sort of systematization of secondary rules for accommodating intercity legal pluralism. However, according to some historiographies of private law, these conflict-of-law rules previously emerged within cannon law as a means to accommodate relations among different polities under the unifying criteria of a common law of Western Christendom. On this, see Harold J. Berman, 'Is Conflict-of-Laws Becoming Passe? An Historical Response', in Hans E. Rasmussen-Bonne et al. (eds.), *Balancing of Interests: Liber Americorum Peter Hay zum 70. Geburtstag* (Frankfurt a.M.: Recht und Wirtschaft, 2005), p. 43, pp. 46–48. Be it as it may, the important point here is that conflict-of-law-style rules, often the nucleus of contemporary theories on global legal pluralism, are inspired by these legal evolutions which show that, in the end, the diversity is to be settled within an overarching scheme of systemic principles or secondary rules, bringing it thus closer to a constitutional framework. The patterns of co-ordination I have in mind are not concerned with the unity of a normative system.

[44] See Andreas Fischer-Lescano and Gunther Teubner, *Regime-Kollisionen* (Frankfurt: Suhrkamp, 2006), pp. 57–65, and 170–171.

[45] Nico Krisch, *Beyond Constitutionalism: The Pluralist Structure of International Law* (Oxford: Oxford University Press, 2010), pp. 285–296.

[46] Neil Walker, *Intimations of Global Law* (Cambridge: Cambridge University Press, 2015), p. 165.

[47] Referring to the rule-of-law ideals attached to the conception of international law as a legal system, see Benvenisti, 'The Conception of International Law'.

224 COALITIONS OF THE WILLING AND THE ROLE OF LAW

these controls and constraints (to power, in the end) are what regime complexity is there to bypass in the first place.

The patterns of co-ordination I am referring to are there for managing complexity, and hence, they are better called *pragmatic correspondences*. It should thus come as no surprise that in the specialized literature on climate change governance, very similar patterns of pragmatic management have been observed and described.[48] This literature is not concerned with centrality aspirations of an international legal order, nor whether such aspirations are worth preserving the constant changes in the global setting notwithstanding; it rather explains what is going on out there. Whether this can be captured according to pluralism or other narratives of normative order seems not be its priority. I am not judging this approach; the only point I am trying to make here is that when looking at such a complex phenomenon as regime complexity (*the complexities of complexity*), the first step to make should be descriptive. If this then throws out a blurry, quite incomprehensible picture of a game that is about constant change (and constantly changing), we may learn that accommodation is not part of the normative *telos* of that game.[49] In this sense, any kind of secondary rules assigned to that game become a normative enterprise, which may be very much desirable, but they are informed by a different *telos*, and then it is not clear whether as prescriptions they are suited for something that still needs to be diagnosed.

In the game enabled by pragmatic correspondences, the spheres of authority involved give up their claims to exclusive competences (and characteristics in the sense of properties) for the sake of overall efficiency, empowering (and defining) each other along the way according to the general goals of the regime complex (which are also redefined along the way).[50] I have argued that the coalition of the willing approach is part and parcel of global governance. With this I mean that coalitions are not

---

[48] For an illustrative overview, see Sebastian Oberthür, 'Regime-Interplay Management – Lessons from Environmental Policy and Law' in Kerstin Blome, Andreas Fischer-Lescano, Hannah Franzki, Nora Markard, and Stefan Oeter (eds.), *Contested Regime Collisions – Norm Fragmentation in World Society* (Cambridge: Cambridge University Press, 2016), pp. 88–108.

[49] Thus, global law is not only multilevel in the sense of being the expression of different spheres of authority tied to different spaces, but it is also synchronic and diachronic at the same time. In other words, global law is to be understood as configuring and reconfiguring 'chronotopes'; see Mariana Valverde, *Chronotopes of Law*, pp. 9–14.

[50] These pragmatic correspondences build upon the notion of 'metaphorical correspondences', suggesting thus that meaning and similarities are construed through cross-domain correlations; see Lakoff and Johnson, *Metaphors We Live By*, pp. 96 and 113; see also Chapter 2, pp. 23–24.

6.1 THE INTERPLAY BETWEEN FORMALITY AND INFORMALITY 225

only tools of the latter, but that the ideas that inform the conceptual metaphor 'coalition of the willing' are also significant for the very concept of global governance. The practical correspondences that enable the interplay within global governance regime complexes reflect this: defining (and empowering) each other according to the complexes' goals is no different from the maxim of the coalition of the willing approach as defined by Donald Rumsfeld, namely that 'the mission must determine the coalition; the coalition must not determine the mission'.[51] Former US Secretary of State Colin Powell referred to this as 'coalitions' fluidity'.[52] I have called this the *amorphousness* of coalitions of the willing,[53] a characteristic that fits perfectly into the scheme of fluid authorities operating within regime complexes.[54]

The interactions I have referred to so far apparently take place within one regime, be it counter-terrorism, non-proliferation, or climate change. Although fragmentation problems also arise within single regimes, the greater challenges are definitely those that concern the relations across them.[55] The intra-regime perspective suggests that the multilayered approach may be a case of limited disaggregation, so to speak, where the different spheres are ultimately united around a common subject-matter, and a shared purpose. So, it could be argued, the different layers complement the implementation of one set of norms, fortifying the central authority of that set; for example, when different international and transnational players, including IOs, global coalitions of cities (or 'coalitions of global cities'),[56] private actors, and all-encompassing part-nerships,[57] ultimately contribute together through their juxtaposing

---

[51] Rumsfeld, 'Transforming the Military', 31.

[52] Cf. Colin Powell (Interview), *Frontline* (2 June, 2002).

[53] See Chapter 1, as well as Rodiles, '*Coalitions of the Willing: Coyuntura, Contexto y Propiedades*', 693–695.

[54] For a similar account on the kind of authority exercised in global governance, see Nico Krisch, 'Liquid Authority in Global Governance' (2017) 9 *International Theory* 237.

[55] See *Fragmentation of International Law: Difficulties Arising from the Diversification and Expansion of International Law, Report of the Study Group of the International Law Commission Finalized by Martti Koskenniemi*, UN Doc. A/CN.4/L.682 (13 April 2006), paras. 272–282.

[56] A common example in regard to climate change is the *C40 Cities Climate Leadership Group* (information at www.c40.org/); for a legal analysis of this intercity coalition, see Helmut Philipp Aust, *Das Recht der globalen Stadt* (Tübingen: Mohr Siebeck, 2017), pp. 293–298.

[57] Interesting in this regard is the *Climate and Clean Air Coalition to Reduce Short-Lived Climate Pollutants*, which comprises states, IOs, global city coalitions, NGOs, the private sector, and other informal networks; information at www.ccacoalition.org/.

measures and co-ordinated interplay to trying to fulfil the object and purpose of the Paris Agreement.[58]

But co-ordination should neither be taken for granted nor described uncritically as a neutral operation, as the managerial vocabulary in which these correspondences are framed suggests.[59] Orchestrated regime complexity has the purpose of shaping pre-existing regimes and it produces change, sometimes fundamental change. Let me reframe this: it is not orchestrated regime complexity that is actually conveyed but rather *complexity-driven regime orchestration*. And a regime complex is more than *a* complex regime; it is usually an *assemblage of regimes*, provided these are broadly understood in the sense of encompassing norms and institutions, formal and informal, and from different scales (from the subnational to the transnational).[60] The interactions in the fields of counter-proliferation and counter-terrorism have contributed to the edification of a single rationale of security governance: the construction of a nuclear security regime. This regime has fortified counter-terrorism in critical aspects, but it has also altered the legal non-proliferation and law of the sea regimes in ways that are not satisfactory to everyone, weakening the disarmament component of non-proliferation law that is

[58] This is the transnational regime complex of climate change that Abbott calls upon to strengthen, and which has been incorporated into the Paris Agreement's architecture through the category of 'non-party stakeholders', which includes cities, civil society, and the private sector, *inter alia*. Moreover, the 'Non-State Actor Zone for Climate Action Platform' creates a mechanism for these *non-party participants* to engage in concrete terms by registering their pledges as well. These categories and mechanisms are not in the *corpus* of the treaty but in the decision of the COP in which the former was adopted and which contains the treaty as an annex (see UN Doc. FCCC/CP/2015/10/Add.1 (29 January 2016), paras. 117–119, and 133–136). Hence, Decision 1/CP.21 can be regarded as an agreement in terms of Art. 31 (2) (a) VCLT and, as such, as an important means of interpretation of the Paris Accord. Through this interpretative agreement, the treaty regime is expanded significantly.

[59] A point repeatedly made by Koskenniemi, see, *inter alia*, Koskenniemi, 'Hegemonic Regimes', p. 308 (mentioning that "regime interaction' cannot be meaningful reduced to technical coordination and the very suggestion that it can will appear as a linguistic strategy to make the speaker's preferences appear somehow natural because they are, for example, 'scientific' or 'methodological'").

[60] Although I use the notion of 'assemblage' here in its ordinary sense, i.e. as a collection of things, it certainly matches the work on 'transnational legal assemblages', in the sense of 'the symbiotic co-functioning ... of heterogonous elements ... that helps to apprehend (rather than flatten) [the] variegated normative topology' of regime complexes; see Gavin Sullivan, 'Transnational Legal Assemblages and Global Security Law: Topologies and Temporalities of the List' (2014) 5 *Transnational Legal Theory* 81, at 91–92 (with further references).

6.1 THE INTERPLAY BETWEEN FORMALITY AND INFORMALITY 227

crucial to non-nuclear power states, and arguably shifting the foundational principle of the law of the sea from the *mare liberum* to the *mare securum*. The continuous expansion of the FATF's mandate and the recognition it receives from the SC is a case in point for understanding to what extent terrorism, criminal activities (money laundering and corruption), and themes pertaining to national economic policies (informal economy sector) are increasingly viewed under a single rationale of counter-terrorism work. Likewise, the memoranda of the GCTF and their reception by the SC favour the conception of the rule of law as a counter-terrorism tactic. By framing counter-terrorism as a rule-of-law matter, a spin allows to subsume the rule of law under counter-terrorism work without alienating the understanding of the rule-of-law concept in a too evident fashion and, thus, probably discouraging protest.[61] Therefore, in regime complexes, different regimes – including legal ones – tend to conflate under an overarching objective – a *mission* indeed – so that the problems identified in fragmentation debates on competing rationalities[62] are not absent from regime complexity but just seen and promoted by its advocates in a different, 'positive light'.[63]

Now, whether this complexity-driven regime orchestration is beneficial for the efficiency of a given field of global regulation is not questioned here *per se*. The question is rather who defines the regimes' and ultimately the complexes' goals? And here the issue is not only – not even mainly – that the indeterminacy of legal language leaves room for interpreting and reinterpreting these goals according to political preferences; that is a well-known problem that would lead to a very different discussion, and the Vienna rules of interpretation[64] offer a variety of

---

[61] See the several memoranda on good practices produced by the *Criminal Justice and Rule of Law Working Group* of the GCTF, at www.thegctf.org/Working-Groups/Criminal-Justice-and-Rule-of-Law. The Counter-Terrorism Committee (CTC) also frames its activities as rule-of-law promotion. On framing certain policies (which are not always compatible with actual rule-of-law ideas) in the rule-of-law vernacular, see the excellent book by Stephen Humphreys, *Theatre of the Rule of Law: Transnational Legal Intervention in Theory and Practice* (Cambridge: Cambridge University Press, 2012).

[62] For a view on fragmentation as competing rationality maximizations of autonomous regimes, see Fischer-Lescano and Teubner, *Regime-Kollisionen*, pp. 25–33.

[63] Speaking of 'fragmentation in a positive light' calls to mind Bruno Simma's 2004 article; however, in that essay, Simma refers mainly to the proliferation of tribunals and the opportunities for diversification and expansion of international law arising from the proliferation of legal regimes; it does not concern regime complexity in the sense treated here; cf. Bruno Simma, 'Fragmentation in a Positive Light' (2003–2004) 25 *Michigan Journal of International Law* 845.

[64] See VCLT, Arts. 31–33.

228 COALITIONS OF THE WILLING AND THE ROLE OF LAW

methods, which, all their own indeterminacy notwithstanding, provide for means to accommodating divergent interpretations within a common frame of reference – i.e., a shared understanding of admissible arguments for the legal community.[65] In regime complexity, the problems of indeterminacy of the rules involved are significantly augmented by the own indeterminacy of the managerial vocabulary, which is actually greater than the one pertaining to legal rules with their whole systemic backup of methods of interpretation, importantly including systemic integration.[66] 'Outreach', 'awareness raising', and 'capacity building', e.g., leave far more room for filling and refilling these slogans with meanings on a case-by-case basis, and there are no clear methods available for limiting the range of admissible (re)interpretations. Furthermore, the problem is more fundamental as it involves creation of norms; it is a jurisgenerative rather than a hermeneutical question – though the line between both is certainly thin. Through selective enforcement, targeted normative developments, and the assemblage of different pieces picked and chosen from different regimes, pre-established regimes are deeply transformed, or new ones are even created. International non-proliferation law based on the delicate balance between nuclear disarmament and the non-acquisition of nuclear weapons by non-nuclear states[67] probably has been replaced by a regime complex of proliferation and nuclear security, composed of formal and informal rules, and jointly and flexibly managed according to risk-management criteria by formal and informal entities alike.

So, again, who defines which, and in which ways international regimes are shaped, or even transformed? This question cannot be disentangled from power considerations. As Abbott makes clear, orchestration presupposes an 'orchestrator ... with sufficient authority, legitimacy and/or resources',[68] a sort of 'focal point' 'with an accepted leadership position in an issue area and strong connections with other institutions'.[69] Thus, we need to refine our question once more: Who has the ability to set the

---

[65] See Aust, Rodiles and Staubach, 'Unity or Uniformity? Domestic Courts and Treaty Interpreation', 78–79.

[66] VCLT, Art. 31 (3) (c).

[67] See NPT, 729 UNTS 161, Art. VI; on this delicate balance underlying non-proliferation law, see Joyner, *International Law and the Proliferation of Weapons of Mass Destruction*, pp. xiv–xvii.

[68] Abbott, 'Strengthening the Transnational Regime Complex', 83.

[69] Ibid., at note 177. Compare this to the simultaneous roles of the USA as the PSI's focal point, a P5 in the SC, a leading member of the 1540 Committee, and the convener of the NSS.

6.1 THE INTERPLAY BETWEEN FORMALITY AND INFORMALITY 229

agenda, assemble coalitions broad and fluid enough to navigate across the areas concerned, and, ultimately, to connect the dots? By connecting the dots, I mean: who is at the core of most institutions and informal coalitions and networks in a given 'issue area' and in as many related issue areas as possible? Or, in the words of former President Obama, who has the ability to be 'the hub of alliances'?[70]

Nico Krisch explains that '[t]he semiformal structure of the new order is characterized by largely concentric circles of decision makers: while the United States is always part of the "club", the EU or key European governments are also usually members'.[71] He further adds to this list in order of decreasing importance: China and Russia as permanent members of the SC, the rest of the BRICS, and, finally, other members of the G20, such as Australia, Canada, Japan, Mexico, and South Korea. Krisch's theses are also premised on the notion of regime complexes as a mixture of formal and informal authorities. He importantly unravels that behind this apparent heterarchical order, which does not function on the basis of '"legalized" hegemonies in a formal sense',[72] there are, nonetheless, hierarchies in play;[73] and, literally speaking, one may add, as these emerge from the interplay among the different spheres involved. It is the 'patterned' disaggregation described by Rosenau that, through increasing co-ordination, evolves into a system of rule: *regime complexity as a power game.*

The rise of regime complexes as a preferred means of global governance can hardly be denied, and it is increasingly observed by IR scholars.[74] By drawing the attention to them from the legal perspective, Krisch accurately points to how this global governance technique is shifting patterns in international law-making: a move from consent to consultation – among friends, I would add – and from co-operation

---

[70] Obama, *West Point Commencement Address* (2014).

[71] Krisch, 'The Decay of Consent', 30.

[72] Ibid., 31.

[73] This was already noted by Christopher Daase, 'Die Informalisierung internationaler Politik: Beobachtungen zum Stand der internationalen Organisation', in Klaus Dingwerth, Dieter Kerwer and Andreas Nölke (eds.), *Die Organisierte Welt. Internationale Beziehungen und Organisationsforschung* (Baden-Baden: Nomos, 2009) (mentioning that informality's 'structural effect ... [lies in that] it tends to replace the formal anarchical structure of the international system by an informal hierarchical one').

[74] Apart from the specialized literature in IR (see Chapter 5, note 8, and accompanying text), see, e.g., Stewart Patrick, 'The Unruled World: The Case for Good Enough Global Governance' (January/February 2014) *Foreign Affairs* 58.

230   COALITIONS OF THE WILLING AND THE ROLE OF LAW

under the promise of equal participation to forum shopping and the shaping of institutions.[75] This results in the creation of newer forms of global regulation that mostly benefit powerful actors. What is important to add to this description is that the role of the USA has not only been predominant in this power game because it (still) is the most powerful state (and actor) in global affairs. All the relative loss of its power notwithstanding, this is true, and without it, the USA would just not be able to be at the core of most institutions and informal coalitions. In Chapter 3, I described how the coalition of the willing approach has been conceptually developed in US foreign policy circles and strategically promoted from Washington, D.C., since at least the late 1990s. Coalition diplomacy and regime complexity have been conceived as part of a strategy for maintaining US hegemony in a rapidly changing, networked world.[76] This is what Anne-Marie Slaughter and others have been successfully promoting in academia and government, and it is not that far away from the 'empire' described by Michael Hardt and Antonio Negri.[77] It is a grand strategy of foreign policy described by Francis Fukuyama as 'multi-multilateralism',[78] which consists precisely in adding layers to global governance through the 'Gs', coalitions, and other networks, in addition to formal institutions.[79] It emerged out of the necessity to deal with the shifting world order in the aftermath of the Cold War and has experienced important evolutions since then, but remains, in essence, the same.

I started this section by noticing that the description of coalitions of the willing as parallel multilateral venues is quite common but not really accurate. A closer look at what might cause this misrepresentation is revealing in terms of the development that the coalition of the willing approach has experienced in the past fifteen years or so. Indeed, besides

---

[75] Krisch, 'The Decay of Consent', 30.

[76] For an outspoken articulation of this, although avoiding the word 'hegemony', see Slaughter, 'America's Edge: Power in the Networked Century'; and Jones, *Still Ours to Lead.*

[77] See Michael Hardt and Antonio Negri, *Empire* (Cambridge, Massachusetts: Harvard University Press, 2001) pp. 160–180. Making the same comparison but in regard to the final report of the *Princeton Project on National Security*, see Mazower, *No Enchanted Palace*, pp. 102–103.

[78] Francis Fukuyama, 'The Paradox of International Action', *The American Interest* (1 March 2006).

[79] Cf. Drezner, 'The New New World Order', 36; see also Chapter 3, p. 73.

6.1 THE INTERPLAY BETWEEN FORMALITY AND INFORMALITY 231

unintended imprecisions, this terminological confusion has its roots in the aggressive rhetoric of the Bush Jr. administration, especially during its first term, which portrayed coalitions as the better alternatives to standing institutions:

> Existing international institutions have a role to play, but in many cases coalitions of the willing may be able to respond more quickly and creatively'.[80]

One is here reminded of the discourse that surrounded the creation of the PSI and its initial phase, especially as promoted by his main architect, former Undersecretary of State and Permanent Representative of the USA to the UN and National Security Advisor of the Trump administration, John Bolton. This discourse even resembles the one that framed the US-led military coalition that attacked Iraq in 2003: coalitions of the willing represent the venues that allow willing and able states to do what they consider to be the 'right thing' in the face of unable institutions.[81] But none of these anti-terrorism coalitions are parallel venues. The latter heavily interfered with standing institutions and international law by transgressing them, and the former was conceived from the outset to interact with the SC and other institutions and legal regimes. Actually, the aggressive rhetoric surrounding the PSI was soon abandoned, still under the Bush Jr. administration, also because one of its main missions consists of 'outreaching' as broad as possible.

But the perception that the USA was going all its own way, in clear disregard of organized multilateralism (the description of Thomas Risse of coalitions of the willing as 'unilateralism in disguise' captures this image)[82] became so strong with the Iraq invasion of 2003 that it would take a change in administration to modify it. The *Major Economies Process on Energy Security and Climate Change* (MEM), launched by the government of George W. Bush, in 2007,[83] reveals this very clearly. By that time it was perceived by states and leading NGOs as a parallel venue to the UN climate-change forum – i.e., the Conference of the Parties to the UNFCCC, and the Meeting of the Parties to the Kyoto Protocol. The fear was that the initiative of a government that was openly

---

[80] *US National Security Strategy 2006*, p. 48.
[81] See Rodiles, '*Coalitions of the Willing: Coyuntura, Contexto y Propiedades*', 677–680.
[82] Risse, 'The Crisis of the Transatlantic Security Community', p. 91.
[83] MEM, *Information website*, at http://2001-2009.state.gov/g/oes/climate/mem/.

232   COALITIONS OF THE WILLING AND THE ROLE OF LAW

against the Kyoto Protocol[84] would mainly serve to undermine the UN process.[85] If such perceptions were right, Bush's climate-change coalition would be a case in point for what Eyal Benvenisti and George Downs describe as 'regime or venue shifting': a fragmentation strategy whereby '[t]ypically, one or more powerful states become dissatisfied with the trajectory of negotiations and decide to exit the negotiations and exploit their agenda-setting power to set up a parallel and competing set of negotiations with other powerful states'.[86] There are many reasons to regard Bush's climate change partnership in the sense described by these authors (including its emphasis on 'energy security'), which very accurately explains what lies behind the worries concerning parallel venues. However, this coalition was also meant from the beginning to interact with the UN, complementing it in the sense of regime complexity.

It is interesting to observe how the Obama administration relaunched the initiative, renaming it the *Major Economies Forum on Energy and Climate Change* (MEF), as a venue that 'is intended to facilitate a candid dialogue among major developed and developing economies, help generate the political leadership necessary to achieve a successful outcome at the annual UN climate negotiations'.[87] This clearly shows the change in US foreign policy discourse on coalitions of the willing from the Bush to the Obama administrations, a change I have characterized as 'from rivalry to complementary'.[88] But this is mainly a rhetorical change, a spin in terms of frame theory. Bush's multilateral strategy also consisted of adding layers to the pre-existing standing institutions. Yet, Obama's spin on the issue proved to be an important one since it significantly contributed to the change of perception in the international community (reminding that, in diplomacy, form is often substance), and to refine the methods employed, making them more efficient in an era that is

---

[84] See David E. Sanger, 'Bush Will Continue to Oppose Kyoto Pact on Global Warming', *The New York Times* (12 June 2001), A12.

[85] See Philip Rucker and Juliet Eilperin, 'Obama Sets International Climate Forum', *The Washington Post* (online) (28 March 2009), at http://voices.washingtonpost.com/44/2009/03/28/obama_sets_international_clima.html; this was also the position of *Greenpeace*, see 'Bush Major Emitter Meetings (MEM): Wrong Way on Climate Change' (Greenpeace Briefing, January 2008), at www.greenpeace.org/international/Global/international/planet-2/report/2008/1/bush-mem.pdf.

[86] Benvenisti and Downs, 'The Empire's New Clothes', 615; see also Rodiles, 'La Fragmentación del Derecho Internacional', 403–404.

[87] See MEF, *Information website*, at https://2009-2017.state.gov/e/oes/climate/mem/index.htm.

[88] See chapter 2, section 3.2.2.4.

6.1 THE INTERPLAY BETWEEN FORMALITY AND INFORMALITY 233

increasingly perceived and described as a world of non-polarity,[89] including by the proponents of the coalition of the willing approach.[90]

But let us recall that the NDCs of the Paris Agreement – these highly innovative ruling devices that defy *pacta sunt servanda* while being praised as the future of international law-making – are, to a great extent, the result of the interplay between the MEM, first, and the MEF, later, and the formal UN process, as well as with other informal fora like the *Petersberg Climate Dialogue*, and, at least as mimesis is concerned, with the NSS.[91]

Although some elements of this proclaimed co-operation, or complementarity, are already present in the 2002 and 2006 security strategies of the USA, it is most straightforwardly stated in the *2010 National Security Strategy* of the Obama administration:

> **Pursue Decisions though a Wide Range of Frameworks and Coalitions**: We need to spur and harness a new diversity of instruments, alliances, and institutions in which a division of labor emerges on the basis of effectiveness, competency, and long-term reliability. This requires enhanced coordination among the United Nations, regional organizations, international financial institutions, specialized agencies, and other actors that are better placed or equipped to manage certain threats and challenges.[92]

This is regime complexity at its best, and it is one that emphasizes the role of informal entities along IOs.

Adding complexity to international regimes brings, in principle, opportunities for all the actors willing and able to join each layer, beyond the USA and the West. However, this game will always benefit most those with the ability to play at different levels at the same time and to understand the connections among them, which again is mainly possible due to the opportunity of participating in the different layers simultaneously. This presupposes resources – human and otherwise. One of the most serious problems arising from the fragmentation of international law, and indeed from its diversification and expansion even in a 'positive light',[93] is the very big disparity in resources among governments, and

---

[89] See Haass, 'The Age of Nonpolarity'; see also Kupchan, *No One's World*.
[90] See Haass, 'The Age of Nonpolarity'; also advocating coalition diplomacy as the most suitable strategy for maintaining US predominance in a world marked by these power redistributions, see Jones, *Still Ours to Lead*; and this is also the message of Slaughter's 'America's Edge'.
[91] See Chapter 5, pp. 197–201.
[92] US *National Security Strategy* (May 2010), p. 46.
[93] See note 63, and accompanying text.

234   COALITIONS OF THE WILLING AND THE ROLE OF LAW

among non-state actors across the globe.[94] This is probably more of a problem the more it is seen from the perspective of regime complexity where strength resides in juxtaposition and multiple interactions. And finally, the deformalization inherent to this approach also suits better those who are culturally more comfortable with flexible, fluid frameworks of co-operation. It is anecdotic but (because of it) very telling that when the USA proposed an interactional and dynamic format for the discussions among the heads of state and government at the first plenary meeting of the NSS, held in Washington, D.C., in April 2010, away from the rigid and time-consuming format of the UN General Assembly, several representatives from the 'South' expressed much concern about the host's proposal.[95]

Koskenniemi sharply observes that the move 'from institutions to regimes'[96] is representative of the broader transformations that international law is experiencing since the end of the Cold War, in the sense that the interdisciplinary agenda of IR and international law, 'an academic intelligentsia that has been thoroughly committed to smoothening the paths of the hegemon',[97] as he calls it elsewhere, is converting the latter into a new kind of post-modern natural law, 'a fully instrumentalist discipline dedicated to serving the interests of power'.[98] In Chapters 2 and 3, I made the point that coalitions of the willing are fundamentally instrumental in their conception and functioning, something that is most evidently articulated in the oft-quoted *Rumsfeld maxim*. By interacting with formal institutions and law, coalitions tend to instrumentalize them too; this is another component of deformalization. Institutionally, this manifests in transforming IOs into flexible and efficient 'platforms' of inter-institutional (formal and informal) relations. Normatively speaking, we have also seen how coalitions' informal standards have clear and important effects on (formal) international legal rules once they interact with each other. Taken together, these effects highlight desired aspects of rules and legal regimes to the detriment of others, especially undermining law's formal rationality as expressed in the values of equal participation and general application, favouring instead a function of international law

---

[94] See Rodiles, 'La Fragmentación del Derecho Internacional', 407–409.

[95] Based on the recollections of the present author as Mexican *sous-sherpa* to the NSS, from 2009 to 2011.

[96] Koskenniemi, 'Miserable Comforters', 406–407.

[97] Martti Koskenniemi, 'Carls Schmitt, Hans Morgenthau, and the Image of Law in International Relations', in Byers, *The Role of Law in International Politics*, p. 17.

[98] Koskenniemi, 'Miserable Comforters', 395.

as a means to an end, among the many other means, vocabularies, and instruments involved in regime complexes. But it still remains to be clarified whether these informal norms – and, more broadly speaking, coalitions' innovative regulatory devices – can and should be regarded as law at all. In other words, it is necessary to face the dilemma of whether it is better to expand or adapt international law's categories in order to capture newer and all important global regulatory developments that do not easily correspond to the canons of the discipline or if it is better to avoid this risky adventure altogether.

6.1.2 Coalition's Fluctuant Informality and Informal International Law

The informal international law-making project (IN-LAW) conducted by Joost Pauwelyn, Ramses A. Wessel, and Jan Wouters[99] is an important attempt to connect the discipline with innovative developments in global rule-making –[100] i.e., on the international and transnational levels. This includes the work performed by coalitions of the willing.

Regarding 'output informality',[101] it is quite clear that the outcomes of coalitions are not treaties, nor are participating states interested in generating international custom through the co-ordinated action performed within their framework, as these informal groups of states expressly deny any intention to create legal rules. International co-operation undertaken within coalitions leads to the same outcomes as those mentioned in the IN-LAW project, namely 'a guideline, standard, declaration, or even more informal policy coordination or exchange'.[102] 'Process informality' understood as 'cooperation ... that ... occurs in a loosely organized network or forum rather than a traditional

---

[99] See note 6.

[100] Other projects pursue the same goal, such as GAL, or the Heidelberg-based project on International Public Authority (IPA). The added value I see in the IN-LAW project for the purposes of this section is that it brings together the insights from the other projects, with particular consideration to the specific question of whether informal international law is a meaningful concept and, if so, how it is made. On the relation between GAL, IN-LAW, and IPA, see Philipp Dann and Marie von Engelhardt, 'Legal Approaches to Global Governance and Accountability: Informal Lawmaking, International Public Authority, and Global Administrative Law Compared', in Pauwelyn, Wessel, and Wouters (eds.), p. 106.

[101] See Joost Pauwelyn, 'Informal International Lawmaking: Framing the Concept', in Pauwelyn, Wessel, and Wouters (eds.), p. 13, at pp. 15–20.

[102] Ibid., p. 15.

236   COALITIONS OF THE WILLING AND THE ROLE OF LAW

organization (IO)',[103] is applicable to coalitions of the willing as well, and the fact that different coalitions exhibit varying degrees of procedural organization is also covered in the description of process informality, which is perhaps more aptly described as 'forum informality',[104] another term used in this project. Finally, on 'actor informality', the IN-LAW project attributes this feature to the circumstance that this sort of international co-operation 'does not engage traditional diplomatic actors (such as heads of State, foreign ministries, or embassies) but rather other ministries, domestic regulators, independent or semi-independent agencies … sub-federal entities … or the legislative or judicial branch'.[105] This is clearly influenced by the work on trans-governmental networks, particularly by Anne-Marie Slaughter, since one of the major characteristics of the networks described in her book *New World Order* is the direct agency-to-agency co-operation on a transnational plane performed by the 'new diplomats',[106] instead of traditional interstate co-operation through senior state representatives holding 'full powers'.[107] Here, the correspondence to coalitions is problematic. Most coalitions bring together state representatives of a high political level on their plenary meetings. There is the Ministerial Plenary of the GCTF where foreign ministers gather and adopt the memoranda of this forum (the guidance and best practices documents), the High-Level Political Meetings of the PSI (HLPM), usually at the level of undersecretaries of foreign ministries, and others such as the GICNT's Plenary Meeting, or the Climate and Clear Coalition's High-Level Assembly. IN-LAW's definition of 'actor informality' seems thus to leave several international coalitions, partnerships, initiatives, or however called, out of the picture. On the other hand, however, the working definition of informal international law-making provided in this project reflects crucial characteristics and recurrent themes treated in the present book:

> Cross-border cooperation between public authorities, with or without the participation of private actors and/or international organizations, in a forum other than a traditional international organization (process informality), and/or as between actors other than traditional diplomatic actors (such as regulators or agencies) (actor informality) and/or which does not

---

[103] Ibid., p. 17 (including the FATF in 'process informality').
[104] Ibid., p. 21.
[105] Ibid., p. 19.
[106] See Slaughter, *A New World Order*, pp. 36–64.
[107] See VCLT, Art. 7 (Pauwelyn refers to this too; see note 105).

6.1 THE INTERPLAY BETWEEN FORMALITY AND INFORMALITY 237

> result in a formal treaty or other traditional source of international law (output informality).[108]

It is true that the three elements need not all be present in order for international co-operation to be considered as informal international law-making in the sense of this project,[109] and the working definition reflects this clearly with the alternative use of conjunctions and disjunctions. However, Pauwelyn also mentions that the 'focus of the project is mainly on IN-LAW which is informal in all three ways'.[110] This is understandable since international co-operation in which only 'actor informality' is present includes a broad range of decisions that are hardly conceivable as informal, such as, for instance, many subsequent treaty evolutions that take place within the framework of COPs, where other ministries and domestic agencies, in contrast to foreign ministries, integrate the countries' delegations and take decisions. And more broadly and for quite some time, in (formal) international environmental law, foreign ministries are no longer the leading voices, but instead the ministries of the environment; and the same holds true for international communications law, where the delegates to conferences of the International Telecommunications Union (ITU) come mainly from national regulatory agencies on the sector (international intellectual property, and international trade law are further examples). This suggests that the notion of 'actor informality' provided by the IN-LAW project is problematic.

It is so since it is deeply formalistic and traditionalistic, as the relation to 'full powers' according to the Vienna Convention on the Law Treaties (VCLT) makes clear. Neither is article 7 VCLT so restrictive itself as to exclude state representatives other than 'traditional diplomatic actors', nor is the subsequent practice of states parties to the VCLT that traditionalistic at all. There are, of course, persisting and reasonable worries in foreign ministries regarding the eventual loss of centrality and coherence of a state's foreign policy due to the internal disaggregation that is promoted globally. I have argued that this decentralization of diplomacy is often used as a tactic by powerful states to circumvent central channels, mostly foreign ministries of less powerful states – a tactic that in Mexican foreign policy

---

[108] Pauwelyn, 'Informal International Lawmaking: Framing the Concept', p. 22.
[109] Ibid., p. 21.
[110] Ibid.

238   COALITIONS OF THE WILLING AND THE ROLE OF LAW

circles has been described as 'knocking on several doors at the same time'.[111] Combined with informality, it certainly generates problems of transparency and responsiveness at the domestic level, and if pursued through serial bilateralism, it obscures the creation of plurilateral regimes and the shaping of multilateral ones. So, one should remain alert to the disadvantages caused by the decentralization of states' diplomatic channels. However, taken on its own, it can hardly constitute an element defining informal international law-making.[112] It is far more telling, in my opinion, that many coalitions and networks avoid talking about 'parties', or 'members', making instead very conscious use of terms like 'participants', or 'participating states', and at times 'endorsing states'. This is actually encouraged by the *Guidance on Non-Binding Documents* of the US Department of State Office of the Legal Advisor Treaty Section:

> We advise negotiators to avoid using the term "Parties" in non-binding documents. Rather, we encourage the use of other terms such as "Participants".[113]

The main purpose of the usage of terms like 'participant' is to make clear that these schemes of international co-operation 'are better understood as an activity than an organization'.[114]

Nonetheless, the tripartite notion proposed by IN-LAW is very useful for present purposes, if slightly modified or adapted to what we could observe from the phenomena analyzed in the previous chapters. In this sense, coalitions of the willing are informal actors composed primarily (but not exclusively) of states, in the sense that the *participants* decide to co-ordinate their actions and take decisions outside any formal structure anchored in an instrument under international law (*actor informality*). This does not hinder the introduction of measures related to procedural organization and even some elementary rules of procedure, as long as these are not incorporated into a formal, legal document, which would endanger their flexibility in composition and functioning (*process informality*) – i.e., the efficiency paradigm – which is their *raison d'être*. And coalitions do not intend to create any legal instrument whatsoever,

---

[111] See Chapter 4, p. 139–140.
[112] This shows the difficulties of adopting working definitions on rapidly evolving phenomena that hardly denote 'inherent' or 'defining' properties. On this, see Chapter 2.
[113] See above Chapter 1, note 12.
[114] Haass, *The Reluctant Sheriff*, p. 95.

6.1 THE INTERPLAY BETWEEN FORMALITY AND INFORMALITY 239

renouncing to the advantages of legal obligation in order to maintain the ability 'to respond more quickly and creatively' to pressing global risks (*output informality*).[115]

From this reformulation of the features that characterize, or allow one to talk about, coalitions' informality (and of much of the informality of 'cross-border cooperation between public authorities' more generally),[116] several elements deserve further attention as they help explain the arguments made in the previous chapters, namely that coalitions' informality is itself fluctuant (i.e. marked by *quasi-formalization* processes) and that the informal international law that stems from coalitions of the willing is not a sort of new global soft law, but is best described as an *anti-law law*.[117]

6.1.2.1 On Quasi-Formalization and Reformalization

Informality is at times followed by formalization processes. The FATF is the role model in regard to these developments, and it has been mimicked by other coalitions over time, so that we can fairly speak of these processes as a recurrent theme of coalitions of the willing. This move to a rather limited formality obeys to coalitions' necessity to improve their inner organization, to streamline decision-making, and to provide better outreach to external actors, since, for such purposes, it is indispensable that those outside the club recognize key aspects of the club's organization and work, something that is obscured by a high degree of informality as the early days of the PSI evidenced. Moreover, the attempt to bring in some recognizable structures and processes – i.e., some formality – is also related to achieving a moderate degree of certainty and predictability, and thereby to counter some of the legitimacy – and rule of law – deficits commonly attributed to these loosely organized entities. But, at the same time, coalitions have to remain highly efficient: no issues of procedural fairness can stand in the way of the mission's accomplishment. Any prioritization that would run counter the *Rumsfeld maxim* would transform a coalition into something else, bringing it closer to the process of the UN General Assembly, something every coalition is there to avoid. So, these formalization attempts have to be contained, limited to quasi-formalization, in order to retain the built-in flexibility that informality guarantees best.

---

[115] *US National Security Strategy 2006*, p. 48.
[116] Pauwelyn, 'Informal International Lawmaking: Framing the Concept', p. 22.
[117] See Chapter 5, Section 5.1.2, and Chapter 4, Section 4.1.2.1.

240   COALITIONS OF THE WILLING AND THE ROLE OF LAW

Formal international law – with its rigidity, insistence on predictability, and the respect for sovereign equality – is a bad candidate for assuring this built-in flexibility. But trying to give (whatever) form to political decisions, to make an activity that involves parameters of behaviour durable,[118] and to reach out beyond the inner circle (i.e., to get recognition on the value if not the validity of such decisions by those not involved in making them) is best achieved through law. Coalitions' fluctuant informality – i.e. the shifts from informality to formality, and back again – seems to have emerged as a viable solution to this tension: it is the means for transforming coalitions into 'durable efforts', for 'institutionalizing informality'.[119] The FATF epitomizes this fluctuant form of organization and decision-making, which has been amply mimicked by other coalitions. In this sense, a *prima facie* political process of consultation among friends is increasingly resorting to law-like properties, so to speak. It is a process of global rule-making that remains outside the strictures of law – especially in its rigidity – but takes advantage of the latter's appealing, normative, and legitimizing force. And this, I submit, is the underlying theme of informal international law-making as it explains to a great degree why resorting to informal law is done in the first place.

The interplay between formality and informality happens also through *reformalization processes* in the sense of the reception that informal standards experience in formal law.[120] Suffice it here to recall the influence of the PSI's *Statement of Interdiction Principles* (SIP) on the adoption of a binding treaty in the framework of the IMO, as well as on the drafting of SC resolution 1540 (2004); or the incorporation of crucial elements of the GCTF's memoranda in relation to kidnapping for ransoms and FTF into SC resolutions. Likewise, when the SC strongly urges states to implement the FATF recommendations in relation to the financing of terrorism and targeted sanctions, a reformalization of

---

[118] On the importance of the 'enduring and settled character' of law, see Hart, *The Concept of Law*, pp. 23–24.

[119] The expression is taken from the project conducted at the Goethe University in Frankfurt a.M., and headed by political scientist Christopher Daase, *Die Institutionalisierung von Informalität*, at www.fb03.uni-frankfurt.de/42800816/Forschung-Projekt-A1.

[120] For a similar point, see Christopher Daase, 'The ILC and Informalization', in Georg Nolte (ed.), *Peace through International Law: The Role of the International Law Commission* (Heidelberg: Springer, 2009), p. 179, at p. 182.

6.1 THE INTERPLAY BETWEEN FORMALITY AND INFORMALITY 241

informal standards takes place.[121] Reformalization processes can be surprisingly fast, but usually we are talking about long-lasting efforts of ongoing adaptation of (formal) institutions, which are embedded in a 'reform-unfriendly environment'.[122] Coalitions' durability can therefore be regarded as a prerequisite for a fruitful interplay with institutions; in other words, coalitions' fluctuant informality facilitates reformalization processes.

Such reformalization processes make associations of coalitions' outcomes with international soft law tempting.[123] It is true that we are in the presence of standards, guidelines, best practices, and recommendations, all of which do not intend to create legally binding obligations but nevertheless are normative enunciations that establish parameters of behaviour. However, similarities notwithstanding,[124] there are important differences that call this comparison into question. First, most soft-law instruments are 'soft' in the sense that they do not establish legal obligations, but not necessarily in the sense of emanating from what at times are called 'soft institutions',[125] a term used by Jan Klabbers to describe phenomena related to those I am dealing with here. Softness and informality should not be equated because a soft-law instrument can perfectly and does usually emanate from formal institutions and according to formal procedures. Second, informal norms emanating from coalitions are also directed towards non-participants, or third parties, and

---

[121] For these examples, see Chapter 4, Section 4.1.2; Chapter 5, Section 5.2.2; and Chapter 6, Section 6.1.1.1.

[122] Daase, 'The ILC and Informalization', p. 180.

[123] There are, of course, different conceptions of soft law, and the diversity of instruments that have fallen under this rubric has always made it a challenge to define the concept (see Christine Chinkin, 'The Challenge of Soft Law: Development and Change in International Law' (1989) 38 *International and Comparative Law Quarterly* 850). According to Klabbers, the description as 'soft-law' of normative manifestations that come along with global governance is 'misleading and unhelpful' (Klabbers, *International* Law, p. 38), but this relates to his general skepticism towards the usefulness of the concept as a normative category and does not limit itself to newer normative manifestations (see Jan Klabbers, 'The Redundancy of Soft Law' [1996] 65 *Nordic Journal of International Law* 167).

[124] For instance, many of the advantages of resorting to informal international law-making are very similar to the reasons why states opt for soft law; cf. *inter alia*: Alan Boyle, 'Reflections on the Treaty as a Law-Making Instrument', in Alexander Orakhelashvili and Sarah Williams, *40 Years of the Vienna Convention on the Law of Treaties* (London: British Institute of International and Comparative Law, 2010), p. 9, at pp. 11–12.

[125] Klabbers, 'Institutional Ambivalence by Design'.

242   COALITIONS OF THE WILLING AND THE ROLE OF LAW

compliance is monitored from lesser to stronger degrees –[126] i.e., from outreach activities and capacity building to aggressive and multilayered compliance mechanisms in which even very hard institutions take part – like the case of FATF recommendations in the compliance of which the SC plays a crucial role. Finally, and perhaps most importantly, according to a recurrent understanding of soft law, these are norms of 'nascent legal force', or 'quasi-legal rules',[127] which at times reflect existing international custom and, at other times, give expression to emerging customary rules, thus contributing to their crystallization. Hence, soft-law instruments are normative instances that can be captured according to international law's traditional categories and ultimately form part of the machinery of formal international law-making.[128] As we have seen throughout the book, coalitions of the willing make a strong claim about the non-legal nature of their products, often expressly denying any role in the creation of legal rules, and states acting within coalitions do not usually make assertions about custom. This makes the emergence of customary international law problematic, to say the least, and the location of these instruments within the fabric of international law troublesome.[129]

Reformalization is rather another game of regime complexity conducted through the pragmatic correspondences outlined above. Coalitions' decisions are negotiated within a selective group of friends rather smoothly; it would take far longer not only if they were to be adopted as legally binding instruments (a reason for resorting to soft law as well). This would also be the case if negotiations would take place in a formal forum, including a selective one such as the SC, where occasional spoilers sit at the negotiation table and where scrutiny is greater, if for no other reason than the public attention that many formal fora receive. The non-binding and non-formal decisions are quickly spread beyond the coalition that creates them through the outreach activities of regional working groups affiliated with the coalition, awareness-raising activities facilitated by platforms (institutions and networks interested in the spread of these

---

[126] See also Eyal Benvenisti, *The Law of Global Governance* (Pocketbooks of The Hague Academy of International Law, 2015), p. 37.

[127] Jorge Castañeda, *Legal Effects of United Nations Resolutions* (New York: Columbia University Press, 1969), p. 176.

[128] This does not mean that every soft-law instrument will eventually harden; this depends on a series of circumstances impossible to establish *a priori*.

[129] See also Rodiles, 'The Design of UN Sanctions through the Interplay with Informal Arrangements', pp. 181–182.

6.1 THE INTERPLAY BETWEEN FORMALITY AND INFORMALITY 243

normative contents), as well as through cross-participation and cross-references among the coalition from which the standard emanates and other institutions and informal entities with a saying on the subject-matter. By this means, the normative content is not transformed into a formal rule of international law, but a given knowledge is disseminated and reiterated over time (e.g., why and how ideologies that lead to violent extremism have to be countered) that shapes the normative understanding of the broader international community on the issue.[130] Once the parliamentary ambience of the formal forum where the content is to be adopted is ripe, also because the reasons and motivations underlying the non-formal norm have been acknowledged by the many (recalcitrant states have been educated),[131] predetermined normative contents find their way into the decision-making processes of competent organs. But let us not confuse these reformalization instances with the usual political negotiation that precedes law creation. Not only do the cases described in this book reflect a systematic coadjutant role of informal venues in determining normative contents, but the very same contents possess normative force by their own – i.e., independently, whether they enter the formal realm or not. As FATF recommendations show, there is a non-legal efficacy attached to them that renders the symbiotic relationship between bindingness and legality doubtful.

States that can perform as orchestrators due to their predominant role across institutions (formal and informal) will seek to transplant the normative contents developed within the coalition into formal law instruments, if and when this move proves to be convenient in terms of maximizing implementation and legitimation. Reformalization processes of coalitions' informal rules *may* thus lead to formal and hard law. In this sense, there are similarities to soft law indeed. However, the process itself is different and not necessarily linear, i.e., from informal to formal law: the formalization of informal rules is not the only means of achieving efficacy. Alternative methods of guiding conduct, such as education, which happens a lot through conceptual framing as explained in the first chapter, may not be described as 'hard' directives, but they are

---

[130] I have referred to this as *paideia's* normative function, a notion related to framing, nudging, and the role of repetition in governance, which remains underexplored in international legal scholarship.

[131] Of course, here, as always, external eventualities play an important role. The transplant of several normative contents developed within the GCTF to SC resolutions (on FTF, violent extremism, and kidnapping for ransom) was clearly favoured and accelerated by the rise of the Islamic State.

244 COALITIONS OF THE WILLING AND THE ROLE OF LAW

highly efficient, especially if woven into a multilayered scheme of compliance, as it is characteristic of regime complexes. That is why these normative trends can – and should – be described as ruling devices.[132]

6.1.2.2 The Borrowing of Legal Language by Coalitions: Ruling via Framing

One of the principal tools for achieving this fluctuant informality is the borrowing of international law's vernacular. The PSI is a case in point for the apparent contradiction of a political commitment that does not intend to create any legal rule whatsoever, and that highlights its voluntary and action-oriented nature, while at the same time it is very actively engaged in improving existing legal frameworks. The closely related CSI, described in Chapter 4 as a paramount example of informal serial bilateralism,[133] is all about advancing certain goals through voluntary bilateral declarations, which, at the same time, are attached to the language of treaties, giving rise to speculations about the precise legal nature of these arrangements, which do not pretend to create rights and obligations but are said to be adopted within the framework of existing bilateral treaties. And the GCTF makes extensive usage of the rule of law moniker to advance its measures.

The FATF borrows most heavily from the language of law, and it does so in a rather systematic way: It describes its mission as a 'mandate'; it speaks of 'counter-measures' when referring to aggressive economic actions members and non-members alike are called upon to implement in regard to 'high risk and non-cooperative *jurisdictions*';[134] while most

---

[132] As mentioned by Neil Walker, contemporary scholarship on global law (to which the attempts at understanding the implications of global governance schemes for international law – and beyond, as the present one – belong) engages more and more in 'trend-spotting' – i.e., identifying the new normative 'trends', or innovative 'legal designs'. It is thus a mapping exercise, but one which refers to a 'shifting sea'. This difficulty is already apparent in that it is not always clear whether we are talking about the implications of these trends for international law, transnational law, or both, so that the moniker 'global law' is used to remedy this lack of reference, while at the same time a reference is being construed from *intimations*, at best. See Walker, *Intimations of Global Law*, pp. 159–162.

[133] See above, Chapter 4, pp. 128–133.

[134] See FATF, *High-Risk and Non-Cooperative Jurisdictions, Public Statement* (3 November 2017), at www.fatf-gafi.org/publications/high-riskandnon-cooperativejurisdictions/documents/public-statement-november-2017.html. The FATF ended the use of the list of non-cooperative jurisdiction (also known as the 'black list') in 2006 (as early as 2002, it ceased to include new states in this review). This was due to increasing legitimacy concerns related to the aggressive measures imposed by a Western dominated group

6.1 THE INTERPLAY BETWEEN FORMALITY AND INFORMALITY 245

coalitions speak of 'participating States', or just 'participants', the FATF uses the term 'members', though it sometimes also employs 'endorsing State'; 'monitoring' and 'implementation' are two key concepts of its elaborated and highly efficient compliance mechanism. Furthermore, its recommendations are followed by 'interpretive notes', and some of its key documents, such as the *Mandate 2012–2020*,[135] are formulated in a way that resembles to a large degree documents of traditional IOs. The extensive reliance on this legal vocabulary further contributes to the perception of the FATF as a 'formal but non-legally binding institution'.[136]

The usage of the term 'counter-measures' by the FATF is particularly perplexing. It suggests that those jurisdictions that persistently fail to implement its recommendations, regardless of if they are members or not, commit thereby an internationally wrongful act and are thus legitimate targets of economic sanctions,[137] even if the sanctions themselves

---

of states that targeted third states. The listing process was replaced in 2007 by the creation of the *International Co-operation Review Group* (ICRG) and a new, more co-operative procedure, which was again hardened in 2010 following calls from the G20. Today, the ICRG conducts reviews of countries with 'strategic deficiencies' in the implementation of its standards (which goes beyond the mere recommendations, including the means the FATF considers appropriate to implement them according to its interpretative notes and other compliance indicators). According to the ability and willingness exhibited by the reviewed countries along this process, the FATF releases several 'public statements' per year, calling its members *and other* jurisdictions to adopt either enhanced due diligence measures regarding these high-risk countries or 'counter-measures' against unwilling states – i.e., non-cooperative jurisdictions. The 'black list' is thus still in place (on the FATF's website), and it still follows the double dichotomy able/unable–willing/unwilling, though in regard to the unable or less able, the approach is less confrontational as it used to be until the early 2000s. Information on this review process and its evolution can be consulted at www.fatf-gafi.org/topics/high-riskandnon-coopera tivejurisdictions/more/moreabouttheinternationalco-operationreviewgroupicrg.html.

[135] See FATF, *Mandate (2012–2020)*, at http://www.fatf-gafi.org/media/fatf/documents/FINAL%20FATF%20MANDATE%202012-2020.pdf.

[136] See Benvenisti, 'Coalitions of the Willing', p. 4. However, more recently, Benvenisti has used the term 'informal inter-governmental agreements', and 'informal institutions' (see Benvenisti, 'Towards a Typology of Informal International Lawmaking Mechanisms and their Distinct Accountability Gaps', pp. 299–301), or 'informal international governmental organizations' ('InGOs') (see Benvenisit, *The Law of Global Governance*, p. 37).

[137] These go from restrictions to prohibitions of business and financial transactions with non-cooperative states; see the Interpretative Note to Recommendation 19, in *FATF Recommendations*, p. 81.

246   COALITIONS OF THE WILLING AND THE ROLE OF LAW

consisted of wrongful acts.[138] At the same time, this seems to run counter the very nature of the recommendations, which are 'non-binding instruments under international law'.[139] It could hardly follow a wrongful act from the non-observance of a political commitment,[140] indeed of a non-legal norm. This again would impede the preclusion of wrongfulness of the acts taken by FATF members in the application of coercive economic measures in the event that these would constitute violations of their obligations under international law, a situation which, in practice, does not always come across as clear. This has raised doubts regarding the use of FATF's counter-measures, with at least one commentator describing them as violations of international law,[141] and others more carefully suggesting 'a potential for recourse to unlawful coercion'.[142] However, the FATF does not seem to employ this term in its technical–legal sense, i.e., as a measure to procure the cessation of an internationally wrongful act and to achieve reparation for the injuries caused by such a wrongful act,[143] but rather as a tool for compliance with its standards, and, more broadly, as a means to *counter* the risks for the international financial system that emanate from unable and unwilling states, more than a reaction to a violation of international law, it has the character of a preventive measure informed by risk-management criteria. So, why the legal framing?[144]

The strategic recourse to legal terms by coalitions of the willing is part of a move to a quasi-formality, which is itself an attempt to better connect to those outside the club, and even to those not pertaining to the core of the club. As explained in Chapter 2, words carry a conceptual package associated with their ordinary sense (surface frames), and, at

---

[138] See *Responsibility of States for Internationally Wrongful Acts*, annexed to UN Doc. A/RES/56/83 (12 December 2001), Art 22.

[139] See FATF, *20 Years of the FAFT Recommendations (1990–2010)*, p. 4.

[140] FATF's Mandate speaks also of the commitment of the members to 'endorse and implement' the recommendations and makes clear that it 'is not intended to create any legal rights or obligations'; see FATF, *Mandate (2012–2020)*, paras. 5 and 48.

[141] See Todd Doyle, 'Cleaning Up Anti-Money Laundering Strategies: Current FATF Tactics Needlessly Violate International Law' (2002) 24 *Houston Journal of International Law* 279, at 294.

[142] Roth, 'Coalitions of the Willing and the International Rule of Law', p. 39

[143] See *ILC Commentaries to the Articles on State Responsibility*, reprinted in ILC, *Report on the Work of Its Fifty-Third Session (23 April–1 June and 2 July–10 August 2001)*, Chapter IV (State Responsibility) p. 20, Art. 22, Commentary, para. 1.

[144] This legal framing goes as far as to mention, in recommendation 19, that FATF counter-measures should be 'proportionate'; see *FATF Recommendations*, 19, p. 19.

6.1 THE INTERPLAY BETWEEN FORMALITY AND INFORMALITY 247

times, such conceptual packages can be representative of deeply rooted ideals, value systems, and cultural preferences (deep frames).[145] The language of law, even if not used in its technical sense, represents a common frame of reference that is crucial for communication. Since this frame of reference is about shared understandings, it evokes notions of fairness and objectivity. In other words, the usage of this language provides coalitions with a ready-made arsenal of input legitimacy that they are very much in need of in the eyes of non-participants, and sometimes even among those who join the club later, when the rules of the game have been set by the coalition's inner circle. In relation to output legitimacy, legal notions bring with them normative force, which contributes to coalitions' benchmark – i.e., efficiency. FATF 'counter-measures' may have little to do with state responsibility, but the idea that non-cooperative jurisdictions are something like 'wrongdoers' is success-fully spread by the non-technical usage of this juridical concept. This shows again how coalitions further the instrumentalization of inter-national law, using it strategically as a legitimacy-conferring device, as *politics of fairness.*

Another example of ruling via framing is the NSS 'gift basket', suc-cessfully imported to international treaty law in the form of the Paris Agreement's NDCs.[146] There, the role of persuasion in mobilizing states to adopt national policies and international measures voluntarily but in a highly co-ordinated way is rather remarkable. In his article on the transnational regime complex for climate change, Abbott speaks about the role of targeted information – i.e., the 'provision of politically useful information' in 'managing' states, as another method for improving regime complexity.[147] This is closely related to the partial briefing func-tion[148] I described in Chapter 2 as one of the principal functions of framing – and it also resembles 'nudging' as a regulation technique based on choice architecture and behavioural psychology.[149] Actually, Abbott explicitly acknowledges in this context the role of 'cognitive framing'.[150] As argued in the present book, 'coalition of the willing' is itself an idea of international co-operation transmitted through a frame (that comes in

---

[145] See Chapter 2, pp. 19 et seq.
[146] See Chapter 5, Section 5.2.4.
[147] Abbott, 'Strengthening the Transnational Regime Complex', 79.
[148] See Chapter 2, pp. 14–15.
[149] See Sunstein, *Why Nudge? The Politics of Libertarian Paternalism.*
[150] Abbott, 'Strengthening the Transnational Regime Complex', 79.

248 COALITIONS OF THE WILLING AND THE ROLE OF LAW

the form of a conceptual metaphor), and the work of coalitions is carried out to a considerable extent via strategic framing and spins (i.e., reframing in order to avoid negative connotations about the frames involved), which are aimed at persuading states to adjust their conduct, voluntarily but in a directed manner, and thereby disciplining them.[151]

What this suggests is that framing and other related persuasion tactics like nudging are becoming more and more important tools of global ruling; it is no exaggeration to say that these techniques – informed by cognitive psychology and linguistics and well-established practice in marketing strategies – are contemporary means for establishing parameters of behaviour that are routinely followed. And this might have impact on the notion of (international) legality, by way of depriving the law of its formality (and the control of power that comes along with it), and finally of its autonomous character: an *anti-law law* that rules efficiently without many of the attributes that have long distinguished the legal materials (as belonging to a legal system), from other normative instances.

6.2 Concluding Remarks on Coalitions' Impact on International Legality

What was discussed in the last section furthermore suggests that the attribute of being legally binding, indeed, of being legal in a formal sense at all, does not hinder rules to be effectively followed. This is a fundamental issue related to the concept of international law as it confronts us with the question to what extent *having an obligation* can still be separated from *being obliged*,[152] the perlocutionary distinction that informs Hart's concept of law.[153] It is clear that states, IOs, and other

---

[151] This could be examined equally from the perspective of Michel Foucault's theses of disciplinary power – in particular, his ideas on 'correction' and 'normalization'. See, for instance, Michel Foucault, *Discipline and Punish – The Birth of the Prison* (New York: Vintage Books, 1997), pp. 135 et seq.

[152] Also alluding to this distinction in the context of the deformalization of non-proliferation law, see Joyner, *International Law and the Proliferation of Weapons of Mass Destruction*, p. 354. I have referred elsewhere to Hart's distinction in relation to coalitions of the willing in general, see Rodiles, 'Coalitions of the Willing', 701.

[153] Hart, *The Concept of Law*, pp. 6, 82–91 (on the said distinction). I use here the notion 'perlocutionary' because this distinction is based on the ordinary usage of language – i.e., the ordinary usage of these utterances and what they reveal for the concept of law. Hart follows the theory of speech acts of philosopher John Langshaw Austin (the seminal work being J. L. Austin, *How to Do Things with Words*, second edition (Oxford: Oxford University Press, 1976) as he explicitly refers to in p. 14 of *The Concept of Law*.

6.2 CONCLUDING REMARKS ON INTERNATIONAL LEGALITY 249

actors follow international political and moral rules; there is nothing new to the observation that there are reasons for the conduct of behaviour other than legal. Hart's distinction, however, implies that rules are followed over time (out of a general habit of obedience) based on the fact that they emanate from an authority recognized as legitimate by society,[154] and due to the fact that they form part of a system unified by the 'authoritative mark'[155] provided by the recognized authority (the identification of law as valid that permits to trace back this recognition).

In classical international law, this authority resides ultimately in states, and identification occurs by tracing back the validity of international rules according to the principle of state consent, using the guide that Article 38 of the Statute of the ICJ offers to that court. Now, as global governance advances, and more broadly, as globalization continues to give rise to new constituencies, a doctrine of sources based on state consent is increasingly regarded as insufficiently covering the fundamental task of identifying (and uniting) international or global law's materials.[156] That also relinquishes international law's aspiration of centrality as a legal system. States still enjoy this recognized authority, but no longer exclusively so. Coalitions of the willing are states' creatures, and the innovative rule-making they engage in is followed effectively – at times more than treaties and custom – by an increasing number of states and within states, regardless of inside or outside a given coalition. The protests and other objections that emerged in regard to the PSI in its early years are less frequent today as a result, in part, of the successful spin exercises of the Obama administration, which present coalitions and other informal networks not in a confrontational manner but as complementary and co-operative venues. This posits the question whether the work of coalitions and other related phenomena of global governance has an influence deep enough that it is changing states' 'internal point of view'[157] about the *reasons* that explain patterns of behaviour. I will address this far-reaching question by way of some tentative remarks in the next and concluding chapter.

---

[154] Ibid., pp. 20–25.

[155] Ibid., p. 95.

[156] For a skeptical view on the attempts to capture these materials, see d'Aspremont, *Formalism and the Sources of International Law*, p. 133.

[157] Hart, *The Concept of Law*, pp. 88–91.

7

Conclusion

Fluctuant informality is the benchmark of coalitions of the willing. It has been this dynamic evolutionary practice that has allowed the phenomenon to adapt over time to tectonic shifts in world affairs: from post–Cold War anxieties to the challenges of non-polarity. In terms of coalitions' design, it means that these groupings oscillate between amorphousness and a rudimentary form in order to enhance the links among fellow partnerships and become companions of standing institutions, thus being able to shape the latter along the way. Hence, this kind of fluctuant informality, or *quasi-formalization*, facilitates orchestration. Inherently related to the institutional dimension of fluctuant informality, its normative dimension consists of the back-and-forth between informality and formality, the interplay spurred by coalitions of the willing. This interplay manifests in *reformalization* processes. As seen most clearly in Chapter 5 in regard to FATF recommendations, informal standards systematically inform formal law-making via recognition, repetition, and intricate implementation strategies, thus not only preceding the law as prelegal political processes, but already informing how the law should be created, interpreted, and implemented. Therefore, informal standards operate at the interstices between law and non-law, integrated eventually into the meaning and scope of formal norms. Particularly in regard to interpretation and norm evolution, informal law shows its jurisgenerative capacity precisely as 'interstice norms', in the sense described by Vaughan Lowe,[1] which spur change of primary rules of international law via subsequent practice, for instance.[2]

---

[1] See Vaughan Lowe, 'The Politics of Law-Making: Are the Method and Character of Norm Creation Changing?', in Byers, *The Role of Law in International Politics*, p. 207, at pp. 212–219.

[2] For a similar reading of 'indicators' as interstice norms, see Guadalupe Barrena Nájera, *Human Rights Indicators in the Field of Criminal Justice and Crime Control. Implications for the Idea of Law in Governance and Governmentality* (PhD Dissertation, submitted to

CONCLUSION

251

But the normative interplay does not stop there. The borrowing of the legal vernacular by coalitions is part of this mutually reinforcing game of reformalization too. Non-legal norms are framed in legal language, as the observation of FATF's framing tactics in Chapter 6 revealed. It would be rather naïve to think that these interactions do not affect the instances involved. Not only is the non-legal framed as the legal by way of comparison, but also, as explained in Chapter 2, framing *creates* similarities: when voluntary commitments are roped in the legal language, informal norms acquire legal characteristics but without renouncing the advantages of the built-in flexibility that defines efficiency-driven, pragmatic normativity. In Chapter 5, we also saw that innovative regulatory devices developed within coalitions and other networks are not only mimicked in informal frameworks but also imported by formal institutions and law. Regulatory devices that do not prescribe but induce patterns of behaviour, discipline conduct, or just manage relevant actors have become part of transnational law and even international treaty law. It may be an overreaction, but I think that the observations and analysis undertaken throughout this book give strong reasons for regarding the *Paris Agreement on Climate Change* as a silent but profound revolution in the law of treaties. The interplay that manifests there in the non-legal framing of the legal, disturbs the conception of the latter: instead of *pacta sunt servanda*, a compilation of national public policies, a formal multilateral treaty that is about 'best-practices multilateralism' as proposed by Richard Haass;[3] in other words, a non-contractual commitment called treaty.

It is in this sense that the notion of an *anti-law law* introduced towards the end of the preceding chapter (and also mentioned in Chapter 4) is to be understood: a normativity that is mutually defined by the interplay between formality and informality, between law and non-law. Effective ruling devices are deprived of law's formal rationality but connected to the legitimacy-conferring arsenal of the language of law, as well as to the normative force of the legal toolkit. This may bring to mind Fleur Johns' concept of 'non-legality'.[4] But the notion of an *anti-law law* put forward in the present book has a lot to do with international law's deformalization, something with which Johns' important book is not

---

the Legal Research Institute of the National Autonomous University of Mexico (UNAM), Mexico City: October 2017; on file with the author).

[3] See Haass, *A World in Disarray*, pp. 254–255.

[4] See Fleur Johns, *Non-Legality in International Law*.

252 CONCLUSION

primarily concerned.[5] Nonetheless, both are related, especially in the sense that describing the work of coalitions of the willing as something which happens outside the province of international law, without affecting its fundamentals, is fallacious. The many extra- and pre-legalities that coalitions generate transform the legal. Remember the description of the PSI as an entirely voluntary undertaking, respectful of state consent, and in line with the *Lotus presumption*. As a matter of strict legality, this is accurate, so why does this even matter to an international lawyer? I was often confronted with this 'non-issue' during presentations of drafts related to different parts of this book. I decided to problematize this, and made it an issue itself: the *non-issue issue* of coalitions of the willing described in Chapter 4 shows that the extra-legal framing of the PSI is, above all, a distraction from the ways through which the PSI has shaped the law of proliferation and the law of the sea, as subsequently demonstrated in Chapter 5. The relation of coalitions with international law has always been about 'shaping it, not breaking it',[6] but this shaping is quite intense. The 'extra-legal work' of the PSI has profoundly affected international legal regimes, so much so that studying, teaching, practicing, and writing on the applicable law in matters of shipping interdiction or non-proliferation of WMDs, or even about the law of the sea in general, would be incomplete and inaccurate today without addressing the extra-legal 'activity' called PSI.[7]

At the end of the previous chapter, I asked whether the work of coalitions of the willing is having an influence deep enough that it is changing states' 'internal point of view'[8] about the reasons that explain patterns of behaviour. A possible answer to this would be that states are giving up international law as we know it. Due to its lack of enforcement power, the big divisions within the international community, its cumbersome decision-making processes, etc., a deep resignation about the international rule of law (in the sense that *international law rules*) is leading to a fall-back into national policies that are formulated at the global level as voluntary 'pledges' or 'commitments' but efficiently co-ordinated transnationally among friends. The trade-off is not only the abandonment of

[5] Ibid., p. 21.

[6] Cf. Jones, *Still Ours to Lead*, p. 100.

[7] See, for instance, Douglas Guilfoyle, *Shipping Interdiction and the Law of the Sea* (Cambridge: Cambridge University Press, 2009); Joyner, *International Law and the Proliferation of WMD*; Klein, *Maritime Security and the Law of the Sea*; as well as Tanaka, *The International Law of the Sea*.

[8] Hart, *The Concept of Law*, pp. 88–91

CONCLUSION 253

legal certainty, but of the dichotomy legal/illegal altogether, replaced by a more efficient compliance mechanism characterized by pragmatic correspondences, persuasion, conceptual framing, and nudging. This narrative is a crude account of a 'new informal multilateral era',[9] or of 'best practices multilateralism' indeed,[10] in which the role of law at the global level is deeply transformed into the previously described *anti-law law*. A way of global ruling is favoured, which acquires its efficiency precisely by renouncing international law's formality. The new binary code is more rudimentary and politically informed; it replaces the fundamental distinction legal/illegal with one that comes at varying degrees – namely, 'willing and able/unable or unwilling'.

Many of the findings of this book point in that direction. However, two problems persist. First, the recognition of this *anti-law law* cannot be attributed to the international community as a whole – however problematic this concept is to define – but only to some: mostly powerful Western states. In Chapter 3, I argued that powerful states from the so-called 'Global South' disclose a highly ambivalent attitude towards informality, resorting, on the one hand, to it as well, but, on the other, sticking to the legal discourse of formalism. If the internal point of view in Hartian terms is not sufficiently representative of the larger community, then a change of the rule of recognition is hardly sustainable. This poses a conundrum: postulating that state consent has ceased to function as the building block of the law of the international community without sufficient consideration to state consent within that community is tantamount to changing the rules of a game by breaching the rules of that very same game. In that case, only time will tell whether the transgression becomes the new norm. In other words, the impact of coalitions of the willing and global governance more broadly is not deep enough to talk about a new international law, and so we are stacked to the narrative of international law in times of globalization, a law that is changing while resisting change at the same time.

Eyal Benvenisti has argued that coalitions of the willing are 'substituting international law'.[11] One could think in light of the above that this is not entirely accurate, an exaggeration indeed, since international law has not been shoved away, but augmented by and integrated into

---

[9] Haas (interviewee), Gwertzman (interviewer), 'The New Informal Multilateral Era'.
[10] See note 3.
[11] Benvenisti, 'The Move from Institutions'.

254   CONCLUSION

'frameworks'. However, Benvenisti is talking about international law as a legal system,[12] or its conception of it as such, and, therefore, it is the centrality aspiration of international law what has been seriously weakened by the interplay promoted by coalitions and other global governance mechanisms. Through this interplay, international law has entered into the reign of regime complexity, in which its centrality aspiration does not hold water any longer. In this sense – and this is the second, more serious problem with the narrative of disillusion with state consent – the internal point of view becomes pointless precisely because it might tell us something useful about the recognition of one normative order, but only when that normative order is already knotted with others within a broader disorder or complex. Here, the pluralism of Boaventura de Sousa Santos comes to mind:

> [I]n phenomenological terms and as a result of interaction and intersection among legal spaces one cannot properly speak of law and legality but rather of interlaw and interlegality. More important than the identification of the different legal orders is the tracing of the complex and changing relations among them.[13]

One might add that in today's global complex, it is more accurate to talk about 'inter-normativity', and that would probably not stand in the way of de Sousa Santos's pluralism, which is not constitutionalism in disguise. The struggle for the self-preservation of international law's relative autonomy would then become self-defeating violence in the sense of Walter Benjamin.[14] Once we acknowledge that regime complexity is managed and not ordered, and that this management is performed through pragmatic correspondences that evolve spontaneously from the interplay itself, then the interplay between formality and informality is best described as *resilience normativity* under which the primary and secondary levels are superseded, and no second-order rules can accommodate this multilayered and diachronic game.

However, today's global normative pluralism does not emerge spontaneously but is deliberately created by orchestrators, as we learned in Chapters 5 and 6. And although, in principle, it is open to broad participation, not every state and non-state player with a legitimate

---

[12] Ibid., 294.

[13] Santos, 'Law: A Map of Misreading. Toward a Postmodern Conception of Law', at 288.

[14] Walter Benjamin, 'Zur Kritik der Gewalt' in W Benjamin, *Angelus Novus*, volume 2 (Frankfurt a.M.: Suhrkamp, 1988) 42, 61.

CONCLUSION   255

interest have the resources to insert themselves in the creation processes
of the different normative instances – i.e., in the edges of the network.[15]
Such a pluralistic normative order tends to converge in the end into a
highly integrated, though still complex, system controlled by those who
have the power to be at the hub of the network. It is important to
underline that the fact that authority at the global level is disaggregating
into several spheres does not mean that it is not being exercised: 'liquid'[16]
or 'amorphous'[17] authority is nonetheless authority, and it is probably
the most active way of ruling in our contemporary world. As mentioned
in Chapter 6, the lawyer's traditional lens may not be trained in capturing
this amorphousness, or paraphrasing Andrea Bianchi, in catching the
butterflies,[18] but can aptly capture the detrimental effects of not doing so.
This is an uncomfortable position and one of the greatest and inescapable
challenges of our profession today: acknowledging the increasing deformalization of international law as a reality that affects our understanding
of the sources and, more broadly, of the structures of international law
while, at the same time, continuing to pursue the protection of the ideals
that make this legal order a meaningful political and historical project at
the global scale, as argued in Chapter 3. It is particularly perplexing since
this protection has been mainly afforded by formal means, which do not
seem to efficiently respond to informal developments.

   The challenge has to be addressed in a first step by refocusing our
lenses to capture the kaleidoscopic nature of global regulation.[19] Global
administrative law (GAL), pluralist accounts of international law, and
critical legal scholars, among others, have been doing this for quite some
time. The examples analyzed in this book strongly suggest that international lawyers need to look more carefully whenever a 'commitment' to
follow a global standard is raised, even if this is formally non-binding and
derives from no instrument under international law whatsoever; otherwise, the academic discipline may remain pure but detached from the
conduct of world affairs in a significant and growing number of 'issue

---

[15] See Niall Ferguson, *The Square and the Tower – Networks of Power, from the Freemasons
to Facebook* (New York: Penguin Press, 2017).
[16] Krisch, 'Liquid Authority in Global Governance'.
[17] Rodiles, *'Coalitions of the Willing'*.
[18] See Andrea Bianchi, 'Reflexive Butterfly Catching: Insights from a Situated Catcher', in
Pauwelyn, Wessel, and Wouters (eds.), *Informal International Lawmaking*, p. 200.
[19] Borrowing the metaphor from Edith Brown Weiss, 'International Law in a Kaleidoscopic
Word' (2011) 1 *Asian Journal of International Law* 21.

areas'. *Taking trends seriously*[20] might be the new professional motto. This is not a 'self-serving quest for new legal materials' that may help scholars to 'find their niche and distinguish themselves';[21] it is the function of law in contemporary global affairs that is at stake.

More than seventy years ago, Lauterpacht expressed a desire by formulating the function of international law as 'the subjection of the totality of international relations to the rule of law'.[22] This is the basic, indeed tautological, understanding of the rule of law, namely that *law should rule*,[23] and it is in this sense that the global rule of law is, above all, about the role that law occupies (or should occupy) in global affairs – i.e., in today's global complex. Lauterpacht's ambition is equally valid in regard to a rudimentary system defined by anarchy among states, as it is in the face of a networked order driven by complexity; in both cases, the risk of missing the law or shrinking its role is to leave power unconstrained. It is a myth that today's multilayered approach to global rule and action is not about hierarchy; the difference is that predominance is sought through other channels that are very good at disguising hierarchies. Thus, the deformalization of international law, resulting from the proliferation of informal governance schemes and from their interplay with formal institutions and law, represents a threat to the global rule of law in its most fundamental understanding as it considerably reduces the ambit where international law operates with relative autonomy. There is little doubt that international disputes still are (and will continue to be) settled by international tribunals where international law remains (and will remain) largely autonomous and where regime conflicts are more a matter of colliding rules from within a general system that either has the means to resolve them or draw analogies from private international law – if the analogies are not already part of the system. But this does not tell much about the rules that govern today

---

[20] I am referring here to the notion of 'trend-spotting' described in Walker, *Intimations of Global Law*, pp. 159–162.

[21] D'Aspremont, *Formalism and the Sources of International Law*, p. 133.

[22] Hersch Lauterpacht, 'The Grotian Tradition in International Law' (1946) 23 *The British Yearbook of International Law* 1, 19.

[23] On the tautological nature of the concept, see Stephen Humphreys, *Theatre of the Rule of Law: Transnational Legal Intervention in Theory and Practice* (Cambridge: Cambridge University Press, 2012), p. 3. This notion is also present in one of the possible Spanish translations for 'rule of law', namely '*el imperio del derecho*' or 'imperio de la ley', which translates literally as 'law's empire'.

CONCLUSION

the proliferation of WMDs, nuclear security, and counter-terrorism more broadly, or climate change, for example.

Critical legal scholars may escape the risks of stretching the concept of law by limiting themselves to unravelling the hidden power games and the actual regulatory work behind the new managerial vocabularies (the new natural law behind global governance).[24] However, deconstruction should not be seen as the end of this drama but as an enabling interlude for political contestation to take place, thereby allowing the search for the necessary recalibrations of the political ideals that will inform the rule of law in global governance.

There can be little doubt that coalitions are instruments that serve the evasion of legal constraints on transnational executive action.[25] No matter how voluntarily their work might be framed, it creates 'global administrative spaces',[26] which are also aimed at bypassing constitutional controls on the national executives. Rule of law principles at the domestic level are under strain when parliamentary participation is systematically circumvented through informal bilateral arrangements, intergovernmental networks, or commitments made through other innovative devices, such as 'gift baskets'. The hope is that by focusing on how global ruling functions today at different scales at the same time (subnational, national, international, transnational) this *anti-law law* that is also an *anti-politics politics* becomes increasingly subject to political contestation, thus making rule of law expectations more attuned. These expectations have to be the result of spontaneous contestation; it is not an academic enterprise. But the observation and explanation is.

Jan Klabbers mentions that 'if IN-LAW continues to grow in popularity, it is only a matter of time before parliaments will start to demand a right of approval of IN-LAW as well'.[27] We saw some instances in Chapter 4 where the German *Bundestag* has sought clarification from the government on informal coalitions, like the PSI and the CSI. I would like to conclude with another example, from a very different area and region. It is the case of the *Mérida Initiative*, an informal partnership between Mexico and the USA that has defined many aspects of the failed

---

[24] See Martti Koskenniemi, 'Miserable Comforters'.

[25] See, *inter alia*, Roth, 'Coalitions of the Willing and the International Rule of Law', p. 41.

[26] See Kingsbury, Krisch, and Stewart, 'The Emergence of Global Administrative Law', 18-27.

[27] Jan Klabbers, 'International Courts and Informal International Law', in Pauwelyn, Wessel, and Wouters (eds.), p. 219, at p. 235.

258 CONCLUSION

'war on drugs' in Mexico.[28] This 'initiative' affects the day-to-day life of millions of individuals, so that voices in Mexico have emerged, denouncing democratic deficits and lack of control of this trans-governmental programme. On the occasion of the approval process of a new *Mexican Law on Treaties*, in April 2012, Congressman Porfirio Muñoz Ledo (PT – Labour Party), a lawyer who served as Permanent Representative of Mexico to the UN, explained his negative vote by mentioning that informal arrangements, like the *Mérida Initiative*, that affect the legal sphere of people without any accountability mechanism in place, make it necessary to reconsider the parliamentary approval procedures on the 'international commitments' that the Mexican executive enters into.[29] One may only hope that situations derived from informal law need not be that dramatic for further contestation to arise.

---

[28] See Rodiles, 'The Tensions between Local Resilience-Building and Transnational Action'.
[29] See the remarks by Congressman Porfirio Muñoz Ledo (PT – Labor Party), while explaining his vote against the draft for a new Law on Treaties, in Gaceta Parlamentaria, XV, no. 3489-IX, April 12, 2012, *available at* http://gaceta.diputados.gob.mx/Gaceta/61/2012/abr/20120412-IX.html#VotosParticulares - VotosParticulares.

BIBLIOGRAPHY

Abbott, Kenneth W., 'Modern International Relations Theory: A Prospectus for International Lawyers' (1989) 14 *Yale Journal of International Law* 335.

'Strengthening the Transnational Regime Complex for Climate Change' (2014) 3 *Transnational Environmental Law* 57.

Abbott, Kenneth W. and Snidal, Duncan, 'International Regulation without International Government: Improving IO Performance through Orchestration' (2010) 5 *The Review of International Organizations* 315.

Ahmed, Dawood I., 'Defending Weak States against the "Unwilling or Unable" Doctrine of Self-Defense' (2013) 9 *Journal of International Law and International Relations* 1.

Albright, Madeleine K. (interview), *Interview on NBC-TV 'The Today Show' with Matt Lauer* (19 February 1998), at www.state.gov/1997-2001-NOPDFS/state ments/1998/980219a.html.

Allen, Craig H., 'Command of the Commons Boasts: An Invitation to Lawfare?', in Carsten, *Global Legal Challenges: Command of the Commons, Strategic Communications and Natural Disasters* (2007), pp. 21–50.

'The Limits of Intelligence in Maritime Counterproliferation Operations' (2007) 60 *Naval War College Review* 35.

Maritime Counterproliferation Operations and the Rule of Law (Westport: Praeger Security, 2007).

Alston, Philip, 'The Myopia of the Handmaidens: International Lawyers and Globalization' (1997) 8 *European Journal of International Law* 435.

Alston, Philip and Macdonald, Euan (eds.), *Human Rights, Intervention, and the Use of Force* (Oxford: Oxford University Press, 2008).

Alvarez, José E., 'Do Liberal States Behave Better? A Critique of Slaughter's Liberal Theory' (2001) 12 *European Journal of International Law* 183.

'The Move from Institutions: Introductory Remarks' (2006) 100 *Proceedings of the Annual Meeting (American Society of International Law)* 287.

Amsterdam, Anthony G. and Bruner, Jerome, *Minding the Law: How Courts Rely on Storytelling, and How Their Stories Change the Ways We Understand the Law – And Ourselves* (Cambridge, MA: Harvard University Press, 2000).

BIBLIOGRAPHY

Anghie, Antony, *Imperialism, Sovereignty and the Making of International Law* (Cambridge: Cambridge University Press, 2007).

Anghie, Antony and Chimni, B. S., 'Third World Approaches to International Law and Individual Responsibility in Internal Conflicts' (2003) 2 *Chinese Journal of International Law* 77.

Appelbaum, Yoni, 'Trump's Foreign Policy "Adhocracy"', *The Atlantic* (27 June 2017), at www.theatlantic.com/international/archive/2017/06/trumps-for eign-policy-adhocracy/531732/.

Aristotle, *Rhetoric* (New York, NY: Dover Publications, 2004).

Arms Control Association, *Nuclear Security Summit at a Glance* (August 2017), at www.armscontrol.org/factsheets/NuclearSecuritySummit.

Ash, Timothy Garton, *Free World: America, Europe, and the Surprising Future of the West*, reprinted edition with a new postscript (London: Penguin, 2005).

Aust, Anthony, 'The Theory and Practice of Informal International Instruments' (1986) 35 *International and Comparative Law Quarterly* 787.

    Modern Treaty Law and Practice, third edition (Cambridge: Cambridge University Press, 2013).

Aust, Helmut Philipp, *Complicity and the Law of State Responsibility* (Cambridge: Cambridge University Press, 2011).

    Das Recht der globalen Stadt (Tübingen: Mohr Siebeck, 2017).

Aust, Helmut Philipp, Rodiles, Alejandro and Staubach, Peter, 'Unity or Uniformity? Domestic Courts and Treaty Interpretation' (2014) 27 *Leiden Journal of International Law* 75.

Austin, John L., *How to Do Things with Words*, second edition (Oxford: Oxford University Press, 1976).

Axworthy, Lloyd, 'Human Security and Global Governance: Putting People First' (2001) 7 *Global Governance* 19.

Bai, Matt, 'Notion Building', *The New York Times Magazine* (12 October 2003), at www.nytimes.com/2003/10/12/magazine/notion-building.html?pagewanted= print.

    'The Framing Wars', *The New York Times Magazine* (17 July 2005), at www .nytimes.com/2005/07/17/magazine/17DEMOCRATS.html?pagewanted= all&_r=0.

Balser, Markus, 'Frischer Wind in Petersberg', *Süddeutsche Zeitung* (15 July 2014).

Bargh, John A., 'What Have We Been Priming All These Years? On the Development, Mechanisms, and Ecology of Nonconscious Social Behavior' (2006) 36 *European Journal of Social Psychology* 147.

Barrena Nájera, Guadalupe, *Human Rights Indicators in the Field of Criminal Justice and Crime Control. Implications for the Idea of Law in Governance and Governmentality* (unpublished PhD Dissertation, Legal Research Institute of the National Autonomous University of Mexico (UNAM), Mexico City: October 2017).

BIBLIOGRAPHY

Barrett, Scott and Stavins, Robert, 'Increasing Participation and Compliance in International Climate Change Agreements' (2003) 3 *International Environmental Agreements: Politics, Law and Economics* 349.

Beck, Ulrich, *Weltrisikogesellschaft* (Frankfurt: Suhrkamp, 2007).

Becker, Michael A., 'The Shifting Public Order of the Oceans: Freedom of Navigation and the Interdiction of Ships at Sea' (2005) 46 *Harvard International Law Journal* 131.

Belcher, Emma, 'The Proliferation Security Initiative: Lessons for Using Nonbinding Agreements', *Council on Foreign Relations, Working Paper* (July 2011) 1.

Benjamin, Walter, 'Zur Kritik der Gewalt', in W. Benjamin (ed.), *Angelus Novus*, volume 2 (Frankfurt a.M.: Suhrkamp, 1988).

Benvenisti, Eyal, 'Coalitions of the Willing and the Evolution of Informal International Law', in Calliess, Nolte, and Stoll (eds.), *Coalitions of the Willing: Avantgarde or Threat?* (2007), pp. 1–24.

'The Conception of International Law as a Legal System' (2007) 50 *German Yearbook of International Law* 393.

'Towards a Typology of Informal International Lawmaking Mechanisms and their Distinct Accountability Gaps', in Wessel and Wouters (eds.), *Informal International Lawmaking* (Oxford: Oxford University Press, 2012), pp. 297–309.

'Sovereigns as Trustees of Humanity: On the Accountability of States to Foreign Stakeholders' (2013) 107 *The American Journal of International Law* 295.

The Law of Global Governance (Pocketbooks of The Hague Academy of International Law, 2015).

Benvenisti, Eyal and Downs, George W., 'The Empire's New Clothes: Political Economy and the Fragmentation of International Law' (2007) 60 *Stanford Law Review* 595.

Berman, Harold J., 'Is Conflict-of-Laws Becoming Passe? An Historical Response', in Hans E. Rasmussen-Bonne et al. (eds.), *Balancing of Interests: Liber Americorum Peter Hay zum 70. Geburtstag* (Frankfurt: Recht und Wirtschaft, 2005), p. 43.

Besier, Gerhard and Lindemann, Gerhard, *Im Namen der Freiheit: Die amerikanische Mission* (Goettingen: Vandenhoeck & Ruprecht, 2006).

Bianchi, Andrea, 'Textual Interpretation and (International) Law Reading: The Myth of (In)Determinacy and the Genealogy of Meaning', in Pieter H.F. Bekker, Rudolf Dolzer and Michael Waibel (eds.), *Making Transnational Law Work in the Global Economy, Essays in Honour of Detlev Vagts* (Cambridge: Cambridge University Press, 2010), pp. 34–55.

'Reflexive Butterfly Catching: Insights from a Situated Catcher', in Pauwelyn, Wessel, and Wouters (eds.), *Informal International Lawmaking* (Oxford: Oxford University Press, 2012), pp. 200–215.

BIBLIOGRAPHY

Blazejewski, Kenneth S., 'The FATF and Its Institutional Partners: Improving the Effectiveness and Accountability of Transgovernmental Networks' (2008) 22 *Temple International Law and Comparative Law Journal* 1.

Blokker, Niels, 'Is the Authorization Authorized? Powers and Practice of the UN Security Council to Authorize the Use of Force by "Coalitions of the Able and Willing"' (2000) 11 *European Journal of International Law* 541.

Böckenförde, Ernst-Wolfgang, 'Entstehung und Wandel des Rechtsstaatsbegriffs' in E. W. Böckenförde, *Recht, Staat, Freiheit* (Frankfurt a.M.: Surkamp, 2006).

Bolton, John, *Surrender Is Not an Option: Defending America at the United Nations and Abroad* (New York: Threshold Editions, 2008).

Bolton, John R., 'Beyond the Axis of Evil: Additional Threats to Weapons of Mass Destruction', *The Heritage Foundation, Lecture No. 743 on Missile Defense* (6 May 2002), at www.heritage.org/research/lecture/beyond-the-axis-of-evil.

'An All-Out War on Proliferation', *Financial Times* (7 September 2004), at http://2001-2009.state.gov/t/us/rm/36035.htm.

Bond, Richard, 'The Proliferation Security Initiative: Targeting Iran and North Korea?', *British American Security Information Council* (BASIC), Paper No. 53 (January 2007).

Bowett, Derek W., *Self-Defence in International Law* (Manchester: Manchester University Press, 1958).

Bowman, Gregory W., 'Thinking Outside the Border: Homeland Security and the Forward Deployment of the U.S. Border' (2007) 44 *Houston Law Review* 189.

Boyle, Alan, 'Reflections on the Treaty as a Law-making Instrument', in Alexander Orakhelashvili and Sarah Williams, *40 Years of the Vienna Convention on the Law of Treaties* (London: British Institute of International and Comparative Law, 2010), pp. 9–28.

Brummer, Chris, *Minilateralism: How Trade Alliances, Soft Law and Financial Engineering Are Redefining Economic Statecraft* (New York: Cambridge University Press, 2014).

Bunn, Matthew et al., *Advancing Nuclear Security: Evaluating Progress and Setting New Goals* (Harvard Kennedy School, Belfer Center for Science and International Affairs, March 2014).

Bush, George H. W., *Address before a Joint Session of Congress* (11 September 1990), at http://www.presidency.ucsb.edu/ws/?pid=18820.

Address to the Nation on the Invasion of Iraq (16 January 1991), at http://www.americanrhetoric.com/speeches/ghwbushiraqinvasion.htm.

Bush, George W., *President Delivers State of Union Address* (29 January 2002), at http://georgewbush-whitehouse.archives.gov/news/releases/2002/01/20020129-11.html.

President's Statement on the Proliferation Security Initiative (31 March 2005), at http://2001-2009.state.gov/t/isn/rls/prsrl/47260.htm.

BIBLIOGRAPHY 263

Bush, George W. and Blair, Tony, 'Effective Multilateralism to Build a Better World: Joint Statement by President George W. Bush and Prime Minister Tony Blair, November 20, 2003', reprinted in US Government Printing Office, *Weekly Compilation of Presidential Documents*, vol. 39, issue 47 (2003).

Byers, Michael (ed.), *The Role of Law in International Politics. Essays in International Relations and International Law* (Oxford: Oxford University Press, 2000).

'Policing the High Seas: The Proliferation Security Initiative' (2004) 98 *The American Journal of International Law* 526.

Byers, Michael and Nolte, Georg (eds.), *United States Hegemony and the Foundations of International Law* (Cambridge: Cambridge University Press, 2003).

'Preface', in Byers and Nolte (eds.), *United States Hegemony and the Foundations of International Law* (Cambridge: Cambridge University Press, 2003), pp. xv–xvii.

Calliess, Christian, Nolte, Georg, and Stoll, Peter-Tobias (eds.), *Coalitions of the Willing: Avantgarde or Threat?* (Germany: Carl Heymanns, 2007).

Cann, Michelle, Davenport, Kelsey, and Williams, Sarah, *The Nuclear Security Summit: Assessment of Joint Statements* (Arms Control Association/Partnership for Global Security, March 2014).

Carsten, Michael D. (ed.), *Global Legal Challenges: Command of the Commons, Strategic Communications and Natural Disasters, International Law Studies vol. 83* (Newport: Naval War College, 2007).

Castañeda, Jorge, *Legal Effects of United Nations Resolutions* (New York: Columbia University Press, 1969).

Chakrabarty, Dipesh, '*Charlemagne*: Coalitions for the Willing: "Multi-Speed Europe" Is Making a Comeback, along with the Constitution', *The Economist* (1 February 2007).

'*Charlemagne*: A Crisis? Call the F-Team', *The Economist* (4 November 2011).

Provincializing Europe: Postcolonial Thought and Historical Difference, reissue with a new preface by the author (Princeton: Princeton University Press, 2008).

Chen, Ronald and Hanson, Jon, 'Categorically Biased: The Influence of Knowledge Structures on Law and Legal Theory' (2004) 77 *Southern California Law Review* 1103.

Chesterman, Simon, *Just War or Just Peace? Humanitarian Intervention and International Law* (Oxford: Oxford University Press, 2001).

Chilton, Paul and Lakoff, George, 'Foreign Policy by Metaphor', in Christina Schäffner and Anita L. Wenden (eds.), *Language & Peace* (Aldershot: Ashgate, 1995), pp. 37–60.

Chimni, B.S., 'Legitimating the International Rule of Law', in Crawford and Koskenniemi (eds.), *The Cambridge Companion to International Law* (Cambridge: Cambridge University Press, 2012), pp. 290–308.

BIBLIOGRAPHY

Chinkin, Christine, 'The Challenge of Soft Law: Development and Change in International Law' (1989) 38 *International and Comparative Law Quarterly* 850.

Churchill, R. R. and Lowe, A-V., *The Law of the Sea*, third edition, (Manchester: Manchester University Press, 1999).

Clinton, Hillary R., *Hard Choices. A Memoir* (New York: Simon & Schuster, 2014).

Clinton, William J. (interview), *Interview of the President by Sam Donaldson, ABC* (5 June 1994), at www.ibiblio.org/pub/archives/whitehouse-papers/1994/Jun/1994-06-05-Presidents-ABC-Interview-on-USS-George-Washington.

Cowell, Alan, 'Syria, Baking Coalition, Is Still Insistent on Golan', *The New York Times* (15 February 1991).

Crawford, James, *State Responsibility: The General Part* (Cambridge: Cambridge University Press, 2013).

Crawford, James and Koskenniemi, Martti (eds.), *The Cambridge Companion to International Law* (Cambridge: Cambridge University Press, 2012).

D'Argent, Pierre, 'Coalitions of the Willing: Why, How and What?', in Calliess, Nolte, and Stoll (eds.), *Coalitions of the Willing: Avantgarde or Threat?* (2007), pp. 25–32.

D'Aspremont, Jean, *Formalism and the Sources of International Law: A Theory of the Ascertainment of Legal Rules* (Oxford: Oxford University Press, 2013).

Daase, Christopher, 'Die Informalisierung internationaler Politik: Beobachtungen zum Stand der internationalen Organisation', in Klaus Dingwerth, Dieter Kerwer and Andreas Nölke (eds.), *Die Organisierte Welt. Internationale Beziehungen und Organisationsforschung* (Baden-Baden: Nomos, 2009), pp. 290–308.

'The ILC and Informalization', in Georg Nolte (ed.), *Peace through International Law: The Role of the International Law Commission* (Heidelberg: Springer, 2009), pp. 179–182.

'Coercion and the Informalization of Arms Control', in Oliver Meier and Christopher Daase (eds.), *Arms Control in the 21st Century: Between Coercion and Cooperation* (New York: Routledge, 2013), pp. 67–76.

Dal, Bart, Herbach, Jonathan, and Luongo, Kenneth N., *The Strengthening Nuclear Security Implementation Initiative: Evolution, Status and Next Steps* (NSGEG, October 2015).

Dann, Philipp and Von Engelhardt, Marie, 'Legal Approaches to Global Governance and Accountability: Informal Lawmaking, International Public Authority, and Global Administrative Law Compared', in Pauwelyn, Wessel, and Wouters, *Informal International Lawmaking* (Oxford: Oxford University Press, 2012), pp. 106–121.

Davis, Kevin and Kingsbury, Benedict, 'Obligation Overload: Adjusting the Obligations of Fragile or Failed States', preliminary, unpublished paper,

BIBLIOGRAPHY

New York University, School of Law (2010), at www.iilj.org/wp-content/uploads/2016/11/Davis-et-al-Obligation-Overload-2010.pdf.

De Sousa Santos, Boaventura, 'Law: A Map of Misreading. Toward a Postmodern Conception of Law' (1987) 14 *Journal of Law and Society* 279.

De Wet, Erika, *The Chapter VII Powers of the United Nations Security Council* (Oxford/Portland: Hart, 2004).

Deeks, Ashley S., '"Unwilling or Unable": Toward a Normative Framework for Extraterritorial Self-Defense' (2012) 52 *Virginia Journal of International Law* 483.

Deere, Carolyn, *The Implementation Game: The TRIPS Agreement and the Global Politics of Intellectual Property Reform in Developing Countries* (Oxford: Oxford University Press, 2011).

Deibel, Terry L., *Foreign Affairs Strategy: Logic for American Statecraft* (New York: Cambridge University Press, 2007).

Delmas-Marty, Mireille, 'The Paradigm of the War on Crime: Legitimating Inhumane Treatment?' (2007) 5 *Journal of International Criminal Justice* 584.

Doolin, Joel, 'The Proliferation Security Initiative: Cornerstone of a New International Norm' (2006) 59 *Naval War College Review* 29.

Downer, Alexander, *The Threat of Proliferation: Global Resolve and Australian Action* [Speech] (23 February 2004), at www.foreignminister.gov.au/speeches/2004/040223_lowy.html.

Doyle, Todd, 'Cleaning Up Anti-Money Laundering Strategies: Current FATF Tactics Needlessly Violate International Law' (2002) 24 *Houston Journal of International Law* 279.

Drezner, Daniel W., *All Politics Is Global: Explaining International Regulatory Regimes* (Princeton: Princeton University Press, 2007).

'The New New World Order' (March/April 2007) *Foreign Affairs* 36.

Dunne, Aaron, 'The Proliferation Security Initiative: Legal Considerations and Operation Realities', SIPRI Policy Paper 36 (May 2013).

Dunoff, Jeffrey L., 'A New Approach to Regime Interaction', in Young (ed.), *Regime Interaction in International Law: Facing Fragmentation* (Cambridge: Cambridge University Press, 2012), pp. 136–174.

'From Interdisciplinarity to Counterdisciplinarity: Is there Madness in Martti's Method?' (2013) 27 *Temple International and Comparative Law Journal* 309.

Durkalec, Jacek, 'The Proliferation Security Initiative: Evolution and Future Prospects', *EU Non-Proliferation Consortium*, Non-Proliferation Papers No. 16 (June 2012), at www.sipri.org/research/disarmament/eu-consortium/publications/nonproliferation-paper-16.

Erskine, Toni, 'Coalitions of the Willing and Responsibilities to Protect: Informal Associations, Enhanced Capacities, and Shared Moral Burdens' (2014) 28 *Ethics and International Affairs* 115.

266 BIBLIOGRAPHY

Falk, Richard A., 'What Future for the UN Charter System of War Prevention?' (2003) 97 *The American Journal of International Law* 590.

Farley, Robert, 'Managing the United States' Global Naval Partnerships: The U.S. Navy Has Decisions to Make on Cooperation with Other Global Navies. Will It Make the Right Ones?', *The Diplomat* (10 July 2014), at http://thediplomat.com/2014/07/managing-the-united-states-global-naval-partnerships/?allpages=yes&print=yes

Fassbender, Bardo, 'Review Essay: *Quis judicabit*? The Security Council, Its Powers and Its Legal Control' (2000) 11 *European Journal of International Law* 219.

Feinberg, Richard, 'Institutionalized Summitry', in Andrew F. Cooper, Jorge Heine, and Ramish Thakur (eds.), *The Oxford Handbook of Modern Diplomacy* (Oxford: Oxford University Press, 2013), pp. 303–318.

Feinstein, Lee and Slaughter, Anne-Marie, 'A Duty to Prevent', (January/February 2004) *Foreign Affairs* 136.

Ferguson, Niall, *The Square and the Tower - Networks of Power, from the Freemasons to Facebook* (New York: Penguin Press, 2017).

Fischer-Lescano, Andreas and Teubner, Gunther, *Regime-Kollisionen. Zur Fragmentierung des globalen Rechts* (Frankfurt a.M.: Suhrkamp, 2006).

Foucault, Michel, 'Nietzsche, Genealogy, History', in Donald F. Bouchard (ed.), *Language, Counter-Memory, Practice* (Ithaca: Cornell University Press, 1977), pp. 139–164.

Discipline and Punish – The Birth of the Prison (New York: Vintage Books, 1997).

Franck, Thomas, 'The United Nations as Guarantor of International Peace and Security: Past, Present and Future', in Christian Tomuschat (ed.), *The United Nations at Age Fifty: A Legal Perspective* (The Hague: Kluwer Law International, 1995), pp. 25–38.

Franck, Thomas M., 'When, If Ever, May States Deploy Military Force without Prior Security Council Authorization?' (2001) 5 *Washington University Journal of Law & Policy* 51.

Recourse to Force: State Action against Threats and Armed Attacks (Cambridge: Cambridge University Press, 2002).

Franck, Thomas M. and Patel, Faiza, 'UN Police Action in Lieu of War: "The Old Order Changeth"' (1991) 85 *The American Journal of International Law* 63.

Frederking, Brian, *The United States and the Security Council: Collective Security since the Cold War* (London/New York: Routledge, 2007).

Friedman, Thomas L., 'Running the Gulf Coalition Is Tricky Business', *The New York Times* (23 September 1990).

Fukuyama, Francis, 'The Paradox of International Action', *The American Interest* (1 March 2006), at www.the-american-interest.com/2006/03/01/the-paradox-of-international-action/.

Gallie, W. B., 'Essentially Contested Concepts' (1955–1956) 56 *Proceedings of the Aristotelian Society* 193.

BIBLIOGRAPHY

Goffman, Erving, *Frame Analysis: An Essay on the Organisation of Experience* (New York: Harper Colophon, 1974).

Goodman, Ryan, 'International Law on International Airstrikes against ISIS in Syria', blog contribution, *Just Security* (28 August 2014), at http://justsecurity.org/14414/international-law-airstrikes-isis-syria/.

Goodman, Ryan and Knuckey, Sarah, 'Remarkable Statement by UN Secretary General on US Airstrikes in Syria', blog contribution, *Just Security* (23 September 2014), at http://justsecurity.org/15456/remarkable-statement-secretary-general-airstrikes-syria/).

Gougelet, David-Olivier and Feder, Ellen K., 'Genealogies of Race and Gender', in Christopher Falzon, Timothy O'Leary and Jana Sawicki (eds.), *A Companion to Foucault* (Chichester: Willey-Blackwell, 2013), pp. 472–490.

Gray, Christine, *International Law and the Use of Force*, third edition (Oxford: Oxford University Press, 2008).

'The Charter Limitations on the Use of Force: Theory and Practice', in Lowe et al. (eds.), *The United Nations Security Council and War: The Evolution of Thought and Practice since 1945* (Oxford: Oxford University Press, 2008), pp. 89–98.

Greenert, Admiral Jonathan and Foggo III, Rear Admiral James M. (US Navy), 'Forging a Global Network of Navies' (2014) 140 *Proceedings* 335.

Guilfoyle, Douglas, 'The Proliferation Security Initiative: Interdicting Vessels in International Waters to Prevent the Spread of Weapons of Mass Destruction?' (2005) 29 *Melbourne University Law Review* 733.

'Maritime Interdiction of Weapons of Mass Destruction' (2007) 12 *Journal of Conflict & Security Law* 1.

Shipping Interdiction and the Law of the Sea (Cambridge: Cambridge University Press, 2009).

Haass, Richard N., *The Reluctant Sheriff. The United States after the Cold War* (New York: Council on Foreign Relations/Brookings Institution Press, 1997), p. 95.

'From Reluctant to Resolute: American Foreign Policy after September 11', Remarks to the Chicago Council on Foreign Relations (26 June 2002), at http://2001-2009.state.gov/s/p/rem/11445.htm.

'Planning Policy in Today's World', Remarks at the Kennan Institute Annual Dinner (22 May 2003), at http://2001-2009.state.gov/s/p/rem/2003/20910.htm.

The Opportunity: America's Moment to Alter History's Course (New York: Public Affairs, 2005).

'The Age of Nonpolarity. What Will Follow U.S. Dominance' (May/June 2008) *Foreign Affairs* 44.

[Interview], 'The New Informal Multilateral Era' (24 September 2009), at www.cfr.org/international-organizations-and-alliances/new-informal-multilateral-era/p20275.

War of Necessity, War of Choice: A Memoir of Two Iraq Wars (New York: Simon & Schuster, 2009).

'The Unraveling. How to Respond to a Disordered World' (November/December 2014) *Foreign Affairs* 70.

A World in Disarray: American Foreign Policy and the Crisis of the Old Order (New York: Penguin Press, 2017).

Hanson, Jon D. and Yeboah, Mark, 'The Policy IAT', in Jon D. Hanson (ed.), *Ideology, Psychology, and Law* (Oxford: Oxford University Press, 2012), pp. 265–297.

Hardt, Michael and Negri, Antonio, *Empire* (Cambridge, Massachusetts: Harvard University Press, 2001).

Hart, H. L. A., *The Concept of Law*, second edition (Oxford: Clarendon Press, 1997).

Hautecouverture, Benjamin, 'The Container Security Initiative', ONP. 83, *Centre d'Etudes de Sécurité Internationale et des Maîtrise des armements* (CESIM) (2012).

Hegel, G. F. W., *Phänomenologie des Geistes* (Frankfurt a.M.: Suhrkamp, second edition, 1989).

Helfer, Laurence R., 'Regime Shifting: The TRIPS Agreement and New Dynamics of International Intellectual Property Lawmaking' (2004) 29 *Yale Journal of International Law* 1.

Heller, Kevin Jon, 'Ashley Deeks' Problematic Defense of the "Unwilling or Unable" Test', blog contribution, *Opinio Juris* (15 December 2011), at http://opiniojuris.org/2011/12/15/ashley-deeks-failure-to-defend-the-unwilling-or-unable-test/.

Heng, Yee-Kuang and McDonagh, Kenneth, *Risk, Global Governance and Security* (London/New York: Routledge, 2009).

Higgins, Rosalyn, *Problems & Process, International Law and How We Use It* (Oxford: Clarendon Press, 1995).

Honecker, P., 'Vorreformatorische Schlagwörter, Spiegel politischer, religiöser und sozialer Konflikte in der frühen Neuzeit', PhD thesis, University of Trier (2002), at http://ubt.opus.hbz-nrw.de/volltexte/2004/149/pdf/2002 1212.pdf.

Hookway, Christopher, 'Pragmatism', in Zalta, *The Stanford Encyclopedia of Philosophy* (Summer 2016 Edition), at https://plato.stanford.edu/archives/sum2016/entries/pragmatism/.

Howorth, Jolyon, 'From Alliances to Coalitions of the Willing: The New Regional Dynamics of Transatlantic Relations', paper delivered to the Annual Conference of International Studies Association (ISA) (Hawaii, March 2005) (on file with the author).

Humphreys, Stephen, *Theatre of the Rule of Law: Transnational Legal Intervention in Theory and Practice* (Cambridge: Cambridge University Press, 2012).

BIBLIOGRAPHY 269

Huntington, Samuel P., 'Transnational Organizations in World Politics' (1973) 25 *World Politics* 333.

Hurrell, Andrew, 'International Law 1989–2010: A Performance Appraisal', in James Crawford and Sarah Nouwen (eds.), *Select Proceedings of the European Society of International Law: Third Volume, International Law 1989–2010: A Performance Appraisal* (Oxford: Hart Publishing, 2012), pp. 3–20.

Ikenberry, G. John and Slaughter, Anne-Marie, *Forging a World of Liberty under Law: U.S. National Security in the 21st Century* (Final Paper of the Princeton Project on National Security) (Princeton: The Woodrow Wilson School of Public and International Affairs, 27 September 2006).

Johns, Fleur, *Non-Legality in International Law – Unruly Law* (Cambridge: Cambridge University Press, 2013).

Jones, Bruce, *Still Ours to Lead: America, Rising Powers, and the Tension between Rivalry and Restraint* (Washington D.C.: The Brookings Institution Press, 2014).

Joyner, Daniel H., 'The Security Council as Legal Hegemon' (2012) 43 *Georgetown Journal of International Law* 225.

International Law and the Proliferation of Weapons of Mass Destruction (Oxford: Oxford University Press, 2009).

'Fundamental Rights of States in International Law and the Right to Peaceful Nuclear Energy' (2014) 4 *Cambridge International Law Journal* 661.

Ke, Xu, 'Myth and Reality: The Rise and Fall of Contemporary Maritime Piracy in the South China Sea', in Shicun Wu and Keyuan Zou (eds.), *Maritime Security in the South China Sea: Regional Implications and International Cooperation* (Burlington: Ashgate, 2007), pp. 81–98.

Kelsen, Hans, 'Collective Security and Collective Self-Defense under the Charter of the United Nations' (1948) 42 *The American Journal of International Law* 783.

'Is the North Atlantic Treaty a Regional Arrangement?' (1951) 45 *The American Journal of International Law* 162.

Reine Rechtslehre, second edition (1960) (Vienna: Österreichische Staatsdruckerei, 1992).

Was ist Gerechtigkeit? (Stuttgart: Reclam, 2000).

The Law of the United Nations. A Critical Analysis of its Fundamental Problems (Clark, New Jersey: The Lawbook Exchange, LTD., 1950, eighth reprint, 2009).

Kennedy, David, 'The Move to Institutions' (1987) 8 *Cardozo Law Review* 841.

'Lawfare and Warfare', in Crawford and Koskenniemi (eds.), *The Cambridge Companion to International Law* (Cambridge: Cambridge University Press, 2012), pp. 158–184.

Kennedy, Duncan, 'A Left Phenomenological Alternative to the Hart/Kelsen Theory of Legal Interpretation', in Duncan Kennedy (ed.), *Legal Reasoning: Collected Essays* (Aurora: The Davies Group Publishers, 2008), pp. 154–173.

BIBLIOGRAPHY

Kennedy, Paul, *The Rise and Fall of the Great Powers* (New York: Random House, 1987).

Keohane, Robert O. and Nye, Joseph S., 'Transgovernmental Relations and International Organizations' (1974) 27 *World Politics* 39.

'Between Centralization and Fragmentation: The Club Model of Multilateral Cooperation and Problems of Democratic Legitimacy', *KSG Working Paper No. 01–004* (February 2001).

Kingsbury, Benedict, 'Sovereignty and Inequality' (1998) 9 *European Journal of International Law* 599.

'The Concept of "Law" in Global Administrative Law' (2009) 20 *European Journal of International Law* 23.

Kingsbury, Benedict, Krisch, Nico and Stewart, Richard B., 'The Emergence of Global Administrative Law' (2005) 68 *Law and Contemporary Problems* 15.

Kirgis, Frederic L., 'Cruise Missile Strikes in Afghanistan and Sudan', *ASIL Insight* (18 August 1998), at www.asil.org/insights/volume/3/issue/11/cruise-mis sile-strikes-afghanistan-and-sudan.

Klabbers, Jan, 'The Redundancy of Soft Law' (1996) 65 *Nordic Journal of International Law* 167.

'Institutional Ambivalence by Design: Soft Organizations in International Law' (2001) 70 *Nordic Journal of International Law* 403.

'The Relative Autonomy of International Law or the Forgotten Politics of Interdisciplinarity' (2004–2005) 1 *Journal of International Law and International Relations* 35.

'International Courts and Informal International Law', in Pauwelyn, Wessel, and Wouters, (eds.) *Informal International Lawmaking* (Oxford: Oxford University Press, 2012), pp. 219–240.

'Towards a Culture of Formalism? Martti Koskenniemi and the Virtues' (2013) 27 *Temple International & Comparative Law Journal* 417.

International Law, second edition (Cambridge: Cambridge University Press, 2017).

Klein, Natalie, *Maritime Security and the Law of the Sea* (Oxford: Oxford University Press, 2011).

Koh, Harold H., 'The Obama Administration and International Law' (keynote address) (2010) 104 *Proceedings of the Annual Meeting (American Society of International Law)* 207.

Koskenniemi, Martti, 'Carls Schmitt, Hans Morgenthau, and the Image of Law in International Relations', in Byers (ed.), *The Role of Law in International Politics. Essays in International Relations and International Law* (Oxford: Oxford University Press, 2000), pp. 17–34.

'Global Governance and Public International Law' (2004) 37 *Kritische Justiz* 241.

BIBLIOGRAPHY

The Gentle Civilizer of Nations - The Rise and Fall of International Law 1870–1960 (Cambridge: Cambridge University Press, 2005).

'Constitutionalism as Mindset: Reflections on Kantian Themes about International Law and Globalization' (2007) 8 *Theoretical Inquires in Law* 9.

'The Case for Comparative International Law' (2009) 20 *Finnish Yearbook of International Law* 1.

'Miserable Comforters: International Relations as New Natural Law' (2009) 15 *European Journal of International Relations* 395.

'Law, Teleology and International Relations: An Essay in Counterdisciplinarity' (2011) 26 *International Relations* 3.

'Hegemonic Regimes', in Young (ed.), *Regime Interaction in International Law: Facing Fragmentation* (Cambridge: Cambridge University Press, 2012), pp. 305–324.

Koskenniemi, Martti and Leino, Päivi, 'Fragmentation of International Law? Postmodern Anxieties' (2002) 15 *Leiden Journal of International Law* 553.

Kövecses, Zoltan, *Metaphor: A Practical Introduction*, second edition (Oxford: Oxford University Press, 2010).

Krahmann, Elke, 'American Hegemony or Global Governance? Competing Visions of International Security' (2002) 7 *International Studies Review* 531.

Krasner, Stephen D., 'Structural Causes and Regime Consequences: Regimes as Intervening Variables' (1982) 36 *International Organization* 185.

Krauthammer, Charles, 'The Unipolar Moment' (1990) 70 *Foreign Affairs* 23.

Kreps, Sarah E., *Coalitions of Convenience: United States Interventions after the Cold War* (Oxford: Oxford University Press, 2011).

Krieger, Heike, 'Coalitions of the Willing - A Résumé from the General Public International Law Point of View', in Calliess, Nolte, and Stoll (eds.), *Coalitions of the Willing: Avantgarde or Threat?* (2007), pp. 43–50.

Krisch, Nico, 'Unilateral Enforcement of the Collective Will: Kosovo, Iraq and the Security Council' (1999) 3 *Max Planck Yearbook of United Nations Law* 59.

Selbstverteidigung und kollektive Sicherheit (Heidelberg: Springer, 2001).

'International Law in Times of Hegemony: Unequal Power and the Shaping of the International Legal Order' (2005) 16 *European Journal of International Law* 369.

Beyond Constitutionalism: The Pluralist Structure of International Law (Oxford: Oxford University Press, 2010).

'Article 43', in Simma, Khan, Nolte and Paulus (eds.), *The Charter of the United Nations, A Commentary*, third edition, vol. II (Oxford: Oxford University Press, 2012) p. 1351.

'The Decay of Consent: International Law in an Age of Global Public Goods' (2014) 108 *The American Journal of International Law* 1.

'Liquid Authority in Global Governance' (2017) 9 *International Theory* 237.

BIBLIOGRAPHY

Kulovesi, Kati, 'Addressing Sectoral Emissions outside the United Nations Framework Convention on Climate Change: What Roles for Multilateralism, Minilateralism and Unilateralism?' (2012) 21 *Review of European Community & International Environmental Law* 193.

Kumar, Vinod, *India and the Nuclear Non-Proliferation Regime: The Perennial Outlier* (New Delhi: Cambridge University Press, 2014).

Kupchan, Charles A., *No One's World: The West, The Rising Rest, and the Coming Global Turn* (New York: Oxford University Press, 2012).

Kwakwa, Edward, 'The International Community, International Law, and the United States: Three in One, Two against One, Or One and the Same', in Byers and Nolte (eds.), *United States Hegemony and the Foundations of International Law* (Cambridge: Cambridge University Press, 2003), pp. 25–56.

Lakoff, George, *Moral Politics. What Conservatives Know That Liberals Don't,* second edition (Chicago: The University of Chicago Press, 2002).

   Don't Think of an Elephant! Know Your Values and Frame the Debate (Vermont: Chelsea Green Publishing, 2004).

   Thinking Points, Communicating Our American Values and Vision (New York: Farrar, Straus and Giroux, 2006).

   Whose Freedom: The Battle over America's Most Important Idea (New York: Picador/Farrar, Straus and Giroux, 2006).

Lakoff, George and Johnson, Mark, 'The Metaphorical Structure of the Human Conceptual System' (1980) 4 *Cognitive Science* 205.

   Metaphors We Live By, second edition (Chicago: The University of Chicago Press, 2003).

Larsen, Kjetil Mujezinović, 'Attribution of Conduct in Peace Operations: The "Ultimate Authority and Control" Test' (2008) 19 *European Journal of International Law* 509.

Lauterpacht, Hersch, 'The Grotian Tradition in International Law' (1946) 23 *The British Yearbook of International Law* 1.

Liu, Lydia H., *The Clash of Empires: The Invention of China in Modern World Making* (Cambridge, USA: Harvard University Press, 2004).

Lorca, Arnulf Becker, 'Rules for the "Global War on Terror": Implying Consent and Presuming Conditions for Intervention' (2012) 45 *New York University Journal of International Law and Politics* 1.

   Mestizo International Law – A Global Intellectual History 1842-1993 (Cambridge: Cambridge University Press, 2016).

Lowe, Vaughan, 'The Politics of Law-Making: Are the Method and Character of Norm Creation Changing?', in Byers (ed.), *The Role of Law in International Politics. Essays in International Relations and International Law* (Oxford: Oxford University Press, 2000), pp. 207–226.

BIBLIOGRAPHY 273

Lowe, Vaughan et al. (eds.), *The United Nations Security Council and War: The Evolution of Thought and Practice since 1945* (Oxford: Oxford University Press, 2008).

Lynch, Timothy J. and Singh, Robert S., *After Bush: The Case for Continuity in American Foreign Policy* (Cambridge: Cambridge University Press, 2008).

Malirsch, Maximiliam and Prill, Florian, 'The Proliferation Security Initiative and the 2005 Protocol to the SUA Convention' (2007) 67 *Zeitschrift für ausländisches öffentliches Recht und Völkerrecht* 229.

Malone, David M. (ed.), *The UN Security Council, from the Cold War to the 21st Century* (Colorado: International Peace Academy/Lynne Rienner Publishers, 2004).

Margolis, Eric and Laurence, Stephen, 'Concepts', in Zalta (ed.), *The Stanford Encyclopedia of Philosophy* (Spring 2014 Edition), at https://plato.stanford.edu/archives/spr2014/entries/concepts/.

Marquis, Christopher, 'US Declares "Rogue Nations" are now "States of Concern"', *The New York Times* (20 June 2000), at www.nytimes.com/2000/06/20/world/us-declares-rogue-nations-are-now-states-of-concern.html.

Matz-Lück, Nele, 'Norm Interpretation across International Regimes: Competence and Legitimacy', in Young (ed.), *Regime Interaction in International Law: Facing Fragmentation* (Cambridge: Cambridge University Press, 2012), pp. 201–234.

Mazower, Mark, *No Enchanted Palace: The End of Empire and the Ideological Origins of the United Nations* (Princeton: Princeton University Press, 2008).

McDougal, Myres S. and Feliciano, Florentino P., *Law and Minimum World Public Order: The Legal Regulation of International Coercion* (New Haven: Yale University Press, 1961).

Mcgee Jeffrey, Scott, 'Exclusive Minilateralism: An Emerging Discourse within International Climate Change Governance?' (2011) 8 *Portal Journal of Multidisciplinary International* 1.

Miles, Alex, *US Foreign Policy and the Rogue State Doctrine* (New York: Routledge, 2013).

Morgan, Rhiannon, *Transforming Law and Institution: Indigenous Peoples, the United Nations and Human Rights* (Farnham: Ashgate, 2011).

Moroney, Jennifer D. P. et al., *Building Partner Capabilities for Coalition Operations* (Pittsburgh: RAND Corporation, 2007).

Morse, Julia C. and Keohane, Robert O., 'Contested Multilateralism' (2014) 9 *The Review of International Organizations* 385.

Mullen, Admiral Mike, *Remarks As Delivered for the 17th International Seapower Symposium* (21 September 2005), at www.navy.mil/navydata/cno/mullen/speeches/mullen050921.txt.

BIBLIOGRAPHY

Münkler, Herfried, *Imperien. Die Logik der Weltherrschaft – Vom alten Rom bis zu den Vereinigten Staaten* (Berlin: Rowohlt, 2005).

N'Zatioula Grovogui, Siba, *Sovereigns, Quasi Sovereigns and Africans* (Minneapolis: The University of Minnesota Press, 1996).

Naím, Moisés, 'Minilateralism: The Magic Number to Get Real International Action', (July/August 2009) *Foreign Policy* 136.

Neto, Ibrahim Abdul Hak, *Armas de Destruição em Massa no Século XXI: Novas Regras para um Velho Jogo. O Paradigma da Iniciativa de Segurança contra a Proliferação* (Brasilia: FUNAG, 2011).

Nikitin, Mary Beth, 'Proliferation Security Initiative', *Congressional Research Service*, Report for Congress (Washington D.C., 15 July 2012).

Nino, Carlos S., *Introducción al Análisis del Derecho*, second edition, twelfth reprint (Buenos Aires: Astrea, 2013).

Nolte, Georg, 'Die "neuen Aufgaben" von NATO und WEU: Völker- und verfassungsrechtliche Fragen' (1994) 54 *Zeitschrift für ausländisches öffentliches Recht und Völkerrecht* 95.

'Die USA und das Völkerrecht' (2003) 78 *Die Friedens-Warte* 119.

'Kosovo und Konstitutionalisierung: Zur humanitären Intervention der NATO-Staaten' (1999) 59 *Zeitschrift für ausländisches öffentliches Recht und Völkerrecht* 941.

(ed.), *Treaties and Subsequent Practice* (Oxford: Oxford University Press, 2013).

'Treaties over Time in Particular: Subsequent Agreement and Practice', in *Yearbook of the International Law Commission (2008), Volumen 2, Part II* (New York and Geneva, 2015).

Nye, Joseph S., *The Future of Power* (New York: Public Affairs, 2011).

Nye Jr., Joseph S., 'Will the Liberal Order Survive?' (January/February 2017) *Foreign Affairs*.

Obama, Barack H., *Remarks by President Barack Obama, Hradcany Square Prague, Czech Republic* (4 April 2009), at https://obamawhitehouse.archives.gov/the-press-office/remarks-president-barack-obama-prague-delivered.

Remarks by the President at the United States Military Academy Commencement Ceremony (28 May 2014), at: www.whitehouse.gov/the-press-office/2014/05/28/remarks-president-united-states-military-academy-commencement-ceremony.

Oberthür, Sebastian, 'Regime-Interplay Management – *Lessons from Environmental Policy and Law*' in Kerstin Blome, Andreas Fischer-Lescano, Hannah Franzki, Nora Markard, and Stefan Oeter (eds.), *Contested Regime Collisions – Norm Fragmentation in World Socidety* (Cambridge: Cambridge University Press, 2016), pp. 88–108.

Pahuja, Sundhya, *Decolonising International Law: Development, Economic Growth and the Politics of Universality* (Cambridge: Cambridge University Press, 2011).

BIBLIOGRAPHY

Patrick, Stewart, '"The Mission Determines the Coalition": The United States and Multilateral Cooperation after 9/11', in Bruce D. Jones, Shepard Forman and Richard Gowan (eds.), *Cooperating for Peace and Security: Evolving Institutions and Arrangements in a Context of Changing U.S. Security Policy* (New York: Cambridge University Press, 2012), pp. 20–44.

'The Unruled World: The Case for Good Enough Global Governance' (January/ February 2014) *Foreign Affairs* 58.

Patrick, Stewart and Forman, Shepard (eds.), *Multilateralism & U.S. Foreign Policy: Ambivalent Engagement* (London/Boulder: Lynne Rienner Publishers, 2002).

Patterson, Dennis, 'Fashionable Nonsense' (2003) 81 *Texas Law Review* 841.

Paulus, Andreas, 'The War against Iraq and the Future of International Law: Hegemony or Pluralism?' (2004) 25 *Michigan Journal of International Law* 691.

Pauwelyn, Joost, 'Informal International Lawmaking: Framing the Concept', in Pauwelyn, Wessel, and Wouters, *Informal International Lawmaking*, p. 13–34.

Pauwelyn, Joost, Wessel, Ramses A., and Wouters, Jan (eds.), *Informal International Lawmaking* (Oxford: Oxford University Press, 2012).

Penttilä, Risto E. J., *The Role of the G8 in International Peace and Security* (Oxford: Oxford University Press/International Institute for Strategic Studies, 2003).

Pernice, Ingolf, 'Coalitions of the Willing and European Integration: Different Speed? A Core Europe?', in Calliess, Nolte, and Stoll (eds.), *Coalitions of the Willing: Avantgarde or Threat?* (2007), pp. 89–98.

Perry, Timothy C., 'Blurring the Oceans Zones: The Effect of the Proliferation Security Initiative on the Customary International Law of the Sea' (2006) 37 *Ocean Development & International Law* 33.

Pfeil, Julia, 'Völkerrechtliche Praxis der Bundesrepublik Deutschland in den Jahren 2000 bis 2002 (3. Teil Friedenssicherung)' (2004) 64 *Zeitschrift für ausländisches öffentliches Recht und Völkerrecht* 1105.

Phillips, John and Tan, Chrissie, 'Langue and Parole', in *The Literary Encyclopedia*, at www.litencyc.com/php/stopics.php?rec=true&UID=662.

Pinker, Steven, 'Block That Metaphor!', *The New Republic Online* (6 October 2006), at https://newrepublic.com/article/77730/block-metaphor-steven-pinker-whose-freedom-george-lakoff.

The Stuff of Thought. Language as a Window into Human Nature (New York: Penguin Books, 2008).

Posner, Eric, 'Obama's Drone Dilemma', *Slate* (8 October 2012), at www.slate.com/articles/news_and_politics/view_from_chicago/2012/10/obama_s_drone_war_is_probably_illegal_will_it_stop_.html.

Posner, Richard A., *Catastrophe: Risk and Response* (New York: Oxford University Press, 2004).

BIBLIOGRAPHY

Powell, Colin (interview), *Frontline* (7 June, 2002), at www.pbs.org/wgbh/pages/frontline/shows/campaign/interviews/powell.html.

Powell, Colin L., 'A Strategy of Partnerships' (January/February 2004) *Foreign Affairs* 22.

Prantl, Jochen, *The UN Security Council and Informal Groups of States: Complementing or Competing for Governance?* (New York: Oxford University Press, 2006).

Pulkowski, Dirk, 'Structural Paradigms of International Law', in Broude, Tomer and Shany, Yuval (eds.), *The Shifting Allocation of Authority in International Law: Considering Sovereignty, Supremacy and Subsidiarity, Essays in Honour of Professor Ruth Lapidoth* (Oxford: Hart, 2008), pp. 51–78.

Quigley, John, 'The "Privatization" of Security Council Enforcement Action: A Threat to Multilateralism' (1996) 17 *Michigan Journal of International Law* 249.

Rademaker, Steve, 'International Coalitions of the Willing, Introduction' (2005) 99 *Proceedings of the Annual Meeting (American Society of International Law)* 243.

Rahman, Chris, 'The Global Maritime Partnership Initiative: Implications for the Royal Australian Navy', *Papers in Australian Maritime Affairs No. 24* (Canberra: Sea Power Centre Australia, 2008).

Randelzhofer, Albrecht and Nolte, Georg, 'Article 51', in Simma, Khan, Nolte and Paulus (eds.), *The Charter of the United Nations, A Commentary*, third edition, vol. II (Oxford: Oxford University Press, 2012), p. 1397.

Raustiala, Kal, 'The Architecture of International Cooperation: Transgovernmental Networks and the Future of International Law' (2002) 43 *Virginia Journal of International Law* 1.

Reinold, Theresa, 'State Weakness, Irregular Warfare, and the Right to Self-Defense Post 9/11' (2011) 105 *The American Journal of International Law* 244.

Risse, Thomas, 'The Crisis of the Transatlantic Security Community', in Dimitris Bourantonis, Kostas Ifantis and Panayotis Tsakonas (eds.), *Multilateralism and Security Institutions in an Era of Globalization* (New York: Routledge, 2008), pp. 78–100.

Roach, Ashley, 'Container and Port Security: A Bilateral Perspective' (2003) 18 *The International Journal of Marine and Coastal Law* 341.

Roberts, Anthea, 'Legality vs Legitimacy: Can Uses of Force be Illegal but Justified?', in Alston and Macdonald (eds.), *Human Rights, Intervention, and the Use of Force* (Oxford: Oxford University Press, 2008), pp. 179–214.

Is International Law International? (Oxford: Oxford University Press, 2017).

Roberts, Anthea, Stephen, Paul B., Verdier, Pierre-Hughes and Versteeg, Mila (eds.), *Comparative International Law* (Oxford: Oxford University Press, 2018).

BIBLIOGRAPHY 277

Rodiles, Alejandro, '*Coalitions of the Willing*: Coyuntura, Contexto y Propiedades. Un Primer Esbozo' (2007) 7 *Anuario Mexicano de Derecho Internacional* 675.

'After TPP is Before TPP: Mexican Politics for Economic Globalization and the Lost Chance for Reflection', in Benedict Kingsbury et al. (eds.), *Mega-regulation Contested: Global Economic Ordering After TPP* (Oxford: Oxford University Press, forthcoming).

'La Fragmentación del Derecho Internacional. ¿Riesgos u Oportunidades para México?' (2009) 9 *Anuario Mexicano de Derecho Internacional* 373.

'Non-Permanent Members of the United Nations Security Council and the Promotion of the International Rule of Law' (2013) 5 *Goettingen Journal of International Law* 333.

'La Guerra contra el Estado Islámico y el Legado Bush', blog contribution, *Nexos* (2 October 2014), at http://eljuegodelacorte.nexos.com.mx/?p=4111.

'Law and Violence in the Global South: The Legal Framing of Mexico's "NARCO WAR"', *Journal of Conflict & Security Law* (2018, forthcoming).

'El Acuerdo de París: un empujoncito hacia la justicia climática', blog contribution, *Nexos* (25 February 2015), at https://eljuegodelacorte.nexos.com.mx/?p=5680.

'The Design of UN Sanctions through the Interplay with Informal Arrangements', in Larissa van den Herik (ed.), *Research Handbook on UN Sanctions and International Law* (Cheltenham /Northhampton: Edward Elgar, 2017), pp. 177–193.

'The Great Promise of Comparative Public Law for Latin America – Toward Ius Commune Americanum?', in Roberts, Stephen, Verdier and Versteeg (eds.), *Comparative International Law* (Oxford: Oxford University Press, 2018), pp. 501–522.

'The Tensions Between Local Resilience-Building and Transnational Action – US-Mexican Cooperation in Crime Affected Communities in Northern Mexico, And What This Tells About Global Urban Governance', in Helmut P. Aust and Anél du Plessis (eds.), *The Globalisation of Urban Governance - Legal Perspectives on Sustainable Development Goal 11* (Routledge, forthcoming).

Roele, Isobel, 'Disciplinary Power and the UN Security Council Counter Terrorism Committee' (2014) 19 *Journal of Conflict & Security Law* 49.

Roessler, Frieder, 'Law, De Facto Agreements and Declarations of Principle in International Economic Relations' (1978) 21 *German Yearbook of International Law* 27.

Rogers, Peter, 'The Etymology and Genealogy of a Contested Concept', in David Chandler and Jon Coaffee (eds.), *The Routledge Handbook of International Resilience* (Abingdon/New York: Routledge, 2017), pp. 13–25.

Romero, Jessica, 'Prevention of Maritime Terrorism: The Container Security Initiative' (2003) 4 *Chicago Journal of International Law* 597.

Rosand, Eric, 'The UN-Led Multilateral Institutional Response to Jihadist Terrorism: Is a Global Counterterrorism Body Needed?' (2006) 11 *Journal of Conflict & Security Law* 399.

Rosenau, James N., 'Governance, Order, and Change in World Politics', in James N. Rosenau and Ernst-Otto Czempiel (eds.), *Governance without Government: Order and Change in World Politics* (Cambridge: Cambridge University Press, 1992), pp. 1–29.

'Governing the Ungovernable: The Challenge of a Global Disaggregation of Authority' (2007) 88 *Regulation & Governance* 1.

Ross, Alf, 'On Self-Reference and a Puzzle in Constitutional Law' (1969) 78 *Mind* 1.

Rostow, Eugene V., 'Until What? Enforcement Action or Collective Self-Defense?' (1991) 85 *The American Journal of International Law* 505.

Roth, Brad R., 'Coalitions of the Willing and the International Rule of Law', in Calliess, Nolte, and Stoll (eds.), *Coalitions of the Willing: Avantgarde or Threat?* (Germany: Carl Heymanns, 2007), pp. 33–42.

Rudolf, Peter and Wilzewski, Jürgen, 'Beharrung und Alleingang: Das außenpolitische Vermächtnis William Jefferson Clintons' (2000) 44 *Aus Politik und Zeitgeschichte* x.

Rumsfeld, Donald A., 'Transforming the Military' (May/June 2002) *Foreign Affairs* 20.

Ruys, Tom and Verhoeven, Sten, 'Attacks by Private Actors and the Right of Self-Defence' (2005) 10 *Journal of Conflict & Security Law* 289.

Sabel, Charles F. and Victor, David G., 'Making the Paris Process more Effective: A New Approach to Policy Coordination on Global Climate Change', *Policy Analysis Brief* (The Stanley Foundation, February 2016).

Sanger, David E., 'Bush Will Continue to Oppose Kyoto Pact on Global Warming', *The New York Times* (12 June 2001).

Sarooshi, Danesh, *The United Nations and the Development of Collective Security: The Delegation by the UN Security Council of its Chapter VII Powers* (Oxford: Clarendon Press, 1999).

Savaresi, Annalisa, 'The Paris Agreement: A Rejoinder', blog contribution, *EJIL Talk!* (16 February 2016), at www.ejiltalk.org/the-paris-agreement-a-rejoin der/.

Schachter, Oscar, 'The Twilight Existence of Nonbinding International Agreements' (1977) 71 *The American Journal of International Law* 296.

'United Nations Law in the Gulf Conflict' (1991) 85 *The American Journal of International Law* 452.

Scheinin, Martin, 'Back to post 9/11 panic? Security Council Resolution on Foreign Terrorist Fighters', blog contribution, *Just Security* (23 September 2014), at http://justsecurity.org/15407/post-911-panic-security-council-resolution-for eign-terrorist-fighters-scheinin/.

BIBLIOGRAPHY

Schmitt, Carl, *Der Nomos der Erde im Völkerrecht des Jus Publicum Europaeum*, second edition (Berlin: Dunker & Humboldt, 1974).

Schmitt, Eric and Shanker, Thom, 'Washington Recasts Terror War as "Struggle"', *The New York Times* (27 July 2007), at www.nytimes.com/2005/07/26/world/americas/26iht-terror.html.

Shaffer, Gregory, 'International Law and Global Public Goods in a Legal Pluralist World' (2012) 23 *European Journal of International Law* 669.

Shanker, Thom, 'White House Says the U.S. Is Not a Loner, Just Choosy', *The New York Times* (31 July 2001), at www.nytimes.com/2001/07/31/world/white-house-says-the-us-is-not-a-loner-just-choosy.html?src=pm&pagewanted=2.

Simma, Bruno, 'Fragmentation in a Positive Light' (2003–2004) 25 *Michigan Journal of International Law* 845.

'NATO, the UN and the Use of Force: Legal Aspects' (1999) 10 *European Journal of International Law* 1.

Simma, Bruno, Daniel-Erasmus Khan, Georg Nolte and Andreas Paulus (eds.), *The Charter of the United Nations, A Commentary*, third edition, vol. II (Oxford: Oxford University Press, 2012).

Simpson, Gerry, *Great Powers and Outlaw States: Unequal Sovereigns in the International Legal Order* (Cambridge: Cambridge University Press, 2006).

Slaughter, Anne-Marie, 'International Law and International Relations Theory: A Dual Agenda' (1993) 87 *The American Journal of International Law* 205.

'Governing the Global Economy through Government Networks', in Byers (ed.), *The Role of Law in International Politics. Essays in International Relations and International Law* (Oxford: Oxford University Press, 2000), pp. 177–206.

'Agencies on the Loose? Holding Government Networks Accountable', in George A. Bermann, Matthias Herdegen and Peter L. Lindseth (eds.), *Transatlantic Regulatory Cooperation: Legal Problems and Political Prospects* (Oxford: Oxford University Press, 2001), pp. 521–546.

A New World Order (Princeton: Princeton University Press, 2004).

'America's Edge: Power in the Networked Century' (January/February 2009) *Foreign Affairs* 94.

'International Law and International Relations Theory: Twenty Years Later', in Jeffrey L. Dunoff and Mark A. Pollack (eds.), *Interdisciplinary Perspectives on International Law and International Relations: The State of the Art* (New York: Cambridge University Press, 2013), pp. 613–625.

'The Paris Approach to Global Governance', *Project Syndicate* (28 December 2015), at www.project-syndicate.org/commentary/paris-agreement-model-for-global-governance-by-anne-marie-slaughter-2015-12?barrier=accessreg.

The Chessboard & the Web – Strategies of Connection in a Networked World (New Haven and London: Yale University Press, 2017).

BIBLIOGRAPHY

Song, Yann-huei, 'Security in the Strait of Malacca and the Regional Maritime Security Initiative: Responses to the US Proposal', in Carsten (ed.), *Global Legal Challenges: Command of the Commons, Strategic Communications and Natural Disasters*, vol. 83 (Newport: Naval War College, 2007) pp. 97–156.

Spring, Baker, 'Harnessing the Power of Nations for Arms Control: The Proliferation Security Initiative and Coalitions of the Willing', *The Heritage Foundation, Backgrounder # 1737* (18 March 2004), at www.heritage.org/research/reports/2004/03/harnessing-the-power-of-nations-for-arms-control-the-proliferation-security-initiative-and-coalitions-of-the-willing.

Squassoni, Sharon, 'Proliferation Security Initiative (PSI)', *CRS, Report for Congress* (Washington D.C., 14 September 2006).

Staubach, Peter, *The Rule of Unwritten International Law – Customary Law, General Principles, and World Order* (London: Routledge, 2018).

Stewart, Richard, 'The Global Regulatory Challenge to US Administrative Law' (2005) 37 *New York University Journal of International Law and Politics* 695.

Su, Jinyuan, 'The Proliferation Security Initiative and the Interdiction at Sea: A Chinese Perspective' (2012) 43 *Ocean Development and International Law* 96.

Sullivan, Gavin, 'Transnational Legal Assemblages and Global Security Law: Topologies and Temporalities of the List' (2014) 5 *Transnational Legal Theory* 81.

Sunstein, Cass R., *Why Nudge? The Politics of Libertarian Paternalism* (New Haven/London: Yale University Press, 2014).

Székely, Alberto, 'Non-Binding Commitments: A Commentary on the Softening of International Law Evidenced in the Environmental Field', in ILC (ed.), *International Law on the Eve of the Twenty-First Century. Views from the International Law Commission* (New York: United Nations Press, 1997), pp. 173–199.

Talbott, Strobe, *The Great Experiment: The History of Ancient Empires, Modern States, and the Quest for a Global Nation* (New York: Simon & Schuster, 2008).

Talmon, Stefan, 'The Statements by the President of the Security Council' (2003) 2 *Chinese Journal of International Law* 419.

Tams, Christian J., 'The Use of Force against Terrorists' (2009) 20 *European Journal of International Law* 359.

Tanaka, Yoshifumi, *The International Law of the Sea* (Cambridge: Cambridge University Press, 2012).

Tharoor, Shashi, 'Saving Humanity from Hell', in Edward Newman, Ramesh Thakur and John Tirman (eds.), *Multilateralism under Challenge? Power, International Order, and Structural Change* (Tokyo: United Nations University Press, 2002), pp. 21–33.

BIBLIOGRAPHY

Toope, Stephen J., 'Emergent Patterns of Governance and International Law', in Byers (ed.), *The Role of Law in International Politics. Essays in International Relations and International Law* (Oxford: Oxford University Press, 2000), pp. 91–108.

Triepel, Heinrich, *Delegation und Mandat im Öffentlichen Recht. Eine Kritische Studie* (Berlin/Stuttgart: Kohlhammer Verlag, 1942).

Valencia, Mark, 'Is the PSI Really a Cornerstone of a New International Norm?' (2006) 59 *Naval War College Review* 123.

Valverde, Mariana, *Chronotopes of Law – Jurisdiction, Scale and Governance* (Oxon and New York: Routledge, 2015).

Vihma, Antto, 'Friendly Neighbor or Trojan Horse? Assessing the Interaction of Soft Law Initiatives and the UN Climate Regime' (2009) 9 *International Environmental Agreements* 239.

Viñuales, Jorge E., 'The Paris Agreement: An Initial Examination (Part II of III)', blog contribution, *EJIL Talk!* (8 Febraury 2016), at www.ejiltalk.org/the-paris-climate-agreement-an-initial-examination-part-ii-of-iii/.

Waismann, Friedrich, 'Verifiability' (1945) sup. vol. XIX *Proceedings of the Aristotelian Society* 119.

Waldron, Jeremy, 'Is the Rule of Law an Essentially Contested Concept (in Florida)?' (2002) 21 *Law and Philosophy* 137.

Walker, Neil, *Intimations of Global Law* (Cambridge: Cambridge University Press, 2015).

Walsh, Nick Paton and Labott, Elise, 'Security Council Oks Syria Resolution, Warns of Consequences', *CNN* (28 September 2013), at http://edition.cnn .com/2013/09/27/world/meast/un-syria-resolution/.

Weber, Max, *Economy and Society*, Guenther Roth and Claus Wittich (eds.), volume one, (Berkeley, CA: The University of California Press, 1978).

Weil, Prosper, 'Towards Relative Normativity in International Law?' (1977) 77 *The American Journal of International Law* 413.

Weiss, Edith Brown, 'International Law in a Kaleidoscopic Word' (2011) 1 *Asian Journal of International Law* 21.

Weston, Burns H., 'Security Council Resolution 678 and Persian Gulf Decision Making: Precarious Legitimacy' (1991) 85 *The American Journal of International Law* 516.

White, N. D. and Ülgen, Özlem, 'The Security Council and the Decentralized Military Option: Constitutionality and Function' (1997) 44 *Netherlands International Law Review* 378.

Wilson, Gary, 'The Legal, Military and Political Consequences of the "Coalition of the Willing" Approach to UN Military Enforcement Action' (2007) 12 *Journal of Conflict and Security Law* 295.

282 BIBLIOGRAPHY

Winter, Steven L., *A Clearing in the Forest: Law, Life and Mind* (Chicago: The University of Chicago Press, 2001).

Wolfrum, Rüdiger, *Freedom of Navigation: New Challenges* (2008), at www.itlos.org/fileadmin/itlos/documents/statements_of_president/wolfrum/ freedom_navigation_080108_eng.pdf.

Wood, Michael C., 'The Interpretation of Security Council Resolutions', in Jochen A. Frowein and Rüdiger Wolfrum (eds.), *Max Planck Yearbook of United Nations Law*, volume 2 (1998), p. 73.

'The Law on the Use of Force: Current Challenges' (2007) 11 *Singapore Year Book of International Law* 1.

Yoo, John and Sulmasy, Glen, 'The Proliferation Security Initiative: A Model for International Cooperation' (2006) 35 *Hofstra Law Review* 405.

Young, Margaret A. (ed.), *Regime Interaction in International Law: Facing Fragmentation* (Cambridge: Cambridge University Press, 2012).

Zagaris, Bruce, 'The Merging of the Anti-Money Laundering and Counter-Terrorism Financial Enforcement Regimes after September 11, 2001' (2004) 22 *Berkeley Journal of International Law* 123.

Zalta, Edward N. (ed.), *The Stanford Encyclopedia of Philosophy*, at https://plato .stanford.edu/.

INDEX

Al-Qaida and ISIL/Daesh Sanctions
    Committee, 117–118,
    177–178, 187–191
  Monitoring Team, 187–190
Anghie, Antony, 39–40, 42, 110–111
awareness-raising activities, 158, 177,
    181, 242

Benvenisti, Eyal, 74, 137–138, 161, 171,
    232, 253
bilateralism, 116–117, 128–131,
    138–140, 244 *see* bilateral
    arrangements, *see also* serial
    bilateralism
Bolton, John, 77, 97–98, 102, 109,
    203
border, 74, 126, 136, 236
  control, 120, 181–182
  security, 136
Brazil, 85, 112–113, 134
BRICS, 85, 90, 229
Bush, George W., 1, 36, 76, 94, 163, 198,
    231–232

capacity building, 98–99, 106, 154–158,
    165–166, 177–179
catchphrase, 25–26
  buzzword, 16, 18–19
  political catchphrase, 1, 11, 14–16,
    18–21, 83
China, 90, 112–113, 122–123, 171, 177,
    229 *see also* One Belt One
    Road
Clinton, Hillary R., 80
cognitive psychology, 248
Combined Maritime Forces (CMF),
    141–142

conceptual metaphor theory, 7,
    28–38
  expansion, 23
  experience, 22, 24–25, 28–30, 38
  fallacies, 21–25
  interactional properties, 13, 28–30
  metaphorical mappings, 22–23
  political culture, 27–28
conceptual structure, 13
  floodgate concepts, 32
  open texture, 13, 45, 148
  phenomenological trap, 12, 35
consultation, 74–75, 202, 229, 240
Container Security Initiative (CSI),
    126–128
  cargo at ports, 134–135
  declaration of principles, 127–133
  serial bilateralism, 131, 137–139
contestation, 31–33, 41, 86–87,
    257–258
counter-measures, 159, 161, 183,
    244–246
counter-terrorism, 92, 149, 154–155,
    159–160, 177–179, 191,
    204–209, 225–227
Counter-Terrorism Committee (CTC),
    177
  Counter-Terrorism Executive
    Directorate (CTED),
    177–182, 184, 187

division of labour, 82, 85, 102–104, 153,
    155, 193, 197, 202
dynamic of difference, 67, 93, 98, 106,
    110–115, 197, 202, 205, 229
    see also concentric circles
    approach

284 INDEX

dynamic of difference (cont.)
    selectiveness, 39–43, 228, 242
      see selective

efficiency paradigm, 34, 82, 101, 113,
    148, 211, 222, 238
    flexibility, 39–41, 85–86, 162–163,
    167
    pragmatism, 85–89
enforcement, 49, 52–57, 252
    selectiveness, 114–115, 123–124, 228
      see selective enforcement
exclusive jurisdiction, principle of, 115,
    117, 120

Financial Action Task Force (FATF),
    158–164, 167–170, 179–184,
    187–191, 212
    FATF-style regional bodies (FSRBs),
    156–158, 177–179, 181
Financial Intelligence Units (FIUs), 182
fragmentation and re-integration,
    71–72, 138
frames, 7, 16–20, 69, 82, 246–248
    friendship frame, 34, 66, 101,
    110–111
    Western Missionary Deep Frame, 34,
    41–43, 86–87, 98

Germany, 14–15, 100, 125, 199
global administrative law (GAL), 6–7,
    151–152, 255
Global Counterterrorism Forum
    (GCTF), 155–157, 168,
    207–209, 212–213, 227, 236
global governance, 37, 41, 44, 65, 67,
    73–79, 82–85, 88, 146, 149,
    150, 156–157, 198, 202,
    205–206, 210, 229 *see also*
    multilayered
Global Initiative to Combat Nuclear
    Terrorism (GICNT),
    104–105, 153, 161–166
    Implementation and Assessment
    Group (IAG), 105 *see also*
    working group
Global Maritime Partnership (GMP),
    144–146

Guilfoyle, Douglas, 116–120, 176
Gulf War, 1991, 50–52, 67, 77
    Operation Desert Shield, 46
    Operation Desert Storm, 46, 67
    unipolarity, 43–44, 46–47, 64
      see unipolar moment

Haass, Richard N., 3, 67–77, 100,
    201–202, 251
hawala, 182, 187–188
hegemony, 3, 28, 40–41, 65, 72, 76, 84,
    88, 90, 123, 230
    and hegemonic strategy, 116, 138,
    140–141, 234 *see* hegemonic
    law
high seas, 10, 88, 94–95, 115, 120, 170,
    173

India, 101, 110, 112–113
informal international law-making
    project (IN-LAW), 8,
    235–239, 257
innocent passage, right of, 122,
    173–176
instrumentalism, 41, 44, 47, 65, 78–79,
    87–88, 210–211, 234 *see*
    instrumentalist
interdiction, 96, 103, 109, 111, 115–122,
    142, 170–176
International Atomic Energy Agency
    (IAEA), 152, 154, 165–170,
    192, 195–197, 203, 213
International Convention for the
    Suppression of the Financing
    of Terrorism, 182
international co-operation, 13, 27–28,
    34, 41, 46, 66, 94, 143, 236,
    248
    flexibility, 39, 138–139, 144, 147, 218,
    234 *see* flexible
International Court of Justice (ICJ),
    59–60, 63–64, 184
    Art. 38 of the Statute of the ICJ, 217,
    248–249
    Certain Expenses case, 55
interplays (formal–informal), 124, 140,
    149, 151–157, 176, 180, 197,
    204, 211, 254, 256

INDEX

empower, 54, 59, 68, *71*, 224–225
  see empowering
inter-institutional relations, 150–153
jurisgenerative, 169, 227–228, 250
mimesis process, 147–148, 153, 167,
    221, 233 *see* mutual learning
outside orchestration, 205–207, 209,
    220, 226–229, 243
patterns of co-ordination *see*
    pragmatic correspondences
  cross-participation, 222, 241–245
  cross-references, 222, 243
  information sharing, 171–172, 221
interpretation, 30, 183, 227–228
  norm evolution, 169, 181, 187,
    209–210, 250
  subsequent practice, 60, 118, 187,
    200, 237, 250
Iraq War 2003, 53, 96, 231
  associated with, 1, 10, 17, 35, 65, 76
  unilateralism, 36, 65, 231
issue-oriented, 11, 39, 47, 49, 59, 66, 103,
    148–149, 162, 167 *see ad hoc*

Johnson, Mark, 13, 21, 24, 38

Kelsen, Hans, 53, 59–60, 64
Koskenniemi, Martti, 31–32, 43–45,
    215–218, 234
Krasner, Stephen D., 214–215

Lakoff, George, 13, 19–21
law
  of contraband, 118
  and global law, 88, 222–223
  and natural law, 43, 234, 257
  and transnational law, 88, 157, 197
  rule of, 32, 47, 65, 123, 138, 145, 210,
    227, 252–253, 256–257 *see*
    also international law
  anti-law law, 239, 248, 251–253,
    257
    politics of fairness, 216, 247
  autonomy, 212, 215–218, 254, 256
  deformalization, 215–219,
    233–235, 251, 255–256
  quasi-formalization, 148–149, 167,
    239, 250

reformalization, 240–244, 250–
    251
  of the sea, 96, 115–118, 170, 204–
    206, 226
legitimacy, 57–58, 67, 88, 108, 129,
    132, 155, 163, 167, 206,
    246–247
Lotus presumption, 114, 252

mechanisms of co-ordination, 40, 79,
    85, 96, 140, 146, 181–183,
    193, 209–210
  co-ordination of national policies,
    74, 96–97, 247, 252
Mexico, 117, 136, 139, 257
mission, 34, 85, 96, 187, 227, 244
  civilizing, 41–42, 98 *see also* Western
    missionary deep frame
multilateralism, 44, 66, 74, *81*, 94, 139
  and best practices multilateralism,
    75, 201, 251, 253
  and effective multilateralism, 36, 113
  and minilateralism, 98–100
  and multilateral strategy, 69–72,
    75–77, 89, 232
  and multi-multilateralism, 73, 89,
    126, 230
  and organized multilateralism, 40,
    47, 64, *69–71*, 73–79, *82*, 89,
    113, 134, 231 see also
    multilateralism à la carte

N'Zatioula Grovogui, Siba, 42
non-polarity, 72, 79–80, 84, 90, 233
  see also multi-polarity
NSS, 122, 125, 154, 164–168, 192–193,
    203–207 *see* Nuclear Security
    Summit
  gift basket, 193–203, 247
nudge, 33, 200, 247 *see also* nudging

Obama, Barack, 44, 193
  complementarity, 79–80, 93, 126,
    204, 232–233, 249
  doctrine, 78
  hub of alliances, 81, 141
  perceptions, 36, 79–81, 86, 99, 109,
    124, 232

Operation Enduring Freedom, 76, 95, 141
order, 30, 45, 56, 58, 79–86, 89, 91, 150, 174, 255
  global order, 74, 93, 141, 210
  new world order, 43–44, 64–65, 67–68, 72, 74, 217, 223, 229, 236, 253–254 *see also* disorder
  and World Order 1.0, 74, 87
  and World Order 2.0, 75
outreach activities, 99, 106, 155, 165, 241–243

Paris Agreement on Climate Change, 75, 89, 150, 170, 198–202, 247, 251
  Nationally Determined Contributions (NDCs), 200–202, 218, 233, 247
personification of the state, 34, 42
pluralism, 224, 254
posse, 69, 77, 100, 102, 153
  activity, 3, 69, 97, 102, 119–122, 144, 238
  durability, 69, 163, 241
post–Cold War, 3, 43–45, 52, 65, 71, 81
Powell, Colin, 69, 77, 225
practice
  best, 75, 85, 105, 154, 160, 169, 182, 186, 188, 201, 208, 222, 253
  subsequent, 60, 118, 184, 200, 206, 237, 250
preventive measure, 190, 246
Princeton Project on National Security, 80
Proliferation Security Initiative (PSI), 77, 92–95, 133, 145, 153, 163, 170, 203, 244, 252
  High-Level Political Meetings (HLPM), 97, 103, 197, 236
  National Strategy to Combat Weapons of Mass Destruction 2002, 94
  Operation Expert Group (OEG), 97, 104, 125
  Statement of Interdiction Principles (SIP), 96, 100, 102, 111, 117, 133, 145, 171, 240

US *National Security Strategy 2006*, 76, 94, 170
Protocol to the Convention for the Suppression of Unlawful Acts against the Safety of Maritime Navigation 2005 (SUA), 118, 173

regime, *69*
  complex, 5, 8, 73, 152, 212, 223, 241, 247, 253 *see* regime complexity
risk
  based approach, 137, 188
  management, 75, 99, 121, 188, 221
  resilience, 82, 147–148, 200, 220, 222, 254
Rosenau, James N, 149–150, 214, 220, 229
Rumsfeld, Donald, 34, 146, 225, 234, 239
Russia, 46, 101, 104, 166, 207, 229
  see also Soviet Union

security
  collective system, 46, 48–49, 52–59
selectiveness, 39, 67, 72, 98, 209
  and inclusiveness, 6, 34, 159, 213
  see also implementation
self-defense
  pre-emptive, 61, 118
  unwilling or unable test, 61, 63
Slaughter, Anne-Marie, 2, 80, 88, 140, 230, 236
South–South co-operation, 85, 90
sovereignty
  equality, sovereign, 4, 40, 85, 114, 123
  predictability, 4, 239
  State consent, principle of, 5, 9, 249, 252–253
spoilers, 98, 108–111 *see* proliferation concern, States of
standards, 4, 8, 62, 157, 159, 167, 171, 173, 180–184, 188, 206, 212, 216, 240, 250

Treaty on the Non-Proliferation of Nuclear Weapons (NPT), 195, 203

INDEX

Trump, Donald J., 3, 76
  katechon, 90
  katechonic protectionism, 89

United Kingdom (UK), 52, 100, 141,
    154
*United Nations Convention on the Law
    of the Sea* (UNCLOS), 115,
    169, 173
United Nations Security Council (SC)
  Chapter VII Resolutions, 47–48, 54,
    83, 120, 188
  force, use of, 47, 120
United States of America (USA), 2,
    52, 64, 69, 95, 121, 126,
    188
  foreign policy, 3, 8, 35, 44, 75, 108
  predominance, 65, 72

US national maritime security strategy,
    135
  and Megaports, 135–136
  and Secure Freight Initiative,
    135–136 *see also Customs
    Trade Partnership against
    Terrorism* (C-TPAT)

Vienna Convention on the Law of
    Treaties (VCLT), 128, 185,
    237

weapons of mass destruction (WMDs)
  counter-proliferation, 92–93, 120,
    149, 177, 203–204, 226
  disarmament, 202
  non-proliferation, 83, 96, 112, 124,
    204, 226, 228

CAMBRIDGE STUDIES IN INTERNATIONAL AND COMPARATIVE LAW

Books in the Series

135 *Coalitions of the Willing and International Law: The Interplay between Formality and Informality*
Alejandro Rodiles

134 *Self-Determination in Disputed Colonial Territories*
Jamie Trinidad

133 *International Law as a Belief System*
Jean d'Aspremont

132 *Legal Consequences of Peremptory Norms in International Law*
Daniel Costelloe

131 *Third-Party Countermeasures in International Law*
Martin Dawidowicz

130 *Justification and Excuse in International Law: Concept and Theory of General Defences*
Federica Paddeu

129 *Exclusion from Public Space: A Comparative Constitutional Analysis*
Daniel Moeckli

128 *Provisional Measures before International Courts and Tribunals*
Cameron Miles

127 *Humanity at Sea: Maritime Migration and the Foundations of International Law*
Itamar Mann

126 *Beyond Human Rights: The Legal Status of the Individual in International Law*
Anne Peters

125 *The Doctrine of Odious Debt in International Law: A Restatement*
Jeff King

124 *Static and Evolutive Treaty Interpretation: A Functional Reconstruction*
Christian Djeffal

123 *Civil Liability in Europe for Terrorism-Related Risk*
Lucas Bergkamp, Michael Faure, Monika Hinteregger and Niels Philipsen

122 *Proportionality and Deference in Investor-State Arbitration: Balancing Investment Protection and Regulatory Autonomy*
Caroline Henckels

121 *International Law and Governance of Natural Resources in Conflict and Post-Conflict Situations*
Daniëlla Dam-de Jong

120 *Proof of Causation in Tort Law*
Sandy Steel

119 *The Formation and Identification of Rules of Customary International Law in International Investment Law*
Patrick Dumberry

118 *Religious Hatred and International Law: The Prohibition of Incitement to Violence or Discrimination*
Jeroen Temperman

117 *Taking Economic, Social and Cultural Rights Seriously in International Criminal Law*
Evelyne Schmid

116 *Climate Change Litigation: Regulatory Pathways to Cleaner Energy?*
Jacqueline Peel and Hari Osofsky

115 *Mestizo International Law: A Global Intellectual History 1842–1933*
Arnulf Becker Lorca

114 *Sugar and the Making of International Trade Law*
Michael Fakhri

113 *Strategically-Created Treaty Conflicts and the Politics of International Law*
Surabhi Ranganathan

112 *Investment Treaty Arbitration As Public International Law: Procedural Aspects and Implications*
Eric De Brabandere

111 *The New Entrants Problem in International Fisheries Law*
Andrew Serdy

110 *Substantive Protection under Investment Treaties: A Legal and Economic Analysis*
Jonathan Bonnitcha

109 *Popular Governance of Post-Conflict Reconstruction: The Role of International Law*
Matthew Saul

108 *Evolution of International Environmental Regimes: The Case of Climate Change*
Simone Schiele

107 *Judges, Law and War: The Judicial Development of International Humanitarian Law*
Shane Darcy

106 *Religious Offence and Human Rights: The Implications of Defamation of Religions*
Lorenz Langer

105 *Forum Shopping in International Adjudication: The Role of Preliminary Objections*
Luiz Eduardo Ribeiro Salles

104 *Domestic Politics and International Human Rights Tribunals: The Problem of Compliance*
Courtney Hillebrecht

103 *International Law and the Arctic*
Michael Byers

102 *Cooperation in the Law of Transboundary Water Resources*
Christina Leb

101 *Underwater Cultural Heritage and International Law*
Sarah Dromgoole

100 *State Responsibility: The General Part*
James Crawford

99 *The Origins of International Investment Law: Empire, Environment and the Safeguarding of Capital*
Kate Miles

98 *The Crime of Aggression under the Rome Statute of the International Criminal Court*
Carrie McDougall

97 *Crimes against Peace and International Law*
Kirsten Sellars

96 *The Non-Legal in International Law: Unruly Law*
Fleur Johns

95 *Armed Conflict and Displacement: The Protection of Refugees and Displaced Persons under International Humanitarian Law*
Mélanie Jacques

94 *Foreign Investment and the Environment in International Law*
Jorge Viñuales

93 *The Human Rights Treaty Obligations of Peacekeepers*
Kjetil Larsen

92 *Cyber Warfare and the Laws of War*
Heather Harrison Dinniss

91 *The Right to Reparation in International Law for Victims of Armed Conflict*
Christine Evans

90 *Global Public Interest in International Investment Law*
Andreas Kulick

89 *State Immunity in International Law*
Xiaodong Yang

88 *Reparations and Victim Support in the International Criminal Court*
Conor McCarthy

87 *Reducing Genocide to Law: Definition, Meaning, and the Ultimate Crime*
Payam Akhavan

86 *Decolonizing International Law: Development, Economic Growth and the Politics of Universality*
Sundhya Pahuja

85 *Complicity and the Law of State Responsibility*
Helmut Philipp Aust

84 *State Control over Private Military and Security Companies in Armed Conflict*
Hannah Tonkin

83 *'Fair and Equitable Treatment' in International Investment Law*
Roland Kläger

82 *The UN and Human Rights: Who Guards the Guardians?*
Guglielmo Verdirame

81 *Sovereign Defaults before International Courts and Tribunals*
Michael Waibel

80 *Making the Law of the Sea: A Study in the Development of International Law*
James Harrison

79 *Science and the Precautionary Principle in International Courts and Tribunals: Expert Evidence, Burden of Proof and Finality*
Caroline E. Foster

78 *Transition from Illegal Regimes in International Law*
Yaël Ronen

77 *Access to Asylum: International Refugee Law and the Globalisation of Migration Control*
Thomas Gammeltoft-Hansen

76 *Trading Fish, Saving Fish: The Interaction between Regimes in International Law*
Margaret Young

75 *The Individual in the International Legal System: Continuity and Change in International Law*
Kate Parlett

74 *'Armed Attack' and Article 51 of the UN Charter: Evolutions in Customary Law and Practice*
Tom Ruys

73 *Theatre of the Rule of Law: Transnational Legal Intervention in Theory and Practice*
Stephen Humphreys

72 *Science and Risk Regulation in International Law*
Jacqueline Peel

71 *The Participation of States in International Organisations: The Role of Human Rights and Democracy*
Alison Duxbury

70 *Legal Personality in International Law*
Roland Portmann

69 *Vicarious Liability in Tort: A Comparative Perspective*
Paula Giliker

68 *The Public International Law Theory of Hans Kelsen: Believing in Universal Law*
Jochen von Bernstorff

67 *Legitimacy and Legality in International Law: An Interactional Account*
Jutta Brunnée and Stephen J. Toope

66 *The Concept of Non-International Armed Conflict in International Humanitarian Law*
Anthony Cullen

65 *The Principle of Legality in International and Comparative Criminal Law*
Kenneth S. Gallant

64 *The Challenge of Child Labour in International Law*
Franziska Humbert

63 *Shipping Interdiction and the Law of the Sea*
Douglas Guilfoyle

62 *International Courts and Environmental Protection*
Tim Stephens

61 *Legal Principles in WTO Disputes*
Andrew D. Mitchell

60 *War Crimes in Internal Armed Conflicts*
Eve La Haye

59 *Humanitarian Occupation*
Gregory H. Fox

58 *The International Law of Environmental Impact Assessment: Process, Substance and Integration*
Neil Craik

57 *The Law and Practice of International Territorial Administration: Versailles to Iraq and Beyond*
Carsten Stahn

56 *United Nations Sanctions and the Rule of Law*
Jeremy Farrall

55 *National Law in WTO Law: Effectiveness and Good Governance in the World Trading System*
Sharif Bhuiyan

54 *Cultural Products and the World Trade Organization*
Tania Voon

53 *The Threat of Force in International Law*
Nikolas Stürchler

52 *Indigenous Rights and United Nations Standards: Self-Determination, Culture and Land*
Alexandra Xanthaki

51 *International Refugee Law and Socio-Economic Rights: Refuge from Deprivation*
Michelle Foster

50 *The Protection of Cultural Property in Armed Conflict*
Roger O'Keefe

49 *Interpretation and Revision of International Boundary Decisions*
Kaiyan Homi Kaikobad

48 *Multinationals and Corporate Social Responsibility: Limitations and Opportunities in International Law*
Jennifer A. Zerk

47 *Judiciaries within Europe: A Comparative Review*
John Bell

46 *Law in Times of Crisis: Emergency Powers in Theory and Practice*
Oren Gross and Fionnuala Ní Aoláin

45 *Vessel-Source Marine Pollution: The Law and Politics of International Regulation*
Alan Tan

44 *Enforcing Obligations Erga Omnes in International Law*
Christian J. Tams

43 *Non-Governmental Organisations in International Law*
Anna-Karin Lindblom

42 *Democracy, Minorities and International Law*
Steven Wheatley

41 *Prosecuting International Crimes: Selectivity and the International Law Regime*
Robert Cryer

40 *Compensation for Personal Injury in English, German and Italian Law: A Comparative Outline*
Basil Markesinis, Michael Coester, Guido Alpa and Augustus Ullstein

39 *Dispute Settlement in the UN Convention on the Law of the Sea*
Natalie Klein

38 *The International Protection of Internally Displaced Persons*
Catherine Phuong

37 *Imperialism, Sovereignty and the Making of International Law*
Antony Anghie

35 *Necessity, Proportionality and the Use of Force by States*
Judith Gardam

34 *International Legal Argument in the Permanent Court of International Justice: The Rise of the International Judiciary*
Ole Spiermann

32 *Great Powers and Outlaw States: Unequal Sovereigns in the International Legal Order*
Gerry Simpson

31 *Local Remedies in International Law (second edition)*
C. F. Amerasinghe

30 *Reading Humanitarian Intervention: Human Rights and the Use of Force in International Law*
Anne Orford

29 *Conflict of Norms in Public International Law: How WTO Law Relates to Other Rules of International Law*
Joost Pauwelyn

27 *Transboundary Damage in International Law*
Hanqin Xue

25 *European Criminal Procedures* Edited by Mireille Delmas-Marty and John Spencer

24 *The Accountability of Armed Opposition Groups in International Law*
Liesbeth Zegveld

23 *Sharing Transboundary Resources: International Law and Optimal Resource Use*
Eyal Benvenisti

22 *International Human Rights and Humanitarian Law*
René Provost

21 *Remedies against International Organisations*
Karel Wellens

20 *Diversity and Self-Determination in International Law*
Karen Knop

19 *The Law of Internal Armed Conflict*
Lindsay Moir

18 *International Commercial Arbitration and African States: Practice, Participation and Institutional Development*
Amazu A. Asouzu

17 *The Enforceability of Promises in European Contract Law*
James Gordley

16 *International Law in Antiquity*
David J. Bederman

15 *Money Laundering: A New International Law Enforcement Model*
Guy Stessens

14 *Good Faith in European Contract Law*
Reinhard Zimmermann and Simon Whittaker

13 *On Civil Procedure*
   J. A. Jolowicz

12 *Trusts: A Comparative Study*
   Maurizio Lupoi

11 *The Right to Property in Commonwealth Constitutions*
   Tom Allen

10 *International Organizations before National Courts*
   August Reinisch

9 *The Changing International Law of High Seas Fisheries*
   Francisco Orrego Vicuña

8 *Trade and the Environment: A Comparative Study of EC and US Law*
   Damien Geradin

7 *Unjust Enrichment: A Study of Private Law and Public Values*
   Hanoch Dagan

6 *Religious Liberty and International Law in Europe*
   Malcolm D. Evans

5 *Ethics and Authority in International Law*
   Alfred P. Rubin

4 *Sovereignty over Natural Resources: Balancing Rights and Duties*
   Nico Schrijver

3 *The Polar Regions and the Development of International Law*
   Donald R. Rothwell

2 *Fragmentation and the International Relations of Micro-States: Self-Determination and Statehood*
   Jorri Duursma

1 *Principles of the Institutional Law of International Organizations*
   C. F. Amerasinghe

CPSIA information can be obtained
at www.ICGtesting.com
Printed in the USA
LVHW080411250220
648027LV00011BA/126